Vocabulary

Third Edition

Samuel C. Brownstein

Former Chairman, Science Department
George W. Wingate High School, Brooklyn, New York

Mitchel Weiner

Former Member, Department of English
James Madison High School, Brooklyn, New York

Sharon Weiner Green

Former Instructor in English
Merritt College, Oakland, California

Barron's Educational Series, Inc.

© Copyright 1997, 1990, 1984 by Barron's Educational Series, Inc.

All inquiries should be addressed to:
Barron's Educational Series, Inc.
250 Wireless Boulevard
Hauppauge, New York 11788

International Standard Book No. 0-8120-9818-8

Library of Congress Catalog Card No. 97-117

Library of Congress Cataloging-in-Publication Data

Brownstein, Samuel C., 1909–
    A pocket guide to vocabulary / Samuel C. Brownstein, Mitchel
Weiner, Sharon Weiner Green. — 3rd ed.
        p. cm.
    ISBN 0-8120-9818-8
    1. Vocabulary. I. Weiner, Mitchel, 1907– . II. Green, Sharon.
III. Title .
PE1449.B765   1997   97-117
428.1—dc21   CIP

PRINTED IN THE UNITED STATES OF AMERICA
987654321

Contents

Acknowledgments

Special acknowledgment is made to the following
organization for allowing us to reprint copyrighted
or previously published material.

The system of indicating pronunciation is used by
permission. From Merriam-Webster's Collegiate®
Dictionary © 1996 by Merriam-Webster Inc.

Preface

This book is designed to serve as a handy reference to the spelling, syllabication, pronunciation, part of speech, and meaning of over 3,000 words that appear most frequently on standardized exams like the SAT, PSAT, GMAT, and GRE. It is intended for use by students, executives, secretaries, proofreaders, writers, or anyone else in need of a quick, easy-to-use word reference book.

The plan of *A Pocket Guide to Vocabulary* is straightforward. Designed in dictionary format, each entry contains the word broken into syllables, its preferred pronunciation based on *Webster's Tenth New Collegiate Dictionary,* its part of speech, its meaning, and a sentence illustrating its use. Some entries contain other forms of the word as well.

A detailed explanation of the pronunciation symbols precedes the full list of words; a concise pronunciation key appears at the bottom of each page of the list.

A Pocket Guide to Vocabulary is a power tool. Based on computer analysis of actual published standardized tests, this book enables its users to reach their goal: a strong working vocabulary of college-level words.

Pronunciation Symbols

ə ... banana, collide, abut

'ə, ˌə ... humdrum, abut

ə ... immediately preceding \l\, \n\, \m\, \ŋ\, as in batt**le**, mitt**en**, eat**en**, and sometimes open \ˈōp-ᵊn\, lock **and** key \-ᵊŋ-\; immediately following \l\, \m\, \r\, as often in French table, prisme, titre

ər ... fu**r**ther, me**r**ger, bi**r**d

'ər-
'ə-r ... as in two different pronunciations of hu**rr**y \ˈhər-ē, ˈhə-rē\

a ... m**a**t, m**a**p, m**a**d, g**a**g, sn**a**p, p**a**tch

ā ... d**ay**, f**a**de, d**a**te, **a**orta, dr**a**pe, c**a**pe

ä ... b**o**ther, c**o**t, and, with most American speakers, f**a**ther, c**a**rt

à ... f**a**ther as pronounced by speakers who do not rhyme it with *bother*

aů ... n**ow**, l**ou**d, **ou**t

b ... **b**a**b**y, ri**b**

ch ... **ch**in, nature \ˈnā-chər\ (actually, this sound is \t\ + \sh\)

d ... **d**i**d**, a**dd**er

e ... b**e**t, b**e**d, p**e**ck

'ē, ˌē ... b**ea**t, nos**e**bl**ee**d, **e**venly, **ea**sy

ē ... eas**y**, meal**y**

f ... **f**i**f**ty, cu**ff**

g ... **g**o, bi**g**, **g**ift

h ... **h**at, a**h**ead

hw ... **wh**ale as pronounced by those who do not have the same pronunciation for both *whale* and *wail*

i ... t**i**p, ban**i**sh, act**i**ve

ī ... site, side, buy, tripe (actually, this sound is \ä\ + \i\, or \a\ + \i\)

j ... job, gem, edge, join, judge (actually, this sound is \d\ + \zh\)

k ... kin, cook, ache

k̲ ... German ich, Buch; one pronunciation of loch

l ... lily, pool

m ... murmur, dim, nymph

n ... no, own

ⁿ ... indicates that a preceding vowel or diphthong is pronounced with the nasal passages open, as in French *un bon vin blanc* \œⁿ-bōⁿ-vaⁿ-bläⁿ\

ŋ ... sing \'siŋ\, singer \'siŋ-ər\, finger \'fiŋ-gər\, ink, \'iŋk\

ō ... bone, know, beau

ȯ ... saw, all, gnaw, caught

œ ... French boeuf, German Hölle

œ̄ ... French feu, German Höhle

ȯi ... coin, destroy

p ... pepper, lip

r ... red, car, rarity

s ... source, less

sh ... as in shy, mission, machine, special (actually, this is a single sound, not two); with a hyphen between, two sounds as in *grasshopper* \'gras-ˌhäp-ər\

t ... tie, attack, late, later, latter

th ... as in thin, ether (actually, this is a single sound, not two); with a hyphen between, two sounds as in *knighthood* \'nīt-ˌhu̇d\

th̲ ... then, either, this (actually, this is a single sound, not two)

ü ... rule, youth, union \'yün-yən\, few \'fyü\

u̇ ... pull, wood, book, curable \'kyu̇r-ə-bəl\, fury \'fyu̇(ə)r-ē\

ue ... German füllen, hübsch

ūe ... French rue, German fühlen

v ... vivid, give

w ... we, away; in some words having final \\₍ᵢ₎ō\\, \\₍ᵢ₎yü\\, or \\₍ᵢ₎ü\\ a variant \\ə-w\\ occurs before vowels, as in \\'fäl-ə-wiŋ\\ , covered by the variant \\ə(-w)\\ or \\yə(-w)\\ at the entry word

y ... yard, young, cue \\'kyü\\, mute \\'myüt\\, union \\'yün-yən\\

ʸ ... indicates that during the articulation of the sound represented by the preceding character the front of the tongue has substantially the position it has for the articulation of the first sound of *yard,* as in French *digne* \\dēnʸ\\

z ... zone, raise

zh ... as in vision, azure \\'azh-ər\\ (actually, this is a single sound, not two); with a hyphen between, two sounds as in *hogshead* \\'hȯgz-ˌhed, 'hägz-\\

\\ ... slant line used in pairs to mark the beginning and end of a transcription: \\pen\\

′ ... mark preceding a syllable with primary (strongest) stress: \\'pen-mən-ˌship\\

ˌ ... mark preceding a syllable with secondary (medium) stress: \\'pen-mən-ˌship\\

- ... mark of syllable division

( ) ... indicate that what is symbolized between is present in some utterances but not in others: *factory* \\'fak-t(ə-)rē\\

÷ ... indicates that many regard as unacceptable the pronunciation variant immediately following: *cupola* \\'kyü-pə-lə, ÷-ˌlō\\

A

a-base \ə-'bās\ (v) lower; humiliate. His refusal to *abase* himself in the eyes of his followers irritated the king, who wanted to humiliate the proud leader.

a-bash \ə-'bash\ (v) embarrass. He was not at all *abashed* by her open admiration.

a-bate \ə-'bāt\ (v) subside; decrease, lessen. Rather than leaving immediately, they waited for the storm to *abate*. abate-ment \ə-'bāt-mənt\ (n)

ab-bre-vi-ate \ə-'brē-vē-,āt\ (v) shorten. Because we were running out of time, the lecturer had to *abbreviate* her speech.

ab-di-cate \'ab-di-,kāt\ (v) renounce; give up. When Edward VIII *abdicated* the British throne, he surprised the entire world.

ab-er-ra-tion \,ab-ə-'rā-shən\ (n) wandering or straying away; in optics, failure of rays to focus. In designing a good lens for a camera, the problem of correcting chromatic and rectilinear *aberration* was a serious one. ab-er-rant \a-'ber-ənt\ (adj and n)

a-bet-tor \ə-'bet-ər\ (n) encourager. He was accused of being an aider and *abettor* of the criminal. a-bet \ə-'bet\ (v)

a-bey-ance \ə-'bā-ən(t)s\ (n) suspended action. The deal was held in *abeyance* until his arrival.

ab-hor \əb-'hȯ(ə)r\ (v) detest; hate. He *abhorred* all forms of bigotry. ab-hor-rence \əb-'hȯr-ən(t)s\ (n)

ab-jure \ab-'jü(ə)r\ (v) renounce upon oath. He *abjured* his allegiance to the king. ab-ju-ra-tion \,ab-jə'rā-shən\ (n)

ab-lu-tion \ə-'blü-shən\ (n) washing. His daily *ablutions* were accompanied by loud noises that he humorously labeled "Opera in the Bath."

\ə\ abut \ᵊ\ kitten, F table \ər\ further \a\ ash \ā\ ace \ä\ cot, cart
\aů\ out \ch\ chin \e\ bet \ē\ easy \g\ go \i\ hit \ī\ ice \j\ job
\ŋ\ sing \ō\ go \ȯ\ law \ȯi\ boy \th\ thin \t̲h̲\ the \ü\ loot \ů\ foot
\y\ yet \zh\ vision \à, k̲, ⁿ, œ, œ̄, ɶ, ɶ̄, ʸ\ see Pronunciation Symbols

ab-ne-ga-tion \ab-ni-'gā-shən\ (*n*) repudiation; self-sacrifice. No act of *abnegation* was more pronounced than his refusal of any rewards for his discovery.

a-bol-ish \ə-'bäl-ish\ (*v*) cancel; put an end to. The president of the college refused to *abolish* the physical education requirement. ab-o-li-tion \,ab-ə-'lish-ən \ (*n*)

a-bom-i-nate \ə-'bäm-ə-,nāt\ (*v*) loathe; hate. Moses scolded the idol worshippers in the tribe because he *abominated* the custom.

ab-o-rig-i-nal \,ab-ə-'rij-nəl\ (*adj, n*) being the first of its kind in a region; primitive; native. His studies of the primitive art forms of the *aboriginal* Indians were widely reported in the scientific journals. ab-o-rig-i-ne \,ab-ə-'rij-ə$_{(i)}$nē\ (*n*)

a-bor-tive \ə-'bȯrt-iv\ (*adj*) unsuccessful; fruitless. We had to abandon our *abortive* attempts.

a-brade \ə-'brād\ (*v*) wear away by friction; erode. The skin of his leg was *abraded* by the sharp rocks. a-bra-sion \ə-'brā-zhən\ (*n*)

a-bridge \ə-'brij\ (*v*) condense or shorten. Because the publishers felt the public wanted a shorter version of *War and Peace,* they proceeded to *abridge* the novel.

ab-ro-gate \'ab-rə-,gāt\ (*v*) abolish. He intended to *abrogate* the decree issued by his predecessor.

ab-scond \ab-'skänd\ (*v*) depart secretly and hide. The teller *absconded* with the bonds and was not found.

ab-solve \əb-'zälv\ (*v*) pardon (an offense). The father confessor *absolved* him of his sins. ab-so-lu-tion \,ab -sə-'lü-shən\ (*n*)

ab-ste-mi-ous \ab-'stē-mē-əs\ (*adj*) temperate; sparing in drink, etc. The drunkards mocked him because of his *abstemious* habits.

ab-sti-nence \'ab-stə-nən(t)s\ (*n*) restraint from eating or drinking. The doctor recommended total *abstinence* from salted foods. ab-stain \əb-'stān\ (*v*)

\ə\ **abut** \ᵊ\ **kitten**, F **table** \ər\ **further** \a\ **ash** \ā\ **ace** \ä\ **cot, cart**
\au̇\ **out** \ch\ **chin** \e\ **bet** \ē\ **easy** \g\ **go** \i\ **hit** \ī\ **ice** \j\ **job**

ab-stract \ab-'strakt\ (*adj*) theoretical; not concrete; non-representational. To him, hunger was an *abstract* concept; he had never missed a meal.

ab-struse \əb-'strüs\ (*adj*) obscure; profound; difficult to understand. He read *abstruse* works in philosophy.

a-bu-sive \ə-'byü-siv\ (*adj*) coarsely insulting; physically harmful. An *abusive* parent damages a child both mentally and physically.

a-but \ə-'bət\ (*v*) border upon; adjoin. Where our estates *abut,* we must build a fence.

a-bys-mal \ə-'biz-məl\ (*adj*) bottomless. His arrogance is exceeded only by his *abysmal* ignorance.

ac-cede \ak-'sēd\ (*v*) agree. If I *accede* to this demand for blackmail, I am afraid that I will be the victim of future demands.

ac-cel-er-ate \ik-'sel-ə-rāt\ (*v*) move faster. In our science class, we learn how falling bodies *accelerate.*

ac-ces-si-ble \ik-'ses-a-bal\ (*adj*) easy to approach; obtainable. We asked our guide whether the ruins were *accessible* on foot.

ac-ces-so-ry \ik-'ses-(ə-)rē\ (*n*) additional object; useful but not essential thing. The *accessories* she bought cost more than the dress; also (*adj*).

ac-claim \ə-'klām\ (*v*) applaud; announce with great approval. The NBC sportscasters *acclaimed* every American victory in the Olympics and decried every American defeat; also (*adj*).

ac-cli-mate \'ak-lə-ˌmāt\ (*v*) adjust to climate. One of the difficulties of our present air age is the need of travelers to *acclimate* themselves to their new and often strange environments.

ac-cliv-i-ty \ə-'kliv-ət-ē\ (*n*) sharp upslope of a hill. The car could not go up the *acclivity* in high gear.

ac-co-lade \'ak-ə-ˌlād\ (*n*) award of merit. In Hollywood, an "Oscar" is the highest *accolade.*

---

ac-com-plice \ə-'käm-pləs\ (*n*) partner in crime. Because he had provided the criminal with the lethal weapon, he was arrested as an *accomplice* in the murder.

ac-cord \ə-'kȯ(ə)rd\ (*n*) agreement. He was in complete *accord* with the verdict.

ac-cost \ə-'kȯst\ (*v*) approach and speak first to a person. When the two young men *accosted* me, I was frightened because I thought they were going to attack me.

ac-cou-tre \ə-'küt-ər\ (*v*) equip. The fisherman was *accoutred* with the best that the sporting goods store could supply. **ac-cou-tre-ment** \ə-'kü-trə-mənt\ (*n*)

ac-cre-tion \ə-'krē-shən\ (*n*) growth; increase. The *accretion* of wealth marked the family's rise in power.

ac-crue \ə-'krü\ (*v*) come about by addition. You must pay the interest that has *accrued* on your debt as well as the principal sum. **ac-cru-al** \ə-'krü-əl\ (*n*)

a-cer-bi-ty \ə-'sər-bət-ē\ (*n*) bitterness of speech and temper. The meeting of the United Nations Assembly was marked with such *acerbity* that little hope of reaching any useful settlement of the problem could be held.

a-ce-tic \ə-'sēt-ik\ (*adj*) vinegary. The salad had an exceedingly *acetic* flavor.

a-cid-u-lous \ə-'sij-ə-ləs\ (*adj*) slightly sour; sharp, caustic. James was unpopular because of his sarcastic and *acidulous* remarks.

ac-knowl-edge \ik-'näl-ij\ (*v*) recognize; admit. When pressed for an answer, he *acknowledged* the existence of another motive for the crime.

ac-me \'ak-mē\ (*n*) top; pinnacle. His success in this role marked his *acme* as an actor.

a-cous-tic \ə-'kü-stik\ (*n*) science of sound; quality that makes a room easy or hard to hear in. Carnegie Hall is liked by music lovers because of its fine *acoustics*.

ac-qui-esce \ak-wē-'es\ (*v*) assent; agree passively. Although she appeared to *acquiesce* to her employer's

\ə\ abut \ə\ kitten, F table \ər\ further \a\ ash \ā\ ace \ä\ cot, cart \au\ out \ch\ chin \e\ bet \ē\ easy \g\ go \i\ hit \ī\ ice \j\ job

suggestions, I could tell she had reservations about the changes he wanted made. **ac·qui·es·cence** \ak-wē-'es-ᵊn(t)s\ (*n*); **ac·qui·es·cent** \ak-wē-'es-ᵊnt\ (*adj*)

ac·quit·tal \ə-'kwit-ᵊl\ (*n*) deliverance from a charge. His *acquittal* by the jury surprised those who had thought him guilty. **ac·quit** \ə-'kwit\ (*v*)

ac·rid \'ak-rəd\ (*adj*) sharp; bitterly pungent. The *acrid* odor of burnt gunpowder filled the room after the pistol had been fired.

ac·ri·mo·ni·ous \ˌak-rə-'mō-nē-əs\ (*adj*) stinging; caustic. His tendency to utter *acrimonious* remarks alienated his audience. **ac·ri·mo·ny** \'ak-rə-ˌmō-nē\ (*n*)

ac·tu·ar·i·al \ˌak-chə-'wer-ē-əl\ (*adj*) calculating; pertaining to insurance statistics. According to recent *actuarial* tables, life expectancy is greater today than it was a century ago.

ac·tu·ate \'ak-chə-ˌwāt\ (*v*) motivate. I fail to understand what *actuated* you to reply to this letter so nastily.

a·cu·ity \ə-'kyü-ət-ē\ (*n*) sharpness. In time his youthful *acuity* of vision failed him, and he needed glasses.

a·cu·men \ə-'kyü-mən\ (*n*) mental keenness. His business *acumen* helped him to succeed where others had failed.

ad·age \'ad-ij\ (*n*) wise saying; proverb. There is much truth in the old *adage* about fools and their money.

ad·a·mant \'ad-ə-mənt\ (*adj*) hard; inflexible. He was *adamant* in his determination to punish the wrongdoer. **ad·a·man·tine** \'ad-ə-ˌman-'tēn\ (*adj*)

a·dapt \ə-'dapt\ (*v*) alter; modify. Some species of animals have become extinct because they could not *adapt* to a changing environment.

ad·dic·tion \ə-'dik-shən\ (*n*) compulsive, habitual need. His *addiction* to drugs caused his friends much grief.

ad·dle \'ad -ᵊl\ (*adj*) rotten; muddled; crazy. This *addle*-headed plan is so preposterous that it does not deserve any consideration; also (*v*).

\ŋ\ **sing** \ō\ **go** \ȯ\ **law** \ȯi\ **boy** \th\ **thin** \<u>th</u>\ **the** \ü\ **loot** \u̇\ **foot**
\y\ **yet** \zh\ **vision** \à, <u>k</u>, ⁿ, œ, œ̄, ᴜe, ᴜē, ʸ\ *see* Pronunciation Symbols

ad-duce \ə-'d(y)üs\ (*v*) present as evidence. When you *adduce* evidence of this nature, you must be sure of your sources.

a-dept \ə-'dept\ (*adj*) expert at. He was *adept* at the fine art of irritating people. **ad-ept** \'ad-,ept\ (*n*)

ad-here \ad-'hi(ə)r\ (*v*) stick fast to. I will *adhere* to this opinion until proof that I am wrong is presented. **ad-he-sion** \ad-,hē-zhən\ (*n*)

ad-i-pose \'ad-ə-,pōs\ (*adj*) fatty. Excess *adipose* tissue should be avoided by middle-aged people.

ad-junct \'aj-,əŋ(k)t\ (*n*) something attached to but holding an inferior position. I will entertain this concept as an *adjunct* to the main proposal.

ad-ju-ra-tion \,aj-ə-'rā-shən\ (*n*) solemn urging. His *adjuration* to tell the truth did not change the witnesses' testimony.

ad-jure \ə-'jü(ə)r\ (*v*) request solemnly. I must *adjure* you to consider this matter carefully as it is of utmost importance to all of us.

ad-mon-ish \ad-'män-ish\ (*v*) warn; reprove. He *admonished* his listeners to change their wicked ways.

ad-mo-ni-tion \,ad-mə-'nish-ən\ (*n*) warning. After repeated rejections of its *admonitions,* the country was forced to issue an ultimatum.

a-dorn \ə-'dȯ(ə)rn\ (*v*) decorate. Wall paintings and carved statues *adorned* the temple. **adorn-ment** \ə-'dȯ(ə)rn-mənt\ (*n*)

a-droit \ə-'drȯit\ (*adj*) skillful. His *adroit* handling of the delicate situation pleased his employers.

ad-u-la-tion \,aj-ə-'lā-shən\ (*n*) flattery; admiration. He thrived on the *adulation* of his henchmen.

a-dul-ter-ate \ə-'dəl-tə-,rāt\ (*v*) make impure by mixing with baser substances. It is a crime to *adulterate* foods without informing the buyer; also (*adj*).

\ə\ **abut** \ə\ **kitten,** F **table** \ər\ **further** \a\ **ash** \ā\ **ace** \ä\ **cot, cart**
\au̇\ **out** \ch\ **chin** \e\ **bet** \ē\ **easy** \g\ **go** \i\ **hit** \ī\ **ice** \j\ **job**

ad-um-bra-tion \ˌad-ₔₘ-'brā-shən\ (*n*) foreshadowing; outlining. The *adumbration* of the future in science fiction is often extremely fantastic.

ad-vent \'ad-ˌvent\ (*n*) arrival. Most Americans were unaware of the *advent* of the Nuclear Age until the news of Hiroshima reached them.

ad-ven-ti-tious \ˌad-vən-'tish-əs\ (*adj*) accidental; casual. He found this *adventitious* meeting with his friend extremely fortunate.

ad-verse \ad-'vərs\ (*adj*) unfavorable; hostile. *Adverse* circumstances compelled him to close his business.

ad-ver-si-ty \ad-'vər-sət-ē\ (*n*) poverty; misfortune. We must learn to meet *adversity* gracefully.

ad-vert \ad-'vərt\ (*v*) refer to. Since you *advert* to this matter so frequently, you must regard it as important.

ad-vo-cate \'ad-və-ˌkāt\ (*v*) urge; plead for. The abolitionists *advocated* freedom for the slaves; also (*n*).

ae-gis \'ē-jəs\ (*n*) shield; defense. Under the *aegis* of the Bill of Rights, we enjoy our most treasured freedoms.

ae-on \'ē-ən\ (*n*) long period of time; an age. It has taken *aeons* for our civilization to develop.

aes-thet-ic \es-'thet-ik\ (*adj*) artistic, dealing with or capable of appreciation of the beautiful. Because of his *aesthetic* nature, he was emotionally disturbed by ugly things. **aes-thete** \'es-ˌthēt\ (*n*)

af-fa-ble \'af-ə-bəl\ (*adj*) courteous. Although he held a position of responsibility, he was an *affable* individual and could be reached by anyone with a complaint.

af-fect-ed \ə-'fek-təd\ (*adj*) artificial; pretended. His *affected* mannerisms irritated many of us who had known him before his promotion. **af-fec-ta-tion** \ˌaf-ˌek-'tā-shən\ (*n*)

af-fi-da-vit \ˌaf-ə-'dā-vət\ (*n*) written statement made under oath. The court refused to accept his statement unless he presented it in the form of an *affidavit*.

\ŋ\ **sing** \ō\ **go** \ò\ **law** \ òi\ **boy** \th\ **thin** \ṯẖ\ **the** \ü\ **loot** \ù\ **foot** \y\ **yet** \zh\ **vision** \à, ḵ, ⁿ, œ, œ̄, ᵫ, ᵫ̄, ʸ\ *see* Pronunciation Symbols

af-fil-i-a-tion \ə-'fil-ē-ā-shən\ (*n*) joining; associating with. His *affiliation* with the political party was of short duration for he soon disagreed with his colleagues. **affil-i-ate** \ə-'fil-ē-ͺāt\ (*v*)

af-fin-i-ty \ə-'fin-ət-ē\ (*n*) kinship. He felt an *affinity* with all who suffered; their pains were his pains.

af-fir-ma-tion \ͺaf-ər-'mā-shən\ (*n*) solemn pledge by one who refuses to take an oath. The Constitution of this country provides for oath or *affirmation* by officeholders.

af-flu-ence \'af-ͺlü-ən(t)s\ (*n*) abundance; wealth. Foreigners are amazed by the *affluence* and luxury of the American way of life.

af-fray \ə-'frā\ (*n*) public brawl. He was badly mauled by the fighters in the *affray.*

a-gape \ə-'gāp\ (*adj*) openmouthed. He stared, *agape,* at the many strange animals in the zoo.

a-gen-da \ə-'jen-də\ (*n*) items of business at a meeting. We had so much difficulty agreeing upon an *agenda* that there was very little time for the meeting.

ag-glom-er-a-tion \ə-ͺgläm-ə-'rā-shən\ (*n*) collection; heap. It took weeks to assort the *agglomeration* of miscellaneous items he had collected on his trip.

ag-gran-dize \ə-'gran-ͺdīz\ (*v*) increase or intensify. The history of the past quarter century illustrates how a president may *aggrandize* his power to act aggressively in international affairs without considering the wishes of Congress.

ag-gre-gate \'ag-ri-gət\ (*adj*) sum; total. The *aggregate* wealth of this country is staggering to the imagination; also (*v*).

a-ghast \ə-'gast\ (*adj*) horrified. He was *aghast* at the nerve of the speaker who had insulted his host.

a-gil-i-ty \ə-'jil-ət-ē\ (*n*) nimbleness. The *agility* of the acrobat amazed and thrilled the audience.

\ə\ **abut** \ə\ **kitten, F table** \ər\ **further** \a\ **ash** \ā\ **ace** \ä\ **cot, cart**
\au̇\ **out** \ch\ **chin** \e\ **bet** \ē\ **easy** \g\ **go** \i\ **hit** \ī\ **ice** \j\ **job**

ag-i-tate \'aj-ə-ˌtāt\ (*v*) stir up; disturb. His fiery remarks *agitated* the already angry mob.

ag-i-ta-tion \ˌaj-ə-'tā-shən\ (*n*) strong feeling; excitement. We felt that he was responsible for the *agitation* of the mob because of the inflammatory report he had issued.

ag-nos-tic \ag-'näs-tik\ (*n*) one who is skeptical of the existence or knowability of a god or any ultimate reality. The *agnostic* demanded proof before he would accept the minister; also (*adj*).

a-grar-i-an \ə-'grer-ē-ən\ (*adj*) pertaining to land or its cultivation. The country is gradually losing its *agrarian* occupation and turning more and more to an industrial point of view; also (*n*).

a-gron-o-mist \ə-'grän-ə-məst\ (*n*) scientist engaged in the management of land. Because the country failed to heed the warnings of its *agronomists,* it was faced with serious famine.

a-lac-ri-ty \ə-'lak-rət-ē\ (*n*) cheerful promptness. He demonstrated his eagerness to serve by his *alacrity* in executing the orders of his master.

al-che-my \'al-kə-mē\ (*n*) medieval chemistry. The changing of baser metals into gold was the goal of the students of *alchemy.* **al-che-mist** \'al-kə-məst\ (*n*)

a-li-as \'ā-lē-əs\ (*n*) an assumed name. John Smith's *alias* was Bob Jones; also (*adv*).

al-ien-ate \'al-yə-ˌnāt\ (*v*) make hostile; separate. His attempts to *alienate* the two friends failed because they had complete faith.

al-i-men-ta-ry \ˌal-ə-'ment-ə-rē\ (*adj*) supplying nourishment. The *alimentary* canal in our bodies is so named because digestion of foods occurs there.

al-i-mo-ny \'al-ə-ˌmō-nē\ (*n*) payment by a husband to his divorced wife. Mrs. Jones was awarded $200 monthly *alimony* by the court when she was divorced from her husband.

\ŋ\ **sing** \ō\ **go** \ȯ\ **law** \ȯi\ **boy** \th\ **thin** \th̲\ **the** \ü\ **loot** \u̇\ **foot**
\y\ **yet** \zh\ **vision** \à, k̲, ⁿ, œ, œ̄, ᵫ, ᵫ̄, ʸ\ *see* Pronunciation Symbols

al-lay \ə-'lā\ (*v*) calm; pacify. The crew tried to *allay* the fears of the passengers by announcing that the fire had been controlled.

al-lege \ə-'lej\ (*v*) state without proof. It is *alleged* that he had worked for the enemy. **al-le-ga-tion** \ˌal-i'gā-shən\ (*n*)

al-le-go-ry \'al-ə-ˌgōr-ē\ (*n*) story in which characters are used as symbols; fable. *Pilgrim's Progress* is an *allegory* of the temptations and victories of man's soul. **al-le-gor-ical** \ˌal-ə-'gȯr-i-kəl\ (*adj*)

al-le-vi-ate \ə-'lē-vē-ˌāt\ (*v*) relieve. This should *alleviate* the pain; if it does not, we shall have to use stronger drugs.

al-lit-er-a-tion \ə-ˌlit-ə-'rā-shən\ (*n*) repetition of beginning sound in poetry. "The furrow followed free" is an example of *alliteration*.

al-lo-cate \'al-ə-ˌkāt\ (*v*) assign. Even though the Red Cross had *allocated* a large sum for the relief of the sufferers of the disaster, many people perished.

al-loy \'al-ˌȯi\ (*n*) a mixture as of metals. *Alloys* of gold are used more frequently than the pure metal. **al-loy** \ə-'lȯi\ (*v*)

al-lude \ə-'lüd\ (*v*) refer indirectly. Try not to *allude* to this matter in his presence because it annoys him to hear of it.

al-lu-sion \ə-'lü-zhən\ (*n*) indirect reference. The *allusions* to mythological characters in Milton's poems bewilder the reader who has not studied Latin.

al-lu-vi-al \ə-'lü-vē-əl\ (*adj*) pertaining to soil deposits left by rivers, etc. The farmers found the *alluvial* deposits at the mouth of the river very fertile.

a-loft \ə-'lȯft\ (*adv*) upward. The sailor climbed *aloft* into the rigging.

a-loof \ə-'lüf\ (*adj*) apart; reserved. He remained *aloof* while all the rest conversed.

\ə\ **abut** \ə\ **kitten, F table** \ər\ **further** \a\ **ash** \ā\ **ace** \ä\ **cot, cart**
\au̇\ **out** \ch\ **chin** \e\ **bet** \ē\ **easy** \g\ **go** \i\ **hit** \ī\ **ice** \j\ **job**

al·ter·ca·tion \ˌȯl-tər-'kā-shən\ (*n*) wordy quarrel. Throughout the entire *altercation,* not one sensible word was uttered.

al·tru·ism \'al-trü-ˌiz-əm\ (*n*) unselfish aid to others; generosity. The philanthropist was noted for his *altruism.* **al·tru·is·tic** \ˌal-trü-'is-tik\ (*adj*)

a·mal·gam·ate \ə-mal-gə-ˌmāt\ (*v*) combine; unite in one body. The unions will attempt to *amalgamate* their groups into one national body.

a·mass \ə-'mas\ (*v*) collect. The miser's aim is to *amass* and hoard as much gold as possible.

am·a·zon \'am-ə-ˌzän\ (*n*) female warrior. Ever since the days of Greek mythology we refer to strong and aggressive women as *amazons.*

am·bi·dex·trous \ˌam-bi-'dek-strəs\ (*adj*) capable of using either hand with equal ease. A switch-hitter in baseball should be naturally *ambidextrous.*

am·bi·ence \'am-bē-ən(t)s\ (*n*) environment; atmosphere. She went to the restaurant not for the food but for the *ambience.*

am·big·u·ous \am-'big-yə-wəs\ (*adj*) doubtful in meaning. His *ambiguous* direction misled us; we did not know which road to take. **am·bi·gu·i·ty** \ˌam-bə-'gyü-ət-ē\ (*n*)

am·biv·a·lence \am-'biv-ə-lən(t)s\ (*n*) the state of having contradictory or conflicting emotional attitudes. Torn between loving her parents one minute and hating them the next, she was confused by the *ambivalence* of her feelings. **am·biv·a·lent** \am-'biv-ə-lənt\ (*adj*)

am·ble \'am-bəl\ (*n*) moving at an easy pace. When she first mounted the horse, she was afraid to urge the animal to go faster than a gentle *amble;* also (*v*).

am·bro·sia \am-'brō-zh(ē-)ə\ (*n*) food of the gods. *Ambrosia* was supposed to give immortality to any human who ate it.

\ŋ\ si**ng**   \ō\ **go**   \ȯ\ **law**   \ȯi\ **boy**   \th\ **thin**   \t͟h\ **the**   \ü\ **loot**   \u̇\ **foot**
\y\ **yet**   \zh\ **vision**   \à, k̲, ⁿ, œ, œ̄, ue, ūe, ʸ\ *see* Pronunciation Symbols

am-bu-la-tor-y \\'am-byə-lə-ˌtōr-ē\ (*adj*) able to walk. He was described as an *ambulatory* patient because he was not confined to his bed.

a-me-lio-rate \ə-'mēl-yə-ˌrāt\ (*v*) improve. Many social workers have attempted to *ameliorate* the conditions of people living in the slums.

a-me-na-ble \ə-'mē-nə-bəl\ (*adj*) readily managed; willing to be led. He was *amenable* to any suggestions that came from those he looked up to; he resented advice from his inferiors.

a-mend \ə-'mend\ (*v*) correct; change, generally for the better. Hoping to *amend* his condition, he left Vietnam for the United States.

a-me-ni-ties \ə-'men-ət-ēz\ (*n*) agreeable manners; courtesies. She observed the social *amenities*.

a-mi-a-ble \'ā-mē-ə-bəl\ (*adj*) agreeable; lovable. His *amiable* disposition pleased all who had dealings with him.

am-i-ca-ble \'am-i-kə-bəl\ (*adj*) friendly. The dispute was settled in an *amicable* manner with no harsh words.

a-miss \ə-'mis\ (*adj*) wrong; faulty. Seeing her frown, he wondered if anything were *amiss;* also (*adv*).

am-i-ty \'am-ət-ē\ (*n*) friendship. Student exchange programs such as the Experiment in International Living were established to promote international *amity*.

am-ne-sia \am-'nē-zhə\ (*n*) loss of memory. Because she was suffering from *amnesia,* the police could not get the young girl to identify herself.

am-nes-ty \'am-nə-stē\ (*n*) pardon. When his first child was born, the king granted *amnesty* to all in prison.

a-mor-al \(ˈ)ā-'mȯr-əl\ (*adj*) nonmoral. The *amoral* individual lacks a code of ethics; he should not be classified as immoral.

a-mor-phous \ə-'mȯr-fəs\ (*adj*) shapeless. He was frightened by the *amorphous* mass that had floated in from the sea.

\ə\ abut \ə\ kitten, F table \ər\ **further** \a\ ash \ā\ **ace** \ä\ cot, cart
\aů\ **out** \ch\ **chin** \e\ bet \ē\ **easy** \g\ go \i\ hit \ī\ ice \j\ job

am-phib-i-an \am-'fib-ē-ən\ (*adj*) able to live both on land and in water. Frogs are classified as *amphibian;* also (*n*).

am-phi-the-ater \'am(p)-fə-ˌthē-ət-ər\ (*n*) oval building with tiers of seats. The spectators in the *amphitheater* cheered the gladiators.

am-ple \'am-pəl\ (*adj*) abundant. He had *ample* opportunity to dispose of his loot before the police caught up with him.

am-pli-fy \'am-plə-ˌfī\ (*v*) enlarge. His attempts to *amplify* his remarks were drowned out by the jeers of the audience.

am-pu-tate \'am-pyə-ˌtāt\ (*v*) cut off part of body; prune. When the doctors decided to *amputate* his leg to prevent the spread of gangrene, he cried that he preferred death to incapacity.

a-muck \ə-'mək\ (*adv*) in a state of rage. The police had to be called in to restrain him after he ran *amuck* in the department store.

am-u-let \'am-yə-lət\ (*n*) charm; talisman. Around his neck he wore the *amulet* that the witch doctor had given him.

a-nach-ro-nism \ə-'nak-rə-ˌniz-əm\ (*n*) an error involving time in a story. The reference to clocks in *Julius Caesar* is an *anachronism.*

an-al-ge-sic \ˌan-ᵊl-'jē-zik\ (*adj*) causing insensitivity to pain. The *analgesic* qualities of this lotion will provide temporary relief. **an-al-ge-sia** \ˌan-ᵊl-jē-zha\ (*n*)

a-nal-o-gous \ə-'nal-ə-gəs\ (*adj*) comparable. He called our attention to the things that had been done in an *analogous* situation and recommended that we do the same.

a-nal-o-gy \ə-'nal-ə-jē\ (*n*) similarity; parallelism. Your *analogy* is not a good one because the two situations are not similar.

\ŋ\ **sing**   \ō\ **go**   \ȯ\ **law**   \ȯi\ **boy**   \th\ **thin**   \t͟h\ **the**   \ü\ **loot**   \u̇\ **foot**
\y\ **yet**   \zh\ **vision**   \à, k̲, ⁿ, œ, œ̄, ᵫ, ᵫ̄, ʸ\ *see* Pronunciation Symbols

an-ar-chist \\'an-ər-kəst\ (*n*) person who rebels against the established order. Only the total overthrow of all governmental regulations would satisfy the *anarchist*.

an-ar-chy \\'an-ər-kē\ (*n*) absence of governing body; state of disorder. The assassination of the leaders led to a period of *anarchy*.

a-nath-e-ma \ə-'nath-ə-mə\ (*n*) solemn curse. He heaped *anathema* upon his foe.

an-chor \\'aŋ-kər\ (*v*) secure or fasten firmly; be fixed in place. We set the post in concrete to *anchor* it in place. **an-chor-age** \\'aŋ-k(ə-)rij\ (*n*)

an-cil-lar-y \\'an(t)-sə-,ler-ē\ (*adj*) serving as an aid or accessory; auxiliary. In an *ancillary* capacity he was helpful; however, he could not be entrusted with leadership; also (*n*).

a-ne-mi-a \ə-'nē-mē-ə\ (*n*) condition in which blood lacks red corpuscles. The doctor ascribes his tiredness to *anemia*. **a-ne-mic** \ə-nē-mik\ (*adj*).

an-es-thet-ic \,an-əs-'thet-ik\ (*n*) substance that removes sensation with or without loss of consciousness. His monotonous voice acted like an *anesthetic;* his audience was soon asleep. **an-es-the-sia** \,an-əs-'thē-zhə\ (*n*)

an-gu-lar \\'an-gyə-lər\ (*adj*) sharp-cornered; stiff in manner. His features, though *angular,* were curiously attractive.

an-i-mad-ver-sion \,an-ə-,mad-'vər-zhən\ (*n*) critical remark. He resented the *animadversions* of his critics, particularly because he realized they were true.

an-i-mat-ed \\'an-ə-,māt-əd\ (*adj*) lively. Her *animated* expression indicated a keenness of intellect.

an-i-mos-i-ty \,an-ə-'mäs-ət-ē\ (*n*) active enmity. He incurred the *animosity* of the ruling class because he advocated limitations of their power.

an-i-mus \\'an-ə-məs\ (*n*) hostile feeling or intent. The *animus* of the speaker became obvious to all when he began to indulge in sarcastic and insulting remarks.

\ə\ **abut** \ᵊ\ **kitten, F table** \ər\ **further** \a\ **ash** \ā\ **ace** \ä\ **cot, cart**
\au̇\ **out** \ch\ **chin** \e\ **bet** \ē\ **easy** \g\ **go** \i\ **hit** \ī\ **ice** \j\ **job**

an-nals \\'an-ᵊlz\\ (*n*) records; history. In the *annals* of this period, we find no mention of democratic movements.

an-neal \\ə-'nē(ə)l\\ (*v*) reduce brittleness and improve toughness by heating and cooling. After the glass is *annealed,* it will be less subject to chipping and cracking.

an-ni-hi-late \\ə-'nī-ə-ˌlāt\\ (*v*) destroy. The enemy in its revenge tried to *annihilate* the entire population.

an-no-tate \\'an-ə-ˌtāt\\ (*v*) comment; make explanatory notes. In the appendix to the novel, the critic sought to *annotate* many of the more esoteric references.

an-nu-i-ty \\ə-'n(y)ü-ət-ē\\ (*n*) yearly allowance. The *annuity* he set up with the insurance company supplements his social security benefits so that he can live very comfortably without working.

an-nul \\ə-'nəl\\ (*v*) make void. The parents of the eloped couple tried to *annul* the marriage.

a-noint \\ə-'nȯint\\ (*v*) consecrate. The prophet Samuel *anointed* David with oil, crowning him king of Israel.

a-nom-a-lous \\ə-'näm-ə-ləs\\ (*adj*) abnormal; irregular. He was placed in the *anomalous* position of seeming to approve procedures he despised.

a-nom-a-ly \\ə-'näm-ə-lē\\ (*n*) irregularity. A bird that cannot fly is an *anomaly.*

a-non-y-mous \\ə-'nän-ə-məs\\ (*adj*) having no name. He tried to ascertain the identity of the writer of the *anonymous* letter.

an-tag-o-nism \\an-'tag-ə-niz-əm\\ (*n*) active resistance. We shall have to overcome the *antagonism* of the natives before our plans for settling this area can succeed.

an-te-cede \\ˌant-ə-'sēd\\ (*v*) precede. The invention of the radiotelegraph *anteceded* the development of television by a quarter of a century.

an-te-di-lu-vi-an \\ˌant-i-də-'lü-vē-ən\\ (*adj*) antiquated; ancient. The *antediluvian* customs had apparently not changed for thousands of years; also (*n*).

\\ŋ\\ sing \\ō\\ go \\ȯ\\ law \\ȯi\\ boy \\th\\ thin \\th̲\\ the \\ü\\ loot \\u̇\\ foot
\\y\\ yet \\zh\\ vision \\à, k̲, ⁿ, œ, œ̄, ue, ūe, ʸ\\ *see* Pronunciation Symbols

an-thro-poid \\'an(t)-thrə-ˌpȯid\ (*adj*) manlike. The gorilla is the strongest of the *anthropoid* animals; also (*n*).

an-thro-pol-o-gist \ˌan(t)-thrə-'päl-ə-jəst\ (*n*) a student of the history and science of mankind. *Anthropologists* have discovered several relics of prehistoric man in this area.

an-thro-po-mor-phic \ˌan(t)-thrə-pə-'mȯr-fik\ (*adj*) having human form or characteristics. Primitive religions often have dieties with *anthropomorphic* characteristics.

an-ti-cli-max \ˌant-i-'klī-ˌmaks\ (*n*) letdown in thought or emotion. After the fine performance in the first act, the rest of the play was an *anticlimax*. **an-ti-cli-mac-tic** \ˌant-i-'klī-ˌmak-tik\ (*adj*)

an-tip-a-thy \an-'tip-ə-thē\ (*n*) aversion; dislike. His extreme *antipathy* to dispute caused him to avoid argumentative discussions with his friends.

an-ti-sep-tic \ˌant-ə-'sep-tik\ (*n*) substance that prevents infection. It is advisable to apply an *antiseptic* to any wound, no matter how slight or insignificant; also (*adj*).

an-tith-e-sis \an-'tith-ə-səs\ (*n*) contrast; direct opposite of or to. This tyranny was the *antithesis* of all that he had hoped for, and he fought it with all his strength.

ap-a-thy \\'ap-ə-thē\ (*n*) lack of caring; indifference. A firm believer in democratic government, she could not understand the *apathy* of people who never bothered to vote. **ap-a-thet-ic** \ˌàp-ə-'thet-ik\ (*adj*)

ape \āp\ (*v*) imitate or mimic. He was suspended for a week because he had *aped* the principal in front of the whole school.

ap-er-ture \\'ap-ə(r)-ˌchu̇(ə)r\ (*n*) opening; hole. He discovered a small *aperture* in the wall, through which the insects had entered the room.

a-pex \\'ā-ˌpeks\ (*n*) tip; summit; climax. He was at the *apex* of his career.

\ə\ **abut** \ᵊ\ **kitten,** F **table** \ər\ **further** \a\ **ash** \ā\ **ace** \ä\ **cot, cart**
\au̇\ **out** \ch\ **chin** \e\ **bet** \ē\ **easy** \g\ **go** \i\ **hit** \ī\ **ice** \j\ **job**

a-pha-sia \a-'fā-zh(ē-)ə\ (*n*) loss of speech due to injury. After the automobile accident, the victim had periods of *aphasia* when he could not speak at all or could only mumble incoherently.

aph-o-rism \'af-ə-ˌriz-əm\ (*n*) pithy maxim. An *aphorism* differs from an adage in that it is more philosophical or scientific. **aph-o-ris-tic** \af-ə-'ris-tik\ (*adj*)

a-pi-ar-y \'ā-pē-ˌer-ē\ (*n*) a place where bees are kept. Although he spent many hours daily in the *apiary,* he was very seldom stung by a bee.

a-plomb \ə-'pläm\ (*n*) poise. His nonchalance and *aplomb* in times of trouble always encouraged his followers.

a-poc-a-lyp-tic \ə-ˌpäk-ə-'lip-tik\ (*adj*) prophetic; pertaining to revelations. His *apocalyptic* remarks were dismissed by his audience as wild surmises.

a-poc-ry-phal \ə-'päk-rə-fəl\ (*adj*) not genuine; sham. His *apocryphal* tears misled no one.

ap-o-gee \'ap-ə-⁽ˡ⁾jē\ (*n*) highest point. When the moon in its orbit is furthest away from the earth, it is at its *apogee.*

a-po-plex-y \'ap-ə-ˌplek-sē\ (*n*) stroke; loss of consciousness followed by paralysis. He was crippled by an attack of *apoplexy.*

a-pos-tate \ə-'päs-ˌtat\ (*n*) one who abandons his or her religious faith or political beliefs. Because he switched from one party to another, his former friends shunned him as an *apostate.*

a-poth-e-cary \ə-'päth-ə-ˌker-ē\ (*n*) druggist. In the *apothecaries'* weight, twelve ounces equal one pound.

ap-o-thegm \'ap-ə-ˌthem\ (*n*) pithy, compact saying. Proverbs are *apothegms* that have become familiar sayings.

a-po-the-o-sis \ə-ˌpäth-ē-'ō-səs\ (*n*) deification; glorification. The *apotheosis* of a Roman emperor was designed to insure his eternal greatness.

\ŋ\ **sing**   \ō\ **go**   \ȯ\ **law**   \ȯi\ **boy**   \th\ **thin**   \t̲h̲\ **the**   \ü\ **loot**   \u̇\ **foot**
\y\ **yet**   \zh\ **vision**   \à, k̲, ⁿ, œ, œ̄, ᵫ, ᵫ̄, ʸ \ *see* Pronunciation Symbols

ap-pall \ə-'pȯl\ (*v*) dismay; shock. We were *appalled* by the horrifying conditions in the city's jails.

ap-pa-ri-tion \ˌap-ə-'rish-ən\ (*n*) ghost; phantom. Hamlet was uncertain about the identity of the *apparition* that had appeared and spoken to him.

ap-pease \ə-'pēz\ (*v*) pacify; soothe. We have discovered that, when we try to *appease* our enemies, we encourage them to make additional demands.

ap-pel-la-tion \ˌap-ə-'lā-shən\ (*n*) name; title. He was amazed when the witches hailed him with his correct *appellation*.

ap-pend \ə-'pend\ (*v*) attach. I shall *append* this chart to my report.

ap-po-site \'ap-ə-zət\ (*adj*) appropriate; fitting. He was always able to find the *apposite* phrase, the correct expression for every occasion.

ap-praise \ə-'prāz\ (*v*) estimate value of. It is difficult to *appraise* the value of old paintings; it is easier to call them priceless. **ap-prais-al** \ə-'prā-zəl\ (*n*)

ap-pre-hend \ˌap-ri-'hend\ (*v*) arrest (a criminal); dread; perceive. The police will *apprehend* the culprit and convict him before long.

ap-pre-hen-sive \ap-ri-'hen(t)-siv\ (*adj*) fearful; discerning. His *apprehensive* glances at the people who were walking in the street revealed his nervousness.

ap-prise \ə-'prīz\ (*v*) inform. When he was *apprised* of the dangerous weather conditions, he decided to postpone his trip.

ap-pro-ba-tion \ˌap-rə-'bā-shən\ (*n*) approval. She looked for some sign of *approbation* from her parents.

ap-pro-pri-ate \ə-'prō-prē-ˌāt\ (*v*) acquire; take possession of for one's own use. The ranch owners *appropriated* the lands that had originally been set aside for the Indians' use.

\ə\ abut \ᵊ\ kitten, F table \ər\ further \a\ ash \ā\ ace \ä\ cot, cart
\au̇\ out \ch\ chin \e\ bet \ē\ easy \g\ go \i\ hit \ī\ ice \j\ job

ap-pur-te-nance \ə-'pərt-nən(t)s\ (*n*) subordinate possession. He bought the estate and all its *appurtenances*.

ap-ro-pos \ˌap-rə-'pō\ (*prep*) with reference to; properly. I find your remarks *apropos* of the present situation timely and pertinent; also (*adj* and *adv*).

ap-ti-tude \'ap-tə-ˌt(y)üd\ (*n*) fitness; talent. The counselor gave him an *aptitude* test before advising him about the career he should follow.

aq-ui-line \'ak-wə-ˌlīn\ (*adj*) curved, hooked. He can be recognized by his *aquiline* nose, curved like the beak of the eagle.

ar-a-ble \'ar-ə-bəl\ (*adj*) fit for plowing. The land was no longer *arable;* erosion had removed the valuable topsoil.

ar-bi-ter \'är-bət-ər\ (*n*) a person with power to decide a dispute; judge. As an *arbiter* in labor disputes, he has won the confidence of the workers and the employers.

ar-bi-trar-y \'är-bə-ˌtrer-ē\ (*adj*) fixed or decided; despotic. Any *arbitrary* action on your part will be resented by the members of the board whom you do not consult.

ar-cade \är-'kād\ (*n*) a covered passageway, usually lined with shops. The *arcade* was popular with shoppers because it gave them protection from the summer sun and the winter rain.

ar-cane \är-'kān\ (*adj*) secret; mysterious. What was *arcane* to us was clear to the psychologist.

ar-chae-ol-o-gy \ˌär-kē-'äl-əjē\ (*n*) study of artifacts and relics of early mankind. The professor of *archaeology* headed an expedition to the Gobi Desert in search of ancient ruins.

ar-cha-ic \är-'kā-ik\ (*adj*) antiquated. "Methinks," "thee," and "thou" are *archaic* words that are no longer part of our normal vocabulary.

ar-che-type \'är -ki-ˌtīp\ (*n*) prototype; primitive pattern. The Brooklyn Bridge was the *archetype* of the many

---

\ŋ\ sing \ō\ go \ȯ\ law \ȯi\ boy \th\ thin \t͟h\ the \ü\ loot \u̇\ foot
\y\ yet \zh\ vision \à, k̲, ⁿ, œ, œ̄, ᴜe, ᴜē, ʸ\ *see* Pronunciation Symbols

spans that now connect Manhattan with Long Island and New Jersey.

ar-chi-pel-a-go \\är-kə-'pel-ə-gō\ (*n*) group of closely located islands. When he looked at the map and saw the *archipelagoes* in the South Seas, he longed to visit them.

ar-chive \'är-ˌkīv\ (*n*) public records; place where public records are kept. These documents should be part of the *archives* so that historians may be able to evaluate them in the future.

ar-dor \'ärd-ər\ (*n*) heat; passion; zeal. His *ardor* was contagious; soon everyone was eagerly working.

ar-du-ous \'ärj-(ə-)wəs\ (*adj*) hard; strenuous. His *arduous* efforts had sapped his energy.

ar-got \'är-gət\ (*n*) slang. In the *argot* of the underworld, he "was taken for a ride."

a-ri-a \'är-ē-ə\ (*n*) operatic solo. At her Metropolitan Opera audition, Marian Anderson sang an *aria* from *Norma.*

ar-id \'ar-əd\ (*adj*) dry; barren. The cactus has adapted to survive in an *arid* environment.

ar-ma-da \är-'mäd-ə\ (*n*) fleet of warships. Queen Elizabeth's navy defeated the mighty *armada* that threatened the English coast.

ar-o-mat-ic \ˌar-ə-'mat-ik\ (*adj*) fragrant. Medieval sailing vessels brought *aromatic* herbs from China to Europe; also (*n*).

ar-raign \ə-'rān\ (*v*) charge in court; indict. After his indictment by the Grand Jury, the accused man was *arraigned* in the County Criminal Court.

ar-ray \ə-'rā\ (*v*) marshal; place in proper or desired order. His actions were bound to *array* public sentiment against him; also (*n*).

ar-ray \ə-'rā\ (*v*) clothe; adorn. She liked to watch her mother *array* herself in her finest clothes before going out for the evening; also (*n*).

\ə\ **abut** \ᵊ\ kitten, F table \ər\ **further** \a\ **ash** \ā\ **ace** \ä\ **cot, cart**
\aů\ **out** \ch\ **chin** \e\ bet \ē\ **easy** \g\ go \i\ hit \ī\ ice \j\ job

ar-rears \ə-'ri(ə)rz\ (*n*) being in debt. He was in *arrears* with his payments on the car.

ar-ro-gance \'ar-ə-gən(t)s\ (*n*) haughtiness. The *arrogance* of the nobility was resented by the middle class. **ar-ro-gant** \'ar-ə-gənt\ (*adj*)

ar-ro-gate \'ar-ə-ˌgāt\ (*v*) claim without reasonable grounds. I am afraid that the manner in which he *arrogates* power to himself indicates that he is willing to ignore Constitutional limitations.

ar-roy-o \ə-'rȯi-ə\ (*n*) gully. Until the heavy rains of the past spring, this *arroyo* had been a dry bed.

ar-tic-u-late \är-'tik-yə-lət\ (*adj*) effective; distinct. Her *articulate* presentation of the advertising campaign impressed her employers; also (*v*).

ar-tic-u-late \är-'tik-yə-ˌlāt\ (*v*) to utter distinctly. The singer *articulated* every consonant.

ar-ti-fact \'ärt-ə-ˌfakt\ (*n*) product of primitive culture. Archaeologists debated the significance of the *artifacts* discovered in the ruins of Asia Minor and came to no conclusion.

ar-ti-fice \'ärt-ə-fəs\ (*n*) deception, trickery. The Trojan War proved to the Greeks that cunning and *artifice* were often more effective than military might.

ar-ti-san \'ärt-ə-zən\ (*n*) a manually skilled worker. Artists and *artisans* alike are necessary to the development of a culture.

as-cen-dan-cy \ə-'sen-dən-sē\ (*n*) controlling influence. President Marcos failed to maintain his *ascendancy* over the Philippines.

as-cer-tain \ˌas-ər-'tān\ (*v*) find out for certain. Please *ascertain* his present address.

as-cet-ic \ə-'set-ik\ (*adj*) practicing self-denial; austere. The cavalier could not understand the *ascetic* life led by the monks; also (*n*).

\ŋ\ **sing**   \ō\ **go**   \ȯ\ **law**   \ȯi\ **boy**   \th\ **thin**   \t͟h\ **the**   \ü\ **loot**   \u̇\ **foot**
\y\ **yet**   \zh\ **vision**   \à, k̲, ⁿ, œ, œ̄, ᵫ, ᵫ̄, ʸ\ *see* Pronunciation Symbols

as-cet-i-cism \ə-'set-ə-ˌsiz-əm\ (*n*) doctrine of self-denial. We find *asceticism* carried on in many parts of the world.

as-cribe \ə-'skrīb\ (*v*) refer; attribute; assign. I can *ascribe* no motive for his acts.

a-sep-tic \ˌ(ˌ)ā-'sep-tik\ (*adj*) preventing putrefaction or blood poisoning by killing bacteria. Hospitals succeeded in lowering the mortality rate as soon as they introduced *aseptic* conditions.

ash-en \'ash-ən\ (*adj*) ash-colored. His face was *ashen* with fear.

as-i-nine \'as-ᵊn-ˌīn\ (*adj*) stupid. Your *asinine* remarks prove that you have not given this problem any serious consideration.

a-skance \ə-'skan(t)s\ (*adv*) with a sideways or indirect look. Looking *askance* at her questioner, she displayed her scorn.

a-skew \ə-'skyü\ (*adv*) crookedly; slanted; at an angle. When he placed his hat *askew* upon his head, his observers laughed.

as-per-i-ty \a-'sper-ət-ē\ (*n*) sharpness (of temper). These remarks, spoken with *asperity,* stung the boys to whom they had been directed.

as-per-sion \ə-'spər-zhən\ (*n*) slanderous remark. Do not cast *aspersions* on his character.

as-pi-rant \'as-p(ə-)rənt\ (*n*) seeker after position or status. Although I am an *aspirant* for public office, I am not willing to accept the dictates of the party bosses; also (*adj*).

as-pi-ra-tion \ˌas-pə-'rā-shən\ (*n*) noble ambition. One's *aspirations* should be as lofty as the stars.

as-sail \ə-'sā(ə)l\ (*v*) assault. He was *assailed* with questions after his lecture.

as-say \ a-'sā\ (*v*) analyze; evaluate. When they *assayed* the ore, they found that they had discovered a very rich vein. **as-say** \'as-ˌā\ (*n*)

\ə\ **abut** \ᵊ\ **kitten,** F **table** \ər\ **further** \a\ **ash** \ā\ **ace** \ä\ **cot, cart**
\au̇\ **out** \ch\ **chin** \e\ **bet** \ē\ **easy** \g\ **go** \i\ **hit** \ī\ **ice** \j\ **job**

as·sess·ment \ə-'ses-mənt\ (*n*) appraisal; estimation. I would like to have your *assessment* of the situation in South Africa.

as·sid·u·ous \ə-'sij-(ə-)wəs\ (*adj*) diligent. He worked *assiduously* at this task for weeks before he felt satisfied with his results. **as·si·du·i·ty** \as-ə-'d(y)ü-ət-ē\ (*n*)

as·sim·i·late \ə-'sim-ə-,lāt\ (*v*) absorb; cause to become homogeneous. The manner in which the United States was able to *assimilate* the hordes of immigrants during the nineteenth and the early part of the twentieth centuries will always be a source of pride; also (*n*).

as·suage \ə-'swāj\ (*v*) ease; lessen (pain). Your messages of cheer should *assuage* his suffering. **as·suage·ment** \ə-'swāj-mənt\ (*n*)

as·sumed \ə-'sümd\ (*adj*) pretended; feigned, fictitious. The forger used an *assumed* name when passing bad checks.

as·sump·tion \ə-'səm(p)-shən\ (*n*) the act of taking something upon oneself; the act of taking ownership of; a thing taken for granted. Never cosign a loan application unless you are willing to risk the *assumption* of the other party's debts.

as·ter·oid \'as-tə-,ròid\ (*n*) small planet. *Asteroids* have become commonplace to the readers of interstellar travel stories in science fiction magazines.

a·stig·ma·tism \ə-'stig-mə-,tiz-əm\ (*n*) eye defect that prevents proper focus. As soon as his parents discovered that the boy suffered from *astigmatism,* they took him to the optometrist for corrective glasses.

as·tral \'as-trəl\ (*adj*) relating to the stars. He was amazed at the number of *astral* bodies the new telescope revealed.

as·trin·gent \ə-'strin-jənt\ (*adj*) binding; causing contraction. The *astringent* quality of the unsweetened lemon juice made swallowing difficult; also (*n*).

\ŋ\ sing   \ō\ go   \ò\ law   \òi\ boy   \th\ thin   \t͟h\ the   \ü\ loot   \u̇\ foot
\y\ yet   \zh\ vision   \à, k̲, ⁿ, œ, œ̄, ue, ūe, ʸ\ *see* Pronunciation Symbols

as-tro-nom-i-cal \as-trə-'näm-i-kəl\ (*adj*) enormously large or extensive. The government seems willing to spend *astronomical* sums on weapons development.

as-tute \ə-'st(y)üt\ (*adj*) wise; shrewd. That was a very *astute* observation. I shall heed it.

a-sy-lum \ə-'sī-ləm\ (*n*) place of refuge or shelter; protection. The refugees sought *asylum* from religious persecution in a new land.

at-a-vism \'at-ə-ˌviz-əm\ (*n*) resemblance to remote ancestors rather than to parents; deformity returning after passage of two or more generations. The doctors ascribed the child's deformity to an *atavism*.

a-te-lier \ˌat-əl-'yā\ (*n*) workshop; studio. Stories of Bohemian life in Paris are full of tales of artists' starving or freezing in their *ateliers*.

a-the-is-tic \ˌā-thē-'is-tik\ (*adj*) denying the existence of God. His *atheistic* remarks shocked the religious worshippers. **a-the-ist** \ˌā-thē-əst\ (*n*)

a-troc-i-ty \ə-'träs-ət-ē\ (*n*) brutal deed. In time of war, many *atrocities* are committed by invading armies.

at-ro-phy \'a-trə-fē\ (*n*) wasting away. Polio victims need physiotherapy to prevent the *atrophy* of affected limbs; also (*v*).

at-ten-u-ate \ə-'ten-yə-ˌwāt\ (*v*) make thin; weaken. By withdrawing their forces, the generals hoped to *attenuate* the enemy lines.

at-test \ə-'test\ (*v*) testify, bear witness. Having served as a member of the Grand Jury, I can *attest* that our system of indicting individuals is in need of improvement.

at-tri-bute \'a-trə-ˌbyüt\ (*n*) essential quality. His outstanding *attribute* was his kindness.

at-tri-bute \a-'trib-yət, -yüt\ (*v*) ascribe; explain. I *attribute* her success in science to the encouragement she received from her parents.

\ə\ abut \ə\ kitten, F table \ər\ further \a\ ash \ā\ ace \ä\ cot, cart
\au̇\ out \ch\ chin \e\ bet \ē\ easy \g\ go \i\ hit \ī\ ice \j\ job

at-tri-tion \ə-'trish-ən\ (*n*) gradual wearing down. They decided to wage a war of *attrition* rather than to rely on an all-out attack.

a-typ-i-cal \ₒā-'tip-i-kəl\ (*adj*) not normal. You have taken an *atypical* case. It does not prove anything.

au-dac-i-ty \ò-'das-ət-ē\ (*n*) boldness. His *audacity* in this critical moment encouraged us.

au-dit \'òd-ət\ (*n*) examination of accounts. When the bank examiners arrived to hold their annual *audit,* they discovered the embezzlements of the chief cashier; also (*v*).

aug-ment \òg-'ment\ (*v*) increase. How can we hope to *augment* our forces when our allies are deserting us?

au-gu-ry \'ò-gyə-rē\ (*n*) omen; prophecy. He interpreted the departure of the birds as an *augury* of evil. au-gur \'ò-gər\ (*v, n*)

aus-pi-cious \ò-'spish-əs\ (*adj*) favoring success. With favorable weather conditions, it was an *auspicious* moment to set sail.

aus-tere \ò-'sti(ə)r\ (*adj*) strict, stern. His *austere* demeanor prevented us from engaging in our usual frivolous activities.

aus-ter-i-ty \ò-'ster-ət-ē\ (*n*) sternness; severity. The *austerity* and dignity of the court were maintained by the new justices.

au-then-ti-cate \ə-'thent-i͵-kāt\ (*v*) prove genuine. An expert was needed to *authenticate* the original Van Gogh painting from its imitation.

au-thor-i-ta-tive \ə-'thär-ə-͵tāt-iv\ (*adj*) having the weight of authority; dictatorial. We accepted her analysis of the situation as *authoritative.*

au-to-crat \'òt-ə-͵krat\ (*n*) monarch with supreme power. The nobles tried to limit the powers of the *autocrat* without success. au-toc-ra-cy \ò-'täk-rə-sē\ (*n*)

\ŋ\ **sing**   \ō\ **go**   \ò\ **law**   \òi\ **boy**   \th\ **thin**   \th̲\ **the**   \ü\ **loot**   \u̇\ **foot**
\y\ **yet**   \zh\ **vision**   \à, k̲, ⁿ, œ, œ̄, ue, u̅e, ʸ\ *see* Pronunciation Symbols

au·tom·a·ton \ȯ-'täm-ət-ən\ (*n*) mechanism that imitates actions of humans. Long before science fiction readers became aware of robots, writers were presenting stories of *automatons* who could outperform men.

au·ton·o·mous \ȯ-'tän-ə-məs\ (*adj*) self-governing. This island is a colony; however, in most matters, it is *autonomous* and receives no orders from the mother country. au·ton·o·my\ȯ-'tän-ə-mē\ (*n*)

au·top·sy \'ȯ-ˌtäp-sē\ (*n*) examination of a dead body; post mortem. The medical examiner ordered an *autopsy* to determine the cause of death; also (*v*).

aux·il·ia·ry \ȯg-'zil-yə-rē\ (*adj*) helper, additional or subsidiary. To prepare for the emergency, they built an *auxiliary* power station; also (*n*).

av·a·rice \'av-(ə-)rəs\ (*n*) greediness for wealth. King Midas's *avarice* has been famous for centuries. av·a·ri·cious \ˌav-ə-'rish-əs\ (*adj*)

av·a·tar \'av-ə-ˌtär\ (*n*) incarnation. In Hindu mythology, the *avatar* of Vishnu is thoroughly detailed.

a·ver \ə-'vər\ (*v*) state confidently. I wish to *aver* that I am certain of success.

a·verse \ə-'vərs\ (*adj*) reluctant. He was *averse* to revealing the sources of his information.

a·ver·sion \ə-'vər-zhən\ (*n*) firm dislike. Their mutual *aversion* was so great that they refused to speak to one another.

a·vert \ə-'vərt\ (*v*) prevent; turn away. She *averted* her eyes from the dead cat on the highway.

av·id \'av-əd\ (*adj*) greedy; eager for. He was *avid* for learning and read everything he could get. a·vid·i·ty \ə-vid ət-ē\ (*n*).

av·o·ca·tion \ˌav-ə-'kā-shən\ (*n*) secondary or minor occupation. His hobby proved to be so fascinating and profitable that gradually he abandoned his regular occupation and concentrated on his *avocation*.

\ə\ **abut** \ᵊ\ **kitten, F table** \ər\ **further** \a\ **ash** \ā\ **ace** \ä\ **cot, cart**
\au̇\ **out** \ch\ **chin** \e\ **bet** \ē\ **easy** \g\ **go** \i\ **hit** \ī\ **ice** \j\ **job**

a-vow \ə-'vaů\ (*v*) declare openly. I must *avow* that I am innocent.

a-vun-cu-lar \ə-'vəŋ-kyə-lər\ (*adj*) like an uncle. *Avancular* pride did not prevent him from noticing his nephew's shortcomings.

awe \ȯ\ (*n*) solemn wonder. The tourists gazed with *awe* at the tremendous expanse of the Grand Canyon.

a-wry \ə-'rī\ (*adv*) distorted; crooked. He held his head *awry,* giving the impression that he had caught cold in his neck during the night; also (*adj*).

ax-i-om \'ak-sē-əm\ (*n*) self-evident truth requiring no proof. Before a student can begin to think along the lines of Euclidean geometry, he must accept certain principles or *axioms.*

az-ure \'azh-ər\ (*adj*) sky blue. *Azure* skies are indicative of good weather.

\ŋ\ **sing**   \ō\ **go**   \ȯ\ **law**   \ȯi\ **boy**   \th\ **thin**   \t̲h̲\ **the**   \ü\ **loot**   \ů\ **foot**
\y\ **yet**   \zh\ **vision**   \à, k̲, ⁿ, œ, œ̄, ue, īe, ʸ\ *see* Pronunciation Symbols

B

bab-ble \\'bab-əl\\ (v) chatter idly. The little girl *babbled* about her doll; also (n).

bad-ger \\'baj-ər\\ (v) pester; annoy. She was forced to change her telephone number because she was *badgered* by obscene phone calls.

ba-di-nage \\,bad-ᵊn-'äzh\\ (n) teasing conversation. Her friends at work greeted the news of her engagement with cheerful *badinage.*

baf-fle \\'baf-əl\\ (v) frustrate; perplex. The new code *baffled* the enemy agents; also (n).

bait \\'bāt\\ (v) harass; tease. The soldiers *baited* the prisoners, terrorizing them.

bale-ful \\'bā(ə)l-fəl\\ (adj) deadly; destructive. The drought was a *baleful* omen.

balk \\'bók\\ (v) foil. When the warden learned that several inmates were planning to escape, he took steps to *balk* their attempt; also (n).

bal-last \\'bal-əst\\ (n) heavy substance used to add stability or weight. The ship was listing badly to one side; it was necessary to shift the *ballast* in the hold to get it back on an even keel; also (v).

balm \\'bä(l)m\\ (n) something that relieves pain. Friendship is the finest *balm* for the pangs of disappointed love.

balm-y \\'bäm-ē\\ (adj) mild; fragrant. A *balmy* breeze refreshed us after the sultry blast.

ba-nal \\bə-'näl\\ (adj) hackneyed; commonplace; trite. His frequent use of clichés made his essay seem *banal.* ba-nal-i-ty \\bə-'nal-ət-ē\\ (n)

ban-dy \\'ban-dē\\ (v) discuss lightly; exchange blows or words. The president refused to *bandy* words with the reporters at the press conference.

bane \\'bān\\ (n) cause of ruin; poison. Lack of public transportation is the *bane* of urban life. bane-ful \\bān-fəl\\ (adj)

\\ə\\ **abut** \\ᵊ\\ **kitten, F table** \\ər\\ **further** \\a\\ **ash** \\ā\\ **ace** \\ä\\ **cot, cart** \\aú\\ **out** \\ch\\ **chin** \\e\\ **bet** \\ē\\ **easy** \\g\\ **go** \\i\\ **hit** \\ī\\ **ice** \\j\\ **job**

bane-ful \'bān-fəl\ (*adj*) ruinous; poisonous. His *baneful* influence was feared by all.

ban-ter \'bant-ər\ (*n*) good-natured ridiculing. They resented his *banter* because they thought he was being sarcastic; also (*v*).

barb \'bärb\ (*n*) sharp projection from fishhook, etc. The *barb* from the fishhook caught in his finger as he grabbed the fish; also (*v*).

ba-roque \bə-'rōk\ (*adj*) highly ornate. They found the *baroque* architecture amusing.

bar-rage \bə-'räzh\ (*n*) barrier laid down by artillery fire. The company was forced to retreat through the *barrage* of heavy cannons; also (*v*).

bar-ris-ter \'bar-ə-stər\ (*n*) counselor-at-law. Galsworthy started as a *barrister,* but when he found the practice of law boring, turned to writing.

bar-ter-er \'bärt-ər-ər\ (*n*) trader. The *barterer* exchanged trinkets for the natives' furs. **bar-ter** \'bärt-ər\ (*v*)

bask \'bask\ (*v*) luxuriate; take pleasure in warmth. *Basking* on the beach, she relaxed so completely that she fell asleep.

bas-tion \'bas-chən\ (*n*) fortress; defense. Once a *bastion* of democracy, under its new government the island became a dictatorship.

bate \'bāt\ (*v*) let down; restrain. Until it was time to open the presents, the children had to *bate* their curiosity.

bat-ten \'bat-ᵊn\ (*v*) grow fat; thrive upon others. We cannot accept a system where a favored few can *batten* in extreme comfort while others toil.

bau-ble \'bȯ-bəl\ (*n*) trinket; trifle. The child was delighted with the *bauble* she had won in the grab bag.

bawdy \'bȯd-ē\ (*adj*) indecent; obscene. She took offense at his *bawdy* remarks.

be-a-ti-fic \ˌbē-ə-'tif-ik\ (*adj*) giving bliss; blissful. The *beatific* smile on the child's face made us very happy.

---

be·at·i·tude \bē-'at-ə-ˌt(y)üd\ (*n*) blessedness; state of bliss. Growing closer to God each day, the mystic achieved a state of indescribable *beatitude.*

be·di·zen \bi-'dīz -ᵊn\ (*v*) dress with vulgar finery. The witch doctors were *bedizened* in all their gaudiest costumes.

be·drag·gle \bi-'drag-əl\ (*v*) wet thoroughly. We were so *bedraggled* by the severe storm that we had to change into dry clothing. **be·drag·gled** \bi-'drag-əld\ (*adj*)

be·guile \bi-'gī(ə)l \ (*v*) delude; cheat; amuse. He *beguiled* himself during the long hours by playing solitaire.

be·he·moth \bi-'hē-məth\ (*n*) huge creature; something of monstrous size or power. Sportscasters nicknamed the linebacker "The *Behemoth.*"

be·hold·en \bi-'hōl-dən\ (*adj*) obligated; indebted. Since I do not wish to be *beholden* to anyone, I cannot accept this favor.

be·hoove \bi-'hüv\ (*v*) suited to; incumbent upon. In this time of crisis, it *behooves* all of us to remain calm and await the instructions of our superiors.

be·la·bor \bi-'lā-bər\ (*v*) beat soundly; assail verbally. He was *belaboring* his opponent.

be·lat·ed \bi-'lāt-əd\ (*adj*) delayed. He apologized for his *belated* note of condolence to the widow of his friend and explained that he had just learned of her husband's untimely death.

be·lea·guer \bi-'lē-gər\ (*v*) besiege. As soon as the city was *beleaguered,* life became more subdued as the citizens began their long wait for outside assistance.

be·lie \bi-'lī\ (*v*) contradict; give a false impression. His coarse, hard-bitten exterior *belied* his inner sensitivity.

be·lit·tle \bi-'lit-ᵊl\ (*v*) disparage; deprecate. Although I do not wish to *belittle* your contribution, I feel I must place it in its proper perspective.

bel·li·cose \'bel-i-ˌkōs\ (*adj*) warlike. His *bellicose* disposition alienated his friends.

\ə\ **abut** \ᵊ\ **kitten,** F **table** \ər\ **further** \a\ **ash** \ā\ **ace** \ä\ **cot, cart**
\au̇\ **out** \ch\ **chin** \e\ **bet** \ē\ **easy** \g\ **go** \i\ **hit** \ī\ **ice** \j\ **job**

bel·lig·er·ent \bə-'lij(ə)-rənt\ (*adj*) quarrelsome. Whenever he had too much to drink, he became *belligerent* and tried to pick fights with strangers.

ben·e·dic·tion \ˌben-ə-'dik-shən\ (*n*) blessing. The appearance of the sun after the many rainy days was like a *benediction.*

ben·e·fac·tor \'ben-ə-ˌfak-tər\ (*n*) gift-giver; patron. Scrooge later became Tiny Tim's *benefactor.*

ben·e·fi·ci·ary \ˌben-ə-'fish-ē-er-ē\ (*n*) person entitled to benefits or proceeds of an insurance policy or will. You may change your *beneficiary* as often as you wish; also (*adj*).

be·nev·o·lent \bə-'nev(-ə)-lənt\ (*adj*) generous; charitable. His *benevolent* nature prevented him from refusing any beggar who accosted him.

be·night·ed \bi-'nīt-əd\ (*adj*) overcome by darkness. In the *benighted* Middle Ages, intellectual curiosity was discouraged by the authorities.

be·nign \bi-'nīn\ (*adj*) kindly; favorable; not malignant. The old man was well liked because of his *benign* attitude toward friend and stranger alike.

be·nig·ni·ty \bi-'nig-nət-ē\ (*n*) state of being kind, benign, gracious. We have endowed our Creator with a *benignity* that permits forgiveness of our sins and transgressions.

be·rate \bi-'rāt\ (*v*) scold strongly. He feared she would *berate* him for his forgetfulness.

be·reave·ment \bi-'rēv-mənt\ (*n*) state of being deprived of something valuable or beloved. His friends gathered to console him upon his sudden *bereavement.*

be·reft \bi-'reft\ (*adj*) deprived of; lacking. The foolish gambler soon found himself *bereft* of funds.

ber·serk \bə(r)-'sərk\ (*adv*) frenzied. Angered, he went *berserk* and began to wreck the room; also (*n*).

be·smirch \bi-'smərch\ (*v*) soil, defile. The scandalous remarks in the newspaper *besmirch* the reputations of every member of the society.

\ŋ\ sing   \ō\ go   \ȯ\ law   \ȯi\ boy   \th\ thin   \t̲h̲\ the   \ü\ loot   \u̇\ foot
\y\ yet   \zh\ vision   \à, k̲, ⁿ, œ, œ̄, ᵫ, ᵫ̄, ʸ\ *see* Pronunciation Symbols

bes·tial \'bes(h)-chəl\ (*adj*) beastlike; brutal. We must suppress our *bestial* desires and work for peaceful and civilized ends.

be·stow \bi-'stō\ (*v*) confer. He wished to *bestow* great honors upon the hero.

be·troth \bi-'träth\ (*v*) become engaged to marry. The announcement that they had become *betrothed* surprised their friends who had not suspected any romance. **be·troth·al** \bi-'trōth-əl\ (*n*)

be·vy \'bev-ē\ (*n*) large group. The movie actor was surrounded by a *bevy* of starlets.

bi·cam·er·al \(ˈ)bī-'kam-(ə-)rəl\ (*adj*) two-chambered, as a legislative body. The United States Congress is a *bicameral* body.

bick·er \'bik-ər\ (*v*) quarrel. The children *bickered* morning, noon, and night, exasperating their parents.

bi·en·ni·al \(ˈ)bī-'en-ē-əl\ (*adj*) every two years. The plant bore *biennial* flowers; also (*n*)

bi·fur·cate \(ˈ)bi-'fər-kət\ (*adj*) divided into two branches; forked. With a *bifurcate* branch and a piece of elastic rubber, he made a crude but effective slingshot.

big·ot·ry \'big-ə-trē\ (*n*) stubborn intolerance. Brought up in a democratic atmosphere, the student was shocked by the *bigotry* and narrowness expressed by several of his classmates.

bil·ious \'bil-yəs\ (*adj*) suffering from indigestion; irritable. His *bilious* temperament was apparent to all who heard him rant about his difficulties.

bilk \'bilk\ (*v*) swindle; cheat. The con man specialized in *bilking* insurance companies.

bi·zarre \bə-'zär\ (*adj*) fantastic; violently contrasting. The plot of the novel was too *bizarre* to be believed.

blanch \'blanch\ (*v*) bleach; whiten. Although age had *blanched* his hair, he was still vigorous and energetic.

\ə\ abut \ə\ kitten, F table \ər\ further \a\ ash \ā\ ace \ä\ cot, cart
\aù\ out \ch\ chin \e\ bet \ē\ easy \g\ go \i\ hit \ī\ ice \j\ job

bland \'bland\ (*adj*) soothing; mild. She used a *bland* ointment for her sunburn.

blan·dish·ment \'blan-dish-mənt\ (*n*) flattery. Despite the salesperson's *blandishments,* the customer did not buy the outfit.

bla·sé \blä-'zā\ (*adj*) bored with pleasure or dissipation. Your *blasé* attitude gives your students an erroneous impression of the joys of scholarship.

blas·phe·mous \'blas-fə-məs\ (*adj*) profane; impious. The people in the room were shocked by his *blasphemous* language.

bla·tant \'blāt-ᵊnt\ (*adj*) loudly offensive. I regard your remarks as *blatant* and ill-mannered. **bla·tan·cy** \'blāt-ᵊn-sē\ (*n*)

bla·zon \'blāz-ᵊn\ (*v*) decorate with an heraldic coat of arms. *Blazoned* on his shield were the two lambs and the lion, the traditional coat of arms of his family; also (*n*).

bleak \'blēk\ (*adj*) cold; cheerless. The Aleutian Islands are *bleak* military outposts.

blight·ed \'blīt-əd\ (*adj*) suffering from a disease; destroyed. The extent of the *blighted* areas could be seen only when viewed from the air. **blight** \'blīt\ (*n*)

blithe \'blīth\ (adj) gay; joyous. Shelley called the skylark a *"blithe* spirit" because of its happy song.

bloat·ed \'blōt-əd\ (*adj*) swollen or puffed as with water or air. The *bloated* corpse was taken from the river. **bloat** \'blōt\ (*n, v*)

blud·geon \'bləj-ən\ (*n*) club; heavy-headed weapon. His walking stick served him as a *bludgeon* on many occasions; also (*v*).

blun·der \'blən-dər\ (*n*) error. The criminal's fatal *blunder* led to his capture; also (*v*).

blurt \'blərt\ (*v*) utter impulsively. Before she could stop him, he *blurted* out the news.

bode \'bōd\ (*v*) foreshadow; portend. The gloomy skies and the sulphurous odors from the mineral springs seemed to *bode* evil to those who settled in the area.

bo-gus \'bō-gəs\ (*adj*) counterfeit; not authentic. The police quickly found the distributors of the *bogus* twenty-dollar bills.

bois-ter-ous \'bȯi-st(ə-)rəs\ (*adj*) violent; rough; noisy. The unruly crowd became even more *boisterous* when he tried to quiet them.

bol-ster \'bōl-stər\ (*v*) support; prop up. I do not intend to *bolster* your hopes with false reports of outside assistance; the truth is that we must face the enemy alone; also (*n*).

bom-bas-tic \bäm-'bas-tik\ (*adj*) pompous; using inflated language. The orator spoke in a *bombastic* manner. **bom-bast** \'bäm-ˌbast\ (*n*)

boor-ish \'bu̇(ə)r-ish\ (*adj*) rude; clownish. Your *boorish* remarks to the driver of the other car were not warranted by the situation and served merely to enrage him.

boun-ti-ful \'bau̇nt-i-fəl\ (*adj*) generous; showing bounty. She distributed gifts in a *bountiful* and gracious manner.

bour-geois \'bu̇(ə)rzh-ˌwä\ (*n*) middle class. The French Revolution was inspired by the *bourgeois;* also (*adj*).

brack-ish \'brak-ish\ (*adj*) somewhat saline. He found the only wells in the area were *brackish;* drinking the water made him nauseated.

brag-ga-do-ci-o \ˌbrag-ə-'dō-s(h)ē-ˌō\ (*n*) boasting. He was disliked because his manner was always full of *braggadocio.*

bra-va-do \brə-'väd-ˌ(ˌ)ō\ (*n*) swagger; assumed air of defiance. The *bravado* of the young criminal disappeared when he was confronted by the victims of his brutal attack.

bra-zen \'brāz-ᵊn\ (*adj*) insolent. Her *brazen* contempt for authority angered the officials; also (*v*).

\ə\ abut \ᵊ\ kitten, F table \ər\ **further** \a\ ash \ā\ **ace** \ä\ cot, cart
\au̇\ **out** \ch\ **chin** \e\ bet \ē\ **easy** \g\ go \i\ hit \ī\ ice \j\ **job**

breach \'brēch\ (*n*) breaking of contract or duty; fissure; gap. They found a *breach* in the enemy's fortifications and penetrated their lines; also (*v*).

breadth \'bretth\ (*n*) width; extent. We were impressed by the *breadth* of her knowledge.

brev-i-ty \'brev-ət-ē\ (*n*) conciseness. *Brevity* is essential when you send a telegram or cablegram; you are charged for every word.

bris-tling \'bris-(ə-)liŋ\ (*adj*) rising like bristles, showing irritation. The dog stood there, *bristling* with anger. **bris-tle** \'bris-əl\ (*n, v*)

broach \'brōch\ (*v*) open up. He did not even try to *broach* the subject of poetry.

bro-chure \brō-'shú(ə)r\ (*n*) pamphlet. This *brochure* on farming was issued by the Department of Agriculture.

brusque \'brəsk\ (*adj*) blunt; abrupt. She was offended by his *brusque* reply.

bu-col-ic \byü-'käl-ik\ (*adj*) rustic; pastoral. The meadow was the scene of *bucolic* gaiety.

buf-foon-er-y \(')bə-'fün-(ə-)rē\ (*n*) clowning. Jimmy Durante's *buffoonery* was hilarious.

bul-lion \'bùl-yən\ (*n*) gold and silver in the form of bars. Much *bullion* is stored in the vaults at Fort Knox.

bul-wark \'bùl-(')wərk\ (*n*) earthwork or other strong defense; person who defends. The navy is our principal *bulwark* against invasion.

bun-gle \'bəŋ-gəl\ (*v*) spoil by clumsy behavior. I was afraid you would *bungle* this assignment but I had no one else to send.

bu-reau-cra-cy \byù-'räk-rə-sē\ (*n*) government by bureaus. Many people fear that the constant introduction of federal agencies will create a government by *bureaucracy*.

bur-geon \'bər-jən\ (*v*) grow forth; send out buds. In the spring, the plants that burgeon are a promise of the beauty that is to come.

\ŋ\ **sing** \ō\ **go** \ò\ **law** \òi\ **boy** \th\ **thin** \th̲\ **the** \ü\ **loot** \ù\ **foot**
\y\ **yet** \zh\ **vision** \à, k̲, ⁿ, œ, œ̄, ᴜe, ᴜ̄e, ʸ\ *see* Pronunciation Symbols

bur-lesque \⁽ʼ⁾bər-ˈlesk\ (*v*) give an imitation that ridicules. In his caricature, he *burlesqued* the mannerisms of his adversary; also (*n*).

bur-ly \ˈbər-lē\ (*adj*) husky; muscular. The *burly* mover lifted the packing crate with ease.

bur-nish \ˈbər-nish\ (*v*) make shiny by rubbing; polish. The *burnished* metal reflected the lamplight; also (*n*).

but-tress \ˈbə-trəs\ (*n*) support or prop. The huge cathedral walls were supported by flying *buttresses;* also (*v*).

bux-om \ˈbək-səm\ (*adj*) plump; vigorous; jolly. The soldiers remembered the *buxom* nurse who had always been so pleasant to them.

C

ca-bal \kə-'bal\ (*n*) small group of persons secretly united to promote their own interests. The *cabal* was defeated when their scheme was discovered; also (*v*).

cache \'kash\ (*n*) hiding place. The detectives followed the suspect until he led them to the *cache* where he had stored his loot; also (*v*).

ca-coph-o-ny \ka-'käf-ə-nē\ (*n*) discord. Some people seem to enjoy the *cacophony* of an orchestra that is tuning up.

ca-dav-er \kə-'dav-ər\ (*n*) corpse. In some states, it is illegal to dissect *cadavers*.

ca-dav-er-ous \kə-'dav-(ə-)rəs\ (*adj*) like a corpse; pale. By his *cadaverous* appearance, we could see how the disease had ravaged him.

ca-jole \kə-'jōl\ (*v*) coax; wheedle. I will not be *cajoled* into granting you your wish.

cal-i-ber \'kal-ə-bər\ (*n*) ability; capacity. A man of such *caliber* should not be assigned such menial tasks.

cal-lig-ra-phy \kə-'lig-rə-fē\ (*n*) beautiful writing; excellent penmanship. As we examine ancient manuscripts, we become impressed with the *calligraphy* of the scribes.

cal-lous \'kal-əs\ (*adj*) hardened; unfeeling. He had worked in the hospital for so many years that he was *callous* to the suffering in the wards. **cal-lus** \'kal-əs\ (*n*)

cal-low \'kal-ˌō\ (*adj*) unfledged; youthful. In that youthful movement, the leaders were only a little less *callow* than their immature followers.

cal-o-rif-ic \kal-ə-'rif-ik\ (*adj*) heat-producing. Coal is much more *calorific* than green wood.

cal-um-ny \'kal-əm-nē\ (*n*) malicious misrepresentation; slander. He could endure his financial failure, but he could not bear the *calumny* that his foes heaped upon him.

\ŋ\ **sing** \ō\ **go** \ȯ\ **law** \ȯi\ **boy** \th\ **thin** \t͟h\ **the** \ü\ **loot** \u̇\ **foot**
\y\ **yet** \zh\ **vision** \à, ᵏ, ⁿ, œ, œ̄, ̣ue, ̣œ, ʸ\ *see* Pronunciation Symbols

cam-e-o \\'kam-ē-ˌō\ (*n*) shell or jewel carved in relief. Tourists are advised not to purchase *cameos* from the street peddlers of Rome who sell poor specimens of the carver's art.

ca-nard \kə-'närd\ (*n*) unfounded rumor; exaggerated report. It is almost impossible to protect oneself from such a base *canard.*

can-dor \\'kan-dər\ (*n*) frankness. The *candor* and simplicity of his speech impressed all. **can-did** \\'kan-dəd\ (*adj*)

ca-nine \\'kā-ˌnīn\ (*adj*) related to dogs; doglike. Some days the *canine* population of Berkeley seems almost to outnumber the human population.

can-ny \\'kan-ē\ (*adj*) shrewd; thrifty. The *canny* Scotsman was more than a match for the swindlers.

cant \\'kant\ (*n*) jargon of thieves; pious phraseology. Many listeners were fooled by the *cant* and hypocrisy of his speech; also (*v*).

can-tan-ker-ous \kan-'tan-k(ə)rəs\ (*adj*) ill humored; irritable. Constantly complaining about his treatment and refusing to cooperate with the hospital staff, he was a *cantankerous* patient.

can-ter \\'kant-ər\ (*n*) slow gallop. Because the racehorse had outdistanced its competition so easily, the reporter wrote that the race was won in a *canter;* also (*v*).

can-vass \\'kan-vəs\ (*v*) determine votes, etc. After *canvassing* the sentiments of his constituents, the congressman was confident that he represented the majority opinion of his district; also (*n*).

ca-pa-cious \kə-'pā-shəs\ (*adj*) spacious. In the *capacious* areas of the railroad terminal, thousands of travelers lingered while waiting for their train.

ca-par-i-son \kə-'par-ə-sən\ (*n*) showy harness or ornamentation for a horse. The audience admired the *caparison* of the horses as they made their entrance into the circus ring; also (*v*).

\ə\ **abut** \ˈə\ **kitten, F table** \ər\ **further** \a\ **ash** \ā\ **ace** \ä\ **cot, cart**
\au̇\ **out** \ch\ **chin** \e\ **bet** \ē\ **easy** \g\ **go** \i\ **hit** \ī\ **ice** \j\ **job**

cap-il-lar-y \\'kap-ə-ˌler-ē\\ (*adj*) having a very fine bore. The changes in surface tension of liquids in *capillary* vessels is of special interest to physicists; also (*n*).

ca-pit-u-late \\kə-'pich-ə-ˌlāt\\ (*v*) surrender. The enemy was warned to *capitulate* or face annihilation.

ca-price \\kə-'prēs\\ (*n*) whim. Do not act on *caprice*. Study your problem.

ca-pri-cious \\kə-'prish-əs\\ (*adj*) fickle; incalculable. The storm was *capricious* and changed course constantly.

cap-tion \\'kap-shən\\ (*n*) title; chapter heading; text under illustration. I find the *captions* that accompany these cartoons very clever and humorous; also (*v*).

cap-tious \\'kap-shəs\\ (*adj*) faultfinding. His criticisms were always *captious* and frivolous, never offering constructive suggestions.

ca-rafe \\kə-'raf\\ (*n*) glass water bottle; decanter. With each dinner, the patron receives a *carafe* of red or white wine.

car-at \\'kar-ət\\ (*n*) unit of weight for precious stones; measure of fineness of gold. He gave her a three-*carat* diamond mounted in an eighteen-*carat* gold band.

car-cin-o-gen-ic \\kär-sin-ə-'jen-ik\\ (*adj*) causing cancer. Many supposedly harmless substances have been revealed to be *carcinogenic*.

car-di-nal \\'kärd-nəl\\ (*adj*) chief. If you want to increase your word power, the *cardinal* rule of vocabulary-building is to read.

ca-reen \\kə-'rēn\\ (*v*) lurch; sway from side to side. The taxicab *careened* wildly as it rounded the corner.

car-i-ca-ture \\'kar-i-kə-ˌchu̇(ə)r\\ (*n*) distortion; burlesque. The *caricatures* he drew always emphasized a personal weakness of the people he burlesqued; also (*v*).

car-nage \\'kär-nij\\ (*n*) destruction of life. The *carnage* that can be caused by atomic warfare adds to the responsibilities of our statesmen.

\\ŋ\\ sing \\ō\\ go \\ȯ\\ law \\ȯi\\ boy \\th\\ thin \\t͟h\\ the \\ü\\ loot \\u̇\\ foot
\\y\\ yet \\zh\\ vision \\à, k̲, ⁿ, œ, œ̄, ue, œ, ʸ\\ *see* Pronunciation Symbols

car-nal \\'kärn-əl\ (*adj*) fleshly. The public was more interested in *carnal* pleasures than in spiritual matters.

car-niv-o-rous \kär-'niv-(ə-)rəs\ (*adj*) meat-eating. The lion is a *carnivorous* animal. **car-ni-vore** \\'kär-nə-‚vō(ə)r\ (*n*)

ca-rous-al \kə-'raů-zəl\ (*n*) drunken revel. The party degenerated into an ugly *carousal.*

carp-ing \\'kär-piŋ\ (*adj*) finding fault. A *carping* critic disturbs sensitive people.

car-ri-on \\'kar-ē-ən\ (*n*) rotting flesh of a dead body. Buzzards are nature's scavengers; they eat the *carrion* left behind by other predators.

car-tog-ra-pher \kär-'täg-rə-fər\ (*n*) maker of maps or charts. *Cartographers* are unable to provide accurate maps of legal boundaries in the Near East because of the unsettled political situation in that part of the world following the recent military actions.

cas-cade \⁽ʲ⁾kas-'kād\ (*n*) small waterfall. We could not appreciate the beauty of the many *cascades* as we were forced to make detours around each of them; also (*v*).

caste \\'kast\ (*n*) one of the hereditary classes in Hindu society. The differences created by the *caste* system in India must be eradicated if true democracy is to prevail in that country.

cas-ti-gate \\'kas-tə-‚gāt\ (*v*) punish. He decided to *castigate* the culprit personally.

ca-su-al-ty \\'kazh-əl-tē\ (*n*) serious or fatal accident. The number of *casualties* on this holiday weekend was high.

ca-su-ist-ry \\'kazh-(ə-)wə-strē\ (*n*) subtle or sophisticated reasoning resulting in minute distinctions. You are using *casuistry* to justify your obvious violation of decent behavior.

cat-a-clysm \\'kat-ə-‚kliz-əm\ (*n*) deluge, upheaval. A *cataclysm* such as the French Revolution affects all countries. **cat-a-clys-mic** \\'kat-ə-‚kliz-mik\ (*adj*)

\ə\ abut \ᵊ\ kitten, F table \ər\ **further** \a\ ash \ā\ **ace** \ä\ cot, cart
\aů\ **out** \ch\ **chin** \e\ bet \ē\ **easy** \g\ go \i\ hit \ī\ ice \j\ **job**

cat-a-lyst \'kat-ᵊl-əst\ (*n*) agent that brings about a chemical change while it remains unaffected and unchanged. Many chemical reactions cannot take place without the presence of a *catalyst.*

cat-a-pult \'kat-ə-ˌpəlt\ (*n*) slingshot; a hurling machine. Airplanes are sometimes launched from battleships by *catapults;* also (*v*).

cat-a-ract \'kat-ə-ˌrakt\ (*n*) great waterfall; eye abnormality. She gazed with awe at the mighty *cataract* known as Niagara Falls.

ca-tas-tro-phe \kə-'tas-trə-₍ᵢ₎fē\ (*n*) calamity. The Johnstown flood was a *catastrophe.*

cat-e-chism \'kat-ə-ˌkiz-əm\ (*n*) book for religious instruction; instruction by question and answer. He taught by engaging his pupils in a *catechism* until they gave him the correct answer.

ca-thar-sis \ka-'thär-səs\ (*n*) purging or cleansing of any passage of the body. Aristotle maintained that tragedy created a *catharsis* by purging the soul of base concepts.

ca-thar-tic \kə-'thärt-ik\ (*n*) purgative. Some drugs act as laxatives when taken in small doses but act as *cathartics* when taken in much larger doses; also (*adj*).

cath-o-lic \ˌkath-(ə-)lik\ (*adj*) broadly sympathetic; liberal. He was extremely *catholic* in his reading tastes.

cau-cus \'kȯ-kəs\ (*n*) private meeting of members of a party to select officers or determine policy. At the opening of Congress, the members of the Democratic Party held a *caucus* to elect the Majority Leader of the House and the Party Whip; also (*v*).

caus-tic \'kȯ-stik\ (*adj*) burning; sarcastically biting. The critic's *caustic* remarks angered the hapless actors who were the subjects of his sarcasm; also (*n*).

cav-al-cade \'kav-əl-ˌkād\ (*n*) procession; parade. As described by Chaucer, the *cavalcade* by Canterbury pilgrims was a motley group.

\ŋ\ sing   \ō\ go   \ȯ\ law   \ȯi\ boy   \th\ thin   \t͟h\ the   \ü\ loot   \u̇\ foot
\y\ yet   \zh\ vision   \à, k̲, ⁿ, œ, œ̄, ᵫ, œ̄, ʸ\ *see* Pronunciation Symbols

cav·il \\'kav-əl\ (*v*) make frivolous objections. I respect your sensible criticisms, but I dislike the way you *cavil* about unimportant details; also (*n*).

cede \\'sēd\ (*v*) transfer; yield title to. I intend to *cede* this property to the city.

ce·ler·i·ty \sə-'ler-ət-ē\ (*n*) speed; rapidity. Hamlet re- sented his mother's *celerity* in remarrying within a month after his father's death.

ce·les·tial \sə-'les(h)-chəl\ (*adj*) heavenly. He wrote about the music of "*celestial* spheres"; also (*n*).

cel·i·bate \\'sel-ə-bət\ (*adj*) unmarried; abstaining from sexual intercourse. He vowed to remain *celibate*. **cel·i·ba·cy** \\'sel-ə-bə-sē\ (*n*)

cen·sor \\'sen(t)-sər\ (*n*) overseer of morals; person who studies material to eliminate inappropriate remarks. Soldiers dislike having their mail read by a *censor* but understand the need for this precaution; also (*v*).

cen·so·ri·ous \sen-'sōr-ē-əs\ (*adj*) critical. *Censorious* people delight in casting blame.

cen·sure \\'sen-chər\ (*v*) blame; criticize. He was *censured* for his ill-advised act; also (*n*).

cen·ti·grade \\'sent-ə-ˌgrād\ (*adj*) measure of temperature used widely in Europe. On the *centigrade* thermometer, the freezing point of water is zero degrees.

cen·trif·u·gal \sen-'trif-yə-gəl\ (*adj*) radiating; departing from the center. Many automatic drying machines re- move excess moisture from clothing by *centrifugal* force; also (*n*).

cen·trip·e·tal \sen-'trip-ət-ᵊl\ (*adj*) tending toward the center. Does *centripetal* force or the force of gravity bring orbiting bodies to the earth's surface?

ce·re·bral \sə-'rē-brəl\ (*adj*) pertaining to the brain or in- tellect. The content of philosophical works is *cerebral* in nature and requires much thought.

cer-e-bra-tion \ˌser-ə-'brā-shən\ (*n*) thought. Mathematics problems sometimes require much *cerebration*. **cer-e-brate** \'ser-ə-ˌbrāt\ (*v*)

ces-sa-tion \se-'sā-shən)\ (*n*) stopping. The workers threatened a *cessation* of all activities if their demands were not met. **cease** \'sēs\ (*v*)

ces-sion \'sesh-ən\ (*n*) yielding to another; ceding. The *cession* of Alaska to the United States is discussed in this chapter.

chafe \'chāf\ (*v*) warm by rubbing; make sore by rubbing. The collar *chafed* his neck; also (*n*).

chaff \'chaf\ (*n*) worthless products of an endeavor. When you separate the wheat from the chaff, be sure you throw out the *chaff.*

chaff-ing \'chaf-iŋ\ (*adj*) bantering; joking. Sometimes his flippant and *chaffing* remarks annoy us.

cha-grin \sha-'grin\ (*n*) vexation; disappointment. His refusal to go with us filled us with *chagrin;* also (*v*).

chal-ice \'chal-əs\ (*n*) goblet; consecrated cup. In a small room adjoining the cathedral, many ornately decorated *chalices* made by the most famous European goldsmiths were on display.

cha-me-leon \kə-'mēl-yən\ (*n*) lizard that changes color in different situations. Like the *chameleon,* he assumed the political thinking of every group he met.

cham-pi-on \'cham-pē-ən\ (*v*) support militantly. Martin Luther King, Jr., won the Nobel Peace Prize because he *championed* the oppressed in their struggle for equality.

cha-ot-ic \kā-ät-ik\ (*adj*) in utter disorder. He tried to bring order into the *chaotic* state of affairs. **cha-os** \'kā-ˌäs\ (*n*)

char-ac-ter-ize \'kar-ik-tə-ˌrīz\ (*v*) describe; distinguish. Heavy use of garlic and tomatoes *characterizes* the food of Provence. **char-ac-ter-is-tic** \ˌkar-ik-tə-'ris-tik\ (*adj*) cha-ris-ma \kə-'riz-mə\ (*n*) divine gift; great popular charm or appeal of a political leader. Political commentators have deplored the importance of a candidate's *charisma* in these days of television campaigning.

char-la-tan \'shär-lə-tən\ (*n*) quack; pretender to knowledge. Because he was unable to substantiate his claim that he had found a cure for the dread disease, he was called a *charlatan* by his colleagues.

char-y \'cha(ə)r-ē\ (*adj*) cautiously watchful. She was *chary* of her favors.

chasm \'kaz-əm\ (*n*) abyss. They could not see the bottom of the *chasm*.

chas-sis \'shas-ē\ (*n*) framework and working parts of an automobile. Examining the car after the accident, the owner discovered that the body had been ruined but that the *chassis* was unharmed.

chaste \'chāst\ (*adj*) pure. Her *chaste* and decorous garb was appropriately selected for the solemnity of the occasion. chas-ti-ty \'chas-tət-ē\ (*n*)

chas-tise \(ⁱ)chas-'tiz\ (*v*) punish. I must *chastise* you for this offense.

chat-tel \'chat'-ᵊl\ (*n*) personal property. When he bought his furniture on the installment plan, he signed a *chattel* mortgage.

chau-vin-ist \'shō-və-nəst\ (*n*) blindly devoted patriot. A *chauvinist* cannot recognize any faults in his country, no matter how flagrant they may be.

check-er \'chek-ər\ (*v*) mark by changes in fortune. His long career was *checkered* by prosperity and failure; also (*n*).

che-ru-bic \chə-'rü-bik\ (*adj*) angelic; innocent-looking. With her cheerful smile and rosy cheeks, she was a particularly *cherubic* child.

chi-ca-ner-y \skik-'ān-(ə-)rē\ (*n*) trickery. Your deceitful tactics in this case are indications of *chicanery*.

---

chide \'chīd\ (*v*) scold. Grandma began to *chide* Steven for his lying.

chi·me·ri·cal \kī-'mer-i-kəl\ (*adj*) fantastic; highly imaginative. Poe's *chimerical* stories are sometimes too morbid for reading in bed. chi·me·ra \kī-'mir-ə\ (*n*)

cho·ler·ic \'käl-ə-rik\ (*adj*) hot-tempered. His flushed, angry face indicated a *choleric* nature.

cho·re·og·ra·phy \ˌkōr-ē-ē-'äg-rə-fē\ (*n*) art of dancing. Martha Graham introduced a form of *choreography* that seemed awkward and alien to those who had been brought up on classic ballet.

chron·ic \'krän-ik\ (*adj*) long established as a disease. The doctors were able finally to attribute his *chronic* headaches and nausea to traces of formaldehyde gas in his apartment.

churl·ish \'chər-lish\ (*adj*) boorish; rude. Dismayed by his *churlish* manners at the party, the girls vowed never to invite him again.

cir·cu·i·tous \ˌsər-'kyü-ət-əs\ (*adj*) roundabout. Because of the traffic congestion on the main highways, he took a *circuitous* route. cir·cuit \'sər-kət\ (*n*, *v*)

cir·cum·lo·cu·tion \ˌsər-kəm-lō-'kyü-shən\ (*n*) indirect or roundabout expression. He was afraid to call a spade a spade and resorted to *circumlocution* to avoid direct reference to his subject.

cir·cum·scribe \'sər-kəm-ˌskrīb\ (*v*) limit; confine. Although I do not wish to *circumscribe* your activities, I must insist that you complete this assignment before you start anything else.

cir·cum·spect \'sər-kəm-ˌspekt\ (*adj*) prudent; cautious. Investigating before acting, he tried always to be *circumspect*.

cir·cum·vent \ˌsər-kəm-'vent\ (*v*) outwit; baffle. In order to *circumvent* the enemy, we will make two preliminary attacks in other sections before starting our major campaign.

\ŋ\ **sing** \ō\ **go** \ȯ\ **law** \ȯi\ **boy** \th\ **thin** \t͟h\ **the** \ü\ **loot** \u̇\ **foot**
\y\ **yet** \zh\ **vision** \à, k̲, ⁿ, œ, œ̄, ue, œ, ʸ\ *see* Pronunciation Symbols

cit-a-del \\'sit-əd-ᵊl\\ (*n*) fortress. The *citadel* overlooked the city like a protecting angel.

cite \\'sīt\\ (*v*) quote; commend. He could *cite* passages in the Bible from memory. ci-ta-tion \\sī-'tā-shən\\ (*n*)

clair-voy-ant \\kla(ə)r-'vȯi-ənt\\ (*adj*) having foresight. Cassandra's *clairvoyant* warning was not heeded by the Trojans; also (*n*). clair-voy-ance \\kla(ə)r-'vȯi-ən(t)s\\ (*n*)

clam-ber \\'klam-(b)ər\\ (*v*) climb by crawling. He *clambered* over the wall.

clan-des-tine \\klan-'des-tən\\ (*adj*) secret. After avoiding their chaperon, the lovers had a *clandestine* meeting.

clar-i-on \\'klar-ē-ən\\ (*adj*) shrill trumpetlike sound. We woke to the *clarion* call of the bugle; also (*n*).

claus-tro-pho-bi-a \\ˌklȯ-strə-'fō-bē-ə\\ (*n*) fear of being locked in. His fellow classmates laughed at his *claustrophobia* and often threatened to lock him in his room.

clav-i-cle \\'klav-i-kəl\\ (*n*) collarbone. Even though he wore shoulder pads, the football player broke his *clavicle* during a practice scrimmage.

cleave \\'klēv\\ (*v*) split asunder. The lightning *cleaves* the tree in two. cleav-age \\'klē-vij\\ (*n*)

cleft \\'kleft\\ (*n*) split. There was a *cleft* in the huge boulder; also (*adj*).

clem-en-cy \\'klem-ən-sē\\ (*n*) disposition to be lenient; mildness, as of the weather. The lawyer was pleased when the case was sent to Judge Smith's chambers because Smith was noted for his *clemency* toward first offenders.

cli-ché \\kli-'shā\\ (*n*) phrase dulled in meaning by repetition. High school compositions are often marred by such *clichés* as "strong as an ox."

cli-mac-tic \\klī-'mak-tik\\ (*adj*) relating to the highest point. When he reached the *climactic* portions of the book, he could not stop reading. cli-max \\'klī-ˌmaks\\ (*n*)

\\ə\\ abut \\ᵊ\\ kitten, F table \\ər\\ **further** \\a\\ ash \\ā\\ **ace** \\ä\\ cot, cart
\\au̇\\ **out** \\ch\\ **chin** \\e\\ bet \\ē\\ **easy** \\g\\ go \\i\\ hit \\ī\\ ice \\j\\ job

clime \'klīm\ (*n*) region; climate. His doctor advised him to move to a milder *clime.*

clique \'klēk\ (*n*) small exclusive group. He charged that a *clique* had assumed control of school affairs.

clois-ter \'klŏi-stər\ (*n*) monastery or convent. The nuns lived in the *cloister;* also (*v*).

clo-ven \'klō-vən\ (*adj*) split. Popular legends maintain that the devil has *cloven* hooves.

co-ad-ju-tor \ˌkō-ə-'jut-ər\ (*n*) assistant; colleague. He was assigned as *coadjutor* of the bishop.

co-a-lesce \ˌkō-ə-'ləs\ (*v*) combine; fuse. The brooks *coalesce* into one large river.

cod-dle \'käd-ᵊl\ (*v*) treat gently; pamper. Don't *coddle* the children so much; they need a taste of discipline.

cod-i-cil \'käd-ə-səl\ (*n*) supplement to the body of a will. This *codicil* was drawn up five years after the writing of the original will.

co-erce \kō-ərs\ (*v*) force; repress. Do not *coerce* me into doing this; I hate force. **co-er-cion** \kō-'ər-zhən\ (*n*)

co-eval \kō-'ē-vəl\ (*adj*) living at the same time as; contemporary. *Coeval* with the dinosaur, the pterodactyl flourished during the Mesozoic era.

cog \'käg\ (*n*) tooth projecting from a wheel. On steep slopes, *cog* railways are frequently used to prevent slipping.

co-gent \'kō-jənt\ (*adj*) convincing. He presented *cogent* arguments to the jury.

cog-i-tate \'käj-ə-ˌtāt\ (*v*) think over. *Cogitate* on this problem; the solution will come.

cog-nate \'käg-ˌnāt\ (*adj*) allied by blood; of the same or kindred nature. In the phrase "die a thousand deaths," the word "death" is a *cognate* object; also (*n*).

cog-ni-zance \'käg-nə-zən(t)s\ (*n*) knowledge. During the election campaign, the two candidates were kept in full *cognizance* of the international situation.

\ŋ\ sing   \ō\ go   \ȯ\ law   \ȯi\ boy   \th\ thin   \<u>th</u>\ the   \ü\ loot   \u̇\ foot
\y\ yet   \zh\ vision   \à, <u>k</u>, ⁿ, œ, ӕ, ue, ɶ, ʸ\ *see* Pronunciation Symbols

cog-no-men \käg-'nō-mən\ (*n*) family name. He asked the court to change his *cognomen* to a more American-sounding name.

co-here \kō-,hi(ə)r\ (*v*) stick together. Solids have a greater tendency to *cohere* than liquids.

co-he-sion \kō-'hē-zhən\ (*n*) force that keeps parts together. In order to preserve our *cohesion,* we must not let minor differences interfere with our major purposes.

co-hort \'kō-,hó(ə)rt\ (*n*) armed band. Caesar and his Roman *cohorts* conquered almost all of the known world.

co-in-ci-dent \kō-'in(t)-səd-ənt\ (*adj*) occurring at the same time. Some people find the *coincident* events in Hardy's novels annoying.

col-lab-o-rate \kə-'lab-ə-,rāt\ (*v*) work together. Two writers *collaborated* in preparing this book.

col-late \kə-'lāt\ (*v*) examine in order to verify authenticity; arrange in order. They *collated* the newly found manuscripts to determine their age.

col-lat-er-al \kə-'lat-ə-rəl\ (*n*) security given for loan. The sum you wish to borrow is so large that it must be secured by *collateral.*

col-la-tion \kə-'lā-shən\ (*n*) a light meal. Tea sandwiches and cookies were offered at the *collation.*

col-lier \'käl-yər\ (*n*) worker in coal mine; ship carrying coal. The extended cold spell has prevented the *colliers* from delivering the coal to the docks as scheduled.

col-lo-qui-al \kə-'lō-kwē-əl\ (*adj*) pertaining to conversational or common speech. Your use of *colloquial* expressions in a formal essay such as the one you have presented spoils the effect you hope to achieve.

col-lo-quy \'käl-ə-kwē\ (*n*) informal discussion. I enjoy our *colloquies,* but I sometimes wish that they could be made more formal and more searching.

col-lu-sion \kə-'lü-zhən\ (*n*) conspiring in a fraudulent scheme. The swindlers were found guilty of *collusion.*

\ə\ **abut** \ᵊ\ **kitten,** F **table** \ər\ **further** \a\ **ash** \ā\ **ace** \ä\ **cot, cart**
\aú\ **out** \ch\ **chin** \e\ **bet** \ē\ **easy** \g\ **go** \i\ **hit** \ī\ **ice** \j\ **job**

co-los-sal \kə-'läs-əl\ (*adj*) huge. Radio City Music Hall has a *colossal* stage.

co-ma-tose \'kō-mə-ˌtōs\ (*adj*) in a coma; extremely sleepy. The long-winded orator soon had his audience in a *comatose* state.

com-bus-ti-ble \kəm-'bəs-tə-bəl\ (*adj*) easily burned. After the recent outbreak of fires in private homes, the fire commissioner ordered that all *combustible* materials be kept in safe containers; also (*n*).

come-ly \'kəm-lē\ (*adj*) attractive; aggreeable. I would rather have a *comely* wife than a rich one.

co-mes-ti-ble \kə-'mes-tə-bəl\ (*n*) something fit to be eaten. The roast turkey and other *comestibles,* the wines, and the excellent service made this Thanksgiving dinner particularly memorable.

co-mi-ty \'käm-ət-ē\ (*n*) courtesy; civility. A spirit of *comity* should exist among nations.

com-man-deer \ˌkäm-ən-'di(ə)r\ (*v*) to draft for military purposes; to take for public use. The policeman *commandeered* the first car that approached and ordered the driver to go to the nearest hospital.

com-men-su-rate \kə-'men(t)s(-ə)-rət\ (*adj*) equal in extent. Your reward will be *commensurate* with your effort.

com-mis-er-ate \kə-'miz-ə-ˌrāt\ (*v*) feel or express pity or sympathy for. Her friends *commiserated* with the widow.

com-mo-di-ous \kə-'mōd-ē-əs\ (*adj*) spacious and comfortable. After sleeping in small roadside cabins, they found their hotel suite *commodious*.

com-mu-nal \kə-'myün-əl\ (*adj*) held in common; of a group of people. When they were divorced, they had trouble dividing their *communal* property.

com-pact \'käm-ˌpakt\ (*n*) agreement; contract. The signers of the Mayflower *Compact* were establishing a form of government. com-pact \kəm-'pakt\ (*v, adj*)

\ŋ\ **sing**   \ō\ **go**   \ȯ\ **law**   \ȯi\ **boy**   \th\ **thin**   \th\ **the**   \ü\ **loot**   \u̇\ **foot**
\y\ **yet**   \zh\ **vision**   \à, k̲, ⁿ, œ, œ̄, ue, œ, ʸ\ *see* Pronunciation Symbols

com·pat·i·ble \kəm-'pat-ə-bəl\ (*adj*) harmonious; in harmony with. They were *compatible* neighbors, never quarreling over unimportant matters.

com·pen·di·um \kəm-'pen-dē-əm\ (*n*) brief comprehensive summary. This text can serve as a *compendium* of the tremendous amount of new material being developed in this field.

com·pen·sa·tory \kəm-'pen(t)-sə-ˌtōr-ē\ (*adj*) making up for; repaying. Can a *compensatory* education program make up for the inadequate schooling he received in earlier years?

com·pi·la·tion \ˌkäm-pə-'lā-shən\ (*n*) listing of statistical information in tabular or book form. The *compilation* of available scholarships serves a very valuable purpose.

com·pla·cent \kəm-'plās-ᵊnt\ (*adj*) self-satisfied. There was a *complacent* look on his face as he examined his paintings. com·pla·cen·cy \kəm-'plās-ᵊn-sē\ (*n*)

com·plai·sant \kəm-'plās-ᵊnt\ (*adj*) trying to please; obliging. The courtier obeyed the king's orders in a *complaisant* manner.

com·ple·ment \'käm-plə-mənt\ (*n*) that which completes. The waiter would not seat us until our party's full *complement* had arrived; also (*v*).

com·pli·ant \kəm-'plī-ənt\ (*adj*) yielding. He was *compliant* and ready to conform to the pattern set by his friends.

com·plic·i·ty \kəm-'plis-ət-ē\ (*n*) participation; involvement. You cannot keep your *complicity* in this affair secret very long; you would be wise to admit your involvement immediately.

com·port \kəm-'pō(ə)rt\ (*v*) bear one's self; behave. He *comported* himself with great dignity.

com·po·sure \kəm-'pō-zhər\ (*n*) mental calmness. Even the latest work crisis failed to shake her *composure*.

---

com-pre-hen-sive \ˌkäm-pri-'hen(t)-siv\ *(adj)* thorough; inclusive. This book provides a *comprehensive* review of verbal and math skills for the SAT.

com-press \kəm-'pres\ *(v)* squeeze; contract. She *compressed* the package under her arm. com-pres-sion \kəm-'presh-ən\ *(n)*

com-pro-mise \'käm-prə-ˌmīz\ *(v)* adjust; endanger the interests or reputation of. Your presence at the scene of the dispute *compromises* our claim to neutrality in this matter; also *(n)*.

com-punc-tion \kəm-'pəŋ(k)-shən\ *(n)* remorse. The judge was especially severe in his sentencing because he felt that the criminal had shown no *compunction* for his heinous crime.

com-pute \kəm-'pyüt\ *(v)* reckon; calculate. He failed to *complete* the interest.

con-cave \kän-'kāv\ *(adj)* hollow. The backpackers found partial shelter from the storm by huddling against the *concave* wall of the cliff.

con-cen-tra-tion \'kän(t)-sən-ˌtrā-shən\ *(n)* close attention or focus; density or clustering. The children's playground was closed because of the high *concentration* of toxic chemicals in the soil.

con-cen-tric \kən-'sen-trik\ *(adj)* having a common center. The target was made of *concentric* circles.

con-cep-tion \kən-'sep-shən\ *(n)* beginning; forming of an idea. At the first *conception* of the work, he was consulted. con-ceive \kən-'sēv\ *(v)*

con-ces-sion \kən-'sesh-ən\ *(n)* an act of yielding. Before they could reach an agreement, both sides had to make certain *concessions*.

con-cil-i-ate \kən-'sil-ē-ˌāt\ *(v)* pacify; win over. She tried to *conciliate* me with a gift. con-cil-ia-to-ry \kən-'sil-yə-ˌtōr-ē\ *(adj)*

con-cise \kən-'sīs\ *(adj)* brief and compact. The essay was *concise* and explicit.

con-clave \\'kän-ˌklāv\\ (*n*) private meeting. He was present at all their *conclaves* as a sort of unofficial observer.

con-coct \\kən-'käkt\\ (*v*) prepare by combining; make up in concert. How did you ever *concoct* such a strange dish? **con-coc-tion** \\kən-'käk-shən\\ (*n*)

con-com-i-tant \\kən-'käm-ət-ənt\\ (*n*) that which accompanies. Culture is not always a *concomitant* of wealth; also (*adj*).

con-cor-dat \\kən-'kȯr-ˌdat\\ (*n*) agreement, usually between the papal authority and the secular. One of the most famous of the agreements between a pope and an emperor was the *Concordat* of Worms in 1122.

con-crete \\'kän-ˌkrēt\\ (*adj*) real or substantial. Being busy is no excuse; you must have a more *concrete* reason for postponing taking your exam.

con-cur-rent \\kən-'kər-ənt\\ (*adj*) happening at the same time. In America, the colonists were resisting the demands of the mother country; at the *concurrent* moment in France, the middle class was sowing the seeds of rebellion.

con-de-scend \\ˌkän-di-'send\\ (*v*) bestow courtesies with a superior air. The king *condescended* to grant an audience to the friends of the condemned man. **con-de-scen-sion** \\ˌkän-di-'sen-chən\\ (*n*)

con-di-ment \\'kän-də-mənt\\ (*n*) seasoning; spice. Spanish food is full of *condiments*.

con-dole \\kən-'dōl\\ (*v*) express sympathetic sorrow. His friends gathered to *condole* with him over his loss. **con-do-lence** \\kən-'dō-lən(t)s\\ (*n*)

con-done \\kən-'dōn\\ (*v*) overlook; forgive. We cannot *condone* your recent criminal cooperation with the gamblers.

con-duit \\'kän-ˌd(y)ü-ət\\ (*n*) aqueduct; passageway for fluids. Water was brought to the army in the desert by an improvised *conduit* from the adjoining mountain.

\\ə\\ abut \\ᵊ\\ kitten, F table \\ər\\ **further** \\a\\ ash \\ā\\ **ace** \\ä\\ cot, **cart**
\\au̇\\ **out** \\ch\\ **chin** \\e\\ bet \\ē\\ **easy** \\g\\ **go** \\i\\ hit \\ī\\ **ice** \\j\\ **job**

con-fer \kən-'fər\ (*v*) discuss or compare ideas; grant or bestow. The members of the committee *conferred* before reaching a final decision.

con-fi-dant \'kän-fə-ˌdant\ (*n*) a person to whom one can tell secrets. When my best friend moved, I lost my only *confidant.*

con-fis-cate \'kän-fə-ˌskāt\ (*v*) seize; commandeer. The army *confiscated* all available supplies of uranium; also (*adj*).

con-fla-gra-tion \ˌkän-flə-'grā-shən\ (*n*) great fire. In the *conflagration* that followed the 1906 earthquake, much of San Francisco was destroyed.

con-for-mi-ty \kən-'för-mət-ē\ (*n*) harmony; agreement. In *conformity* with our rules and regulations, I am calling a meeting of our organization.

con-geal \kən-'jē(ə)l\ (*v*) freeze, coagulate. His blood *congealed* in his veins as he saw the dread monster rush toward him.

con-gen-i-tal \kän-'jen-ə-tᵊl\ (*adj*) existing at birth. His *congenital* deformity disturbed his parents.

con-glom-er-a-tion \kən-ˌgläm-ə-'rā-shən\ (*n*) mass of material sticking together. In such a *conglomeration* of miscellaneous statistics, it was impossible to find a single area of analysis.

con-gre-ga-tion \ˌkäŋ-gri-'gā-shən\ (*n*) a gathering or assembly. There was a great *congregation* of protesters outside the courthouse after the verdict was read.

con-gru-ence \kən-'grü-ən(t)s\ (*n*) correspondence of parts; harmonious relationship. The student demonstrated the *congruence* of the two triangles by using the hypotenuse-arm theorem.

co-ni-fer \'kän-ə-fər\ (*n*) pine tree; cone-bearing tree. According to geologists, the *conifers* were the first plants to bear flowers.

\ŋ\ **sing** \ō\ **go** \ȯ\ **law** \ȯi\ **boy** \th\ **thin** \t͟h\ **the** \ü\ **loot** \u̇\ **foot**
\y\ **yet** \zh\ **vision** \à, k̲, ⁿ, œ, œ̄, ue, œ̄, ʸ\ *see* Pronunciation Symbols

con-jec-ture \kən-'jek-chər\ (*n*) surmise; guess. I will end all your *conjectures;* I admit I am guilty as charged; also (*v*).

con-ju-gal \'kän-ji-gəl\ (*adj*) pertaining to marriage. Their dreams of *conjugal* bliss were shattered as soon as their temperaments clashed.

con-jure \'kän-jər\ (*v*) summon a devil; practice magic; imagine; invent. He *conjured* up an image of a reformed city and had the voters completely under his spell.

con-niv-ance \kə-'nī-vən(t)s\ (*n*) pretense of ignorance of something wrong; assistance; permission to offend. With the *connivance* of his friends, he plotted to embarrass the teacher. con-nive \kə-'nīv\ (*v*)

con-nois-seur \,kän-ə-'sər\ (*n*) person competent to act as a judge of art, etc.; a lover of art. He had developed into a *connoisseur* of fine china.

con-no-ta-tion \,kän-ə-'tā-shən\ (*n*) suggested or implied meaning of an expression. Foreigners frequently are unaware of the *connotations* of the words they use.

con-nu-bi-al \kə-'n(y)ü-bē-əl\ (*adj*) pertaining to marriage or the matrimonial state. In his telegram, he wished the newlyweds a lifetime of *connubial* bliss.

con-san-guin-i-ty \,kän-,san-'gwin-ət-ē\ (*n*) kinship. The lawsuit developed into a test of the *consanguinity* of the claimant to the estate.

con-sci-en-tious \,kän-chē-'en-chəs\ (*adj*) scrupulous; careful. A *conscientious* editor, she checked every definition for its accuracy.

con-se-crate \'kän(t)-sə-,krāt\ (*v*) dedicate; sanctify. We shall *consecrate* our lives to this noble purpose; also (*adj*).

con-sen-sus \kən-'sen(t)-səs\ (*n*) general agreement. The *consensus* indicates that we are opposed to entering into this pact.

\ə\ **abut** \ᵊ\ **kitten**, F **table** \ər\ **further** \a\ **ash** \ā\ **ace** \ä\ **cot, cart** \aů\ **out** \ch\ **chin** \e\ **bet** \ē\ **easy** \g\ **go** \i\ **hit** \ī\ **ice** \j\ **job**

con-se-quen-tial \ˌkän(t)-sə-'kwen-chəl\ *(adj)* following as an effect; important; self-important. Convinced of his own importance, the actor strutted about the dressing room with a *consequential* air. con-se-quence \'kän(t)-sə-ˌkwen(t)s\ *(n)*; con-se-quent \'kän(t)-sə-kwent\ *(adj)*

con-so-nance \'kän(t)-s(ə-)nən(t)s\ *(n)* harmony; agreement. Her agitation seemed out of *consonance* with her usual calm.

con-sort \kən-'sȯ(ə)rt\ *(v)* associate with. We frequently judge people by the company with whom they *consort*. con-sort \'kän-ˌsȯ(ə)rt\ *(n)*

con-spic-u-ous \kən-'spik-yə-wəs\ *(adj)* easily seen; noticeable; striking. Janet was *conspicuous* both for her red hair and for her height.

con-spir-a-cy \kən-'spir-ə-sē\ *(n)* treacherous plot. Brutus and Cassius joined in the *conspiracy* to kill Julius Caesar.

con-stit-u-ent \kən-'stich-(ə-)wənt\ *(n)* supporter. The congressman received hundreds of letters from angry *constituents* after the Equal Rights Amendment failed to pass.

con-straint \kən-'strānt\ *(n)* compulsion; repression of feelings. There was a feeling of *constraint* in the room because no one dared to criticize the speaker. con-strain \kən-'strān\ *(v)*

con-strue \kən-'strü\ *(v)* explain; interpret. If I *construe* your remarks correctly, you disagree with the theory already advanced.

con-sum-mate \kən-'səm-ət\ *(adj)* complete. I have never seen anyone who makes as many stupid errors as you do; you must be a *consummate* idiot. con-sum-mate \'kän(t)-sə-ˌmāt\ *(v)*

con-tam-i-nate \kən-'tam-ə-ˌnāt\ *(v)* pollute. The sewage system of the city so *contaminated* the water that swimming was forbidden.

\ŋ\ **sing** \ō\ **go** \ȯ\ **law** \ȯi\ **boy** \th\ **thin** \th̲\ **the** \ü\ **loot** \u̇\ **foot**
\y\ **yet** \zh\ **vision** \à, k̲, ⁿ, œ, œ̄, ue, œ̄, ʸ\ *see* Pronunciation Symbols

con-ten-tious \kən-'ten-chəs\ (*adj*) quarrelsome. We heard loud and *contentious* noises in the next room.

con-text \'kän-ˌtekst\ (*n*) writings preceding and following the passage quoted. Because these lines are taken out of *context,* they do not convey the message the author intended.

con-tig-u-ous \kən-'tig-yə-wəs\ (*adj*) adjacent to; touching upon. The two countries are *contiguous* for a few miles; then they are separated by the gulf.

con-ti-nence \'känt-ᵊn-ən(t)s\ (*n*) self-restraint; sexual chastity. He vowed to lead a life of *continence.* con-ti-nent \känt-ᵊn-ənt\ (*adj*)

con-tin-gent \kən-'tin-jənt\ (*adj*) conditional. The continuation of this contract is *contingent* on the quality of your first output. con-tin-gen-cy \kən-'tin-jən-sē\ (*n*)

con-tor-tion \kən-'tȯr-shən\ (*n*) twisting; distortion. As the effects of the opiate wore away, the *contortions* of the patient became more violent and demonstrated how much pain he was enduring. con-tort \kən-'tȯ(ə)rt\ (*v*)

con-tra-band \'kän-trə-ˌband\ (*adj*) illegal trade; smuggling. The Coast Guard tries to prevent traffic in *contraband* goods; also (*n*).

con-tract \ˌkän-'trakt\ (*v*) to compress or shrink; to enter into a binding agreement. The application of electric current can cause muscles to *contract.*

con-tra-vene \ˌkän-trə-'vēn\ (*v*) contradict; infringe on. I will not attempt to *contravene* your argument for it does not affect the situation.

con-trite \'kän-ˌtrīt\ (*adj*) penitent. Her *contrite* tears did not influence the judge when he imposed sentence. con-tri-tion \kən-'trish-ən\ (*n*)

con-tro-vert \'kän-trə-ˌvərt\ (*v*) oppose with arguments; contradict. To *controvert* your theory will require much time but it is essential that we disprove it.

\ə\ abut \ᵊ\ kitten, F table \ər\ **further** \a\ ash \ā\ **ace** \ä\ cot, cart
\au̇\ **out** \ch\ **chin** \e\ bet \ē\ **easy** \g\ go \i\ hit \ī\ **ice** \j\ **job**

con-tu-ma-cious \ˌkän-t(y)ə-'mā-shəs\ (*adj*) disobedient; resisting authority. The *contumacious* mob shouted defiantly at the police. **con-tu-ma-cy** \kən-'t(y)ü-mə-sē\ (*n*)

con-tume-ly \kən-'t(y)ü-mə-lē\ (*n*) scornful insolence, insult. The "proud man's *contumely*" is distasteful to Hamlet.

con-tu-sion \kən-'t(y)ü-zhən\ (*n*) bruise. He was treated for *contusions* and abrasions.

co-nun-drum \kə-'nən-drəm\ (*n*) riddle; difficult problem. During the long car ride, she invented *conundrums* to entertain the children.

con-vene \kən-'vēn\ (*v*) assemble. Because much needed legislation had to be enacted, the governor ordered the legislature to *convene* in special session by January 15.

con-ven-tion-al \kən-'vench-nəl, -'ven-chən-ᵊl\ (*adj*) ordinary or typical. His *conventional* upbringing left him wholly unprepared for his wife's eccentric family.

con-ver-sant \kən-'vərs-ᵊnt\ (*adj*) familiar with. The lawyer is *conversant* with all the evidence.

con-vey-ance \kən-'vā-ən(t)s\ (*n*) vehicle; transfer. During the transit strike, commuters used various kinds of *conveyances*.

con-vic-tion \kən-'vik-shən\ (*n*) strongly held belief. Nothing could shake his *conviction* that she was innocent. (secondary meaning)

con-viv-ial \kən-'viv-yəl\ (*adj*) festive; gay; characterized by joviality. The *convivial* celebrators of the victory sang their college songs.

con-voke \kən-'vōk\ (*v*) call together. Congress was *convoked* at the outbreak of the emergency. **con-vo-ca-tion** \ˌkän-və-'kā-shən\ (*n*)

con-vo-lut-ed \'kän-və-ˌlüt-əd\ (*adj*) coiled around; involved; intricate. His argument was so *convoluted* that few of us could follow it intelligently.

\ŋ\ **sing**   \ō\ **go**   \ȯ\ **law**   \ȯi\ **boy**   \th\ **thin**   \t͟h\ **the**   \ü\ **loot**   \u̇\ **foot**
\y\ **yet**   \zh\ **vision**   \à, k̲, ⁿ, œ, œ̄, ᵫ, œ̄, ʸ\ *see* Pronunciation Symbols

co-pi-ous \\'kō-pē-əs\ (*adj*) plentiful. He had *copious* reasons for rejecting the proposal.

co-quette \kō-'ket\ (*n*) flirt. Because she refused to give him any answer to his proposal of marriage, he called her a *coquette;* also (*v*).

cor-dial \\'kȯr-jəl\ (*adj*) gracious; heartfelt. Our hosts greeted us at the airport with a *cordial* and a hearty hug.

cor-don \\'kȯrd-ᵊn\ (*n*) extended line of men or fortifications to prevent access or egress. The police *cordon* was so tight that the criminals could not leave the area; also (*v*).

cor-ol-lar-y \\'kȯr-ə-ˌler-ē\ (*n*) consequence; accompaniment. Brotherly love is a complex emotion, with sibling rivalry its natural *corollary.*

cor-po-re-al \kȯr-'pōr-ē-əl\ (*adj*) bodily; material. He was not a churchgoer; he was interested only in *corporeal* matters.

cor-pu-lent \\'kȯr-pyə-1ənt\ (*adj*) very fat. The *corpulent* man resolved to reduce. **cor-pu-lence** \\'kȯr-pyə-lən(t)s\ (*n*)

cor-re-la-tion \ˌkȯr-ə-lā-shən\ (*n*) mutual relationship. He sought to determine the *correlation* that existed between ability in algebra and ability to interpret reading exercises.

cor-rob-o-rate \kə-'räb-ə-ˌrāt\ (*v*) confirm. Unless we find a witness to *corroborate* your evidence, it will not stand up in court.

cor-ro-sive \kə-'rō-siv\ (*adj*) eating away by chemicals or disease. Stainless steel is able to withstand the effects of *corrosive* chemicals.

cor-ru-gat-ed \\'kȯr-ə-ˌgāt-əd\ (*adj*) wrinkled; ridged. She wished she could smooth away the wrinkles from his *corrugated* brow.

cor-tege \kȯr-'tezh\ (*n*) procession. The funeral *cortege* proceeded slowly down the avenue.

\ə\ **abut** \ᵊ\ **kitten, F table** \ər\ **further** \a\ **ash** \ā\ **ace** \ä\ **cot, cart**
\aủ\ **out** \ch\ **chin** \e\ **bet** \ē\ **easy** \g\ **go** \i\ **hit** \ī\ **ice** \j\ **job**

cos-mic \'käz-mik\ (*adj*) pertaining to the universe; vast. *Cosmic* rays derive their name from the fact that they bombard the earth's atmosphere from outer space. **cos-mos** \'käz-məs\ (*n*)

co-te-rie \'kōt-ə-ₒrē\ (*n*) group that meets socially; select circle. After his book had been published, he was invited to join the literary *coterie* that lunched daily at the hotel.

coun-te-nance \'kaŭnt-ᵊn-ən(t)s\ (*v*) approve; tolerate. He refused to *countenance* such rude behavior on their part.

coun-ter-mand \'kaŭnt-ər-ₘmand\ (*v*) cancel; revoke. The general *countermanded* the orders issued in his absence; also (*n*).

coun-ter-part \'kaŭnt-ər-ₚpärt\ (*n*) a thing that completes another; things very much alike. Night and day are *counterparts*.

coup \'kü\ (*n*) highly successful action or sudden attack. As the news of his *coup* spread throughout Wall Street, his fellow brokers dropped by to congratulate him.

cou-ple \'kəp-əl\ (*v*) join; unite. The Flying Karamazovs *couple* expert juggling and amateur joking in their nightclub act.

cou-ri-er \'kur-ē-ər\ (*n*) messenger. The publisher sent a special *courier* to pick up the manuscript.

cov-e-nant \'kəv-(ə-)nənt\ (*n*) agreement. We must comply with the terms of the *convenant;* also (*v*).

co-vert \'kō-ₒvərt\ (*adj*) secret; hidden; implied. He could understand the *covert* threat in the letter; also (*n*).

cov-et-ous \'kəv-ət-əs\ (*adj*) avaricious; eagerly desirous of. The child was *covetous* by nature and wanted to take the toys belonging to his classmates. **cov-et** \'kəv-ət\ (*v*)

cow-er \'kaŭ(-ə)r\ (*v*) shrink quivering, as from fear. The frightened child *cowered* in the corner of the room.

---

coy \\'kȯi\\ (*adj*) shy; modest; coquettish. She was *coy* in her answers to his offer.

coz-en \\'kəz-ᵊn\\ (*v*) cheat; hoodwink; swindle. He was the kind of individual who would *cozen* his friends in a cheap card game but remain eminently ethical in all his business dealings.

crab-bed \\'krab-əd\\ (*adj*) sour; peevish. The *crabbed* old man was avoided by the children because he scolded them when they made noise.

crass \\'kras\\ (*adj*) very unrefined; grossly insensible. The philosophers deplored the *crass* commercialism.

cra-ven \\'krā-vən\\ (*adj*) cowardly. His *craven* behavior in this critical period was criticized.

cre-dence \\'krēd-ᵊn(t)s\\ (*n*) belief. Do not place any *credence* in his promises.

cred-i-bil-i-ty \\,kred-ə-'bil-ət-ē\\ (*n*) believability. The defense attorney tried to destroy the *credibility* of the witness for the prosecution.

cre-do \\'krēd-(ˌ)ō\\ (*n*) creed. I believe we may best describe his *credo* by saying that it approximates the Golden Rule.

cre-du-li-ty \\kri-'d(y)ü-lət-ē\\ (*n*) belief on slight evidence. The witch doctor took advantage of the *credulity* of the superstitious natives. **cred-u-lous** \\'krej-ə-ləs\\ (*adj*)

creed \\'krēd\\ (*n*) system of religious or ethical beliefs. In any loyal American's *creed,* love of democracy must be emphasized.

cre-scen-do \\krə-'shen-(ˌ)dō\\ (*n*) increase in the volume of sound in a musical passage. The overture suddenly changed from a quiet pastoral theme to a *crescendo* featured by blaring trumpets and clashing cymbals; also (*adj, adv*).

crest-fall-en \\'krest-ˌfȯ-lən\\ (*adj*) dejected; dispirited. We were surprised at his reaction to the failure of his pro-

---

\\ə\\ abut \\ᵊ\\ kitten, F table \\ər\\ **further** \\a\\ ash \\ā\\ **ace** \\ä\\ cot, cart
\\au̇\\ **out** \\ch\\ **chin** \\e\\ bet \\ē\\ **easy** \\g\\ go \\i\\ **hit** \\ī\\ ice \\j\\ **job**

ject; instead of being *crestfallen,* he was busily engaged in planning new activities.

crev-ice \\'krev-əs\ (*n*) crack; fissure. The mountain climbers found footholds in the tiny *crevices* in the mountainside.

cringe \\'krinj\ (*v*) shrink back, as if in fear. The dog *cringed,* expecting a blow.

cri-te-ri-on \krī-'tir-ē-ən\ (*n*) standard used in judging. What *criterion* did you use when you selected this essay as the prizewinner?

crone \\'krōn\ (*n*) hag. The toothless *crone* frightened us when she smiled.

crotch-et-y \\'kräch-ət-ē\ (*adj*) eccentric; whimsical. Although he was reputed to be a *crotchety* old gentleman, I found his ideas substantially sound and sensible.

crux \\'krəks\ (*n*) crucial point. This is the *crux* of the entire problem.

crypt \\'kript\ (*n*) secret recess or vault, usually used for burial. Until recently, only bodies of rulers and leading statesmen were interred in this *crypt.*

cryp-tic \\'krip-tik\ (*adj*) mysterious; hidden; secret. His *cryptic* remarks could not be interpreted.

cu-bi-cle \\'kyü-bi-kəl\ (*n*) small chamber used for sleeping. After his many hours of intensive study in the library, he retired to his *cubicle.*

cui-sine \kwi-'zēn\ (*n*) style of cooking. French *cuisine is* noted for its use of sauces and wines.

cul-de-sac \\'kəl-di-ˌsak\ (*n*) blind alley; trap. The soldiers were unaware that they were marching into a *cul-de-sac* when they entered the canyon.

cu-li-nar-y \\'kel-ə-ˌner-ē\ (*adj*) relating to cooking. Many chefs attribute their *culinary* skill to the wise use of spices.

cull \\'kəl\ (*v*) pick out; reject. Every month the farmer *culls* the nonlaying hens from his flock and sells them to the local butcher; also (*n*).

\ŋ\ sing \ō\ go \ò\ law \òi\ boy \th\ thin \th̲\ the \ü\ loot \ u̇\ foot
\y\ yet \zh\ vision \à, k̲, ⁿ, œ, œ̄, ue, œ, ʸ\ *see* Pronunciation Symbols

cul-mi-na-tion \ˌkəl-mə-'nā-shən\ (*n*) attainment of highest point. His inauguration as President of the United States marked the *culmination* of his political career.

cul-pa-ble \'kəl-pə-bəl\ (*adj*) deserving blame. Corrupt politicians who condone the activities of the gamblers are equally *culpable.*

cul-vert \'kəl-vərt\ (*n*) artificial channel for water. If we build a *culvert* under the road at this point, we will reduce the possibility of the road's being flooded during the rainy season.

cum-ber-some \'kəm-bər-səm\ (*adj*) heavy; hard to manage. He was burdened down with *cumbersome* parcels.

cu-pid-i-ty \kyu̇-'pid-ət-ē\ (*n*) greed. The defeated people could not satisfy the *cupidity* of the conquerors, who demanded excessive tribute.

cu-ra-tor \'kyu̇(ə)r-ˌāt-ər\ (*n*) superintendent; manager. The members of the board of trustees of the museum expected the new *curator* to plan events and exhibitions that would make the museum more popular.

cur-mud-geon \ˌkər-'məj-ən\ (*n*) churlish, miserly individual. Although he was regarded by many as a *curmudgeon,* a few of us were aware of the many kindnesses and acts of charity he secretly performed.

cur-ry \'kər-ē\ (*v*) dress; treat leather; seek favor. The courtier *curried* favors of the king.

cur-sive \'kər-siv\ (*adj*) flowing, running. In normal writing we run our letters together in *cursive* form; in printing, we separate the letters; also (*n*).

cur-so-ry \'kərs-(ə-)rē\ (*adj*) casual; hastily done. A *cursory* examination of the ruins indicates the possibility of arson; a more extensive study should be undertaken.

cur-tail \ˌkər-'tā(ə)l\ (*v*) shorten; reduce. During a coal shortage, we must *curtail* our use of this vital commodity.

\ə\ **abut** \ᵊ\ **kitten, F table** \ər\ **further** \a\ **ash** \ā\ **ace** \ä\ **cot, cart**
\au̇\ **out** \ch\ **chin** \e\ **bet** \ē\ **easy** \g\ **go** \i\ **hit** \ī\ **ice** \j\ **job**

cyn-ic \'sin-ik\ (*n*) one who is skeptical or distrustful of human motives. A *cynic* at all times, he was suspicious of all altruistic actions of others. cyn-i-cal \'sin-i-kəl\ (*adj*)

cy-no-sure \'sī-nə-ˌshu̇(ə)r\ (*n*) the object of general attention. As soon as the movie star entered the room, she became the *cynosure* of all eyes.

D

da-is \\'dā-əs\\ (*n*) raised platform for guests of honor. When he approached the *dais,* he was greeted by cheers from the people who had come to honor him.

dal-ly \\'dal-ē\\ (*v*) trifle with; procrastinate. Laertes told Ophelia that Hamlet could only *dally* with her affections.

dank \\'dank\\ (*adj*) damp. The walls of the dungeon were *dank* and slimy.

dap-pled \\'dap-əld\\ (*adj*) spotted. The sunlight filtering through the screens created a *dappled* effect on the wall.

daub \\'dòb\\ (*v*) smear (as with paint). From the way he *daubed* his paint on the canvas, I could tell he knew nothing of oils; also (*n*).

daunt \\'dònt\\ (*v*) intimidate. Your threats cannot *daunt* me.

daunt-less \\'dònt-ləs\\ (*adj*) bold. Despite the dangerous nature of the undertaking, the *dauntless* soldier volunteered for the assignment.

daw-dle \\'dòd-ᵊl\\ (*v*) loiter; waste time. Inasmuch as we must meet a deadline, do not *dawdle* over this work.

dead-lock \\'ded-,läk\\ (*n*) standstill; stalemate. The negotiations had reached a *deadlock;* also (*v*).

dead-pan \\'ded-,pan\\ (*adj*) wooden; impassive. We wanted to see how long he could maintain his *deadpan* expression.

dearth \\'dərth\\ (*n*) scarcity. The *dearth* of skilled labor compelled the employers to open trade schools.

de-ba-cle \\di-'bäk-əl\\ (*n*) breaking up; downfall. This *debacle* in the government can only result in anarchy.

de-base \\di-'bās\\ (*v*) reduce to lower state. Do not *debase* yourself by becoming maudlin.

de-bauch \\di-'bòch\\ (*v*) corrupt; make intemperate. A vicious newspaper can *debauch* public ideals. **de-bauch-er-y** \\di-'bòch-(ə-)rē\\ (*n*)

\\ə\\ **abut** \\ᵊ\\ **kitten, F table** \\ər\\ **further** \\a\\ **ash** \\ā\\ **ace** \\ä\\ **cot, cart**
\\aù\\ **out** \\ch\\ **chin** \\e\\ **bet** \\ē\\ **easy** \\g\\ **go** \\i\\ **hit** \\ī\\ **ice** \\j\\ **job**

de-bil-i-tate \di-'bil-ə-ˌtāt\ (*v*) weaken; enfeeble. Overindulgence *debilitates* character as well as physical stamina.

deb-o-nair \ˌdeb-ə-'na(ə)r\ (*adj*) friendly; aiming to please. The *debonair* youth was liked by all who met him, because of his cheerful and obliging manner.

deb-u-tante \'deb-yü-ˌtänt\ (*n*) young woman making formal entrance into society. As a *debutante,* she was often mentioned in the society columns of the newspapers.

dec-a-dence \'dek-əd-ən(t)s\ (*n*) decay. The moral *decadence* of the people was reflected in the lewd literature of the period.

de-cap-i-tate \di-'kap-ə-ˌtāt\ (*v*) behead. They did not hang Lady Jane Grey; they *decapitated* her.

de-cid-u-ous \di-'sij-ə-wəs\ (*adj*) falling off as of leaves. The oak is a *deciduous* tree.

dec-i-mate \'des-ə-ˌmāt\ (*v*) kill, usually one out of ten. We do more to *decimate* our population in automobile accidents than we do in war.

de-ci-pher \di-'sī-fər\ (*v*) decode. I could not *decipher* the doctor's handwriting.

de-cliv-i-ty \di-'kliv-ət-ē\ (*n*) downward slope. The children loved to ski down the *declivity.*

de-com-po-si-tion \ˌ(ˌ)dē-ˌkäm-pə-'zish-ən\ (*n*) decay. Despite the body's advanced state of *decomposition,* the police were able to identify the murdered man. **de-com-pose** \ˌdē-kəm-'pōz\ (*v*)

dec-o-rous \'dek-ə-rəs\ (*adj*) proper. Her *decorous* behavior was praised by her teachers. **de-co-rum** \di-'kōr-əm\ (*n*)

de-coy \'de-ˌkȯi\ (*n*) lure or bait. The wild ducks were not fooled by the *decoy.* **de-coy** \di-'kȯi \ (*v*)

de-crep-it \di-'krep-ət\ (*adj*) worn out by age. The *decrepit* car blocked traffic on the highway.

de-crep-i-tude \di-'krep-ə-t(y)üd\ (*n*) state of collapse caused by illness or old age. I was unprepared for the

---

\ŋ\ sing \ō\ go \ȯ\ law \ȯi\ boy \th\ thin \th\ the \ü\ loot \u̇\ foot
\y\ yet \zh\ vision \à, k̲, ⁿ, œ, œ̄, ue, œ, ʸ\ *see* Pronunciation Symbols

state of *decrepitude* in which I had found my old friend; he seemed to have aged twenty years in six months.

de-cry \di-'krī\ (v) disparage. Do not attempt to increase your stature by *decrying* the efforts of your opponents.

de-duc-i-ble \di-'d(y)ü-sə-bəl\ (adj) derived by reasoning. If we accept your premise, your conclusions are easily *deducible.*

def-a-ma-tion \‚def-ə-mā-shən\ (n) harming a person's reputation. Such *defamation* of character may result in a slander suit.

de-fault \di-'fȯlt\ (n) failure to do. As a result of her husband's failure to appear in court, she was granted a divorce by *default;* also (v).

de-feat-ist \di-'fēt-əst\ (adj) attitude of one who is ready to accept defeat as a natural outcome. If you maintain your *defeatist* attitude, you will never succeed; also (n).

de-fec-tion \di-'fek-shən\ (n) desertion. The children, who had made him an idol, were hurt most by his *defection* from our cause.

def-er-ence \'def-(ə-)rən(t)s\ (n) courteous regard for another's wish. In *deference* to his desires, the employers granted him a holiday.

de-file \di-'fī(ə)l\ (v) pollute; profane. The hoodlums *defiled* the church with their scurrilous writing.

de-fin-i-tive \di-'fin-ət-iv\ (adj) final; complete. Carl Sandburg's *Abraham Lincoln* may be regarded as the *definitive* work on the life of the Great Emancipator.

de-flect \di-'flekt\ (v) turn aside. His life was saved when his cigarette case *deflected* the bullet.

de-fray \di-'frā\ (v) pay the costs of. Her employer offered to *defray* the costs of her postgraduate education.

deft \'deft\ (adj) neat; skillful. The *deft* waiter uncorked the champagne without spilling a drop.

de-funct \di-'fəŋ(k)t\ (adj) dead; no longer in use or existence. The lawyers sought to examine the books of the *defunct* corporation.

\ə\ abut \ᵊ\ kitten, F table \ər\ further \a\ ash \ā\ ace \ä\ cot, cart
\aů\ out \ch\ chin \e\ bet \ē\ easy \g\ go \i\ hit \ī\ ice \j\ job

de-grad-ed \di-'grād-əd\ (*adj*) lowered in rank; debased. The *degraded* wretch spoke only of his past glories and honors.

de-i-fy \'dē-ə-ˌfī\ (*v*) turn into a god; idolize. Admire the rock star all you want; just don't *deify* him.

deign \'dān\ (*v*) condescend. He felt that he would debase himself if he *deigned* to answer his critics.

de-lec-ta-ble \di-'lek-tə-bəl\ (*adj*) delightful; delicious. We thanked our host for a most *delectable* meal.

de-lete \di-'lēt\ (*v*) erase, strike out. If you *delete* this paragraph, the composition will have more appeal.

del-e-te-ri-ous \ˌdel-ə-'tir-ē-əs\ (*adj*) harmful. Workers in nuclear research must avoid the *deleterious* effects of radioactive substances.

de-lib-er-ate \di-'lib-ə-ˌrāt\ (*v*) consider; ponder. The judge took time to *deliberate* before reaching her decision.

de-lin-e-a-tion \di-ˌlin-ē-'ā-shən\ (*n*) portrayal. He is a powerful storyteller, but he is weakest in his *delineation* of character.

de-lir-i-um \di-'lir-ē-əm\ (*n*) mental disorder marked by confusion. The drunkard in his *delirium* saw strange animals.

de-lude \di-'lüd\ (*v*) deceive. Do not *delude* yourself into believing that he will relent.

de-lu-sion \di-'lü-zhən\ (*n*) false belief; hallucination. This scheme is a snare and a *delusion*.

de-lu-sive \di-'lü-siv\ (*adj*) deceptive; raising vain hopes. Do not raise your hopes on the basis of his *delusive* promises.

dem-a-gogue \'dem-ə-ˌgäg\ (*n*) person who appeals to people's prejudice; false leader of people. He was accused of being a *demagogue* because he made promises that aroused futile hopes in his listeners.

de-mean \di-'mēn\ (*v*) degrade; humiliate. He felt that he would *demean* himself if he replied to the scurrilous letter.

\ŋ\ **sing** \ō\ **go** \ȯ\ **law** \ȯi\ **boy** \th\ **thin** \th̲\ **the** \ü\ **loot** \u̇\ **foot**
\y\ **yet** \zh\ **vision** \à, k̲, ⁿ, œ, œ̄, ᵫ, œ̄, ʸ\ *see* Pronunciation Symbols

de-mean-or \di-'mē-nər\ (*n*) behavior; bearing. His sober *demeanor* quieted the noisy revelers.

de-ment-ed \di-'ment-əd\ (*adj*) insane. She became increasingly *demented* and had to be hospitalized.

de-mise \di-'mīz\ (*n*) death. Upon the *demise* of the dictator, a bitter dispute about succession to power developed; also (*v*).

de-mo-li-tion \,dem-ə-'lish-ən\ (*n*) destruction. One of the major aims of the air force was the complete *demolition* of all means of transportation by bombing of rail lines and terminals.

de-mo-ni-ac \di-'mō-nē-,ak\ (*adj*) fiendish. The Spanish Inquisition devised many *demoniac* means of torture. **de-mon** \'dē-mən\ (*n*)

de-mur \di-'mər\ (*v*) delay; object. To *demur* at this time will only worsen the already serious situation; now is the time for action; also (*n*).

de-mure \di-'myu̇(ə)r\ (*adj*) grave; serious; coy. She was *demure* and reserved.

den-i-grate \'den-i-,grāt\ (*v*) blacken. All attempts to *denigrate* the character of our late president have failed; the people still love him and cherish his memory.

den-i-zen \'den-ə-zən\ (*n*) inhabitant of. Ghosts are *denizens* of the land of the dead who return to earth.

de-no-ta-tion \,dē-nō-'tā-shən\ (*n*) meaning; distinguishing by name. A dictionary will always give us the *denotation* of a word; frequently, it will also give us its connotation.

de-noue-ment \,dā-,nü-'mä^n\ (*n*) outcome; final development of the plot of a play. The play was childishly written; the *denouement* was obvious to sophisticated theatergoers as early as the middle of the first act.

de-pict \di-'pikt\ (*v*) portray. In this book, the author *depicts* the slave owners as kind and benevolent masters.

\ə\ abut \ᵊ\ kitten, F table \ər\ further \a\ ash \ā\ ace \ä\ cot, cart
\au̇\ out \ch\ chin \e\ bet \ē\ easy \g\ go \i\ hit \ī\ ice \j\ job

de-plete \di-'plēt\ (*v*) reduce; exhaust. We must wait until we *deplete* our present inventory before we order replacements.

de-ploy \di-'plȯi\ (*v*) move troops so that the battle line is extended at the expense of depth. The general ordered the battalion to *deploy* in order to meet the offensive of the enemy.

de-pose \di-'pōz\ (*v*) dethrone; remove from office. The army attempted to *depose* the king and set up a military government.

de-po-si-tion \ˌdep-ə-'zish-ən\ (*n*) testimony under oath. He made his *deposition* in the judge's chamber.

de-prav-i-ty \di-'prav-ət-ē\ (*n*) corruption, wickedness. The *depravity* of his behavior shocked all.

dep-re-cate \'dep-ri-ˌkāt\ (*v*) disapprove regretfully. I must *deprecate* your attitude and hope that you will change your mind.

dep-re-ca-to-ry \'dep-ri-kə-ˌtōr-ē\ (*adj*) disapproving. Your *deprecatory* criticism has offended the author.

de-pre-ci-ate \di-'prē-shē-ˌāt\ (*v*) lessen in value. If you neglect this property, it will *depreciate*.

dep-re-da-tion \ˌdep-rə-'dā-shən\ (*n*) plundering. After the *depredations* of the invaders, the people were penniless.

de-range \di-'rānj\ (*v*) make insane. He was mentally *deranged*.

der-e-lict \'der-ə-ˌlikt\ (*adj*) abandoned. The *derelict* craft was a menace to navigation; also (*n*).

de-ride \di-'rīd\ (*v*) scoff at. The people *derided* his grandiose schemes.

de-ri-sion \di-'rizh-ən\ (*n*) ridicule. They greeted his proposal with *derision* and refused to consider it seriously.

de-riv-a-tive \di-'riv-ət-iv\ (*adj*) unoriginal; derived from another source. Although her early poetry was clearly *derivative* in nature, the critics thought she had promise and eventually would find her own voice.

---

der-ma-tol-o-gist \,der-mə-'täl-ə-jəst\ (*n*) one who studies the skin and its disease. I advise you to consult a *dermatologist* about your acne.

de-rog-a-to-ry \di-'räg-ə-,tōr-ē\ (*adj*) expressing a low opinion. I resent your *derogatory* remarks.

des-cant \'des-,kant\ (*v*) discuss fully. He was willing to *descant* upon any topic of conversation, even when he knew very little about the subject under discussion; also (*n*).

de-scry \di-'skrī\ (*v*) catch sight of. In the distance, we could barely *descry* the enemy vessels.

des-e-crate \'des-i-,krāt\ (*v*) profane; violate the sanctity of. The soldiers *desecrated* the temple.

des-ic-cate \'des-i-,kāt\ (*v*) dry up. A tour of this smoke-house will give you an idea of how the pioneers used to *desiccate* food in order to preserve it.

de-sid-er-a-tum \di-,sid-ə-'rät-əm\ (*n*) that which is desired. Our first *desideratum* must be the establishment of peace; we can then attempt to remove the causes of the present conflict.

de-spi-ca-ble \di-'spik-ə-bəl\ (*adj*) contemptible. Your *despicable* remarks call for no reply.

de-spise \di-'spīz\ (*v*) scorn. I *despise* your attempts at a reconciliation at this time.

de-spoil \di-'spói(ə)l\ (*v*) plunder. If you do not yield, I am afraid the enemy will *despoil* the buildings.

de-spon-dent \di-'spän-dənt\ (*adj*) depressed, gloomy. To the dismay of his parents, he became more and more *despondent* every day. **de-spon-den-cy** \di-'spän-dən-sē\ (*n*)

des-po-tism \'des-pə-,tiz-əm\ (*n*) tyranny. The people rebelled against the *despotism* of the king.

des-ti-tute \'des-tə-,t(y)üt\ (*adj*) extremely poor. The illness left the family *destitute*.

des-ul-to-ry \'des-el-,tōr-ē\ (*adj*) aimless; jumping around. The animals' *desultory* behavior indicated that they had no awareness of their predicament.

\ə\ **abut** \ᵊ\ **kitten,** F **table** \ər\ **further** \a\ **ash** \ā\ **ace** \ä\ **cot, cart**
\au̇\ **out** \ch\ **chin** \e\ **bet** \ē\ **easy** \g\ **go** \i\ **hit** \ī\ **ice** \j\ **job**

de-tached \di-'tacht\ (*adj*) emotionally removed; calm and objective; indifferent. Psychoanalysts must remain *detached* and stay uninvolved in their patients' personal lives.

de-ter-gent \di-'tər-jənt\ (*n*) cleansing agent. Many new *detergents* have replaced soap.

de-ter-mi-nate \di-'tərm-(ə-)nət\ (*adj*) having a fixed order of procedure; invariable. At the royal wedding, the procession of the nobles followed a *determinate* order of precedence.

det-o-na-tion \ˌdet-ᵊn-'ā-shən\ (*n*) initiation of an explosion. The *detonation* could be heard miles away.

de-trac-tion \di-'trak-shən\ (*n*) slandering; aspersion. He is offended by your frequent *detractions* of his ability as a leader.

det-ri-ment \'de-trə-mənt\ (*n*) harm; damage. Your acceptance of his support will ultimately prove to be a *detriment* rather than an aid to your cause.

de-vi-ate \'dē-vē-ˌāt\ (*v*) turn away from. Do not *deviate* from the truth. **de-vi-ate** \dē-vē-ət\ (*adj*)

de-vi-ous \'dē-vē-əs\ (*adj*) going astray; erratic. Your *devious* behavior in this matter puzzles me since you are usually direct and straightforward.

de-void \di-'void\ (*adj*) lacking. He was *devoid* of any personal desire for gain in his endeavor to secure improvement in the community.

de-volve \di-'välv\ (*v*) deputize; pass to others. It *devolved* upon us, the survivors, to arrange peace terms with the enemy.

de-vout \di-'vaut\ (*adj*) pious. The *devout* man prayed daily.

dex-ter-ous \'dek-st(ə-)rəs\ (*adj*) skillful. The magician was so *dexterous* that we could not follow him as he performed his tricks.

di-a-bol-i-cal \ˌdī-ə-'bäl-i-kəl\ (*adj*) devilish. This scheme is so *diabolical* that I must reject it.

\ŋ\ **sing** \ō\ **go** \o\ **law** \oi\ **boy** \th\ **thin** \th\ **the** \ü\ **loot** \u\ **foot** \y\ **yet** \zh\ **vision** \à, k̲, ⁿ, œ, œ̄, ue, œ̄, ʸ\ *see* Pronunciation Symbols

di-a-lec-tic \ˌdī-ə-'lek-tik\ (*n*) art of debate. I am not skilled in *dialectic* and, therefore, cannot answer your arguments as forcefully as I wish.

di-aph-a-nous \dī-'af-ə-nəs\ (*adj*) sheer; transparent. They admired her *diaphanous* and colorful dress.

di-a-tribe \'dī-ə-ˌtrīb\ (*n*) bitter scolding; invective. During the lengthy *diatribe* delivered by his opponent he remained calm and self-controlled.

di-chot-o-my \dī-'kät-ə-mē\ (*n*) branching into two parts. The *dichotomy* of our legislative system provides us with many safeguards.

dic-tum \'dik-təm\ (*n*) authoritative and weighty statement. He repeated the statement as though it were the *dictum* of the most expert worker in the group.

di-dac-tic \dī-'dak-tik\ (*adj*) teaching; instructional. The *didactic* qualities of his poetry overshadow its literary qualities; the lesson he teaches is more memorable than the lines.

dif-fi-dence \'dif-əd-ən(t)s\ (*n*) shyness. You must overcome your *diffidence* if you intend to become a salesperson.

dif-fu-sion \dif-'yü-zhən\ (*n*) wordiness; spreading in all directions like a gas. Your composition suffers from a *diffusion* of ideas; try to be more compact. **dif-fuse** \dif-'yüs\ (*adj*); \dif-'yüz\ (*v*)

di-gres-sive \dī-'gres-iv\ (*adj*) wandering away from the subject. His book was marred by his many *digressive* remarks.

di-lap-i-da-tion \də-ˌlap-ə-'dā-shən\ (*n*) ruin because of neglect. We felt that the *dilapidation* of the building could be corrected by several coats of paint.

di-late \dī-'lāt\ (*v*) expand. In the dark, the pupils of your eyes *dilate*.

dil-a-to-ry \'dil-ə-ˌtōr-ē\ (*adj*) delaying. Your *dilatory* tactics may compel me to cancel the contract.

\ə\ **abut** \ᵊ\ kitten, F table \ər\ **further** \a\ **ash** \ā\ **ace** \ä\ **cot, cart** \aů\ **out** \ch\ **chin** \e\ **bet** \ē\ **easy** \g\ **go** \i\ **hit** \ī\ **ice** \j\ **job**

di-lem-ma \də-'lem-ə\ (*n*) problem; choice of two unsatis-factory alternatives. In this *dilemma,* he knew no one to whom he could turn for advice.

dil-et-tante \'dil-ə-tänt\ (*n*) aimless follower of the arts; amateur; dabbler. He was not serious in his painting; he was rather a *dilettante.*

dim-i-nu-tion \,dim-ə-'n(y)ü-shən\ (*n*) lessening; reduction in size. The blockaders hoped to achieve victory as soon as the *diminution* of the enemy's supplies became serious.

dint \'dint\ (*n*) means; effort. By *dint* of much hard work, the volunteers were able to place the raging forest fire under control; also (*v*).

dip-so-ma-ni-ac \,dip-sə-'mā-nē-,ak\ (*n*) one who has a strong craving for intoxicating liquor. The movie *The Lost Weekend* was an excellent portrayal of the strug-gles of the *dipsomaniac.*

dire \'dī(ə)r\ (*adj*) disastrous. People ignored his *dire* pre-dictions of an approaching depression.

dirge \'dərj\ (*n*) lament with music. The funeral *dirge* stirred us to tears.

dis-a-buse \,dis-ə-'byüz\ (*v*) correct a false impression; undeceive. I will attempt to *disabuse* you of your impression of my client's guilt; I know he is innocent.

dis-ar-ray \,dis-ə-'rā\ (*n*) a disorderly or untidy state. After the New Year's party, the once orderly house was in total *disarray.*

dis-a-vow-al \,dis-ə-'vaù(-ə)l\ (*n*) denial; disclaiming. His *disavowal* of his part in the conspiracy was not believed by the jury.

dis-burse \dis-'bərs\ (*v*) pay out. When you *disburse* money on the company's behalf, be sure to get a receipt.

dis-cern-i-ble \dis-'ər-nə-bəl\ (*adj*) distinguishable; per-ceivable. The ships in the harbor were not *discernible* in the fog.

\ŋ\ sing \ō\ go \ò\ law \òi\ boy \th\ thin \th\ the \ü\ loot \ù\ foot
\y\ yet \zh\ vision \à, k̲, ⁿ, œ, œ̄, ɥe, œ̄, ʸ\ *see* Pronunciation Symbols

dis-cern-ing \dis-'ər-niŋ\ (*adj*) mentally quick and observant; having insight. Because he was considered the most *discerning* member of the firm, he was assigned the most difficult cases.

dis-claim \dis-'klām\ (*v*) disown; renounce claim to. If I grant you this privilege, will you *disclaim* all other rights?

dis-close \dis-'klōz\ (*v*) reveal. Although competitors offered him bribes, he refused to *disclose* any information about his company's forthcoming product. **dis-clo-sure** \dis-'klō-zhər\ (*n*)

dis-com-fit \dis-'kəm(p)-fət\ (*v*) put to rout; defeat; disconcert. This ruse will *discomfit* the enemy. **dis-com-fi-ture** \dis-'kəm(p)-fə-,chu̇(ə)r\ (*n*)

dis-con-cert \,dis-kən-'sərt\ (*v*) confuse; upset; embarrass. The lawyer was *disconcerted* by the evidence produced by his adversary.

dis-con-so-late \dis-'kän(t)-s(ə-)lət\ (*adj*) sad. The death of his wife left him *disconsolate.*

dis-cor-dant \dis-'kȯrd-ənt\ (*adj*) inharmonious; conflicting. He tried to unite the *discordant* factions.

dis-count \'dis-,kau̇nt\ (*v*) disregard. Be prepared to *discount* what he has to say about his ex-wife. (secondary meaning)

dis-cred-it \(⁽⁾)dis-'kred-ət\ (*v*) defame; destroy confidence in; disbelieve. The campaign was highly negative in tone; each candidate tried to *discredit* the other.

dis-crep-an-cy \dis-'krep-ən-sē\ (*n*) lack of consistency; difference. The police noticed some *discrepancies* in his description of the crime and did not believe him.

dis-crete \dis-'krēt\ (*adj*) separate; unconnected. The universe is composed of *discrete* bodies.

dis-cre-tion \dis-'kresh-ən\ (*n*) prudence; ability to adjust actions to circumstances. Use your *discretion* in this matter.

\ə\ **abut** \ᵊ\ **kitten, F table** \ər\ **further** \a\ **ash** \ā\ **ace** \ä\ **cot, cart**
\au̇\ **out** \ch\ **chin** \e\ **bet** \ē\ **easy** \g\ **go** \i\ **hit** \ī\ **ice** \j\ **job**

dis-crim-i-nat-ing \dis-'krim-ə-nāt-iŋ\ (*adj*) able to see differences. They feared he was not sufficiently *discriminating* to judge complex works of modern art. (secondary meaning) **dis-crim-i-na-tion** \dis-ˌkrim-ə-'nā-shən\ (*n*); **dis-crim-i-nate** \dis-'krim-ə-nāt\ (*v*)

dis-cur-sive \dis-'kər-siv\ (*adj*) digressing; rambling. They were annoyed and bored by his *discursive* remarks.

dis-dain \dis-'dān\ (*v*) treat with scorn or contempt. You make enemies of all you *disdain;* also (*n*).

dis-grun-tle \dis-'grənt-əl\ (*v*) make discontented. The passengers were *disgruntled* by the numerous delays.

dis-heart-ened \⁽ʲ⁾dis-'härt-ənd\ (*adj*) lacking courage and hope. His failure to pass the bar exam *disheartened* him.

di-shev-eled \dish-'ev-əld\ (*adj*) untidy. Your *disheveled* appearance will hurt your chances in this interview.

dis-in-gen-u-ous \ˌdis-ən-'jen-yə-wəs\ (*adj*) not naive; sophisticated. Although he was young, his remarks indicated that he was *disingenuous.*

dis-in-ter-est-ed \⁽ʲ⁾dis-'in-trəst-əd\ (*adj*) unprejudiced. The only *disinterested* person in the room was the judge.

dis-joint-ed \⁽ʲ⁾dis-'jöint-əd\ (*adj*) disconnected. His remarks were so *disjointed* that we could not follow his reasoning.

dis-mem-ber \⁽ʲ⁾dis-'mem-bər\ (*v*) cut into small parts. When the Austrian Empire was *dismembered,* several new countries were established.

dis-par-age \dis-'par-ij\ (*v*) belittle. Do not *disparage* anyone's contribution; these little gifts add up to large sums.

dis-pa-rate \dis-'par-ət\ (*adj*) basically different; unrelated. It is difficult, if not impossible, to organize these *disparate* elements into a coherent whole.

\ŋ\ sing   \ō\ go   \ȯ\ law   \ȯi\ boy   \th\ thin   \t͟h\ the   \ü\ loot   \u̇\ foot
\y\ yet   \zh\ vision   \à, k̲, ⁿ, œ, œ̄, ᵫ, œ̣, ʸ\ *see* Pronunciation Symbols

dis-par-i-ty \dis-'par-ət-ē\ (*n*) difference; condition of inequality. The *disparity* in their ages made no difference at all.

dis-pas-sion-ate \⁽ʼ⁾dis-'pash-(ə-)nət\ (*adj*) calm; impartial. In a *dispassionate* analysis of the problem, he carefully examined the causes of the conflict and proceeded to suggest suitable remedies.

dis-per-sion \dis-'pər-zhən\ (*n*) scattering. The *dispersion* of this group throughout the world may be explained by their expulsion from their homeland.

dis-pir-it-ed \⁽ʼ⁾dis-'pir-ət-əd\ (*adj*) lacking in spirit. The coach used all the tricks at his command to buoy up the enthusiasm of his team, which had become *dispirited* at the loss of the star player.

dis-pu-ta-tious \ˌdis-pyə-'tā-shəs\ (*adj*) argumentative; fond of argument. People avoided discussing contemporary problems with him because of his *disputatious* manner.

dis-qui-si-tion \ˌdis-kwə-'zish-ən\ (*n*) a formal systematic inquiry; an explanation of the results of a formal inquiry. In his *disquisition,* he outlined the steps he had taken in reaching his conclusions.

dis-sec-tion \dis-'ek-shən\ (*n*) analysis; cutting apart in order to examine. The *dissection* of frogs in the laboratory is particularly unpleasant to some students.

dis-sem-ble \dis-'em-bəl\ (*v*) disguise; pretend. Even though you are trying to *dissemble* your motive in joining this group, we can see through your pretense.

dis-sem-i-nate \dis-'em-ə-ˌnāt\ (*v*) scatter (like seeds). The invention of the radio has helped propagandists to *disseminate* their favorite doctrines very easily.

dis-sent \dis-'ent\ (*v*) disagree. In that Supreme Court decision, Justice Marshall *dissented* from the majority opinion; also (*n*).

\ə\ **abut** \ᵊ\ **kitten, F table** \ər\ **further** \a\ **ash** \ā\ **ace** \ä\ **cot, cart**
\aů\ **out** \ch\ **chin** \e\ **bet** \ē\ **easy** \g\ **go** \i\ **hit** \ī\ **ice** \j\ **job**

dis·ser·ta·tion \ˌdis-ər-'tā-shən\ (*n*) formal essay. In order to earn a graduate degree from many of our universities, a candidate is frequently required to prepare a *dissertation* on some scholarly subject.

dis·sim·u·late \ˌdis-'im-yə-ˌlāt\ (*v*) pretend; conceal by feigning. She tried to *dissimulate* her grief by her gay attitude.

dis·si·pate \'dis-ə-ˌpāt\ (*v*) squander. The young man quickly dissipated his inheritance.

dis·so·lute \'dis-ə-ˌlüt\ (*adj*) loose in morals. The *dissolute* life led by these people is indeed shocking.

dis·so·nance \'dis-ə-nən(t)s\ (*n*) discord. Some contemporary musicians deliberately use *dissonance* to achieve certain effects.

dis·suade \dis-'wād\ (*v*) advise against. He could not *dissuade* his friend from joining the conspirators.

dis·sua·sion \dis-'wā-zhən\ (*n*) advice against. All his powers of *dissuasion* were useless.

dis·tend \dis-'tend\ (*v*) expand; swell out. I can tell when he is under stress by the way the veins *distend* on his forehead.

dis·tinct \dis-'tiŋ(k)t\ (*adj*) separate; clear or plain. No one could fail to notice the *distinct* odor of skunk while driving down that country road.

dis·tor·tion \dis-'tȯr-shən\ (*n*) twisting out of shape. It is difficult to believe the newspaper accounts of this event because of the *distortions* and exaggerations written by the reporters.

dis·traught \dis-'trȯt\ (*adj*) upset; distracted by anxiety. The *distraught* parents searched the ravine for their lost child.

di·ur·nal \dī-'ərn-əl\ (*adj*) daily. A farmer cannot neglect his *diurnal* tasks at any time; cows, for example, must be milked regularly.

\ŋ\ **sing** \ō\ **go** \ȯ\ **law** \ȯi\ **boy** \th\ **thin** \th̲\ **the** \ü\ **loot** \u̇\ **foot**
\y\ **yet** \zh\ **vision** \à, k̲, ⁿ, œ, œ̄, ue, œ̄, ʸ\ *see* Pronunciation Symbols

di-va \\'dē-və\ (*n*) operatic singer; prima donna. Although world famous as a *diva,* she did not indulge in fits of temperament.

di-verge \də-'vərj\ (*v*) vary; go in different directions from the same point. The spokes of the wheel *diverge* from the hub.

di-vers \\'dī-vərz\ (*adj*) several; differing. We could hear *divers* opinions of his ability.

di-verse \dī-'vərs\ (*adj*) differing in some characteristics; various. There are *diverse* ways of approaching the problem.

di-ver-si-ty \də-'vər-sət-ē\ (*n*) variety; dissimilitude. The *diversity* of colleges in this country indicates that many levels of ability are being cared for.

di-vest \dī-'vest\ (*v*) strip; deprive. He was *divested* of his power to act.

div-i-na-tion \ˌdiv-ə-'nā-shən\ (*n*) foreseeing the future with aid of magic. I base my opinions not on any special gift of *divination* but on the laws of probability.

di-vulge \də-'vəlj\ (*v*) reveal. I will not tell you this news because I am sure you will *divulge* it prematurely.

doc-ile \\'däs-əl\ (*adj*) obedient; easily managed. As *docile* as he seems today, that old lion was once a ferocious, snarling beast.

dock-et \\'däk-ət\ (*n*) program as for trial; book where such entries are made. The case of Smith vs. Jones was entered in the *docket* for July 15; also (*v*).

doc-u-ment \\'däk-yə-ˌment\ (*v*) provide written evidence. She kept all the receipts from her business trip in order to *document* her expenses for the firm; also (*n*).

dod-der-ing \\'däd-(ə-)riŋ\ (*adj*) shaky; infirm from old age. Although he is not as yet a *doddering* and senile old man, his ideas and opinions no longer can merit the respect we gave them years ago.

doff \\'däf\ (*v*) take off. He *doffed* his hat to the lady.

\ə\ **abut** \ᵊ\ **kitten, F table** \ər\ **further** \a\ **ash** \ā\ **ace** \ä\ **cot, cart**
\au̇\ **out** \ch\ **chin** \e\ **bet** \ē\ **easy** \g\ **go** \i\ **hit** \ī\ **ice** \j\ **job**

dog-ger-el \'dȯg-(ə-)rəl\ (*n*) poor verse. Although we find occasional snatches of genuine poetry in his work, most of his writing is mere *doggerel.*

dog-mat-ic \dȯg-'mat-ik\ (*adj*) positive; arbitrary. Do not be so *dogmatic* about that statement; it can be easily refuted.

dol-drums \'dōl-drəmz\ (*n*) blues; listlessness; slack period. Once the excitement of meeting her deadline was over, she found herself in the *doldrums.*

do-lor-ous \'dō-lə-rəs\ (*adj*) sorrowful. He found the *dolorous* lamentations of the bereaved family emotionally disturbing and he left as quickly as he could.

dolt \'dōlt\ (*n*) stupid person. I thought I was talking to a mature audience; instead, I find myself addressing a pack of *dolts* and idiots.

do-mi-cile \'däm-ə-ˌsīl\ (*n*) home. Although his legal *domicile* was in New York City, his work kept him away from his residence for many years; also (*v*).

dor-mant \'dȯr-mənt\ (*adj*) sleeping; lethargic; torpid. Sometimes *dormant* talents in our friends surprise those of us who never realized how gifted our acquaintances really are. **dor-man-cy** \'dȯr-mən-sē\ (*n*)

dor-sal \'dȯr-səl\ (*adj*) relating to the back of an animal. A shark may be identified by its *dorsal* fin, which projects above the surface of the ocean; also (*n*).

dot-age \'dōt-ij\ (*n*) senility. In his *dotage,* the old man bored us with long tales of events in his childhood.

dough-ty \'daȯt-ē\ (*adj*) courageous. Many folk tales have sprung up about this *doughty* pioneer who opened up the New World for his followers.

dour \'daȯ(ə)r\ (*adj*) sullen; stubborn. The man was *dour* and taciturn.

douse \'daȯs\ (*v*) plunge into water; drench; extinguish. They *doused* each other with hoses and water balloons.

---

dowdy \'daủd-ē\ (*adj*) slovenly; untidy. She tried to change her *dowdy* image by buying a new fashionable wardrobe.

dreg \'dreg\ (*n*) sediment; worthless residue. The *dregs* of society may be observed in this slum area of the city.

droll \'drōl\ (*adj*) queer and amusing. He was a popular guest because his *droll* anecdotes were always amusing; also (*n*).

drone \'drōn\ (*n*) idle person; male bee. Content to let his wife support him, the would-be writer was in reality nothing but a *drone*.

drone \'drōn\ (*v*) talk dully; buzz or murmur like a bee. On a gorgeous day, who wants to be stuck in a class-room listening to the teacher *drone*.

dross \'dräs\ (*n*) waste matter; worthless impurities. Many methods have been devised to separate the valu-able metal from the *dross*.

drudg-ery \'drəj-(ə-)rē\ (*n*) menial work. Cinderella's fairy godmother rescued her from a life of *drudgery*.

du-bi-ous \'d(y)ü-bē-əs\ (*adj*) doubtful. He has the *dubi-ous* distinction of being the lowest man in his class.

du-en-na \d(y)ü-'en-ə\ (*n*) attendant of young female; chaperone. Their romance could not flourish because of the presence of her *duenna*.

dul-cet \'dəl-sət\ (*adj*) sweet sounding. The *dulcet* sounds of the birds at dawn were soon drowned out by the roar of traffic passing our motel.

du-plic-i-ty \d(y)ủ-'plis-ət-ē\ (*n*) double-dealing; hypocrisy. People were shocked and dismayed when they learned of his *duplicity* in this affair for he had always seemed honest and straightforward.

du-ress \d(y)ủ-'res\ (*n*) forcible restraint, especially unlawfully. The hostages were held under *duress* until the prisoners' demands were met.

\ə\ **abut** \ᵊ\ **kitten**, F **table** \ər\ **further** \a\ **ash** \ā\ **ace** \ä\ **cot, cart**
\aủ\ **out** \ch\ **chin** \e\ **bet** \ē\ **easy** \g\ **go** \i\ **hit** \ī\ **ice** \j\ **job**

dwin-dle \\'dwin-dəl\\ (*v*) shrink; reduce. They spent so much money that their funds *dwindled* to nothing.

dy-nam-ic \\dī-'nam-ik\\ (*adj*) active; efficient. A *dynamic* government is necessary to meet the demands of a changing society; also (*n*).

dys-pep-tic \\dis-'pep-tik\\ (*adj*) suffering from indigestion. All the talk about rich food made him feel *dyspeptic*. **dys-pep-sia** \\dis-'pep-shə\\ (*n*)

E

earth-y \ 'ər-thē\ (*adj*) unrefined; coarse. His *earthy* remarks often embarrassed the women in his audience.

e-bul-lient \ i-'bu̇l-yənt\ (*adj*) showing excitement; overflowing with enthusiasm. His *ebullient* nature could not be repressed; he was always laughing and gay. **e-bul-lience** \ i-'bu̇l-yən(t)s\ (*n*)

ec-cen-tric-i-ty \ ,ek-,sen-'tris-ət-ē\ (*n*) oddity; idiosyncrasy. Some of his friends tried to account for his rudeness to strangers as the *eccentricity* of genius. **ec-cen-tric** \ ik-'sen-trik\ (*adj, n*)

ec-cle-si-as-tic \ ik-,lē-zē-'as-tik\ (*adj*) pertaining to the church. The minister donned his *ecclesiastic* garb and walked to the pulpit; also (*n*).

e-clec-ti-cism \ e-'klek-tə-,siz-əm\ (*n*) selection of elements from various sets of opinions or systems. The *eclecticism* of the group was demonstrated by their adoption of principles and practices of many forms of government.

eclipse \ i-'klips\ (*v*) darken; extinguish; surpass. The new stock market high *eclipsed* the previous record set in 1989.

ec-sta-sy \ 'ek-stə-sē\ (*n*) rapture; joy; any overpowering emotion. The announcement that the war had ended brought on an *ecstasy* of joy that resulted in many uncontrolled celebrations.

ed-i-fy \ 'ed-ə-,fī\ (*v*) instruct; correct morally. Although his purpose was to *edify* and not to entertain his audience, many of his listeners were amused and not enlightened.

e-duce \ i-'d(y)üs\ (*v*) draw forth; elicit. He could not *educe* a principle that would encompass all the data.

ee-rie \ 'i(ə)r-ē\ (*adj*) weird. In that *eerie* setting, it was easy to believe in ghosts and other supernatural beings.

ef-face \ i-'fās\ (*v*) rub out. The coin had been handled so many times that its date had been *effaced*.

---

ef-fec-tu-al \i-'fek-chə(-wə)l\ (*adj*) efficient. If we are to succeed in this endeavor, we must seek *effectual* means of securing our goals.

ef-fem-i-nate \ə-'fem-ə-nət\ (*adj*) having womanly traits. His voice was high-pitched and *effeminate;* also (*n*).

ef-fer-vesce \,ef-ər-'ves\ (*v*) bubble over; show excitement. Some of us cannot stand the way she *effervesces* over trifles.

ef-fete \e-'fēt\ (*adj*) worn out; exhausted; barren. The literature of the age reflected the *effete* condition of the writers; no new ideas were forthcoming.

ef-fi-ca-cy \'ef-i-kə-sē\ (*n*) power to produce desired effect. The *efficacy* of this drug depends on the regularity of the dosage.

ef-fi-gy \'ef-ə-jē\ (*n*) dummy. The mob showed its irritation by hanging the judge in *effigy.*

ef-flu-vi-um \e-'flü-vē-əm\ (*n*) noxious smell. Air pollution has become a serious problem in our major cities; the *effluvium* and the poisons in the air are hazards to life.

ef-fron-ter-y \i-'frənt-ə-rē\ (*n*) shameless boldness. He had the *effrontery* to insult the guest.

ef-fu-sion \i-'fyü-zhən\ (*n*) pouring forth. The critics objected to his literary *effusion* because it was too flowery.

ef-fu-sive \i-'fyü-siv\ (*adj*) pouring forth; gushing. Her *effusive* manner of greeting her friends finally began to irritate them.

e-go-ism \'e-gə-,wiz-əm\ (*n*) excessive interest in one's self; belief that one should be interested in one's self rather than in others. His *egoism* prevented him from seeing the needs of his colleagues.

e-go-tism \'ē-gə-,tiz-əm\ (*n*) conceit; vanity. We found his *egotism* unwarranted and irritating.

e-gre-gious \i-'grē-jəs\ (*adj*) gross; shocking. He was an *egregious* liar.

\ŋ\ sing \ō\ go \o\ law \oi\ boy \th\ thin \th\ the \ü\ loot \u\ foot
\y\ yet \zh\ vision \à, k, n, œ, œ̄, ue, ūe, y\ *see* Pronunciation Symbols

e-gress \ˈē-ˌgres\ (*n*) exit. Barnum's sign "To the *Egress*" fooled many people who thought they were going to see an animal and instead found themselves in the street. **e-gress** \ē-ˈgres\ (*v*)

e-jac-u-la-tion \i-ˌjak-yə-ˈlā-shən\ (*n*) exclamation. He could not repress an *ejaculation* of surprise when he heard the news.

e-lab-o-ra-tion \i-ˌlab-ə-ˈrā-shən\ (*n*) addition of details; intricacy. Tell what happened simply, without any *elaboration*. **e-lab-o-rate** \i-ˈlab-ə-ˌrāt\ (*v*)

e-la-tion \i-ˈlā-shən\ (*n*) a rise in spirits; exaltation. She felt no *elation* at finding the purse.

el-e-gi-a-cal \ˌel-ə-ˈjī-ə-kəl\ (*adj*) like an elegy; mournful. The essay on the lost crew was *elegiacal* in mood. **el-e-gy** \ˈel-ə-jē\ (*n*)

e-lic-it \i-ˈlis-ət\ (*v*) draw out by discussion. The detectives tried to *elicit* where he had hidden his loot.

e-lix-ir \i-ˈlik-sər\ (*n*) cure-all; something invigorating. The news of her chance to go abroad acted on her like an *elixir*.

el-o-quence \ˈel-ə-kwən(t)s\ (*n*) expressiveness; persuasive speech. The crowds were stirred by Martin Luther King's *eloquence*.

e-lu-ci-date \i-ˈlü-sə-ˌdāt\ (*v*) explain; enlighten. He was called upon to *elucidate* the disputed points in his article.

e-lu-sive \ē-ˈlü-siv\ (*adj*) evasive; baffling; hard to grasp. His *elusive* dreams of wealth were costly to those of his friends who supported him financially.

e-lu-so-ry \e-ˈlüs-(ə-)rē\ (*adj*) tending to deceive expectations; elusive. He argued that the project was an *elusory* one and would bring disappointment to all.

e-ly-sian \i-ˈlizh-ən\ (*adj*) relating to paradise; blissful. An afternoon sail on the bay was for her an *elysian* journey.

e-ma-ci-ate \i-ˈmā-shē-ˌāt\ (*v*) to make thin and wasted. He was wan and *emaciated* after his long period of starvation.

em-a-nate \\'em-ə-ˌnāt\\ (*v*) issue forth. A strong odor of sulphur *emanated* from the spring.

e-man-ci-pate \\i-'man(t)-sə-ˌpāt\\ (*v*) set free. At first, the attempts of the Abolitionists to *emancipate* the slaves were unpopular in New England as well as in the South.

em-bark \\im-'bärk\\ (*v*) commence; go on a boat or airplane; begin a journey. In devoting herself to the study of gorillas, Dian Fossey *embarked* on a course of action that was to cost her her life.

em-bed \\im-'bed\\ (*v*) enclose; place in something. Tales of actual historical figures like King Alfred have become *embedded* in legends.

em-bel-lish \\im-'bel-ish\\ (*v*) adorn. His handwriting was *embellished* with flourishes.

em-bez-zle-ment \\im-'bez-əl-mənt\\ (*n*) stealing. The bank teller confessed his *embezzlement* of the funds.

em-bla-zon \\im-'blāz-ᵊn\\ (*v*) deck in brilliant colors. *Emblazoned* on his shield was his family coat of arms.

em-broil \\im-'broi(ə)l\\ (*v*) throw into confusion; involve in strife; entangle. He became *embroiled* in the heated discussion when he tried to arbitrate the dispute.

em-bry-on-ic \\ˌem-brē-'än-ik\\ (*adj*) undeveloped; rudimentary. The evil of class and race hatred must be eliminated while it is still in an *embryonic* state; otherwise, it may grow to dangerous proportions.

e-mend \\ē-'mend\\ (*v*) correct; correct by a critic. The critic *emended* the book by selecting the passages that he thought most appropriate to the text.

e-men-da-tion \\ˌē-ˌmen-'dā-shən\\ (*n*) correction of errors; improvement. Please initial all the *emendations* you have made in this contract.

e-mer-i-tus \\i-'mer-ət-əs\\ (*adj*) retired but retained in an honorary capacity. As professor *emeritus,* he retained all his honors without having to meet the obligations of daily assignments; also (*n*).

\\ŋ\\ si**ng**   \\ō\\ **go**   \\ȯ\\ **law**   \\ȯi\\ **boy**   \\th\\ **thin**   \\t͟h\\ **the**   \\ü\\ **loot**   \\u̇\\ **foot**
\\y\\ **yet**   \\zh\\ **vision**   \\à, k̲, ⁿ, œ, œ̄, ᵫ, ᵭ, ʸ\\ *see* Pronunciation Symbols

em-i-nent \\'em-ə-nənt\\ (*adj*) high; lofty. After his appointment to this *eminent* position, he seldom had time for his former friends.

em-is-sary \\'em-ə-ˌser-ē\\ (*n*) agent; messenger. The secretary of state was sent as the president's special *emissary* to the conference on disarmament.

e-mol-lient \\i-'mäl-yənt\\ (*n*) soothing or softening remedy. He applied an *emollient* to the inflamed area; also (*adj*).

em-pir-i-cal \\im-'pir-i-kəl\\ (*adj*) based on experience. He distrusted hunches and intuitive flashes; he placed his reliance entirely on *empirical* data.

em-u-late \\'em-yə-ˌlāt\\ (*v*) rival; imitate. As long as our political leaders *emulate* the virtues of the great leaders of this country, we shall flourish.

en-am-or \\in-'am-ər\\ (*v*) overwhelmed by love. Narcissus was *enamored* of his own beauty.

en-clave \\'en-ˌklāv\\ (*n*) territory enclosed within an alien land. The Vatican is an independent *enclave* in Italy.

en-co-mi-um \\en-'kō-mē-əm\\ (*n*) praise; eulogy. He was sickened by the *encomiums* and panegyrics expressed by speakers who had previously been among the first to vilify the man they were now honoring.

en-com-pass \\in-'kəm-pəs\\ (*v*) surround. Although we were *encompassed* by enemy forces, we were cheerful for we were well stocked and could withstand a siege until our allies joined us.

en-coun-ter \\in-'kaůnt-ər\\ (*n*) meeting. Native Americans suffered from new diseases after their first *encounters* with Europeans; also (*v*).

en-croach-ment \\in-'krōch-mənt\\ (*n*) gradual intrusion. The *encroachment* of the factories upon the neighborhood lowered the value of the real estate.

en-cum-ber \\in-'kəm-bər\\ (*v*) burden. Some people *encumber* themselves with too much luggage when they take short trips.

\\ə\\ abut \\ᵊ\\ kitten, F table \\ər\\ **further** \\a\\ ash \\ā\\ ace \\ä\\ cot, cart
\\aů\\ **out** \\ch\\ **chin** \\e\\ bet \\ē\\ **easy** \\g\\ go \\i\\ hit \\ī\\ ice \\j\\ job

en·dear·ment \in-'di(ə)r-mənt\ (*n*) fond statement. Your gifts and *endearments* cannot make me forget your earlier insolence.

en·dem·ic \en-'dem-ik\ (*adj*) prevailing among a specific group of people or in a specific area or country. This disease is *endemic* in this part of the world; more than 80 percent of the population are at one time or another affected by it.

en·dorse \in-'dȯ(ə)rs\ (*v*) approve; support. Everyone waited to see which one of the rival candidates for the city council the mayor would *endorse*. (secondary meaning) **en·dorse·ment** \in-'dȯr-smənt\ (*n*)

en·er·gize \'en-ər-ˌjīz\ (*v*) invigorate; make forceful and active. We shall have to re-*energize* our activities by getting new members to carry on.

e·ner·vate \'en-ər-ˌvāt\ (*v*) weaken. The hot days of August are *enervating*. **e·ner·vate** \i-'nər-vət\ (*adj*)

en·gen·der \in-'jen-dər\ (*v*) cause; produce. This editorial will *engender* racial intolerance unless it is denounced.

en·grossed \in-'grōst\ (*adj*) occupied fully. John was so *engrossed* in his studies that he did not hear his mother call. **en·gross** \in-'grōs\ (*v*)

en·hance \in-'han(t)s\ (*v*) advance; improve. Your chances for promotion in this department will be *enhanced* if you take some more courses in evening school.

e·nig·ma \i-'nig-mə\ (*n*) puzzle. Despite all attempts to decipher the code, it remained an *enigma*.

e·nig·mat·ic \ˌen-(ˌ)ig-'mat-ik\ (*adj*) obscure; puzzling. Many have sought to fathom the *enigmatic* smile of the *Mona Lisa*.

en·join \in-'jȯin\ (*v*) command; order; forbid. The owners of the company asked the court to *enjoin* the union from picketing the plant.

en·mi·ty \'en-mət-ē\ (*n*) ill will; hatred. At Camp David, President Carter labored to bring an end to the *enmity*

\ŋ\ **sing** \ō\ **go** \ȯ\ **law** \ȯi\ **boy** \th\ **thin** \t͟h\ **the** \ü\ **loot** \u̇\ **foot** \y\ **yet** \zh\ **vision** \à, k̲, ⁿ, œ, œ̄, ᵫ, ᵫ̄, ʸ\ *see* Pronunciation Symbols

that prevented the peaceful coexistence of Egypt and Israel.

en-nui \\'än-'wē\\ (*n*) boredom. The monotonous routine of hospital life induced a feeling of *ennui* that made him moody and irritable.

e-nor-mi-ty \\i-'nȯr-mət-ē\\ (*n*) hugeness (in a bad sense). He did not realize the *enormity* of his crime until he saw what suffering he had caused.

en-rap-ture \\in-'rap-chər\\ (*v*) please intensely. The audience was *enraptured* by the freshness of the voices and the excellent orchestration.

en-sconce \\in-'skän(t)s\\ (*v*) settle comfortably. The parents thought that their children were *ensconced* safely in the private school and decided to leave for Europe.

en-sue \\in-'sü\\ (*v*) follow. The evils that *ensued* were the direct result of the miscalculations of the leaders.

en-thrall \\in-'thrȯl\\ (*v*) capture; enslave. From the moment he saw her picture, he was *enthralled* by her beauty.

en-tice \\in-'tīs\\ (*v*) lure; attract; tempt. She always tried to *entice* her baby brother into mischief.

en-ti-ty \\'en(t)-ət-ē\\ (*n*) real being. As soon as the Charter was adopted, the United Nations became an *entity* and had to be considered as a factor in world diplomacy.

en-to-mol-o-gy \\,ent-ə-'mäl-ə-jē\\ (*n*) study of insects. I found *entomology* the least interesting part of my course in biology; studying insects bored me.

en-trance \\in-'tran(t)s\\ (*v*) put under a spell; carry away with emotion. Shafts of sunlight on a wall could *entrance* her and leave her spellbound.

en-treat \\in-'trēt\\ (*v*) plead; ask earnestly. She *entreated* her father to let her stay out till midnight.

en-trée \\'än-,trā\\ (*n*) entrance. Because of his wealth and social position, he had *entrée* into the most exclusive circles.

\\ə\\ **abut** \\ᵊ\\ **kitten, F table** \\ər\\ **further** \\a\\ **ash** \\ā\\ **ace** \\ä\\ **cot, cart**
\\au̇\\ **out** \\ch\\ **chin** \\e\\ **bet** \\ē\\ **easy** \\g\\ **go** \\i\\ **hit** \\ī\\ **ice** \\j\\ **job**

en-tre-pre-neur \ˌäⁿn-trə-p(r)ə-'nər\ (*n*) businessman; contractor. Opponents of our present tax program argue that it discourages *entrepreneurs* from trying new fields of business activity.

en-vi-ron \in-'vī-rən\ (*v*) enclose; surround. In medieval days, Paris was *environed* by a wall. **en-vi-rons** \in-'vī-rənz\ (*n*)

e-phem-er-al \i-'fem(-ə)-rəl\ (*adj*) short-lived; fleeting. The mayfly is an *ephemeral* creature; also (*n*).

ep-ic \'ep-ik\ (*n*) long heroic poem, novel, or similar work of art. Kurosawa's film *Seven Samurai* is an epic portraying the struggle of seven warriors to destroy a band of robbers.

ep-ic \'ep-ik\ (*adj*) unusually great in size or extent; heroic; impressive. The task of renovating the decrepit subway system was one of truly *epic* dimensions; it would cost millions of dollars and involve thousands of laborers working night and day.

ep-i-cure \'ep-i-ˌkyu̇(ə)r\ (*n*) connoisseur of food and drink. *Epicures* frequent this restaurant because it features exotic wines and dishes.

ep-i-cu-re-an \ˌep-i-kyu̇-'rē-ən\ (*n*) person who devotes himself to pleasures of the senses, especially to food. This restaurant is famous for its menu, which can cater to the most exotic whim of the *epicurean;* also (*adj*).

ep-i-gram \'ep-ə-ˌgram\ (*n*) witty thought or saying, usually short. Poor Richard's *epigrams* made Benjamin Franklin famous.

ep-i-logue \'ep-ə-ˌlȯg\ (*n*) short speech at conclusion of dramatic work. The audience was so disappointed in the play that many did not remain to hear the *epilogue.*

ep-i-taph \'ep-ə-ˌtaf\ (*n*) inscription in memory of a dead person. In his will, he dictated the *epitaph* he wanted placed on his tombstone.

\ŋ\ sing \ō\ go \ȯ\ law \ȯi\ boy \th\ thin \th̲\ the \ü\ loot \u̇\ foot
\y\ yet \zh\ vision \à, k̲, ⁿ, œ, œ̄, ue, ūe, ʸ\ *see* Pronunciation Symbols

ep-i-thet \\'ep-ə-ˌthet\\ (*n*) descriptive word or phrase. Homer's writings featured the use of such *epithets* as "rosy-fingered dawn."

e-pit-o-me \\i-'pit-ə-mē\\ (*n*) summary; concise abstract. This final book is the *epitome* of all his previous books. **e-pit-o-mize** \\i-'pit-ə-ˌmīz\\ (*v*)

ep-och \\'ep-ək\\ (*n*) period of time. The glacial *epoch* lasted for thousands of years.

eq-ua-ble \\'ek- wə-bəl\\ (*adj*) tranquil; steady; uniform. After the hot summers and cold winters of New England, he found the climate of the West Indies *equable* and pleasant.

e-qua-nim-i-ty \\ˌē-kwə-'nim-ət-ē\\ (*n*) calmness of temperament. In his later years, he could look upon the foolishness of the world with *equanimity* and humor.

e-ques-tri-an \\i-'kwes-trē-ən\\ (*n*) rider on horseback. These paths in the park are reserved for *equestrians* and their steeds; also (*adj*).

e-qui-lib-ri-um \\ˌē-kwə-'lib-rē-əm\\ (*n*) balance. After the divorce, he needed some time to regain his *equilibrium*.

e-qui-nox \\'e-kwə-ˌnäks\\ (*n*) period of equal days and nights; the beginning of spring and autumn. The vernal *equinox* is usually marked by heavy rainstorms.

eq-ui-ta-ble \\'ek-wət-ə-bəl\\ (*adj*) fair; impartial. I am seeking an *equitable* solution to this dispute, one that will be fair and acceptable to both sides.

eq-ui-ty \\'ek-wət-ē\\ (*n*) fairness; justice. Our courts guarantee *equity* to all.

e-quiv-o-cal \\i-'kwiv-ə-kəl\\ (*adj*) doubtful; ambiguous. Macbeth was misled by the *equivocal* statements of the witches.

e-quiv-o-cate \\i-'kwiv-ə-ˌkāt\\ (*v*) lie; mislead; attempt to conceal the truth. The audience saw through his attempts to *equivocate* on the subject under discussion and ridiculed his remarks.

\\ə\\ **abut** \\ᵊ\\ **kitten**, F **table** \\ər\\ f**urther** \\a\\ **ash** \\ā\\ **ace** \\ä\\ **cot, cart** \\au̇\\ **out** \\ch\\ **chin** \\e\\ **bet** \\ē\\ **easy** \\g\\ **go** \\i\\ **hit** \\ī\\ **ice** \\j\\ **job**

e-rode \i-'rōd\ (*v*) eat away. The limestone was *eroded* by the dripping water.

e-rot-ic \i-'rät-ik\ (*adj*) pertaining to passionate love. The *erotic* passages in this novel should be removed as they are merely pornographic.

er-rant \'er-ənt\ (*adj*) wandering. Many a charming tale has been written about the knights-*errant* who helped the weak and punished the guilty during the Age of Chivalry.

er-rat-ic \ir-'at-ik\ (*adj*) odd; unpredictable. Investors become anxious when the stock market appears *erratic*.

er-ro-ne-ous \ir-'ō-nē-əs\ (*adj*) mistaken; wrong. I thought my answer was correct, but it was *erroneous*.

er-u-dite \'er-(y)ə-ˌdīt\ (*adj*) learned; scholarly. His *erudite* writing was difficult to read because of the many allusions that were unfamiliar to most readers.

er-u-di-tion \ˌer-(y)ə-'dish-ən\ (*n*) high degree of knowledge and learning. Although they respected his *erudition*, the populace refused to listen to his words of caution and turned to less learned leaders.

es-ca-pade \'es-kə-ˌpād\ (*n*) prank; flighty conduct. The headmaster could not regard this latest *escapade* as a boyish joke and expelled the young man.

es-chew \is(h)-'chü\ (*v*) avoid. He tried to *eschew* all display of temper.

es-o-ter-ic \ˌes-ə-'ter-ik\ (*adj*) known only to the chosen few. Those students who had access to his *esoteric* discussions were impressed by the scope of his thinking.

es-pi-o-nage \'es-pē-ə-ˌnäzh\ (*n*) spying. In order to maintain its power, the government developed a system of *espionage* that penetrated every household.

es-pouse \is-'pauz\ (*v*) adopt; support. She was always ready to *espouse* a worthy cause.

es-prit de corps \is-ˌprēd-ə-'kō(ə)r\ (*n*) comradeship; spirit. West Point cadets are proud of their *esprit de corps*.

\ŋ\ sing \ō\ go \ȯ\ law \ȯi\ boy \th\ thin \t͟h\ the \ü\ loot \u̇\ foot
\y\ yet \zh\ vision \à, k̲, ⁿ, œ, œ̄, ᵫ, ᵫ̄, ʸ\ *see* Pronunciation Symbols

es-trange \is-'trānj\ (*v*) alienate. The wife was *estranged* from her husband and sought a divorce.

e-the-re-al \i-'thir-ē-əl\ (*adj*) light; heavenly; fine. Visitors were impressed by her *ethereal* beauty, her delicate charm.

eth-nic \'eth-nik\ (*adj*) relating to races. Intolerance between *ethnic* groups is deplorable and usually is based on lack of information; also (*n*).

eth-nol-o-gy \eth-'näl-ə-jē\ (*n*) study of man. Sociology is one aspect of the science of *ethnology*.

et-y-mol-o-gy \ˌet-ə-'mäl-ə-jē\ (*n*) study of derivation, structure and development of words. To the student of *etymology*, the dictionary is a tremendous source of information.

eu-gen-ic \yù-'jen-ik\ (*adj*) pertaining to the improvement of race. It is easier to apply *eugenic* principles to the raising of racehorses or prize cattle than to the development of human beings. **eu-gen-ics** \yù-'jen-iks\ (*n*)

eu-lo-gis-tic \ˌyü-lə-'jis-tik\ (*adj*) praising. To everyone's surprise, the speech was *eulogistic* rather than critical in tone.

eu-lo-gy \'yü-lə-jē\ (*n*) praise. All the *eulogies* of his friends could not remove the sting of the calumny heaped upon him by his enemies.

eu-phe-mism \'yü-fə-ˌmiz-əm\ (*n*) mild expression in place of an unpleasant one. The expression "He passed away" is a *euphemism* for "He died."

eu-pho-ni-ous \yù-'fō-nē-əs\ (*adj*) pleasing in sound. Italian and Spanish are *euphonious* languages and therefore easily sung.

eu-tha-na-sia \ˌyü-thə-'nā-zh(ē-)ə\ (*n*) mercy killing. Many people support *euthanasia* for terminally ill patients who wish to die.

ev-a-nes-cent \ˌev-ə-'nes-ᵊnt\ (*adj*) fleeting; vanishing. For a brief moment, the entire skyline was bathed in an orange-red hue in the *evanescent* rays of the sunset.

---

e·va·sive \i-'vā-siv\ (*adj*) not frank; eluding. Your *evasive* answers convinced the judge that you were withholding important evidence. **e·vade** \i-'vād\ (*v*)

e·vince \i-'vin(t)s\ (*v*) show clearly. When he tried to answer the questions, he *evinced* his ignorance of the subject matter.

e·vis·cer·ate \i-'vis-ə-ˌrāt\ (*v*) disembowel; remove entrails. The medicine man *eviscerated* the animal and offered the entrails to the angry gods.

e·voke \i-'vōk\ (*v*) call forth. He *evoked* much criticism by his hostile manner.

ex·ac·er·bate \ig-'zas-ər-ˌbāt\ (*v*) worsen; embitter. This latest arrest will *exacerbate* the already existing discontent of the people and enrage them

ex·ac·tion \ig-'zak-shən\ (*n*) exorbitant demand; extortion. The colonies rebelled against the *exactions* of the mother country.

ex·alt \ig-'zȯlt\ (*v*) raise in rank or dignity; praise. The actor Alec Guinness was *exalted* to the rank of knighthood by the queen.

ex·as·per·ate \ig-'zas-pə-ˌrāt\ (*v*) vex. Johnny often *exasperates* his mother with his pranks.

ex·ci·sion \ik-'sizh-ən\ (*n*) act of cutting away. With the *excision* of the dead and dying limbs of this tree, you have not only improved its appearance but you have enhanced its chances of bearing fruit. **ex·cise** \ik-'sīz\ (*v*)

ex·co·ri·ate \ek-'skȯr-ē-ˌāt\ (*v*) flay; abrade. These shoes are so ill-fitting that they will *excoriate* the feet and create blisters.

ex·cul·pate \'ek-(ˌ)skəl-ˌpāt\ (*v*) clear from blame. He was *exculpated* of the crime when the real criminal confessed.

ex·e·cra·ble \'ek-si-krə-bəl\ (*adj*) very bad. The anecdote was in *execrable* taste.

---

ex-e-crate \\'ek-sə-ˌkrāt\\ (v) curse; express abhorrence for. The world *execrates* the memory of Hitler and hopes that genocide will never again be the policy of any nation.

ex-e-cute \\'ek-si-ˌkyüt\\ (v) put into effect; carry out. The choreographer wanted to see how well she could *execute* a pirouette. (secondary meaning) **ex-e-cu-tion** \\ˌek-si-'kyü-shən\\ (n)

ex-e-ge-sis \\ˌek-sə-'jē-səs\\ (n) explanation, especially of Biblical passages. I can follow your *exegesis* of this passage to a limited degree; some of your reasoning eludes me.

ex-em-pla-ry \\ig-'zem-plə-rē\\ (adj) serving as a model; outstanding. Her *exemplary* behavior was praised at Commencement.

ex-haus-tive \\ig-'zȯ-stiv\\ (adj) thorough; comprehensive. We have made an *exhaustive* study of all published SAT tests and are happy to share our research with you.

ex-hort \\ig-'zȯ(ə)rt\\ (v) urge. The evangelist will *exhort* all sinners in his audience to reform.

ex-hume \\igz-'(y)üm\\ (v) dig out of the ground; remove from a grave. Because of the rumor that he had been poisoned, his body was *exhumed* in order that an autopsy might be performed.

ex-i-gen-cy \\'ek-sə-jən-sē\\ (n) urgent situation. In this *exigency,* we must look for aid from our allies.

ex-ig-u-ous \\ig-'zig-yə-wəs\\ (adj) small; minute. Grass grew there, an *exiguous* outcropping among the rocks.

ex-o-dus \\'ek-səd-əs\\ (n) departure. The *exodus* from the hot and stuffy city was particularly noticeable on Friday evenings.

ex of-fi-ci-o \\ˌek-sə-'fish-ē-ˌō\\ (adj) by virtue of one's office. The mayor was *ex officio* chairman of the committee that decided the annual tax rate; also (adv).

ex-on-er-ate \\ig-'zän-ə-ˌrāt\\ (v) acquit; exculpate. I am sure this letter will *exonerate* you.

\\ə\\ **abut** \\ᵊ\\ **kitten,** F **table** \\ər\\ **further** \\a\\ **ash** \\ā\\ **ace** \\ä\\ **cot, cart**
\\au̇\\ **out** \\ch\\ **chin** \\e\\ **bet** \\ē\\ **easy** \\g\\ **go** \\i\\ **hit** \\ī\\ **ice** \\j\\ **job**

ex·or·bi·tant \ig-'zor-bət-ənt\ *(adj)* excessive. The people grumbled at his *exorbitant* prices but paid them because he had a monopoly.

ex·or·cise \'ek-ˌsor-ˌsīz\ *(v)* drive out evil spirits. By incantation and prayer, the medicine man sought to *exorcise* the evil spirits that had taken possession of the young warrior.

ex·ot·ic \ig-'zät-ik\ *(adj)* not native; strange. Because of his *exotic* headdress, he was followed in the streets by small children who laughed at his strange appearance; also *(n)*.

ex·pa·ti·ate \ek-'spā-shē-ˌāt\ *(v)* talk at length. At this time, please give us a brief resumé of your work; we shall permit you to *expatiate* later.

ex·pa·tri·ate \ek-'spā-trē-ˌāt\ *(n)* exile; someone who has withdrawn from his native land. Henry James was an American *expatriate* who settled in England; also *(v, adj)*.

ex·pe·di·en·cy \ik-'spēd-ē-ən-sē\ *(n)* that which is advisable or practical. He was guided by *expediency* rather than by ethical considerations.

ex·pe·di·tious·ly \ˌek-spə-'dish-əs-lē\ *(adv)* rapidly and efficiently. Please adjust this matter as *expeditiously* as possible as it is delaying important work.

ex·per·tise \ˌek-(ˌ)spər-'tēz\ *(n)* specialized knowledge; expert skill. Although she was knowledgeable in a number of fields, she was hired for her particular *expertise* in computer programming.

ex·pi·ate \'ek-spē-ˌāt\ *(v)* make amends for (a sin). He tried to *expiate* his crimes by a full confession to the authorities.

ex·ple·tive \'ek-splət-iv\ *(n)* interjection; profane oath. The sergeant's remarks were filled with *expletives* that reflected on the intelligence and character of the new recruits; also *(adj)*.

ex-plic-it \ik-'splis-ət\ *(adj)* definite; open. Your remarks are *explicit;* no one can misinterpret them.

ex-ploit \'ek-ˌsplȯit\ *(n)* deed or action, particularly a brave deed. Raoul Wallenberg was noted for his *exploits* in rescuing Jews from Hitler's forces.

ex-ploit \ik-'splȯit\ *(v)* make use of, sometimes unjustly. Cesar Chavez fought attempts to *exploit* migrant farmworkers in California. **ex-ploi-ta-tion** \ˌek-ˌsplȯi-'tā-shən\ *(n)*

ex-pos-tu-la-tion \ik-ˌspäs-chə-'lā-shən\ *(n)* remonstrance. Despite the teacher's scoldings and *expostulations,* the class remained unruly.

ex-punge \ik-'spənj\ *(v)* cancel; remove. If you behave, I will *expunge* this notation from your record.

ex-pur-gate \'ek-spər-ˌgāt\ *(v)* clean; remove offensive parts of a book. The editors felt that certain passages in the book had to be *expurgated* before it could be used in this classroom.

ex-tant \'ek-stənt\ *(adj)* still in existence. Although the authorities suppressed the book, many copies are *extant* and may be purchased at exorbitant prices.

ex-tem-po-ra-ne-ous \ₐek-ˌstem-pə-'rā-nē-əs\ *(adj)* not planned; impromptu. Because his *extemporaneous* remarks were misinterpreted, he decided to write all his speeches in advance.

ex-ten-sive \ik-'sten(t)-siv\ *(adj)* vast; comprehensive. The real estate magnate built up his *extensive* holdings over a number of years.

ex-ten-u-ate \ik-'sten-yə-ˌwāt\ *(v)* weaken; mitigate. It is easier for us to *extenuate* our own shortcomings than those of others.

ex-tir-pate \'ek-stər-ˌpāt\ *(v)* root up. We must *extirpate* and destroy this monstrous philosophy.

ex-tol \ik-'stōl\ *(v)* praise; glorify. The astronauts were *extolled* as the pioneers of the Space Age.

\ə\ **abut** \ᵊ\ **kitten, F table** \ər\ **further** \a\ **ash** \ā\ **ace** \ä\ **cot, cart**
\au̇\ **out** \ch\ **chin** \e\ **bet** \ē\ **easy** \g\ **go** \i\ **hit** \ī\ **ice** \j\ **job**

ex-tort \ik-'stȯ(ə)rt\ (*v*) wring from; get money by threats, etc. The blackmailer *extorted* money from his victim.

ex-tra-di-tion \ˌek-strə-'dish-ən\ (*n*) surrender of prisoner by one state to another. The lawyers opposed the *extradition* of their client on the grounds that for more than five years he had been a model citizen.

ex-tra-ne-ous \ek-'strā-nē-əs\ (*adj*) not essential; external. Do not pad your paper with *extraneous* matters; stick to essential items only.

ex-tra-vert \'ek-strə-ˌvərt\ (*n*) person interested mostly in external objects and actions. A good salesman is usually an *extravert,* who likes to mingle with people; also **ex-tro-vert.**

ex-tri-cate \'ek-strə-ˌkāt\ (*v*) free; disentangle. He found that he could not *extricate* himself from the trap.

ex-trin-sic \ek-'strin-zik\ (*adj*) external; not inherent; foreign. Do not be fooled by *extrinsic* causes. We must look for the intrinsic reason.

ex-trude \ik-'strüd\ (*v*) force or push out. Much pressure is required to *extrude* these plastics.

ex-u-ber-ant \ig-'zü-b(ə-)rənt\ (*adj*) abundant; effusive; lavish. His speeches were famous for his *exuberant* language and vivid imagery.

ex-ude \ig-'züd\ (*v*) discharge; give forth. The maple syrup is obtained from the sap that *exudes* from the trees in early spring. **ex-u-da-tion** \ˌek-s(y)ü-dā-shən\ (*n*)

ex-ult \ig-'zəlt\ (*v*) rejoice. We *exulted* when our team won the victory.

\ŋ\ **sing** \ō\ **go** \ȯ\ **law** \ȯi\ **boy** \th\ **thin** \t̲h̲\ **the** \ü\ **loot** \u̇\ **foot**
\y\ **yet** \zh\ **vision** \à, k̲, ⁿ, œ, œ̄, ue, ūe, ʸ\ *see* Pronunciation Symbols

F

fab·ri·cate \\'fab-ri-ˌkāt\\ (*v*) build; lie. If we pre*fabricate* the buildings in this project, we can reduce the cost considerably.

fa·cade \\fə-'säd\\ (*n*) front of the building. The *facade* of the church has often been photographed by tourists.

fac·et \\'fas-ət\\ (*n*) small plane surface (of a gem); a side. The stonecutter decided to improve the rough diamond by providing it with several *facets*.

fa·ce·tious \\fə-'sē-shəs\\ (*adj*) humorous; jocular. Your *facetious* remarks are not appropriate at this serious moment.

fac·ile \\'fas-əl\\ (*adj*) easy; expert. Because he was a *facile* speaker, he never refused a request to address an organization.

fa·cil·i·tate \\fa-'sil-ə-ˌtāt\\ (*v*) make less difficult. He tried to *facilitate* matters at home by getting a part-time job.

fac·tion \\'fak-shən\\ (*n*) party; clique; dissension. The quarrels and bickering of the two small *factions* within the club disturbed the majority of the members.

fac·tious \\'fak-shəs\\ (*adj*) inclined to form factions; causing dissension. Your statement is *factious* and will upset the harmony that now exists.

fac·ti·tious \\fak-'tish-əs\\ (*adj*) artificial; sham. Hollywood actresses often create *factitious* tears by using glycerine.

fac·ul·ty \\'fak-əl-tē\\ (*n*) mental or bodily power; teaching staff. As he grew old, he feared he might lose his *faculties* and become useless to his employer.

fal·la·cious \\fə-'lā-shəs\\ (*adj*) misleading. Your reasoning must be *fallacious* because it leads to a ridiculous answer.

fal·li·ble \\'fal-ə-bəl\\ (*adj*) liable to err. I know I am *fallible*, but I feel confident that I am right this time.

\\ə\\ **abut** \\ᵊ\\ **kitten, F table** \\ər\\ **further** \\a\\ **ash** \\ā\\ **ace** \\ä\\ **cot, cart**
\\au̇\\ **out** \\ch\\ **chin** \\e\\ **bet** \\ē\\ **easy** \\g\\ **go** \\i\\ **hit** \\ī\\ **ice** \\j\\ **job**

fal-low \'fal-(,)ō\ (*adj*) plowed but not sowed; uncultivated. Farmers have learned that it is advisable to permit land to lie *fallow* every few years; also (*n, v*).

fal-ter \'fȯl-tər\ (*v*) hesitate. When told to dive off the high board, she did not *falter,* but proceeded at once.

fa-nat-i-cism \fə-'nat-ə-ˌsiz-əm\ (*n*) excessive zeal. The leader of the group was held responsible even though he could not control the *fanaticism* of his followers.

fan-cied \'fan(t)-sēd\ (*adj*) imagined; unreal. You are resenting *fancied* insults. No one has ever said such things about you.

fan-ci-er \'fan(t)-sē-ər\ (*n*) breeder or dealer of animals. The dog *fancier* exhibited his prize collie at the annual Kennel Club show.

fan-ci-ful \'fan(t)-si-fəl\ (*adj*) whimsical; visionary. This is a *fanciful* scheme because it does not consider the facts.

fan-fare \'fan-ˌfa(ə)r\ (*n*) call by bugles or trumpets. The exposition was opened with a *fanfare* of trumpets and the firing of a cannon.

fan-tas-tic \fan-'tas-tik\ (*adj*) unreal; grotesque; whimsical. Your fears are *fantastic* because no such animal as you have described exists.

farce \'färs\ (*n*) broad comedy; mockery. Nothing went right; the entire interview degenerated into a *farce.* **far-ci-cal** \'fär-si-kəl\ (*adj*)

fas-tid-i-ous \fa-'stid-ē-əs\ (*adj*) difficult to please; squeamish. The waitresses disliked serving him dinner because of his very *fastidious* taste.

fa-tal-ism \'fāt-əl-ˌiz-əm\ (*n*) belief that events are determined by forces beyond one's control. With *fatalism,* he accepted the hardships that beset him. **fa-tal-is-tic** \ˌfāt-əl-'is-tik\ (*adj*)

fath-om \'fath-əm\ (*v*) comprehend; investigate. I find his motives impossible to *fathom.*

\ŋ\ si**ng** \ō\ go \ȯ\ law \ȯi\ boy \th\ thin \th\ the \ü\ loot \u̇\ foot
\y\ yet \zh\ vision \à, k̲, ⁿ, œ, œ̄, ue, ūe, ʸ\ *see* Pronunciation Symbols

fat·u·ous \ˈfach-(ə-)wəs\ (*adj*) foolish; inane. He is far too intelligent to utter such *fatuous* remarks.

fau·na \ˈfȯn-ə\ (*n*) animals of a period or region. The scientist could visualize the *fauna* of the period by examining the skeletal remains and the fossils.

faux pas \ˈfō-ˌpä\ (*n*) an error or slip (in manners or behavior). Your tactless remarks during dinner were a *faux pas.*

fe·al·ty \ˈfē(-ə)l-tē\ (*n*) loyalty; faithfulness. The feudal lord demanded *fealty* of his vassals.

fea·si·ble \ˈfē-zə-bəl\ (*adj*) practical. This is an entirely *feasible* proposal. I suggest we adopt it.

fe·brile \ˈfeb-ˌrīl\ (*adj*) feverish. In his *febrile* condition, he was subject to nightmares and hallucinations.

fe·cun·di·ty \fi-ˈkən-dət-ē\ (*n*) fertility; fruitfulness. The *fecundity* of his mind is illustrated by the many vivid images in his poems.

feign \ˈfān\ (*v*) pretend. Lady Macbeth *feigned* illness in the courtyard.

feint \ˈfānt\ (*n*) trick; shift; sham blow. The boxer was fooled by his opponent's *feint* and dropped his guard; also (*v*).

fe·lic·i·tous \fi-ˈlis-ət-əs\ (*adj*) apt; suitably expressed, well chosen. He was famous for his *felicitous* remarks and was called upon to serve as master-of-ceremonies at many a banquet.

fell \ˈfel\ (*adj*) cruel; deadly. Henley writes of the "*fell* clutch of circumstance" in his poem "Invictus"; also (*n*).

fell \ˈfel\ (*v*) to knock or cut down. The environmentalists protested the *felling* of the old growth redwoods.

fel·on \ˈfel-ən\ (*n*) person convicted of a grave crime. A convicted *felon* loses the right to vote.

fer·ment \ˈfər-ˌment\ (*n*) agitation; commotion. The entire country was in a state of *ferment.* **fer·ment** \fər-ˈment\ (*v*)

\ə\ abut \ˈə\ kitten, F table \ər\ further \a\ ash \ā\ ace \ä\ cot, cart \au̇\ out \ch\ chin \e\ bet \ē\ easy \g\ go \i\ hit \ī\ ice \j\ job

fer-ret \'fer-ət\ (*v*) drive or hunt out of hiding. He *ferreted* out their secret; also (*n*).

fer-vent \'fər-vənt\ (*adj*) ardent; hot. He felt that the *fervent* praise was excessive and somewhat undeserved.

fer-vid \'fər-vəd\ (*adj*) ardent. His *fervid* enthusiasm inspired all of us to undertake the dangerous mission.

fer-vor \'fər-vər\ (*n*) glowing ardor. Their kiss was full of the *fervor* of first love.

fes-ter \'fes-tər\ (*v*) generate pus. When his finger began to *fester*, the doctor lanced it and removed the splinter that had caused the pus to form; also (*n*).

fes-tive \'fes-tiv\ (*adj*) joyous; celebratory. Their wedding in the park was a *festive* occasion.

fete \'fāt\ (*v*) honor at a festival. The returning hero was *feted* at a community supper and dance; also (*n*).

fet-id \'fet-əd\ (*adj*) malodorous. The neglected wound became *fetid*.

fe-tish \'fet-ish\ (*n*) object supposed to possess magical powers; an object of special devotion. The native wore a *fetish* around his peck to ward off evil spirits.

fet-ter \'fet-ər\ (*v*) shackle. The prisoner was *fettered* to the wall; also (*n*).

fi-as-co \fē-'äs-ₒkō\ (*n*) total failure. Our ambitious venture ended in a *fiasco*.

fi-at \'fē-ət\ (*n*) command. I cannot accept government by *fiat*; I feel that I must be consulted.

fick-le \'fik-əl\ (*adj*) changeable; faithless. He discovered she was *fickle*.

fic-ti-tious \fik-'tish-əs\ (*adj*) imaginary. Although this book purports to be a biography of George Washington, many of the incidents are *fictitious*.

fi-del-i-ty \fə-'del-ət-ē\ (*n*) loyalty. A dog's *fidelity* to its owner is one of the reasons why that animal is a favorite household pet.

\ŋ\ sing \ō\ go \ȯ\ law \ȯi\ boy \th\ thin \<u>th</u>\ the \ü\ loot \u̇\ foot
\y\ yet \zh\ vision \à, <u>k</u>, ⁿ, œ, œ̄, ue, ūe, ʸ\ *see* Pronunciation Symbols

fi-du-ci-ar-y \fe-'d(y)ü-shē-ˌer-ē\ *(adj)* pertaining to a position of trust. In his will, he stipulated that the bank act in a *fiduciary* capacity and manage his estate until his children became of age; also *(n)*.

fig-ment \'fig-mənt\ *(n)* invention; imaginary thing. That incident is a *figment* of your imagination.

filch \'filch\ *(v)* steal. The boys *filched* apples from the fruit stand.

fil-i-al \'fil-ē-əl\ *(adj)* pertaining to a son or daughter. Many children forget their *filial* obligations and disregard the wishes of their parents.

fi-na-le \fə-'nal-ē\ *(n)* conclusion. It is not until we reach the *finale* of this play that we can understand the author's message.

fi-nesse \fə-'nes\ *(n)* delicate skill. The *finesse* and adroitness of the surgeon impressed the observers in the operating room; also *(v)*.

fin-ick-y \'fin-i-kē\ *(adj)* too particular; fussy. The old lady was *finicky* about her food.

fi-nite \'fī-ˌnīt\ *(adj)* limited. It is difficult for humanity with its *finite* existence to grasp the infinite.

fire-brand \'fī(ə)r-ˌbrand\ *(n)* hothead; troublemaker. The police tried to keep track of all the local *firebrands* when the president came to town.

fis-sure \'fish-ər\ *(n)* crevice. The mountain climbers secured footholds in tiny *fissures* in the rock; also *(v)*.

fit-ful \'fit-fəl\ *(adj)* spasmodic; intermittent. After several *fitful* attempts, he decided to postpone the start of the project until he felt more energetic.

flac-cid \'flak-səd\ *(adj)* flabby. His sedentary life had left him with *flaccid* muscles.

fla-gel-late \'flaj-ə-ˌlāt\ *(v)* flog; whip. The Romans used to *flagellate* criminals with a whip that had three knotted strands. **fla-gel-late** \'flaj-ə-lət\ *(adj, n)*

\ə\ **abut** \ᵊ\ **kitten, F table** \ər\ **further** \a\ **ash** \ā\ **ace** \ä\ **cot, cart**
\aú\ **out** \ch\ **chin** \e\ **bet** \ē\ **easy** \g\ **go** \i\ **hit** \ī\ **ice** \j\ **job**

flag-ging \'flag-iŋ\ (*adj*) weak; drooping. The encouraging cheers of the crowd lifted the team's *flagging* spirits.

fla-grant \'fla-grənt\ (*adj*) conspicuously wicked. We cannot condone such *flagrant* violations of the rules.

flail \'flā(ə)l\ (*v*) thresh grain by hand; strike or slap. In medieval times, warriors *flailed* their foe with a metal ball attached to a handle; also (*n*).

flair \'fla(ə)r\ (*n*) talent. He has an uncanny *flair* for discovering new artists before the public has become aware of their existence.

flam-boy-ant \flam-'böi-ənt\ (*adj*) ornate. Modern architecture has discarded the *flamboyant* trimming on buildings and emphasizes simplicity of line.

flaunt \'flȯnt\ (*v*) display ostentatiously. She is not one of those actresses who *flaunt* their physical charms; she can act.

flay \'flā\ (*v*) strip off skin; plunder. The criminal was condemned to be *flayed* alive.

fleck \'flek\ (*v*) spot. Her cheeks, *flecked* with tears, were testimony to the hours of weeping; also (*n*).

fledg-ling \'flej-liŋ\ (*adj*) inexperienced. While it is necessary to provide these *fledgling* poets with an opportunity to present their work, it is not essential that we admire everything they write; also (*n*).

fleece \'flēs\ (*n*) wool coat of a sheep. They shear sheep of their *fleece,* which they then comb into separate strands of wool.

fleece \'flēs\ (*v*) rob; plunder. The tricksters *fleeced* him of his inheritance.

flick \'flik\ (*n*) light stroke as with a whip. The horse needed no encouragement; only one *flick* of the whip was all the jockey had to apply to get the animal to run at top speed; also (*v*).

flinch \'flinch\ (*v*) hesitate; shrink. He did not *flinch* in the face of danger but fought back bravely.

\ŋ\ si**ng**   \ō\ **go**   \ȯ\ **law**   \ȯi\ **boy**   \th\ **thin**   \<u>th</u>\ **the**   \ü\ **loot**   \u̇\ **foot**
\y\ **yet**   \zh\ **vision**   \à, <u>k</u>, ⁿ, œ, œ̄, ue, ūe, ʸ\ *see* Pronunciation Symbols

flip-pan-cy \\'flip-ən-sē\ (*n*) trifling gaiety. Your *flippancy* at this serious moment is offensive.

floe \\'flō\ (*n*) mass of floating ice. The ship made slow progress as it battered its way through the ice *floes*.

flo-ra \\'flōr-ə\ (*n*) plants of a region or era. Because she was a botanist, she spent most of her time studying the *flora* of the desert.

flor-id \\'flòr-əd\ (*adj*) flowery; ruddy. His complexion was even more *florid* than usual because of his anger.

flo-til-la \\flō-'til-ə\ (*n*) small fleet. It is always an exciting and interesting moment when the fishing *flotilla* returns to port.

flot-sam \\'flät-səm\ (*n*) drifting wreckage. Beachcombers eke out a living by salvaging the *flotsam* and jetsam of the sea.

flout \\'flaùt\ (*v*) reject; mock. The headstrong youth *flouted* all authority; he refused to be curbed.

fluc-tu-a-tion \\flək-chə-'wā-shən\ (*n*) wavering. Meteorologists watch the *fluctuations* of the barometer in order to predict the weather.

flu-en-cy \\'flü-ən-sē\ (*n*) smoothness of speech. He spoke French with *fluency* and ease.

flus-ter \\'fləs-tər\ (*v*) confuse. The teacher's sudden question *flustered* him and he stammered his reply; also (*n*).

flux \\'fləks\ (*n*) flowing series of changes. While conditions are in such a state of *flux*, I do not wish to commit myself too deeply in this affair; also (*v*).

foi-ble \\'fòi-bəl\ (*n*) weakness; slight fault. We can overlook the *foibles* of our friends.

foil \\'fòi(ə)l\ (*n*) contrast. In *Star Wars,* dark, evil Darth Vader is a perfect *foil* for fair-haired, naive Luke Skywalker.

foil \\'fòi(ə)l\ (*v*) defeat; frustrate. In the end, Skywalker is able to *foil* Vader's diabolical schemes.

---

foist \'fȯist\ (*v*) insert improperly; palm off. I will not permit you to *foist* such ridiculous ideas upon the membership of this group.

fo-ment \'fō-ˌment\ (*v*) stir up; instigate. This report will *foment* dissension in the club.

fool-har-dy \'fül-ˌhärd-ē\ (*adj*) rash. Don't be *foolhardy*. Get the advice of experienced people before undertaking this venture.

fop-pish \'fäp-ish\ (*adj*) vain about dress and appearance. He tried to imitate the *foppish* manner of the young men of the court.

for-ay \'fȯr-ˌā\ (*n*) raid. The company staged a midnight *foray* against the enemy outpost; also (*v*).

for-bear-ance \fȯr-'bar-ən(t)s\ (*n*) patience. We must use *forbearance* in dealing with him because he is still weak from his illness.

fore-bod-ing \fōr-'bōd-iŋ\ (*n*) premonition of evil. Caesar ridiculed his wife's *forebodings* about the Ides of March; also (*adj*).

fo-ren-sic \fə-'ren(t)-sik\ (*adj*) suitable to debate or courts of law. In his best *forensic* manner, the lawyer addressed the jury; also (*n*).

fore-sight \'fō(ə)r-ˌsīt\ (*n*) ability to foresee future happenings; prudence. A wise investor, she had the *foresight* to buy land just before the current real estate boom.

for-mal-i-ty \fȯr-'mal-ət-ē\ (*n*) adherence to established rules or procedures. Signing this is a mere *formality;* it does not obligate you in any way.

for-mi-da-ble \'fȯr-məd-ə-bəl\ (*adj*) menacing; threatening. We must not treat the battle lightly for we are facing a *formidable* foe.

forte \'fō(ə)rt\ (*n*) strong point or special talent. I am not eager to play this rather serious role, for my *forte* is comedy.

\ŋ\ **sing** \ō\ **go** \ȯ\ **law** \ȯi\ **boy** \th\ **thin** \tẖ\ **the** \ü\ **loot** \u̇\ **foot**
\y\ **yet** \zh\ **vision** \à, k̲, ⁿ, œ, œ̄, ᵫe, ᵫē, ʸ\ *see* Pronunciation Symbols

for-ti-tude \'fȯrt-ə-ˌt(y)üd\ (*n*) bravery; courage. He was awarded the medal for his *fortitude* in the battle.

for-tu-i-tous \fȯr-'t(y)ü-ət-əs\ (*adj*) accidental; by chance. There is no connection between these two events; their timing is entirely *fortuitous*.

fos-ter \'fȯs-tər\ (*v*) rear; encourage. According to the legend, Romulus and Remus were *fostered* by a she-wolf; also (*adj*).

fra-cas \'frāk-əs\ (*n*) brawl, melee. The military police stopped the *fracas* in the bar and arrested the belligerents.

frac-tious \'frak-shəs\ (*adj*) unruly. The *fractious* horse unseated its rider.

frail-ty \'frā(-ə)l-tē\ (*n*) weakness. Hamlet says, "*Frailty*, thy name is woman."

fran-chise \'fran-ˌchīz\ (*n*) right granted by authority. The city issued a *franchise* to the company to operate surface transit lines on the streets for ninety-nine years; also (*v*).

fran-tic \'frant-ik\ (*adj*) wild. At the time of the collision, many people became *frantic* with fear.

fraud-u-lent \'frȯ-jə-lənt\ (*adj*) cheating; deceitful. The government seeks to prevent *fraudulent* and misleading advertising.

fraught \'frȯt\ (*adj*) filled. Since this enterprise is *fraught* with danger, I will ask for volunteers who are willing to assume the risks.

fray \'frā\ (*n*) brawl. The three musketeers were in the thick of the *fray*; also (*v*).

fre-net-ic \fri-'net-ik\ (*adj*) frenzied; frantic. His *frenetic* activities convinced us that he had no organized plan of operation.

fren-zied \'fren-zēd\ (*adj*) madly excited. As soon as they smelled smoke, the *frenzied* animals milled about in their cages.

\ə\ **abut** \ə\ kitten, F **table** \ər\ f**urther** \a\ **ash** \ā\ **ace** \ä\ **cot, cart**
\au̇\ **out** \ch\ **chin** \e\ **bet** \ē\ **easy** \g\ **go** \i\ **hit** \ī\ **ice** \j\ **job**

fres-co \\'fres-₍ᵢ₎kō\\ (*n*) painting on plaster (usually fresh). The cathedral is visited by many tourists who wish to admire the *frescoes* by Giotto.

fret \\'fret\\ (*v*) to be annoyed or vexed. To *fret* over your poor grades is foolish; instead, decide to work harder in the future.

fric-tion \\'frik-shən\\ (*n*) clash in opinion; rubbing against. At this time when harmony is essential, we cannot afford to have any *friction* in our group.

frieze \\'frēz\\ (*n*) ornamental band on a wall. The *frieze* of the church was adorned with sculpture.

frig-id \\'frij-əd\\ (*adj*) intensely cold. Alaska is in the *frigid* zone.

frit-ter \\'frit-ər\\ (*v*) waste. He could not apply himself to any task and *frittered* away his time in idle conversation.

fri-vol-i-ty \\friv-'äl-ət-ē\\ (*n*) lack of seriousness. We were distressed by his *frivolity* during the recent grave crisis. **friv-o-lous** \\'friv-(ə-)ləs\\ (*adj*)

frol-ic-some \\'fräl-ik-səm\\ (*adj*) prankish; gay. The *frolicsome* puppy tried to lick the face of its master.

fruc-ti-fy \\'frək-tə-ˌfī\\ (*v*) bear fruit. This tree should *fructify* in three years.

fru-gal-i-ty \\frü-'gal-ət-ē\\ (*n*) thrift. In these difficult days, we must live with *frugality*.

fru-i-tion \\frü-'ish-ən\\ (*n*) bearing of fruit; fulfillment; realization. This building marks the *fruition* of all our aspirations and years of hard work.

frus-trate \\'frəs-ˌtrāt\\ (*v*) thwart; defeat. We must *frustrate* this dictator's plan to seize control of the government.

ful-crum \\'ful-krəm\\ (*n*) support on which a lever rests. If we use this stone as a *fulcrum* and the crowbar as a lever, we may be able to move this boulder.

ful-mi-nate \\'ful-mə-ˌnāt\\ (*v*) thunder; explode. The people against whom he *fulminated* were innocent of any wrongdoing.

\\ŋ\\ **sing** \\ō\\ **go** \\ȯ\\ **law** \\ȯi\\ **boy** \\th\\ **thin** \\<u>th</u>\\ **the** \\ü\\ **loot** \\u̇\\ **foot** \\y\\ **yet** \\zh\\ **vision** \\à, <u>k</u>, ⁿ, œ, œ̄, ᵫ, ᵫ̄, ʸ\\ *see* Pronunciation Symbols

ful-some \'fül-səm\ (*adj*) disgustingly excessive. His *fulsome* praise of the dictator annoyed his listeners.

func-tion-ar-y \'fəŋ(k)-shə-ˌner-ē\ (*n*) official. As his case was transferred from one *functionary* to another, he began to despair of ever reaching a settlement.

fu-ne-re-al \fyü-'nir-ē-əl\ (*adj*) sad; solemn. I fail to understand why there is such a *funereal* atmosphere; we have lost a battle, not a war.

fu-ror \'fyü(ə)r-ˌó(ə)r\ (*n*) frenzy; great excitement. The story of his embezzlement of the funds created a *furor* on the Stock Exchange.

fur-tive \'fərt-iv\ (*adj*) stealthy. The boy took a *furtive* look at his classmate's test paper.

fu-sion \'fyü-zhən\ (*n*) union; coalition. The opponents of the political party in power organized a *fusion* of disgruntled groups and became an important element in the election.

fu-tile \'fyüt-ᵊl\ (*adj*) ineffective; fruitless. Why waste your time on *futile* pursuits?

\ə\ **abut** \ᵊ\ kitten, F table \ər\ **further** \a\ **ash** \ā\ **ace** \ä\ **cot, cart**
\aú\ **out** \ch\ **chin** \e\ **bet** \ē\ **easy** \g\ **go** \i\ **hit** \ī\ **ice** \j\ **job**

G

gad-fly \\'gad-ˌflī\\ (*n*) animal-biting fly; an irritating person. Like a *gadfly,* he irritated all the guests at the hotel; within forty-eight hours, everyone regarded him as an annoying busybody.

gain-say \\ gān-'sā\\ (*v*) deny. He could not *gainsay* the truth of the report.

gait \\'gāt\\ (*n*) manner of walking or running; speed. The lame man walked with an uneven *gait.*

gal-a-xy \\'gal-ək-sē\\ (*n*) the Milky Way; any collection of brilliant personalities. The deaths of such famous actors as Clark Gable, Gary Cooper, and Spencer Tracy demonstrate that the *galaxy* of Hollywood superstars is rapidly disappearing.

gall \\'gȯl\\ (*n*) bitterness; nerve. The knowledge of his failure filled him with *gall.*

gall \\'gȯl\\ (*v*) annoy; chafe. Their taunts *galled* him.

gal-le-on \\'gal-ē-ən\\ (*n*) large sailing ship. The Spaniards pinned their hopes on the *galleon,* the large warship; the British, on the smaller and faster pinnace.

gal-va-nize \\'gal-və-ˌnīz\\ (*v*) stimulate by shock; stir up. The entire nation was *galvanized* into strong military activity by the news of the attack on Pearl Harbor.

gam-bit \\'gam-bət\\ (*n*) opening in chess in which a piece is sacrificed. The player was afraid to accept his opponent's *gambit* because he feared a trap that as yet he could not see.

gam-bol \\'gam-bəl\\ (*v*) skip; leap playfully. Watching children *gamboling* in the park is a pleasant experience; also (*n*).

game-ly \\'gām-lē\\ (*adv*) in a plucky manner. Because he had fought *gamely* against a much superior boxer, the crowd gave him a standing ovation when he left the arena.

\\ŋ\\ sing \\ō\\ go \\ȯ\\ law \\ȯi\\ boy \\th\\ thin \\th\\ the \\ü\\ loot \\u̇\\ foot
\\y\\ yet \\zh\\ vision \\à, k̲, ⁿ, œ, œ̄, ue, œ̄, ʸ\\ *see* Pronunciation Symbols

gam·ut \\'gam-ət\ (*n*) entire range. In this performance, the leading lady was able to demonstrate the complete *gamut* of her acting ability.

gape \\'gāp\ (*v*) open widely. The huge pit *gaped* before him; if he stumbled, he would fall in; also (*n*).

gar·ble \\'gär-bəl\ (*v*) mix up; change meaning by distortion. Because the report was *garbled,* it confused many readers who were not familiar with the facts; also (*n*).

gar·goyle \\'gär-ˌgȯil\ (*n*) waterspout carved in grotesque figures on building. The *gargoyles* adorning the Cathedral of Notre Dame in Paris are amusing in their grotesqueness.

gar·ish \\'ga(ə)r-ish\ (*adj*) gaudy. She wore a *garish* rhinestone necklace.

gar·ner \\'gär-nər\ (*v*) gather; store up. He hoped to *garner* the world's literature in one library; also (*n*).

gar·nish \\'gär-nish\ (*v*) decorate. Parsley was used to *garnish* the boiled potato; also (*n*).

gar·ru·li·ty \ gə-'rü-lət-ē\ (*n*) talkativeness. The office manager fired her assistant because her *garrulity* distracted her coworkers.

gar·ru·lous \\'gar-ə-ləs\ (*adj*) loquacious; wordy. Many members avoided the company of the *garrulous* old gentleman because his constant chatter on trivial matters bored them.

gas·tron·o·my \ ga-'strän-ə-mē\ (*n*) science of preparing and serving good food. One of the by-products of his trip to Europe was his interest in *gastronomy;* he enjoyed preparing and serving foreign dishes to his friends.

gauche \\'gōsh\ (*adj*) clumsy; boorish. Such remarks are *gauche* and out of place; you should apologize for making them.

gaunt \\'gȯnt\ (*adj*) lean and angular; barren. His once round face looked surprisingly *gaunt* after he had lost weight.

\ə\ abut \ᵊ\ kitten, F table \ər\ further \a\ ash \ā\ ace \ä\ cot, cart
\au̇\ out \ch\ chin \e\ bet \ē\ easy \g\ go \i\ hit \ī\ ice \j\ job

gaunt-let \'gȯnt-lət\ (*n*) leather glove. Now that we have been challenged, we must take up the *gauntlet* and meet our adversary fearlessly.

ge-ne-al-o-gy \ jē-nē-äl-ə-jē\ (*n*) record of descent; lineage. He was proud of his *genealogy* and constantly referred to the achievements of his ancestors.

gen-er-al-i-ty \ jen-ə-'ral-ət-ē\ (*n*) vague statement. This report is filled with *generalities;* you must be more specific in your statements.

ge-ner-ic \jə-'ner-ik\ (*adj*) characteristic of a class or species. You have made the mistake of thinking that his behavior is *generic;* actually, very few of his group behave the way he does; also (*n*).

ge-ni-al-i-ty \ jē-nē-'al-ət-ē\ (*n*) cheerfulness; kindliness; sympathy. This restaurant is famous and popular because of the *geniality* of the proprietor who tries to make everyone happy.

gen-re \'zhän-rə\ (*n*) kind, sort; a category of artistic, musical, or literary composition characterized by a particular style, form, or content. The sonnet is one example of the *genre* of poetry.

gen-teel \jen-'tē(ə)l\ (*adj*) well-bred; elegant. We are looking for a man with a *genteel* appearance who can inspire confidence by his cultivated manner.

gen-til-i-ty \jen-'til-ət-ē\ (*n*) those of gentle birth; refinement. Her family was proud of its *gentility.*

gen-try \'jen-trē\ (*n*) people of standing; class of people just below nobility. The local *gentry* did not welcome the visits of the summer tourists and tried to ignore their presence in the community.

gen-u-flect \'jen-yə-ˌflekt\ (*v*) bend the knee as in worship. A proud democrat, he refused to *genuflect* to any man.

ger-mane \₍ₒ₎jər-'mān\ (*adj*) pertinent; bearing upon the case at hand. The lawyer objected that the testimony being offered was not *germane* to the case at hand.

\ŋ\ **sing** \ō\ **go** \ȯ\ **law** \ȯi\ **boy** \th\ **thin** \th̲\ **the** \ü\ **loot** \u̇\ **foot**
\y\ **yet** \zh\ **vision** \à, k̲, ⁿ, œ, œ̄, ᴜe, ᴜē, ʸ\ *see* Pronunciation Symbols

ger·mi·nal \\'jərm-nəl\\ (*adj*) pertaining to a germ; creative. Such an idea is *germinal;* I am certain that it will influence thinkers and philosophers for many generations.

ger·mi·nate \\'jər-mə-ˌnāt\\ (*v*) cause to sprout; sprout. After the seeds *germinate* and develop their permanent leaves, the plants may be removed from the cold frames and transplanted to the garden.

ger·ry·man·der \\jer-ē-'man-dər\\ (*v*) change voting district lines in order to favor a political party. The illogical pattern of the map of this congressional district is proof that the State Legislature *gerrymandered* this area in order to favor the majority party; also (*n*).

ges·tate \\'jes-ˌtāt\\ (*v*) evolve, as in prenatal growth. While this scheme was being *gestated* by the conspirators, they maintained complete silence about their intentions.

ges·tic·u·la·tion \\je-ˌstik-yə-'lā-shən\\ (*n*) motion; gesture. Operatic performers are trained to make exaggerated *gesticulations* because of the large auditoriums in which they appear.

ghast·ly \\'gast-lē\\ (*adj*) horrible. The murdered man was a *ghastly* sight.

gib·ber \\'jib-ər\\ (*v*) speak foolishly. The demented man *gibbered* incoherently.

gibe \\'jīb\\ (*v*) mock. As you *gibe* at their superstitious beliefs, do you realize that you, too, are guilty of similarly foolish thoughts?

gig \\'gig\\ (*n*) two-wheeled carriage. As they drove down the street in their new *gig,* drawn by the dappled mare, they were cheered by the people who recognized them.

gin·ger·ly \\'jin-jər-lē\\ (*adv*) very carefully. To separate egg whites, first crack the egg *gingerly;* also (*adj*).

gist \\'jist\\ (*n*) essence. She was asked to give the *gist* of the essay in two sentences.

glaze \\'glāz\\ (*v*) cover with a thin and shiny surface. The freezing rain *glazed* the streets and made driving hazardous; also (*n*).

\\ə\\ **abut** \\ᵊ\\ **kitten,** F **table** \\ər\\ **further** \\a\\ **ash** \\ā\\ **ace** \\ä\\ **cot, cart**
\\aů\\ **out** \\ch\\ **chin** \\e\\ **bet** \\ē\\ **easy** \\g\\ **go** \\i\\ **hit** \\ī\\ **ice** \\j\\ **job**

glean \'glēn\ (*v*) gather leavings. After the crops had been harvested by the machines, the peasants were permitted to *glean* the wheat left in the fields. **glean-ings** \'gle-niŋz\ (*n*)

glib \'glib\ (*adj*) fluent. He is a *glib* speaker.

gloat \'glōt\ (*v*) express evil satisfaction; view malevolently. As you *gloat* over your ill-gotten wealth, do you think of the many victims you have defrauded?; also (*n*).

glos-sa-ry \'gläs-(ə-)rē\ (*n*) brief explanation of words used in the text. I have found the *glossary* in this book very useful; it has eliminated many trips to the dictionary.

glos-sy \'gläs-ē\ (*adj*) smooth and shining. I want this photograph printed on *glossy* paper; also (*n*).

glower \'glaů(-ə)r\ (*v*) scowl. The angry boy *glowered* at his father.

glut \'glət\ (*v*) overstock; fill to excess. The manufacturers *glutted* the market and could not find purchasers for the many articles they had produced; also (*n*).

glu-ti-nous \'glüt-nəs\ (*adj*) sticky; viscous. Molasses is a *glutinous* substance.

glut-ton-ous \'glət-nəs\ (*adj*) greedy for food. The *gluttonous* boy ate all the cookies.

gnarled \'när(-ə)ld\ (*adj*) twisted. The *gnarled* oak tree had been a landmark for years and was mentioned in several deeds.

gnome \'nōm\ (*n*) dwarf; underground spirit. In medieval mythology, *gnomes* were the special guardians and inhabitants of subterranean mines.

goad \'gōd\ (*v*) urge on. He was *goaded* by his friends until he yielded to their wishes; also (*n*).

gorge \'go(ə)rj\ (*v*) stuff oneself. The gluttonous guest *gorged* himself with food as though he had not eaten for days; also (*n*).

gor-y \'gō(ə)r-ē\ (*adj*) bloody. The audience shuddered as they listened to the details of the *gory* massacre.

gos·sa·mer \\'gäs-ə-mər\\ (*adj*) sheer; like cobwebs. Nylon can be woven into *gossamer* or thick fabrics; also (*n*).

gouge \\'gaúj\\ (*v*) tear out. In that fight, all the rules were forgotten; the adversaries bit, kicked, and tried to *gouge* each other's eyes out; also (*n*).

gour·mand \\'gú(ə)r-ˌmänd\\ (*n*) epicure; person who takes excessive pleasure in food and drink. The *gourmand* liked the French cuisine.

gour·met \\'gú(ə)r-ˌmā\\ (*n*) connoisseur of food and drink. The *gourmet* stated that this was the best onion soup he had ever tasted.

gra·na·ry \\'grān-(ə-)rē\\ (*n*) storehouse for grain. We have reason to be thankful, for our crops were good and our *granaries* are full.

gran·dil·o·quent \\gran-'dil-ə-kwənt\\ (*adj*) pompous; bombastic; using high-sounding language. The politician could never speak simply; he was always *grandiloquent.*

gran·di·ose \\'gran-dē-ˌōs\\ (*adj*) imposing; impressive. His *grandiose* manner impressed those who met him for the first time.

gran·u·late \\'gran-yə-ˌlāt\\ (*v*) form into grains. Sugar that has been *granulated* dissolves more readily than lump sugar. **gran·ule** \\'gran-yü(ə)l⁽ʲ⁾\\ (*n*).

graph·ic \\'graf-ik\\ (*adj*) pertaining to the art of delineating; vividly described. I was particularly impressed by the *graphic* presentation of the story; also (*n*).

gra·tis \\'grat-əs\\ (*adv*) free. The company offered to give one package *gratis* to every purchaser of one of their products; also (*adj*).

gra·tu·i·tous \\grə-'t(y)ü-ət-əs\\ (*adj*) given freely; unwarranted. I resent your *gratuitous* remarks because no one asked for them.

gra·tu·i·ty \\grə-'t(y)ü-ət-ē\\ (*n*) tip. Many service employees rely more on *gratuities* than on salaries for their livelihood.

\\ə\\ **abut** \\ᵊ\\ **kitten, F table** \\ər\\ **further** \\a\\ **ash** \\ā\\ **ace** \\ä\\ **cot, cart**
\\aú\\ **out** \\ch\\ **chin** \\e\\ **bet** \\ē\\ **easy** \\g\\ **go** \\i\\ **hit** \\ī\\ **ice** \\j\\ **job**

gre-gar-i-ous \gri-'gar-ē-əs\ (*adj*) sociable. He was not *gregarious* and preferred to be alone most of the time.

gri-mace \'grim-əs\ (*n*) a facial distortion to show feeling such as pain, disgust, etc. Even though he remained silent, his *grimace* indicated his displeasure; also (*v*).

gris-ly \'griz-lē\ (*adj*) ghastly. She shuddered at the *grisly* sight.

gro-tesque \grō-'tesk\ (*adj*) fantastic; comically hideous. On Halloween people enjoy wearing *grotesque* costumes.

grot-to \'grät-(ı)ō\ (*n*) small cavern. The Blue *Grotto* in Capri can be entered only by small boats rowed by natives through a natural opening in the rocks.

grov-el \'gräv-əl\ (*v*) crawl or creep on ground; remain prostrate. Even though we have been defeated, we do not have to *grovel* before our conquerors.

grudg-ing \'grəj-iŋ\ (*adj*) unwilling; reluctant; stingy. We received only *grudging* support from the mayor despite his earlier promises of aid.

gru-el-ing \'grü-ə-liŋ\ (*adj*) exhausting. The marathon is a *grueling* race.

grue-some \'grü-səm\ (*adj*) grisly. People screamed when his *gruesome* appearance was flashed on the screen.

gruff \'grəf\ (*adj*) rough-mannered. Although he was blunt and *gruff* with most people, he was always gentle with children.

guf-faw \(ı)gə-'fó\ (*n*) boisterous laughter. The loud *guffaws* that came from the closed room indicated that the members of the committee had not yet settled down to serious business; also (*v*).

guile \'gī(ə)l\ (*n*) deceit; duplicity. He achieved his high position by *guile* and treachery.

guile-less \'gī(ə)l-ləs\ (*adj*) without deceit. He is naive, simple, and *guileless;* he cannot be guilty of fraud.

\ŋ\ sing \ō\ go \ó\ law \ói\ boy \th\ thin \t̲h̲\ the \ü\ loot \u̇\ foot
\y\ yet \zh\ vision \à, k̲, ⁿ, œ, œ̄, ue, ūe, ʸ\ *see* Pronunciation Symbols

guise \'gīz\ (*n*) appearance; costume. In the *guise* of a plumber, the detective investigated the murder case.

gull-i-ble \'gəl-ə-bəl\ (*adj*) easily deceived. He preyed upon *gullible* people who believed his stories of easy wealth.

gus-ta-to-ry \'gəs-tə-ˌtōr-ē\ (*adj*) affecting the sense of taste. This food has great *gustatory* appeal because of the spices it contains.

gus-to \'gəs-ₒtō\ (*n*) enjoyment; enthusiasm. He accepted the assignment with such *gusto* that I feel he would have been satisfied with a smaller salary.

gus-ty \'gəs-tē\ (*adj*) windy. The *gusty* weather made sailing precarious.

gut-tur-al \'gət-ə-rəl\ (*adj*) pertaining to the throat. *Guttural* sounds are produced in the throat or in the back of the tongue and palate.

H

hack-les \\'hak-əls\ (*n*) hairs on back and neck of a dog. The dog's *hackles* rose and he began to growl as the sound of footsteps grew louder; also (*v*).

hack-neyed \\'hak-nēd\ (*adj*) commonplace; trite. The English teacher criticized his story because of his *hackneyed* plot.

hag-gard \\'hag-ərd\ (*adj*) wasted away; gaunt. After his long illness, he was pale and *haggard*.

hag-gle \\'hag-əl\ (*v*) argue about prices. I prefer to shop in a store that has a one-price policy because whenever I *haggle* with a shopkeeper I am never certain that I paid a fair price for the articles I purchased; also (*n*).

hal-cy-on \\'hal-sē-ən\ (*adj*) calm; peaceful. In those *halcyon* days, people were not worried about sneak attacks and bombings.

hale \\'hā(ə)l\ (*adj*) healthy. After a brief illness, he was *hale* again.

hal-lowed \\'hal-₍ₒ₎ōd\ (*adj*) blessed; consecrated. He was laid to rest in *hallowed* ground.

hal-lu-ci-na-tion \hə-,lüs-ᵊn-'ā-shən\ (*n*) delusion. I think you were frightened by an *hallucination* that you created in your own mind.

ham-per \\'ham-pər\ (*v*) obstruct. The minority party agreed not to *hamper* the efforts of the leaders to secure a lasting peace.

hap \\'hap\ (*n*) chance; luck. In his poem *Hap*, Thomas Hardy objects to the part chance plays in our lives.

hap-haz-ard \ ⁽⁾hap-'haz-ərd\ (*adj*) random; by chance. His *haphazard* reading left him unacquainted with authors of the books.

hap-less \\'hap-ləs\ (*adj*) unfortunate. This *hapless* creature had never known a moment's pleasure.

ha-rangue \hə-'raŋ\ (*n*) noisy speech. In his lengthy *harangue*, the principal berated the offenders; also (*v*).

---

ha-rass \hə-'ras\ (*v*) to annoy by repeated attacks. When he could not pay his bills as quickly as he had promised, he was *harassed* by his creditors.

har-bin-ger \'här-bən-jər\ (*n*) forerunner. The crocus is an early *harbinger* of spring; also (*v*).

har-bor \'här-bər\ (*v*) provide a refuge for; hide. The church *harbored* illegal aliens who were political refugees.

harp-ing \'härp-iŋ\ (*n*) tiresome dwelling on a subject. After he had reminded me several times about what he had done for me, I told him to stop *harping* on my indebtedness to him. **harp** \'härp\ (*v*)

har-ri-dan \'har-əd-ᵊn\ (*n*) shrewish hag. Most people avoided the *harridan* because they feared her abusive and vicious language.

har-row \'har-(ˌ)ō\ (*v*) break up ground after plowing; torture. I don't want to *harrow* you at this time by asking you to recall the details of your unpleasant experience; also (*n*).

har-ry \'har-ē\ (*v*) raid; annoy. The guerrilla band *harried* the enemy nightly.

haugh-ti-ness \'hȯt-ē-nəs\ (*n*) pride; arrogance. I resent his *haughtiness* because he is no better than we are.

hau-teur \hȯ-'tər\ (*n*) haughtiness. His snobbishness is obvious to all who witness his *hauteur* when he talks to those whom he considers his social inferiors.

haz-ard-ous \'haz-ərd-əs\ (*adj*) dangerous. Your occupation is too *hazardous* for insurance companies to consider your application.

haz-y \'hā-zē\ (*adj*) slightly obscure. In *hazy* weather, you cannot see the top of this mountain.

heck-ler \'hek-(ə)lər\ (*n*) person who verbally harasses others. The *heckler* kept interrupting the speaker with rude remarks. **heck-le** \'hek-əl\ (*v*)

he-do-nism \'hēd-ᵊn-ˌiz-əm\ (*n*) belief that pleasure is the sole aim in life. *Hedonism* and asceticism are opposing philosophies of human behavior.

\ə\ abut \ᵊ\ kitten, F table \ər\ further \a\ ash \ā\ ace \ä\ cot, cart
\au̇\ out \ch\ chin \e\ bet \ē\ easy \g\ go \i\ hit \ī\ ice \j\ job

heed-less \'hēd-ləs\ (*adj*) not noticing; disregarding. He drove on, *heedless* of the warnings placed at the side of the road that it was dangerous.

hei-nous \'hā-nəs\ (adj) atrocious; hatefully bad. Hitler's *heinous* crimes will never be forgotten.

her-biv-o-rous \ͺ(h)ər-'biv-ə-rəs\ (*adj*) grain-eating. Some *herbivorous* animals have two stomachs for digesting their food. **her-bi-vore** \'(h)ər-bə-ͺvō(ə)r\ (*n*)

her-e-sy \'her-ə-sē\ (*n*) opinion contrary to popular belief; opinion contrary to accepted religion. He was threatened with excommunication because his remarks were considered to be pure *heresy.*

her-e-tic \'her-ə-ͺtik\ (*n*) person who maintains opinions contrary to the doctrines of the church. She was punished by the Spanish Inquisition because she was a *heretic.*

her-met-i-cal-ly \ͺ(ı)hər-'met-i-k(ə-)lē\ (*adv*) sealed by fusion so as to be airtight. After these bandages are sterilized, they are placed in *hermetically* sealed containers.

her-mit-age \'hər-mət-ij\ (*n*) home of a hermit. Even in his remote *hermitage* he could not escape completely from the world.

het-er-o-ge-ne-ous \ͺhet-ə-rə-'jē-nē-əs\ (*adj*) dissimilar. In *heterogeneous* groupings, we have an unassorted grouping, while in homogeneous groupings we have people or things that have common traits.

hew \'hyü\ (*v*) cut to pieces with ax or sword. The cavalry rushed into the melee and *hewed* the enemy with their swords.

hi-a-tus \hī-'āt-əs\ (*n*) gap; pause. There was a *hiatus* of twenty years in the life of Rip van Winkle; also (*adj*).

hi-ber-nal \hī-'bərn-ᵊl\ (*adj*) wintry. Bears prepare for their long *hibernal* sleep by overeating.

hi-ber-nate \'hī-bər-ͺnāt\ (*v*) sleep throughout the winter. Bears are one of the many species of animals that *hibernate.*

---

hi-er-ar-chy \\'hī-(ə-),rär-kē\ (*n*) body divided into ranks. It was difficult to step out of one's place in this *hierarchy.*

hi-ero-glyph-ic \,hī-(ə-)rə-'glif-ik\ (*n*) picture writing. The discovery of the Rosetta Stone enabled scholars to read the ancient Egyptian *hieroglyphics.*

hi-lar-i-ty \hil-'ar-ət-ē\ (*n*) boisterous mirth. This *hilarity* is improper on this solemn day of mourning.

hind-most \\'hīn(d)-,mōst\ (*adj*) furthest behind. The coward could always be found in the *hindmost* lines whenever a battle was being waged.

hire-ling \\'hī(ə)r-liŋ\ (*n*) one who serves for hire [usually contemptuously]. In a matter of such importance, I do not wish to deal with *hirelings;* I must meet with the chief.

hir-sute \\'hər-,süt\ (*adj*) hairy. He was a *hirsute* individual with a heavy black beard.

his-tri-on-ic \,his-trē-'än-ik\ (*adj*) theatrical. He was proud of his *histrionic* ability and wanted to play the role of Hamlet. **his-tri-on-ics** \,his-tre-'än-iks\ (*n*)

hoar-y \\'hō(ə)r-ē\ (*adj*) white with age. The man was *hoary* and wrinkled.

hoax \\'hōks\ (*n*) trick; practical joke. Embarrassed by the *hoax,* he reddened and left the room; also (*v*).

ho-lo-caust \\'häl-ə-,kȯst\ (*n*) destruction by fire. Citizens of San Francisco remember that the destruction of the city was caused not by the earthquake but by the *holocaust* that followed.

hom-age \\'(h)äm-ij\ (*n*) honor; tribute. In her speech she tried to pay *homage* to a great man.

home-spun \\'hōm-,spən\ (*adj*) domestic; made at home. *Homespun* wit like *homespun* cloth was often coarse and plain; also (*n*).

hom-i-ly \\'häm-ə-lē\ (*n*) sermon; serious warning. His speeches were always *homilies,* advising his listeners to repent and reform.

---

ho-mo-ge-ne-ous \ˌhō-mə-ˈjē-nē-əs\ (*adj*) of the same kind. Educators try to put pupils of similar abilities into classes because they believe that this *homogeneous* grouping is advisable. **ho-mo-ge-ne-i-ty** \ˌhō-mə-jə-ˈnē-ət-ē\ (*n*)

hone \ˈhōn\ (*v*) sharpen. To make shaving easier, he *honed* his razor with great care.

hood-wink \ˈhùd-ˌwiŋk\ (*v*) deceive; delude. Having been *hoodwinked* once by the fast-talking salesman, he was extremely cautious when he went to purchase a used car.

hor-ta-to-ry \ˈhòrt-ə-ˌtōr-ē\ (*adj*) encouraging; exhortive. The crowd listened to his *hortatory* statements with ever growing excitement; finally they rushed from the hall to carry out his suggestions.

hor-ti-cul-tur-al \ˌhòrt-ə-ˈkəlch(-ə)-rəl\ (*adj*) pertaining to cultivation of gardens. When he bought his house, he began to look for flowers and decorative shrubs, and began to read books dealing with *horticultural* matters.

hos-tel-ry \ˈhäs-tᵊl-rē\ (*n*) inn. Travelers interested in economy should stay at *hostelries* and pensions rather than fashionable hotels.

hov-el \ˈhəv-əl\ (*n*) shack; small, wretched house. He wondered how poor people could stand living in such a *hovel*.

hov-er \ˈhəv-ər\ (*v*) hang about; wait nearby. The police helicopter *hovered* above the accident.

hub-bub \ˈhəb-ˌəb\ (*n*) confused uproar. The marketplace was a scene of *hubbub* and excitement; in all the noise, we could not distinguish particular voices.

hu-bris \ˈhyü-brəs\ (*n*) arrogance; excessive self-conceit. Filled with *hubris,* Lear refused to heed his friends' warnings.

hue \ˈhyü\ (*n*) color; aspect. The aviary contained birds of every possible *hue*.

\ŋ\ **sing** \ō\ **go** \ò\ **law** \òi\ **boy** \th\ **thin** \th̲\ **the** \ü\ **loot** \ù\ **foot**
\y\ **yet** \zh\ **vision** \à, k̲, ⁿ, œ, œ̄, ᵫ, ᵫ̄, ʸ\ *see* Pronunciation Symbols

hu-mane \hyü-'mān\ (*adj*) kind. His *humane* and consid-
erate treatment of the unfortunate endeared him to all.

hum-drum \'həm-‚drəm\ (*adj*) dull; monotonous. After his
years of adventure, he could not settle down to a *hum-
drum* existence.

hu-mid \'hyü-məd\ (*adj*) damp. He could not stand the
humid climate and moved to a drier area.

hu-mil-i-ty \hyü-'mil-ət-ē\ (*n*) humbleness of spirit. He
spoke with a *humility* and lack of pride that impressed
his listeners.

hum-mock \'həm-ək\ (*n*) small hill. The ascent of the
hummock is not difficult and the view from the hilltop
is ample reward for the effort.

hur-tle \'hərt-ᵊl\ (*v*) rush headlong. The runaway train
hurtled toward disaster.

hus-band-ry \'həz-bən-drē\ (*n*) frugality; thrift; agriculture. He accumulated his small fortune by diligence and
husbandry.

hy-brid \'hī-brəd\ (*n*) mongrel; mixed breed. Mendel's
formula explains the appearance of *hybrids* and pure
species in breeding; also (*adj*).

hy-dro-pho-bi-a \‚hī-drə-'fō-bē-ə\ (*n*) rabies; fear of water.
A dog that bites a human being must be observed for
symptoms of *hydrophobia*.

hy-per-bo-le \hī-'pər-bə-⁽ʲ⁾lē\ (*n*) exaggeration; overstate-
ment. This salesman is guilty of *hyperbole* in describing his product; it is wise to discount his claims.

hy-per-crit-i-cal \‚hī-pər-'krit-i-kəl\ (*adj*) excessively ex-
acting. You are *hypercritical* in your demands for
perfection; we all make mistakes.

hy-po-chon-dri-ac \‚hī-pə-'kän-drē-‚ak\ (*n*) person unduly
worried about his or her health; worrier without cause
about illness. The doctor prescribed chocolate pills for
his patient who was a *hypochondriac*.

\ə\ **abut** \ᵊ\ **kitten, F table** \ər\ **further** \a\ **ash** \ā\ **ace** \ä\ **cot, cart**
\au̇\ **out** \ch\ **chin** \e\ **bet** \ē\ **easy** \g\ **go** \i\ **hit** \ī\ **ice** \j\ **job**

hyp-o-crit-i-cal \ˌhip-ə-'krit-i-kəl\ (*adj*) pretending to be virtuous; deceiving. I resent his *hypocritical* posing as a friend for I know he is interested only in his own advancement.

hy-po-thet-i-cal \ˌhī-pə-'thet-i-kəl\ (*adj*) based on assumptions or hypotheses. Why do we have to consider *hypothetical* cases when we have actual case histories that we may examine? **hy-poth-e-sis** \hī-'päth-ə-səs\ (*n*)

I

ich-thy-ol-o-gy \ˌik-thē-'äl-ə-jē\ (*n*) study of fish. Jacques Cousteau's programs about sea life have advanced the cause of *ichthyology.*

icon \'ī-ˌkän\ (*n*) religious image; idol. The *icons* on the walls of the church were painted in the thirteenth century.

i-con-o-clas-tic \ˌ(ˌ)ī-ˌkän-ə-'klas-tik\ (*adj*) attacking cherished traditions. George Bernard Shaw's *iconoclastic* plays often startled people.

i-de-ol-o-gy \ˌīd-ē-'äl-ə-jē\ (*n*) ideas of a group of people. That *ideology* is dangerous to this country because it embraces undemocratic philosophies.

id-i-om \'id-ē-əm\ (*n*) special usage in language. I could not understand their *idiom* because literal translation made no sense.

id-i-o-syn-cra-sy \ˌid-ē-ə-'siŋ-krə-sē\ (*n*) peculiarity; eccentricity. One of his personal *idiosyncrasies* was his habit of rinsing all cutlery given him in a restaurant.

id-i-o-syn-crat-ic \ˌid-ē-ō-ˌ(ˌ)sin-'krat-ik\ (*adj*) private; peculiar to an individual. Such behavior is *idiosyncratic;* it is as easily identifiable as a signature.

i-dol-a-try \ī-'däl-ə-trē\ (*n*) worship of idols; excessive admiration. Such *idolatry* of singers of popular ballads is typical of the excessive enthusiasm of youth.

i-dyl-lic \ī-'dil-ik\ (*adj*) charmingly carefree; simple. Far from the city, she led an *idyllic* existence in her rural retreat.

ig-ne-ous \'ig-nē-əs\ (*adj*) produced by fire; volcanic. Lava, pumice, and other *igneous* rocks are found in great abundance around Mount Vesuvius near Naples.

ig-no-ble \ig-'nō-bəl\ (*adj*) of lowly origin; unworthy. This plan is inspired by *ignoble* motives and I must, therefore, oppose it.

ig-no-min-i-ous \ˌig-nə-'min-ē-əs\ (*adj*) disgraceful. The country smarted under the *ignominious* defeat and dreamed of the day when it would be victorious. ig-no-mi-ny \'ig-nə-ˌmin-ē\ (*n*)

il-lim-it-a-ble \ (ᵒ)il-'(l)im-ət-ə-bəl\ (*adj*) infinite. Having explored the far corners of the earth, we are now reaching out into *illimitable* space.

il-lu-mi-nate \il-'ü-mə-ˌnāt\ (*v*) to light; make clear or understandable; enlighten. Just as a lamp can *illuminate* a dark room, a perceptive comment can *illuminate* a knotty problem.

il-lu-sion \il-'ü-zhən\ (*n*) misleading vision. It is easy to create an optical *illusion* in which lines of equal length appear different. il-lu-so-ry \il-'üs-(ə-)rē\ (*adj*)

il-lu-sive \il-'ü-siv\ (*adj*) deceiving. This mirage is an illusion; let us not be fooled by its *illusive* effect.

im-be-cil-i-ty \ˌim-bə-'sil-ət-ē\ (*n*) weakness of mind. I am amazed at the *imbecility* of the readers of these trashy magazines.

im-bibe \im-'bīb\ (*v*) drink in. The dry soil *imbibed* the rain quickly.

im-bro-glio \im-'brōl-₍ᵢ₎yō\ (*n*) a complicated situation; perplexity; entanglement. He was called in to settle the *imbroglio* but failed to bring harmony into the situation.

im-brue \im-'brü\ (*v*) drench, stain, especially with blood. As the instigator of this heinous murder, he is as much *imbrued* in blood as the actual assassin.

im-bue \im-'byü\ (*v*) saturate, fill. His visits to the famous Gothic cathedrals *imbued* him with feelings of awe and reverence.

im-mac-u-late \im-'ak-yə-lət\ (*adj*) pure; spotless. The West Point cadets were *immaculate* as they lined up for inspection.

im-mi-nent \'im-ə-nənt\ (*adj*) impending; near at hand. The *imminent* battle will determine our success or failure in this conflict.

\ŋ\ sing \ō\ go \o\ law \oi\ boy \th\ thin \th̲\ the \ü\ loot \u̇\ foot
\y\ yet \zh\ vision \à, k̲, ⁿ, œ, œ̄, ue, ūe, ʸ\ *see* Pronunciation Symbols

im-mo-bil-i-ty \,im-$_{(,)}$ō-'bil-ət-ē\ (*n*) state of being immovable. Modern armies cannot afford the luxury of *immobility,* as they are vulnerable to attack while standing still.

im-mo-late \'im-ə-,lāt\ (*v*) offer as a sacrifice. The tribal king offered to *immolate* his daughter to quiet the angry gods.

im-mune \im-'yün\ (*adj*) exempt. He was fortunately *immune* from the disease and could take care of the sick.

im-mure \im-'yu̇(ə)r\ (*v*) imprison; shut up in confinement. For the two weeks before the examination, the student *immured* himself in his room and concentrated upon his studies.

im-mu-ta-ble \$^{(')}$im-'(m)yüt-ə-bəl\ (*adj*) unchangeable. Scientists are constantly seeking to discover the *immutable* laws of nature.

im-pair \im-'pa(ə)r\ (*v*) worsen; diminish in value. This arrest will *impair* his reputation in the community.

im-pale \im-'pā(ə)l\ (*v*) pierce. He was *impaled* by the spear hurled by his adversary.

im-pal-pa-ble \$^{(')}$im-'pal-pə-bəl\ (*adj*) imperceptible; intangible. The ash is so fine that it is *impalpable* to the touch but it can be seen as a fine layer covering the window ledge.

im-par-tial \$^{(')}$im-'pär-shəl\ (*adj*) not biased; fair. As members of the jury, you must be *impartial,* showing no favoritism to either party but judging the case on its merits.

im-passe \'im-,pas\ (*n*) predicament from which there is no escape. In this *impasse,* all turned to prayer as their last hope.

im-pas-sive \$^{(')}$im-'pas-iv\ (*adj*) without feeling; not affected by pain. American Natives have sometimes been incorrectly depicted as *impassive* individuals, undemonstrative and stoical.

\ə\ **abut** \ᵊ\ **kitten, F table** \ər\ **further** \a\ **ash** \ā\ **ace** \ä\ **cot, cart**
\au̇\ **out** \ch\ **chin** \e\ **bet** \ē\ **easy** \g\ **go** \i\ **hit** \ī\ **ice** \j\ **job**

im-peach \im-'pēch\ (*v*) charge with crime in office; indict. The angry congressman wanted to *impeach* the president.

im-pec-ca-ble \(')im-'pek-ə-bəl\ (*adj*) faultless. He was proud of his *impeccable* manners.

im-pe-cu-nious \,im-pi-'kyü-nyəs\ (*adj*) without money. Now that he was wealthy, he gladly contributed to funds to assist the *impecunious* and the disabled.

im-pede \im-'pēd\ (*v*) hinder; block; delay. A series of accidents *impeded* the launching of the space shuttle.

im-ped-i-ment \im-'ped-ə-mənt\ (*n*) hindrance; stumbling-block. She had a speech *impediment* that prevented her speaking clearly.

im-pend-ing \im-'pen-diŋ\ (*adj*) nearing; approaching. The entire country was saddened by the news of his *impending* death.

im-pen-i-tent \(')im-'pen-ə-tənt\ (*adj*) not repentant. We could see by his brazen attitude that he was *impenitent*.

im-pe-ri-ous \im-'pir-ē-əs\ (*adj*) domineering. His *imperious* manner indicated that he had long been accustomed to assuming command.

im-per-me-able \(')im-'pər-mē-ə-bəl\ (*adj*) impervious; not permitting passage through its substance. This new material is *impermeable* to liquids.

im-per-ti-nent \(')im-'pərt-ᵊn-ənt\ (*adj*) insolent. I regard your remarks as *impertinent* and resent them.

im-per-turb-a-bil-i-ty \,im-pər-,tər-bə-'bil-ət-ē\ (*n*) calmness. We are impressed by his *imperturbability* in this critical moment and are calmed by it.

im-per-turb-a-ble \,im-pər-'tər-bə-bəl\ (*adj*) calm; placid. He remained *imperturbable* and in full command of the situation in spite of the hysteria and panic all around him.

im-per-vi-ous \(')im-'pər-vē-əs\ (*adj*) not penetrable; not permitting passage through. You cannot change their habits for their minds are *impervious* to reasoning.

---

im-pet-u-ous \im-'pech-(ə-)wəs\ (*adj*) violent; hasty; rash. We tried to curb his *impetuous* behavior because we felt that in his haste he might offend some people.

im-pe-tus \'im-pət-əs\ (*n*) moving force. It is a miracle that there were any survivors since the two automobiles that collided were traveling with great *impetus*.

im-pi-e-ty \(')im-'pī-ət-ē\ (*n*) irreverence; wickedness. We must regard your blasphemy as an act of *impiety*.

im-pinge \im-'pinj\ (*v*) infringe; touch; collide with. How could they be married without *impinging* on one another's freedom?

im-pi-ous \'im-pē-əs\ (*adj*) irreverent. The congregation was offended by his *impious* remarks.

im-pla-ca-ble \(')im-'plak-ə-bəl\ (*adj*) incapable of being pacified. Madame Defarge was the *implacable* enemy of the Evremonde family.

im-plau-si-ble \(')im-'plȯ-zə-bəl\ (*adj*) unlikely; unbelievable. Though her alibi seemed *implausible,* in fact turned out to be true.

im-ple-ment \'im-plə-,mənt\ (*v*) supply what is needed; furnish with tools. I am unwilling to *implement* this plan until I have assurances that it has the full approval of your officials. **im-ple-ment** \'im-plə-mənt\ (*n*)

im-pli-ca-tion \,im-plə-'kā-shən\ (*n*) that which is hinted at or suggested. If I understand the *implications* of your remark, you do not trust our captain.

im-plic-it \im-'plis-ət\ (*adj*) understood but not stated. It is *implicit* that you will come to our aid if we are attacked.

im-ply \im-'plī\ (*v*) suggest a meaning not expressed; signify. Even though your statement does not declare that you are at war with that country, your actions *imply* that that is the actual situation.

im-pol-i-tic \(')im-'päl-ə-,tik\ (*adj*) not wise. I think it is *impolitic* to raise this issue at the present time because the public is too angry.

---

im-pon-der-a-ble \(')im-'pän-d(ə-)rə-bəl\ (*adj*) weightless. I can evaluate the data gathered in this study; the *imponderable* items are not so easily analyzed.

im-port \'im-ˌpō(ə)rt\ (*n*) significance. I feel that you have not grasped the full *import* of the message sent to us by the enemy. im-port \im-'pō(ə)rt\ (*v*)

im-por-tu-nate \im-'pȯrch-(ə-)nət\ (*adj*) urging; demanding. He tried to hide from his *importunate* creditors until his allowance arrived.

im-por-tune \ˌim-pər-'t(y)ün\ (*v*) beg earnestly. I must *importune* you to work for peace at this time.

im-pos-ture \im-'päs-chər\ (*n*) assuming a false identity; masquerade. She was imprisoned for her *imposture* of a doctor.

im-po-tent \'im-pət-ənt\ (*adj*) weak; ineffective. Although he wished to break the nicotine habit, he found himself *impotent* in resisting the craving for a cigarette.

im-pov-er-ished \im-'päv-(ə-)rishd\ (*adj*) poor. The loss of their farm left the family *impoverished* and hopeless.

im-pre-cate \'im-pri-ˌkāt\ (*v*) curse; pray that evil will befall. To *imprecate* Hitler's atrocities is not enough; we must insure against any future practice of genocide.

im-preg-na-ble \im-'preg-nə-bəl\ (*adj*) invulnerable. Until the development of the airplane as a military weapon, the fort was considered *impregnable*.

im-promp-tu \im-'präm(p)-ˌ(ə)t(y)ü\ (*adj*) without previous preparation. His listeners were amazed that such a thorough presentation could be made in an *impromptu* speech.

im-pro-pri-e-ty \ˌim-p(r)ə-'prī-ət-ē\ (*n*) state of being inappropriate. Because of the *impropriety* of his costume, he was denied entrance into the dining room.

im-prov-i-dent \(')im-'präv-əd-ənt\ (*adj*) thriftless. He was constantly being warned to mend his *improvident* ways and begin to "save for a rainy day."

---

im-pro-vise \ˌim-prə-'vīz\ (*v*) compose on the spur of the moment. He would sit at the piano and *improvise* for hours on themes from Bach and Handel.

im-pru-dent \⁽⁾im-'prüd-ᵊnt\ (*adj*) lacking caution; injudicious. It is *imprudent* to exercise vigorously and become overheated when you are unwell.

im-pugn \im-'pyün\ (*v*) doubt; challenge; gainsay. I cannot *impugn* your honesty without evidence.

im-pu-ni-ty \im-'pyü-nət-ē\ (*n*) freedom from punishment. The bully mistreated everyone in the class with *impunity* for he felt that no one would dare retaliate.

im-pu-ta-tion \ˌim-pyə-'tā-shən\ (*n*) charge; reproach. You cannot ignore the *imputations* in his speech that you are the guilty party.

im-pute \im-'pyüt\ (*v*) attribute; ascribe. If I wished to *impute* blame to the officers in charge of this program, I would come out and state it definitely and without hesitation.

in-ad-ver-tence \ˌin-əd-'vərt-ᵊn(t)s\ (*n*) oversight; carelessness. By *inadvertence,* he omitted two questions on the examination.

in-al-ien-a-ble \⁽⁾in-'āl-yə-nə-bəl\ (*adj*) not to be taken away; nontransferable. The Declaration of Independence mentions the *inalienable* rights that all of us possess.

in-ane \in-'ān\ (*adj*) silly; senseless. Such comments are *inane* because they do not help us solve our problem.
in-an-i-ty \in-'an-ət-ē\ (*n*)

in-an-i-mate \⁽⁾in-'an-ə-mət\ (adj) lifeless. She was asked to identify the still and *inanimate* body.

in-ar-tic-u-late \ˌin-₍₎är-'tik-yə-lət\ (*adj*) speechless; producing indistinct speech. He became *inarticulate* with rage and uttered sounds without meaning.

in-can-des-cent \ˌin-kən-'des-ᵊnt\ (*adj*) strikingly bright; shining with intense heat. If you leave on an *incandescent* light bulb, it quickly grows too hot to touch.

\ə\ **abut** \ᵊ\ **kitten,** F **table** \ər\ **further** \a\ **ash** \ā\ **ace** \ä\ **cot, cart**
\au̇\ **out** \ch\ **chin** \e\ **bet** \ē\ **easy** \g\ **go** \i\ **hit** \ī\ **ice** \j\ **job**

in-can-ta-tion \ˌin-ˌkan-'tā-shən\ (*n*) singing or chanting of magic spells; magical formula. Uttering *incantations* to make the brew more potent, the witch doctor stirred the liquid in the caldron.

in-ca-pac-i-tate \ˌin-kə-'pas-ə-ˌtāt\ (*v*) disable. During the winter, many people were *incapacitated* by respiratory ailments.

in-car-cer-ate \in-'kär-sə-ˌrāt\ (*v*) imprison. The warden will *incarcerate* the felon.

in-car-nate \in-'kär-nət\ (*adj*) endowed with flesh; personified. Your attitude is so fiendish that you must be a devil *incarnate;* also (*v*).

in-car-na-tion \ˌin-ˌkär-'nā-shən\ (*n*) act of assuming a human body and human nature. The *incarnation* of Jesus Christ is a basic tenet of Christian theology.

in-cen-di-ar-y \in-'sen-dē-ˌer-ē\ (*n*) arsonist. The fire spread in such an unusual manner that the fire department chiefs were certain that it had been set by an *incendiary;* also (*adj*).

in-cen-tive \in-'sent-iv\ (*n*) spur, motive. Students who dislike school must be given an *incentive* to learn.

in-ces-sant \⁽ᵗ⁾in-'ses-ᵊnt\ (*adj*) uninterrupted. The crickets kept up an *incessant* chirping that disturbed our attempts to fall asleep.

in-cho-ate \in-'kō-ət\ (*adj*) recently begun; rudimentary; elementary. Before the Creation, the world was an *inchoate* mass.

in-ci-dence \'in(t)-səd-ən(t)s\ (*n*) falling on a body; a casual occurrence. We must determine the angle of *incidence* of the rays of light.

in-ci-den-tal \ˌin(t)-sə-'dent-ᵊl\ (*adj*) not essential; minor. The scholarship covered his major expenses at college and some of his *incidental* expenses as well.

in-cip-i-ent \in-'sip-ē-ənt\ (*adj*) beginning; in an early stage. I will go to sleep early for I want to break an *incipient* cold.

\ŋ\ sing   \ō\ go   \ò\ law   \òi\ boy   \th\ thin   \t̲h̲\ the   \ü\ loot   \u̇\ foot
\y\ yet   \zh\ vision   \à, k̲, ⁿ, œ, œ̄, ᴜe, ᴜ̄e, ʸ\ *see* Pronunciation Symbols

in-ci-sive \in-'sī-siv\ (*adj*) cutting; sharp. His *incisive* remarks made us see the fallacy in our plans.

in-cite \in-'sīt\ (*v*) arouse to action. The demagogue *incited* the mob to take action into its own hands.

in-clem-ent \(ᵗ)in-'klem-ənt\ (*adj*) stormy; unkind. I like to read a good book in *inclement* weather.

in-clu-sive \in-'klü-siv\ (*adj*) tending to include all. This meeting will run from January 10 to February 15 *inclusive.*

in-cog-ni-to \,in-,käg-'nēt-(ᵢ)ō\ (*adv, adj*) with identity concealed; using an assumed name. The monarch enjoyed traveling through the town *incognito* and mingling with the populace; also (*n*).

in-co-her-ence \,in-kō-'hir-ən(t)s\ (*n*) lack of relevance; lack of intelligibility. The bereaved father sobbed and stammered, caught up in the *incoherence* of his grief. **in-co-her-ent** \in-kō-'hir-ənt\ (*adj*)

in-com-mo-di-ous \,in-kə-'mōd-ē-əs\ (*adj*) not spacious. In their *incommodious* quarters, they had to improvise for closet space.

in-com-pat-i-ble \,in-kəm-'pat-ə-bəl\ (*adj*) inharmonious. The married couple argued incessantly and finally decided to separate because they were *incompatible.*

in-con-gru-i-ty \,in-kən-'grü-ət-ē\ (*n*) lack of harmony; absurdity. The *incongruity* of his wearing sneakers with formal attire amused the observers.

in-con-gru-ous \(ᵗ)in-'käŋ-grə-wəs\ (*adj*) not fitting; absurd. These remarks do not have any relationship to the problem at hand; they are *incongruous* and should be stricken from the record.

in-con-se-quen-tial \(ᵢ)in-,kän(t)-sə-kwən-chəl\ (*adj*) of trifling significance. Your objections are *inconsequential* and may be disregarded.

in-con-ti-nent \(ᵗ)in-'känt-ᵊn-ənt\ (*adj*) lacking self-restraint; licentious. His *incontinent* behavior off stage

---

\ə\ **abut** \ᵊ\ **kitten, F table** \ər\ **further** \a\ **ash** \ā\ **ace** \ä\ **cot, cart** \aů\ **out** \ch\ **chin** \e\ **bet** \ē\ **easy** \g\ **go** \i\ **hit** \ī\ **ice** \j\ **job**

shocked many people and they refused to attend the plays and movies in which he appeared.

in-con-tro-vert-i-ble \\,(,)in-ˌkän-trə-ˈvərt-ə-bəl\ *(adj)* indisputable. We must yield to the *incontrovertible* evidence that you have presented and free your client.

in-cor-po-re-al \,in-(,)kȯr-ˈpōr-ē-əl\ *(adj)* immaterial; without a material body. We must devote time to the needs of our *incorporeal* mind as well as our corporeal body.

in-cor-ri-gi-ble \(')in-ˈkȯr-ə-jə-bəl\ *(adj)* uncorrectable. Because he was an *incorrigible* criminal, he was sentenced to life imprisonment.

in-cre-du-li-ty \,in-kri-ˈd(y)ü-lət-ē\ *(n)* a tendency to disbelief. Your *incredulity* in the face of all the evidence is hard to understand.

in-cred-u-lous \(')in-ˈkrej-ə-ləs\ *(adj)* withholding belief; skeptical. The *incredulous* judge refused to accept the statement of the defendant.

in-cre-ment \ˈiŋ-krə-mənt\ *(n)* increase. The new contract calls for a 10 percent *increment* in salary for each employee for the next two years.

in-crim-i-nate \in-ˈkrim-ə-ˌnāt\ *(v)* accuse. The evidence gathered against the racketeers *incriminates* some high public officials as well.

in-cu-bate \ˈiŋ-kyə-ˌbāt\ *(v)* hatch; scheme. Inasmuch as our supply of electricity is cut off, we shall have to rely on the hens to *incubate* these eggs.

in-cu-bus \ˈiŋ-kyə-bəs\ *(n)* burden; mental care; nightmare. The *incubus* of financial worry helped bring on his nervous breakdown.

in-cul-cate \in-ˈkəl-ˌkāt\ *(v)* teach. In an effort to *inculcate* religious devotion, the officials ordered that the school day begin with the singing of a hymn.

in-cum-bent \in-ˈkəm-bənt\ *(n)* officeholder. The newly elected public official received valuable advice from the present *incumbent;* also *(adj)*.

in-cur \in-'kər\ (*v*) bring upon oneself. His parents refused to pay any future debt he might *incur.*

in-cur-sion \in-'kər-zhən\ (*n*) temporary invasion. The nightly *incursions* and hit-and-run raids of our neighbors across the border tried the patience of the country to the point where we decided to retaliate in force.

in-de-fat-i-ga-ble \,in-di-'fat-i-gə-bəl\ (*adj*) tireless. He was *indefatigable* in his constant efforts to raise funds for the Red Cross.

in-dem-ni-fy \in-'dem-nə-,fī\ (*v*) make secure against loss; compensate for loss. The city will *indemnify* all home owners whose property is spoiled by this project.

in-den-ture \in-'den-chər\ (*v*) bind as servant or apprentice to master. Many immigrants could come to America only after they had *indentured* themselves for several years; also (*n*).

in-dict \in-'dīt\ (*v*) charge. If the grand jury *indicts* the suspect, he will go to trial.

in-dig-e-nous \in-'dij-ə-nəs\ (*adj*) native. Tobacco is one of the *indigenous* plants that the early explorers found in this country.

in-di-gent \'in-di-jənt\ (*adj*) poor. Because he was *indigent,* he was sent to the welfare office.

in-dig-ni-ty \in-'dig-nət-ē\ (*n*) offensive or insulting treatment. Although he seemed to accept cheerfully the *indignities* heaped upon him, he was inwardly very angry. **in-dig-nant** \in-'dig-nənt\ (*adj*)

in-dis-put-a-ble \,in-dis-'pyüt-ə-bəl\ (*adj*) too certain to be disputed. In the face of these *indisputable* statements, I withdraw my complaint.

in-dis-sol-u-ble \,in-dis-'äl-yə-bəl\ (*adj*) permanent. The *indissoluble* bonds of marriage are all too often being dissolved.

in-do-lence \'in-də-lən(t)s\ (*n*) laziness. The sultry weather in the tropics encourages a life of *indolence.*

\ə\ **abut** \ᵊ\ **kitten, F table** \ər\ **further** \a\ **ash** \ā\ **ace** \ä\ **cot, cart**
\aù\ **out** \ch\ **chin** \e\ **bet** \ē\ **easy** \g\ **go** \i\ **hit** \ī\ **ice** \j\ **job**

in-dom-i-ta-ble \in-'däm-ət-ə-bəl\ (*adj*) unconquerable. The founders of our country had *indomitable* will-power.

in-du-bi-ta-bly \⁽'⁾in-'d(y)ü-bət-ə-blē\ (*adv*) beyond a doubt. Because his argument was *indubitably* valid, the judge accepted it.

in-duc-tive \in-'dək-tiv\ (*adj*) pertaining to induction or proceeding from the specific to the general. The discovery of the planet Pluto is an excellent example of the results that can be obtained from *inductive* reasoning.

in-dul-gent \in-'dəl-jənt\ (*adj*) humoring; yielding; lenient. An *indulgent* parent may spoil a child by creating an artificial atmosphere of leniency.

in-e-bri-et-y \ˌin-i-'brī-ət-ē\ (*n*) habitual intoxication. Because of his *inebriety*, he was discharged from his position as family chauffeur.

in-ef-fa-ble \⁽'⁾in-'ef-ə-bəl\ (*adj*) unutterable; cannot be expressed in speech. Such *ineffable* joy must be experienced; it cannot be described.

in-ef-fec-tu-al \ˌin-ə-'fek-chə(-wə)l\ (*adj*) not effective; weak. Because the candidate failed to get across his message to the public, his campaign was *ineffectual*.

in-e-luc-ta-ble \ˌin-i-'lək-tə-bəl\ (*adj*) irresistible; not to be escaped. He felt that his fate was *ineluctable* and refused to make any attempt to improve his lot.

in-ept \in-'ept\ (*adj*) unsuited; absurd; incompetent. The constant turmoil in the office proved that he was an *inept* administrator.

in-eq-ui-ty \⁽'⁾in-'ek-wət-ē\ (*n*) unfairness. In demanding equal pay for equal work, women protest the basic *inequity* of a system that gives greater financial rewards to men.

in-er-tia \in-'ər-shə\ (*n*) state of being inert or indisposed to move. Our *inertia* in this matter may prove disastrous; we must move to aid our allies immediately.

\ŋ\ sing \ō\ go \o\ law \oi\ boy \th\ thin \th\ the \ü\ loot \u\ foot
\y\ yet \zh\ vision \à, k, ⁿ, œ, œ̄, ɶ, œ̄, ʸ\ *see* Pronunciation Symbols

in-ex-o-ra-ble \\$^{(')}$in-'eks-(ə-)rə-bəl\ (*adj*) relentless; unyielding; implacable. After listening to the pleas for clemency, the judge was *inexorable* and gave the convicted man the maximum punishment allowed by law.

in-fal-li-ble \\$^{(')}$in-'fal-ə-bəl\ (*adj*) unerring. We must remember that none of us is *infallible.*

in-fa-mous \'in-fə-məs\ (*adj*) notoriously bad. Jesse James was an *infamous* outlaw.

in-fan-tile \'in-fən-ˌtīl\ (*adj*) childish; extremely immature. When will he outgrow such *infantile* behavior?

in-fer \in-'fər\ (*v*) deduce; conclude. We must be particularly cautious when we *infer* that a person is guilty on the basis of circumstantial evidence.

in-fer-ence \ˌin-f(ə-)rən(t)s\ (*n*) conclusion drawn from data. I want you to check this *inference* because it may have been based on insufficient information.

in-fer-nal \in-'fərn-əl\ (*adj*) pertaining to hell; devilish. They could think of no way to hinder his *infernal* scheme.

in-fi-del \'in-fəd-əl\ (*n*) unbeliever. The Saracens made war against the *infidels.*

in-fin-i-tes-i-mal \ˌ$_{(')}$in-ˌfin-ə-'tes-ə-məl\ (*adj*) very small. In the twentieth century, physicists have made their greatest discoveries about the characteristics of *infinitesimal* objects like the atom and its parts.

in-fir-mi-ty \in-'fər-mət-ē\ (*n*) weakness. His greatest *infirmity* was lack of willpower.

in-flat-ed \in-'flāt-əd\ (*adj*) enlarged (with air or gas). After the balloons were *inflated,* they were distributed among the children.

in-flux \'in-ˌfləks\ (*n*) flowing into. The *influx* of refugees into the country has taxed the relief agencies severely.

in-frac-tion \in-'frak-shən\ (*n*) violation. Because of his many *infractions* of school regulations, he was suspended by the dean.

\ə\ **abut** \ᵊ\ **kitten, F table** \ər\ **further** \a\ **ash** \ā\ **ace** \ä\ **cot, cart** \aů\ **out** \ch\ **chin** \e\ **bet** \ē\ **easy** \g\ **go** \i\ **hit** \ī\ **ice** \j\ **job**

in-fringe \in-'frinj\ (*v*) violate; encroach. I think your machine *infringes* on my patent.

in-ge-nue \'an-jə-nü\ (*n*) an artless girl; an actress who plays such parts. Although she was forty, she still insisted that she be cast as an *ingenue* and refused to play more mature roles.

in-gen-u-ous \in-'jen-yə-wəs\ (*adj*) naive; young; unsophisticated. These remarks indicate that you are *ingenuous* and unaware of life's harsher realities.

in-grate \'in-,grāt\ (*n*) ungrateful person . You are an *ingrate* since you have treated my gifts with scorn.

in-gra-ti-ate \in-'grā-shē-,āt\ (*v*) become popular with. He tried to *ingratiate* himself into her parents' good graces.

in-her-ent \in-'hir-ənt\ (*adj*) firmly established by nature or habit. His *inherent* love of justice compelled him to come to their aid.

in-hib-it \in-'hib-ət\ (*v*) prohibit; restrain. The child was not *inhibited* in his responses. in-hi-bi-tion \,in-(h)ə-'bish-ən\ (*n*)

in-im-i-cal \in-'im-i-kəl\ (*adj*) unfriendly; hostile. She felt that they were *inimical* and were hoping for her downfall.

in-im-i-ta-ble \(')in-'im-ət-ə-bəl\ (*adj*) matchless; not able to be imitated. We admire Auden for his *inimitable* use of language; he is one of a kind.

in-iq-ui-tous \in-'ik-wət-əs\ (*adj*) unjust; wicked. I cannot approve of the *iniquitous* methods you used to gain your present position. in-iq-ui-ty \in-'ik-wət-ē\ (*n*)

in-kling \'iŋ-kliŋ\ (*n*) hint. This came as a complete surprise to me as I did not have the slightest *inkling* of your plans.

in-nate \in-'āt\ (*adj*) inborn. His *innate* talent for music was soon recognized by his parents.

in-noc-u-ous \in-'äk-yə-wəs\ (*adj*) harmless. Let him drink it; it is *innocuous*.

\ŋ\ **si**ng   \ō\ **g**o   \ȯ\ **l**aw   \ȯi\ **b**oy   \th\ **th**in   \th̲\ **th**e   \ü\ **l**oot   \u̇\ **f**oot
\y\ **y**et   \zh\ vi**si**on   \à, k̲, ⁿ, œ, œ̄, ᵫ, ᵫ̄, ʸ\ *see* Pronunciation Symbols

in-no-va-tion \\,in-ə-'vā-shən\\ (*n*) change; introduction of something new. He loved *innovations* just because they were new.

in-nu-en-do \\,in-yə-'wen-₍₎dō\\ (*n*) hint; insinuation. I resent the *innuendos* in your statement more than the statement itself.

in-op-por-tune \\₍₎in-,äp-ər-'t(y)ün\\ (*adj*) untimely; poorly chosen. A rock concert is an *inopportune* setting for a quiet conversation.

in-or-di-nate \\in-'órd-ᵊn-ət\\ (*adj*) unrestrained; excessive. She had an *inordinate* fondness for candy.

in-sa-tia-ble \\⁽ⁱ⁾in-'sā-shə-bəl\\ (*adj*) not easily satisfied; greedy. His thirst for knowledge was *insatiable;* he was always in the library.

in-scru-ta-ble \\in-'skrüt-ə-bəl\\ (*adj*) incomprehensible; not to be discovered. I fail to understand the reasons for your outlandish behavior; your motives are *inscrutable.*

in-sen-sate \\⁽ⁱ⁾in-'sen-,sāt\\ (*adj*) without feeling. He lay there as *insensate* as a log.

in-sid-i-ous \\in-'sid-ē-əs\\ (*adj*) treacherous; stealthy; sly. The fifth column is *insidious* because it works secretly within our territory for our defeat.

in-sin-u-ate \\in-'sin-yə-,wāt\\ (*v*) hint; imply. What are you trying to *insinuate* by that remark?

in-sip-id \\in-'sip-əd\\ (*adj*) tasteless; dull. I am bored by your *insipid* talk.

in-so-lent \\'in(t)-s(ə-)lənt\\ (*adj*) haughty and contemptuous. I resent your *insolent* manner.

in-sol-ven-cy \\⁽ⁱ⁾in-'säl-vən-sē\\ (*n*) bankruptcy; lack of ability to repay debts. When rumors of his *insolvency* reached his creditors, they began to press him for payment of the money due them.

in-som-ni-a \\in-'säm-nē-ə\\ (*n*) wakefulness; inability to sleep. He refused to join us in a midnight cup of coffee because he claimed it gave him *insomnia.*

\\ə\\ **abut** \\ᵊ\\ **kitten, F table** \\ər\\ **further** \\a\\ **ash** \\ā\\ **ace** \\ä\\ **cot, cart**
\\aú\\ **out** \\ch\\ **chin** \\e\\ **bet** \\ē\\ **easy** \\g\\ **go** \\i\\ **hit** \\ī\\ **ice** \\j\\ **job**

in-sou-ci-ant \in-'sü-sē-ənt\ (*adj*) indifferent; without concern or care. Your *insouciant* attitude at such a critical moment indicates that you do not understand the gravity of the situation.

in-sti-gate \'in(t)-stə-ˌgāt\ (*v*) urge; start; provoke. I am afraid that this statement will *instigate* a revolt.

in-su-lar \in(t)s-(y)ə-lər\ (*adj*) like an island; narrow-minded. In an age of such rapid means of communication, we cannot afford to be hemmed in by such *insular* ideas.

in-su-per-a-ble \⁽ⁱ⁾in-'sü-p(ə-)rə-bəl\ (*adj*) insurmountable; invincible. In the face of *insuperable* difficulties they maintained their courage and will to resist.

in-sur-gent \in-'sər-jənt\ (*adj*) rebellious. We will not discuss reforms until the *insurgent* troops have returned to their homes; also (*n*).

in-te-grate \'int-ə-ˌgrāt\ (*v*) make whole; combine; make into one unit. He tried to *integrate* all their activities into one program.

in-teg-ri-ty \in-'teg-rət-ē\ (*n*) wholeness; purity; uprightness. He was a man of great *integrity.*

in-tel-lect \'int-ᵊl-ˌekt\ (*n*) higher mental powers. He thought college would develop his *intellect.*

in-tel-li-gen-tsi-a \in-ˌtel-ə-'jen(t)-sē-ə\ (*n*) the intelligent and educated classes [often used derogatorily]. He preferred discussions about sports and politics to the literary conversations of the *intelligentsia.*

in-ter \in-'tər\ (*v*) bury. They are going to *inter* the body tomorrow.

in-ter-dict \ˌint-ər-'dikt\ (*v*) prohibit; forbid. Civilized nations must *interdict* the use of nuclear weapons if we expect our society to live. in-ter-dict \'int-ər-ˌdikt\ (*n*)

in-ter-im \'int-ə-rəm\ (*n*) meantime. The company will not consider our proposal until next week; in the *interim,* let us proceed as we have in the past; also (*adj*).

\ŋ\ **sing** \ō\ **go** \ȯ\ **law** \ȯi\ **boy** \th\ **thin** \<u>th</u>\ **the** \ü\ **loot** \u̇\ **foot**
\y\ **yet** \zh\ **vision** \à, <u>k</u>, ⁿ, œ, œ̄, ᵫ, ᵫ̄, ʸ\ *see* Pronunciation Symbols

in-ter-loc-u-to-ry \,int-ər-'läk-yə-,tōr-ē\ (*adj*) conversational; intermediate, not final. This *interlocutory* decree is only a temporary setback; the case has not been settled.

in-ter-ment \in-'tər-mənt\ (*n*) burial. *Interment* will take place in the church cemetery at 2 P.M. Wednesday.

in-ter-mi-na-ble \(ᵗ)in-'tərm-(ə-)nə-bəl\ (*adj*) endless. Although his speech lasted for only twenty minutes, it seemed *interminable* to his bored audience.

in-ter-mit-tent \,int-ər-'mit-ᵊnt\ (*adj*) periodic; on and off. Our picnic was marred by *intermittent* rains.

in-ter-ne-cine \,int-ər-'nes-,ēn\ (*adj*) mutually destructive. The rising death toll on both sides indicates the *internecine* nature of this conflict.

in-ter-stic-es \in-'tər-stə-,sēz\ (*n*) chinks; crevices. The mountain climber sought to obtain a foothold in the *interstices* of the cliff.

in-ti-mate \'int-ə-,māt\ (*v*) hint. She *intimated* rather than stated her preferences. **in-ti-mate** \'int-ə-mət\ (*adj, n*)

in-tim-i-da-tion \in-,tim-ə-'dā-shən\ (*n*) fear. A ruler who maintains his power by *intimidation* is bound to develop clandestine resistance.

in-trac-ta-ble \(ᵗ)in-'trak-tə-bəl\ (*adj*) unruly; refractory. The horse was *intractable* and refused to enter the starting gate.

in-tran-si-gence \in-'tran(t)s-ə-jən(t)s\ (*n*) state of stubborn unwillingness to compromise. The *intransigence* of both parties in the dispute makes an early settlement almost impossible to obtain.

in-tran-si-gent \in-'tran(t)s-ə-jənt\ (*adj*) refusing any compromise. The strike settlement has collapsed because both sides are *intransigent*.

in-trep-id \in-'trep-əd\ (*adj*) fearless. For his *intrepid* conduct in battle, he was promoted.

\ə\ **abut** \ᵊ\ **kitten, F table** \ər\ **further** \a\ **ash** \ā\ **ace** \ä\ **cot, cart**
\aú\ **out** \ch\ **chin** \e\ **bet** \ē\ **easy** \g\ **go** \i\ **hit** \ī\ **ice** \j\ **job**

in-tri-cate \'in-tri-kət\ *(adj)* complex; knotty; tangled. Philip spent many hours designing mazes so *intricate* that none of his classmates could solve them.

in-trin-sic \in-'trin-zik\ *(adj)* belonging to a thing in itself; inherent. Although the *intrinsic* value of this award is small, I shall always cherish it.

in-tro-vert \'in-trə-ˌvərt\ *(n)* one who is introspective; inclined to think more about oneself. In his poetry, he reveals that he is an *introvert* by his intense interest in his own problems; also *(v)*.

in-trude \in-'trüd\ *(v)* trespass; enter as an uninvited person. He hesitated to *intrude* on their conversation.

in-tu-i-tion \ˌin-t(y)ù-'ish-ən\ *(n)* power of knowing without reasoning. She claimed to know the truth by *intuition*. in-tu-i-tive \in-'t(y)ü-ət-iv\ *(adj)*

in-un-date \'in-(ˌ)ən-ˌdāt\ *(v)* overflow; flood. The tremendous waves *inundated* the town.

in-ure \in-'(y)ù(ə)r\ *(v)* accustom; harden. He was *inured* to the Alaskan cold.

in-val-i-date \(ˌ)in-'val-ə-ˌdāt\ *(v)* weaken; destroy. The relatives who received little or nothing sought to *invalidate* the will by claiming that the deceased had not been in his right mind when he had signed the document.

in-vec-tive \in-'vek-tiv\ *(n)* abuse. He had expected criticism but not the *invective* that greeted his proposal.

in-veigh \in-'vā\ *(v)* denounce; utter censure or invective. He *inveighed* against the demagoguery of the previous speaker and urged that the audience reject his philosophy as dangerous.

in-vei-gle \in-'vā-gəl\ *(v)* lead astray; wheedle. He was *inveigled* into joining the club.

in-verse \(ˌ)in-'vərs\ *(adj)* opposite. There is an *inverse* ratio between the strength of light and its distance. in-verse \'in-ˌvərs\ *(n)*

\ŋ\ **sing** \ō\ **go** \ò\ **law** \òi\ **boy** \th\ **thin** \t͟h\ **the** \ü\ **loot** \ù\ **foot**
\y\ **yet** \zh\ **vision** \à, k̲, ⁿ, œ, œ̄, ᵫ, ᵫ̄, ʸ\ *see* Pronunciation Symbols

in-vet-er-ate \in-'vet-ə-rət\ (*adj*) deep-rooted; habitual. He is an *inveterate* smoker.

in-vid-i-ous \in-'vid-ē-əs\ (*adj*) designed to create ill will or envy. We disregarded her *invidious* remarks because we realized how jealous she was.

in-vin-ci-ble \ ⁽ⁱ⁾in-'vin(t)-sə-bəl\ (*adj*) unconquerable. Superman is *invincible.*

in-vi-o-la-bil-i-ty \ ⁽ⁱ⁾in-ˌvī-ə-lə-'bil-ət-ē\ (*n*) security from being destroyed, corrupted, or profaned. They respected the *inviolability* of her faith and did not try to change her manner of living.

in-voke \in-'vōk\ (*v*) call upon; ask for. She *invoked* her advisor's aid in filling out her financial aid forms.

in-vul-ner-a-ble \ ⁽ⁱ⁾in-'vəln-(ə-)rə-bəl\ (*adj*) incapable of injury. Achilles was *invulnerable* except in his heel.

i-o-ta \ī-'ōt-ə\ (*n*) very small quantity. He hadn't an *iota* of common sense.

ir-as-ci-ble \ir-'as-ə-bəl\ (*adj*) irritable; easily angered. His *irascible* temper frightened me.

i-rate \ī-'rāt\ (*adj*) angry. When John's mother found out he had overdrawn his checking account for the third month in a row, she was so *irate* she could scarcely speak to him.

ir-i-des-cent \ˌir-ə-'des-ᵊnt\ (*adj*) exhibiting rainbowlike colors. He admired the *iridescent* hues of the oil that floated on the surface of the water.

irk-some \'ərk-səm\ (*adj*) repetitious; tedious. He found working on the assembly line *irksome* because of the monotony of the operation he had to perform.

i-ron-i-cal \ī-'rän-i-kəl\ (*adj*) resulting in an unexpected and contrary manner. It is *ironical* that his success came when he least wanted it.

i-ro-ny \'ī-rə-nē\ (*n*) hidden sarcasm or satire; use of words that convey a meaning opposite to the literal meaning. Gradually his listeners began to realize that

---

\ə\ **abut** \ᵊ\ **kitten**, F **table** \ər\ **further** \a\ **ash** \ā\ **ace** \ä\ **cot, cart**
\aů\ **out** \ch\ **chin** \e\ **bet** \ē\ **easy** \g\ **go** \i\ **hit** \ī\ **ice** \j\ **job**

the excessive praise he was lavishing was merely *irony;* he was actually denouncing his opponent.

ir-rec-on-ci-la-ble \ ₍ᵢ₎ir-,(r)ek-ən-'sī-lə-bəl\ (*adj*) incompatible; not able to be resolved. Because the separated couple were *irreconcilable,* the marriage counselor recommended a divorce.

ir-rel-e-vant \ ⁽ⁱ⁾ir-'(r)el-ə-vənt\ (*adj*) not applicable; unrelated. This statement is *irrelevant* and should be disregarded by the jury.

ir-re-me-di-a-ble \ ,ir-i-'mēd-ē-ə-bəl\ (*adj*) incurable, uncorrectable. The error he made was *irremediable.*

ir-rep-a-ra-ble \ ⁽ⁱ⁾ir-'(r)ep-(ə-)rə-bəl\ (*adj*) not able to be corrected or repaired. Your apology cannot atone for the *irreparable* damage you have done to his reputation.

ir-rev-er-ent \ ⁽ⁱ⁾ir-'(r)ev-(ə-)rənt\ (*adj*) lacking proper respect. The worshippers resented his *irreverent* remarks about their faith.

ir-rev-o-ca-ble \ ⁽ⁱ⁾ir-'(r)ev-ə-kə-bəl\ (*adj*) unalterable. Let us not brood over past mistakes since they are *irrevocable.*

it-er-ate \ 'it-ə-,rāt\ (*v*) utter a second time; repeat. I will *iterate* the warning I have previously given to you.

i-tin-er-ant \ī-'tin-ə-rənt\ (*adj*) wandering; traveling. He was an *itinerant* peddler and traveled through Pennsylvania and Virginia selling his wares; also (*n*).

i-tin-er-ar-y \ī-'tin-ə-,rer-ē\ (n) plan of a trip. Before leaving for his first visit to France and England, he discussed his *itinerary* with people who had been there and with his travel agent.

\ŋ\ sing   \ō\ go   \ò\ law   \òi\ boy   \th\ thin   \tẖ\ the   \ü\ loot   \u̇\ foot
\y\ yet   \zh\ vision   \à, ḵ, ⁿ, œ, œ̄, ue, ūe, ʸ\ *see* Pronunciation Symbols

J

jad-ed \'jād-əd\ (*adj*) fatigued; surfeited. He looked for exotic foods to stimulate his *jaded* appetite.

jar-gon \'jär-gən\ (*n*) language used by special group; gibberish. We tried to understand the *jargon* of the peddlers in the marketplace but could not find any basis for comprehension.

jaun-diced \'jȯn-dəst\ (*adj*) yellowed; prejudiced; envious. He gazed at the painting with *jaundiced* eyes.

jaunt \'jȯnt\ (*n*) trip; short journey. He took a quick *jaunt* to Atlantic City.

jaun-ty \'jȯnt-ē\ (*adj*) stylish; perky; carefree. She wore her beret at a *jaunty* angle.

je-june \ji-'jün\ (*adj*) lacking interest; barren; meager. The plot of the play is *jejune* and fails to capture the interest of the audience.

jeop-ar-dy \'jep-ərd-ē\ (*n*) exposure to death or danger. He cannot be placed in double *jeopardy*.

jet-ti-son \'jet-ə-sən\ (*v*) throw overboard. In order to enable the ship to ride safely through the storm, the captain had to *jettison* much of his cargo; also (*n*).

jin-go-ism \'jiŋ-(ˌ)gō-ˌiz-əm\ (*n*) extremely aggressive and militant patriotism. We must be careful to prevent a spirit of *jingoism* from spreading at this time; the danger of a disastrous war is too great.

jo-cose \jō-'kōs\ (*adj*) giving to joking. The salesman was so *jocose* that many of his customers suggested that he become a stand-up comic.

joc-u-lar \'jäk-yə-lər\ (*adj*) said or done in jest. Do not take my *jocular* remarks seriously.

jo-cund \'jäk-ənd\ (*adj*) merry. Santa Claus is always vivacious and *jocund*.

ju-bi-la-tion \ˌjü-bə-'lā-shən\ (*n*) rejoicing. There was great *jubilation* when the armistice was announced.

\ə\ **abut** \ʳ\ **kitten, F table** \ər\ **further** \a\ **ash** \ā\ **ace** \ä\ **cot, cart**
\au̇\ **out** \ch\ **chin** \e\ **bet** \ē\ **easy** \g\ **go** \i\ **hit** \ī\ **ice** \j\ **job**

ju-di-cious \ju-'dish-əs\ (*adj*) wise; determined by sound judgment. I believe that this plan is not *judicious;* it is too risky.

jug-ger-naut \'jəg-ər-ˌnȯt\ (*n*) irresistible crushing force. Nothing could survive in the path of the *juggernaut.*

junc-ture \'jəŋ(k)-chər\ (*n*) crisis; joining point. At this critical *juncture,* let us think carefully before determining the course we shall follow.

jun-ket \'jəŋ-kət\ (*n*) a merry feast or picnic. The opposition claimed that his trip to Europe was merely a political *junket;* also (*v*).

jun-ta \'hün-tə\ (*n*) group of men joined in political intrigue; cabal. As soon as he learned of its existence, the dictator ordered the execution of all of the members of the *junta.*

ju-ris-pru-dence \ jür-ə-'sprüd-ᵊn(t)s\ (*n*) science of law. He was more a student of *jurisprudence* than a practitioner of the law.

jux-ta-pose \'jək-stə-ˌpōz\ (*v*) place side by side. Comparison will be easier if you *juxtapose* the two objects.

K

ka·lei·do·scope \kə-'līd-ə-ˌskōp\ (*n*) tube in which patterns made by the reflection in mirrors of colored pieces of glass, etc., produce interesting symmetrical effects. People found a new source of entertainment while peering through Sir David Brewster's invention, the *kaleidoscope;* they found the everchanging patterns fascinating.

ken \'ken\ (*n*) range of knowledge. I cannot answer your question since this matter is beyond my *ken.*

kin·dred \'kin-drəd\ (*adj*) related; similar in nature or character. Tom Sawyer and Huck Finn were two *kindred* spirits; also (*n*).

ki·net·ic \kə-'net-ik\ (*adj*) producing motion. Designers of the electric automobile find that their greatest obstacle lies in the development of light and efficient storage batteries, the source of the *kinetic* energy needed to propel the vehicle.

ki·osk \'kē-ˌäsk\ (*n*) summerhouse; open pavilion. She waited at the subway *kiosk.*

kis·met \'kiz-ˌmet\ (*n*) fate. *Kismet* is the Arabic word for "fate."

kith \'kith\ (*n*) familiar friends. He always helped both his *kith* and kin.

klep·to·ma·ni·ac \ˌklep-tə-'mā-nē-ˌak\ (*n*) person who has a compulsive desire to steal. They discovered that the wealthy customer was a *kleptomaniac* when they caught her stealing some cheap trinkets.

knav·e·ry \'nāv-(ə-)rē\ (*n*) rascality. We cannot condone such *knavery* in public officials.

knead \'nēd\ (*v*) mix; work dough. Her hands grew strong from *kneading* bread.

knell \'nel\ (*n*) tolling of a bell at a funeral; sound of the funeral bell. "The curfew tolls the *knell* of parting day"; also (*v*).

knoll \'nōl\ (*n*) little round hill. Robert Louis Stevenson's grave is on a *knoll* in Samoa.

\ə\ **abut** \ᵊ\ **kitten, F table** \ər\ **further** \a\ **ash** \ā\ **ace** \ä\ **cot, cart**
\au̇\ **out** \ch\ **chin** \e\ **bet** \ē\ **easy** \g\ **go** \i\ **hit** \ī\ **ice** \j\ **job**

L

lab-y-rinth \\'lab-ə-ˌrin(t)th\\ (*n*) maze. Tom and Betty were lost in the *labyrinth* of secret caves.

lac-er-ate \\'las-ə-ˌrāt\\ (*v*) mangle; tear. Her body was *lacerated* in the automobile crash. **lac-er-ate** \\'las-ə-rət\\ (*adj*)

lach-ry-mose \\'lak-rə-ˌmōs\\ (*adj*) producing tears. His voice has a *lachrymose* quality that is more appropriate at a funeral than a class reunion.

lack-a-dai-si-cal \\ˌlak-ə-'dā-zi-kəl\\ (*adj*) affectedly languid. He was *lackadaisical* and indifferent about his part in the affair.

lack-ey \\'lak-ē\\ (*n*) footman; toady. The duke was followed by his *lackeys;* also (*v*).

lack-lus-ter \\'lak-ˌləs-tər\\ (*adj*) dull. We were disappointed by the *lackluster* performance.

la-con-ic \\lə-'kän-ik\\ (*adj*) brief and to the point. Will Rogers's *laconic* comments on the news made him world famous.

lag-gard \\'lag-ərd\\ (*adj*) slow; sluggish. The sailor had been taught not to be *laggard* in carrying out orders; also (*n*).

la-goon \\lə-'gün\\ (*n*) shallow body of water near a sea; lake. They enjoyed their swim in the calm *lagoon*.

la-i-ty \\'lā-ət-ē\\ (*n*) laymen; persons not connected with the clergy. The *laity* does not always understand the clergy's problems.

lam-i-nat-ed \\'lam-ə-ˌnāt-əd\\ (*adj*) made of thin plates or scales. Banded gneiss is a *laminated* rock.

lam-poon \\lam-'pün\\ (*v*) ridicule. This article *lampoons* the pretensions of some movie moguls; also (*n*).

lan-guid \\'laŋ-gwəd\\ (*adj*) weary; sluggish; listless. Her siege of illness left her *languid* and pallid.

lan-guish \\'laŋ-gwish\\ (*v*) lose animation; lose strength. In stories, lovelorn damsels used to *languish* and pine away.

---

lan-guor \\'laŋ-(g)ər\\ (*n*) lassitude; depression. His friends tried to overcome the *languor* into which he had fallen by taking him to parties and to the theater.

lank \\'laŋk\\ (*adj*) long and thin. *Lank,* gaunt, Abraham Lincoln was a striking figure.

lap-i-dar-y \\'lap-ə-ˌder-ē\\ (*n*) worker in precious stones. He employed a *lapidary* to cut the large diamond; also (*adj*).

lar-ce-ny \\'lärs-nē\\ (*n*) theft. Because of the prisoner's record, the district attorney refused to reduce the charge from grand *larceny* to petit larceny.

lar-gess \\lär-'zhes\\ (*n*) generous gift. Lady Bountiful distributed *largess* to the poor.

las-civ-i-ous \\lə-'siv-ē-əs\\ (*adj*) lustful. The *lascivious* books were confiscated and destroyed.

las-si-tude \\'las-ə-ˌt(y)üd\\ (*n*) languor; weariness. The hot, tropical weather created a feeling of *lassitude* and encouraged drowsiness.

la-tent \\'lāt-ᵊnt\\ (*adj*) dormant; hidden. His *latent* talent was discovered by accident.

lat-er-al \\'lat-ə-rəl\\ (*adj*) coming from the side. In order to get good plant growth, the gardener must pinch off all *lateral* shoots; also (*n, v*).

lat-i-tude \\'lat-ə-ˌt(y)üd\\ (*n*) freedom from narrow limitations. I think you have permitted your son too much *latitude* in this matter.

laud-a-ble \\'lȯd-ə-bəl\\ (*adj*) praiseworthy; commendable. His *laudable* deeds will be remembered by all whom he aided.

lau-da-to-ry \\'lȯd-ə-ˌtōr-ē\\ (*adj*) expressing praise. The critics' *laudatory* comments helped to make her a star.

lave \\'lāv\\ (*v*) wash. The running water will *lave* away all stains.

lav-ish \\'lav-ish\\ (*adj*) liberal; wasteful. The actor's *lavish* gifts pleased her; also (*v*).

\\ə\\ abut \\ᵊ\\ kitten, F table \\ər\\ **further** \\a\\ ash \\ā\\ **ace** \\ä\\ cot, **cart**
\\au̇\\ **out** \\ch\\ **chin** \\e\\ bet \\ē\\ **easy** \\g\\ **go** \\i\\ **hit** \\ī\\ **ice** \\j\\ **job**

lech-er-ous \\'lech-(ə-)rəs\\ (*adj*) impure in thought and act; lustful; unchaste. He is a *lecherous* and wicked old man.

lech-er-y \\'lech-(ə-)rē\\ (*n*) gross lewdness; lustfulness. In his youth he led a life of *lechery* and debauchery, he did not mend his ways until middle age.

lec-tern \\'lek-tərn\\ (*n*) reading desk. The chaplain delivered his sermon from a hastily improvised *lectern.*

lee-way \\'lē-ˌwā\\ (*n*) room to move; margin. When you set a deadline, allow a little *leeway.*

leg-a-cy \\'leg-ə-sē\\ (*n*) a gift made by a will; anything handed down from the past. Part of my *legacy* from my parents is an album of family photographs.

leg-end \\'lej-ənd\\ (*n*) explanatory list of symbols on a map. The *legend* at the bottom of the map made it clear which symbols stood for rest areas along the highway and which stood for public campsites. (secondary meaning)

leg-er-de-main \\ˌlej-ərd-ə-'mān\\ (*n*) sleight of hand. The magician demonstrated his renowned *legerdemain.*

le-ni-en-cy \\'lē-nē-ən-sē\\ (*n*) mildness; permissiveness. Considering the gravity of the offense, we were surprised by the *leniency* of the sentence.

le-o-nine \\'lē-ə-ˌnīn\\ (*n*) like a lion. He was *leonine* in his rage.

le-sion \\'lē-zhən\\ (*n*) unhealthy change in structure, injury. Many *lesions* are the result of disease.

le-thal \\'lē-thəl\\ (*adj*) deadly. It is unwise to leave *lethal* weapons where children may find them.

le-thar-gic \\lə-'thär-jik\\ (*adj*) drowsy; dull. The stuffy room made him *lethargic.*

lev-i-ty \\'lev-ət-ē\\ (*n*) lightness. Such *levity* is improper on this serious occasion.

lewd \\'lüd\\ (*adj*) lustful. They found his *lewd* stories objectionable.

---

lex·i·cog·ra·pher \ˌlek-sə-'käg-rə-fər\ (*n*) compiler of a dictionary. The new dictionary is the work of many *lexicographers* who spent years compiling and editing the work.

lex·i·con \'lek-sə-ˌkän\ (*n*) dictionary. I cannot find this word in any *lexicon* in the library.

li·ai·son \'lē-ə-ˌzän\ (*n*) officer who acts as go-between for two armies. As the *liaison,* he had to avoid offending the leaders of the two armies.

li·ba·tion \lī-'bā-shən\ (*n*) drink. He offered a *libation* to the thirsty prisoner.

li·bel·ous \'lī-b(ə-)ləs\ (*adj*) defamatory; injurious to the good name of a person. He sued the newspaper because of its *libelous* story.

lib·er·tine \'lib-ər-ˌtēn\ (*n*) debauched person, roué. Although she was aware of his reputation as a *libertine,* she felt she could reform him and help him break his dissolute way of life; also (*adj*).

li·bid·i·nous \lə-'bid-ᵊn əs\ (*adj*) lustful. They objected to his *libidinous* behavior.

li·bi·do \lə-'bēd-ˌ(ˌ)ō\ (*n*) emotional urges behind human activity. The psychiatrist maintained that suppression of the *libido* often resulted in maladjustment and neuroses.

li·bret·to \lə-'bret-ˌ(ˌ)ō\ (*n*) text of an opera. The composer of an opera's music is remembered more frequently than the author of its *libretto.*

li·cen·tious \lī-'sen-chəs\ (*adj*) wanton; lewd; dissolute. The *licentious* monarch helped bring about his country's downfall.

lieu \'lü\ (*n*) instead of. They accepted his check in *lieu* of cash.

lil·li·pu·tian \ˌlil-ə-'pyü-shən\ (*adj*) extremely small. The model was built on a *lilliputian* scale; also (*n*).

lim·ber \'lim-bər\ (*adj*) flexible. Hours of ballet classes kept him *limber.*

lim-bo \'lim-(ˌ)bō\ (*n*) region near heaven or hell where certain souls are kept; a prison (slang). Among the divisions of Hell are Purgatory and *Limbo*.

lim-pid \'lim-pəd\ (*adj*) clear. A *limpid* stream ran through his property.

lin-e-a-ments \'lin-ē-ə-mənts\ (*n*) features of the face. She quickly sketched the *lineaments* of his face.

lin-guis-tic \liŋ-'gwis-tik\ (*adj*) pertaining to language. The modern tourist will encounter very little *linguistic* difficulty as English has become an almost universal language.

li-on-ize \'lī-ə-ˌnīz\ (*v*) treat as a celebrity. She enjoyed being *lionized* and adored by the public.

liq-ui-date \'lik-wə-ˌdāt\ (*v*) settle accounts; clear up. He was able to *liquidate* all his debts in a short period of time.

list-less \'list-ləs\ (*adj*) lacking in spirit or energy. We had expected him to be full of enthusiasm and were surprised by his *listless* attitude.

lit-a-ny \'lit-ᵊn-ē\ (*n*) supplicatory prayer. On this solemn day, the congregation responded to the prayers of the priest during the *litany* with fervor and intensity.

lithe \'līth\ (*adj*) flexible; supple. Her figure was *lithe* and willowy.

lit-i-ga-tion \ˌlit-ə-'gā-shən\ (*n*) lawsuit. Try to settle this amicably; I do not want to start *litigation*.

li-to-tes \'līt-ə-ˌtēz\ (*n*) understatement for emphasis. To say, "He little realizes," when we mean that he does not realize at all, is an example of the kind of understatement we call *litotes*.

liv-id \'liv-əd\ (*adj*) lead-colored; black and blue; enraged. His face was so *livid* with rage that we were afraid he might have an attack of apoplexy.

loath \'lōth\ (*adj*) averse; reluctant. They were both *loath* for him to go.

\ŋ\ sing   \ō\ go   \ò\ law   \òi\ boy   \th\ thin   \th̲\ the   \ü\ loot   \u̇\ foot
\y\ yet   \zh\ vision   \à, k̲, ⁿ, œ, œ̄, ue, ūe, ʸ\ *see* Pronunciation Symbols

loathe \\'lōth\\ (*v*) detest. We *loathed* the wicked villain.

lode \\'lōd\\ (*n*) metal-bearing vein. If this *lode* that we have discovered extends for any distance, we have found a fortune.

lofty \\'lȯf-tē\\ (*adj*) very high. They used to tease him about his *lofty* ambitions.

loi·ter \\'lȯit-ər\\ (*v*) hang around; linger. The policeman told him not to *loiter* in the alley.

loll \\'läl\\ (*v*) lounge about. They *lolled* around in their chairs watching television.

lon·gev·i·ty \\län-'jev-ət-ē\\ (*n*) long life. The old man was proud of his *longevity.*

lope \\'lōp\\ (*v*) gallop slowly. As the horses *loped* along, we had an opportunity to admire the ever-changing scenery; also (*n*).

lo·qua·cious \\lō-'kwā-shəs\\ (*adj*) talkative. She is very *loquacious* and can speak on the telephone for hours.

lout \\'laȯt\\ (*n*) clumsy person. The delivery boy is an awkward *lout.*

lu·bric·i·ty \\lü-'bris-ət-ē\\ (*n*) slipperiness; evasiveness. He exasperated the reporters by his *lubricity;* they could not pin him down to a definite answer.

lu·cent \\'lüs-ᵊnt\\ (*adj*) shining. The moon's *lucent* rays silvered the river.

lu·cid \\'lü-səd\\ (*adj*) bright; easily understood. His explanation was *lucid* and to the point.

lu·cra·tive \\'lü-krət-iv\\ (*adj*) profitable. He turned his hobby into a *lucrative* profession.

lu·cre \\'lü-kər\\ (*n*) money. Preferring *lucre* to fame, he wrote stories of popular appeal.

lu·di·crous \\'lüd-ə-krəs\\ (*adj*) laughable; trifling. Let us be serious; this is not a *ludicrous* issue.

lu·gu·bri·ous \\lu̇-'gü-brē-əs\\ (*adj*) mournful. The *lugubrious* howling of the dogs added to our sadness.

---

lu-mi-nous \ˈlü-mə-nəs\ (*adj*) shining; issuing light. The sun is a *luminous* body.

lu-nar \ˈlü-nər\ (*adj*) pertaining to the moon. *Lunar* craters can be plainly seen with the aid of a small telescope.

lu-rid \ˈlu̇r-əd\ (*adj*) wild; sensational. The *lurid* stories he told shocked his listeners.

lus-cious \ˈləsh-əs\ (*adj*) pleasing to taste or smell. The ripe peach was *luscious.*

lus-ter \ˈləs-tər\ (*n*) shine; gloss. The soft *luster* of the silk in the dim light was pleasing; also (*n*).

lus-trous \ˈləs-trəs\ (*adj*) shining. Her large and *lustrous* eyes gave a touch of beauty to an otherwise drab face.

lux-u-ri-ant \ (ₗ)ləg-ˈzhu̇r-ē-ənt\ (*adj*) fertile; abundant; ornate. Farming was easy in this *luxuriant* soil.

M

ma·ca·bre \mə-'käb(-rə)\ (*adj*) gruesome; grisly. The city morgue is a *macabre* spot for the uninitiated.

mac·er·ate \'mas-ə-ˌrāt\ (*v*) to soften by soaking or steeping. The leaves were *macerated* by the damp, boggy soil.

Ma·chi·a·vel·li·an \ˌmak-ē-ə-'vel-ē-ən\ (*adj*) crafty; double-dealing. I do not think he will be a good ambassador because he is not accustomed to the *Machiavellian* maneuverings of foreign diplomats.

mach·i·na·tion \ˌmak-ə-'nā-shən\ (*n*) scheme. I can see through your wily *machinations*.

mad·ri·gal \'mad-ri-gəl\ (*n*) pastoral song. His program of folk songs included several *madrigals* that he sang to the accompaniment of a lute.

mael·strom \'mā(ə)l-strəm\ (*n*) whirlpool. The canoe was tossed about in the *maelstrom*.

mag·nan·i·mous \mag-'nan-ə-məs\ (*adj*) generous. The philanthropist was most *magnanimous*.

mag·nate \'mag-ˌnāt\ (*n*) person of prominence or influence. The steel *magnate* decided to devote more time to city politics.

mag·nil·o·quent \mag-'nil-ə-kwənt\ (*adj*) boastful, pompous. In their stories of the trial, the reporters ridiculed the *magniloquent* speeches of the defense attorney.

mag·ni·tude \'mag-nə-ˌt(y)üd\ (*n*) greatness; extent. It is difficult to comprehend the *magnitude* of his crime.

maim \'mām\ (*v*) mutilate; injure. The hospital could not take care of all who had been wounded or *maimed* in the railroad accident.

mal·a·droit \ˌmal-ə-'dròit\ (*adj*) clumsy; bungling. In his usual *maladroit* way, he managed to upset the cart and spill the food.

mal·aise \mə-'lāz\ (*n*) uneasiness; distress. She felt a sudden vague *malaise* when she heard sounds at the door.

\ə\ **abut** \ᵊ\ **kitten, F table** \ər\ **further** \a\ **ash** \ā\ **ace** \ä\ **cot, cart**
\au̇\ **out** \ch\ **chin** \e\ **bet** \ē\ **easy** \g\ **go** \i\ **hit** \ī\ **ice** \j\ **job**

mal-a-prop-ism \'mal-ə-ˌpräp-ˌiz-əm\ (*n*) comic misuse of a word. When Mrs. Malaprop criticizes Lydia for being "as headstrong as an allegory on the banks of the Nile," she confuses "allegory" and "alligator" in a typical *malapropism.*

mal-con-tent \ˌmal-kən-'tent\ (*n*) person dissatisfied with existing state of affairs. He was one of the few *malcontents* in Congress; he constantly voiced his objections to the presidential program; also (*adj*).

mal-e-dic-tion \ˌmal-ə-'dik-shən\ (*n*) curse. The witch uttered *maledictions* against her captors.

mal-e-fac-tor \'mal-ə-ˌfak-tər\ (*n*) criminal. We must try to bring these *malefactors* to justice.

ma-lev-o-lent \mə-'lev-ə-lənt\ (*adj*) wishing evil. We must thwart his *malevolent* schemes.

ma-li-cious \mə-'lish-əs\ (*adj*) dictated by hatred or spite. The *malicious* neighbor spread the gossip.

ma-lign \mə-'līn\ (*v*) speak evil of; defame. Because of her hatred of the family, she *maligns* all who are friendly to them; also (*adj*).

ma-lig-nant \mə-'lig-nənt\ (*adj*) having an evil influence; virulent. This is a *malignant* disease; we may have to use drastic measures to stop its spread.

ma-lin-ger-er \mə-'liŋ-gər-ər\ (*n*) one who feigns illness to escape duty. The captain ordered the sergeant to punish all *malingerers.*

mall \'mȯl\ (*n*) public walk. The *mall* in Central Park has always been a favorite spot for Sunday strollers.

mal-le-a-ble \'mal-ē-ə-bəl\ (*adj*) capable of being shaped by pounding. Gold is a *malleable* metal.

mam-mal \'mam-əl\ (*n*) a vertebrate animal whose female suckles its young. Many people regard the whale as a fish and do not realize that it is a *mammal.*

mam-moth \'mam-əth\ (*adj*) gigantic. The *mammoth* corporations of the twentieth century are a mixed blessing; also (*n*).

\ŋ\ **sing** \ō\ **go** \ȯ\ **law** \ȯi\ **boy** \th\ **thin** \th̲\ **the** \ü\ **loot** \u̇\ **foot**
\y\ **yet** \zh\ **vision** \à, k̲, ⁿ, œ, œ̄, ue, ue̅, ʸ\ *see* Pronunciation Symbols

man-date \\'man-ˌdāt\\ (*n*) order; charge. In his inaugural address, the president stated that he had a *mandate* from the people to seek an end to social evils such as poverty, poor housing, etc.; also (*v*).

man-da-tor-y \\'man-də-ˌtōr-ē\\ (*adj*) obligatory. These instructions are *mandatory;* any violation will be severely punished.

man-gy \\'mān-jē\\ (*adj*) shabby; wretched. We finally threw out the *mangy* rug that the dog had destroyed.

ma-ni-a-cal \\mə-'nī-ə-kəl\\ (*adj*) raving mad. His *maniacal* laughter frightened us.

man-i-fest \\'man-ə-ˌfest\\ (*adj*) understandable; clear. His evil intentions were *manifest* and yet we could not stop him; also (*v, n*).

man-i-fes-to \\ˌman-ə-'fes-ₗtō\\ (*n*) declaration; statement of policy. This statement may be regarded as the *manifesto* of the party's policy.

man-i-fold \\'man-ə-ˌfōld\\ (*adj*) numerous; varied. I cannot begin to tell you how much I appreciate your *manifold* kindnesses; also (*adv, n*).

ma-nip-u-late \\mə-'nip-yə-ˌlāt\\ (*v*) operate with the hands. How do you *manipulate* these puppets?

ma-raud-er \\mə-'rȯd-ər\\ (*n*) raider; intruder. The sounding of the alarm frightened the *marauders*. **ma-raud** \\mə-'rȯd\\ (*v*)

mar-i-tal \\'mar-ət-ᵊl\\ (*adj*) pertaining to marriage. After the publication of his book on *marital* affairs, he was often consulted by married people on the verge of divorce.

mar-i-time \\'mar-ə-ˌtīm\\ (*adj*) bordering on the sea; nautical. The *Maritime* Provinces depend on the sea for their wealth.

marred \\'märd\\ (*adj*) damaged; disfigured. She had to refinish the *marred* surface of the table. **mar** \\'mär\\ (*v*)

mar-row \\'mar-ₗō\\ (*n*) soft tissue filling the bones. The frigid cold chilled the traveler to the *marrow*.

\\ə\\ **abut** \\ᵊ\\ **kitten, F table** \\ər\\ **further** \\a\\ **ash** \\ā\\ **ace** \\ä\\ **cot, cart**
\\au̇\\ **out** \\ch\\ **chin** \\e\\ **bet** \\ē\\ **easy** \\g\\ **go** \\i\\ **hit** \\ī\\ **ice** \\j\\ **job**

mar-su-pi-al \mär-'sü-pē-əl\ (*n*) one of a family of mammals that nurse their offspring in a pouch. The most common *marsupial* in North America is the opossum; also (*adj*).

mar-tial \'mär-shəl\ (*adj*) warlike. The sound of *martial* music is always inspiring.

mar-ti-net \ˌmärt-ᵊn-'et\ (*n*) strict disciplinarian. The commanding officer was a *martinet* who observed each regulation to the letter.

mas-ti-cate \'mas-tə-ˌkāt\ (*v*) chew. We must *masticate* our food carefully and slowly in order to avoid stomach disorders.

ma-ter-nal \mə-'tərn-ᵊl\ (*adj*) motherly. Many animals display *maternal* instincts only while their offspring are young and helpless.

ma-tri-arch \'mā-trē-ˌärk\ (*n*) woman who rules a family or larger social group. The *matriarch* ruled her gypsy tribe with a firm hand.

ma-tri-cide \'ma-trə-ˌsīd\ (*n*) murder of a mother by a child. A crime such as *matricide* is inconceivable.

ma-trix \'mā-triks\ (*n*) mold or die. The cast around the *matrix* was cracked.

maud-lin \'mȯd-lən\ (*adj*) effusively sentimental. I do not like such *maudlin* pictures. I call them tearjerkers.

maul \'mȯl\ (*v*) handle roughly. The rock star was *mauled* by his overexcited fans.

maun-der \'mȯn-dər\ (*v*) talk incoherently; utter drivel. You do not make sense; you *maunder* and garble your words.

mau-so-le-um \ˌmȯ-sə-'lē-əm\ (*n*) monumental tomb. His body was placed in the family *mausoleum.*

mav-er-ick \'mav-(ə-)rik\ (*n*) rebel; nonconformist. To the masculine literary establishment, George Sand with her insistence on wearing trousers and smoking cigars was clearly a *maverick* who fought her proper womanly role.

\ŋ\ sing \ō\ go \ȯ\ law \ȯi\ boy \th\ thin \th̲\ the \ü\ loot \u̇\ foot
\y\ yet \zh\ vision \à, k̲, ⁿ, œ, œ̄, ᵾe, ᵾē, ʸ\ *see* Pronunciation Symbols

mawk-ish \\'mȯ-kish\\ (*adj*) sickening; insipid. Your *mawk-ish* sighs fill me with disgust.

max-im \\'mak-səm\\ (*n*) proverb; a truth pithily stated. Aesop's fables illustrate moral *maxims*.

may-hem \\'mā-ˌhem\\ (*n*) injury to body. The riot was marked not only by *mayhem* with its attendant loss of life and limb but also by arson and pillage.

mea-ger \\'mē-gər\\ (*adj*) scanty; inadequate. His salary was far too *meager* for him to afford to buy a new car.

me-an-der \\mē-'an-dər\\ (*v*) to wind or turn in its course. It is difficult to sail up this stream because of the way it *meanders* through the countryside; also (*n*).

med-dle-some \\'med-ᵊl-səm\\ (*adj*) interfering. He felt his marriage was suffering because of his *meddlesome* mother-in-law.

me-di-ate \\'mēd-ē-ˌāt\\ (*v*) settle a dispute through the services of an outsider. Let us *mediate* our differences rather than engage in a costly strike. **me-di-ate** \\'mēd-ē-ət\\ (*adj*)

me-di-o-cre \\ˌmēd-ē-'ō-kər\\ (*adj*) ordinary; commonplace. We were disappointed because he gave a rather *mediocre* performance in this role.

med-i-ta-tion \\ˌmed-ə-'tā-shən\\ (*n*) reflection; thought. She reached her decision only after much *meditation*.

med-ley \\'med-lē\\ (*n*) mixture. The band played a *medley* of Gershwin tunes.

meg-a-lo-ma-ni-a \\ˌmeg-ə-lō-'mā-nē-ə\\ (*n*) mania for doing grandiose things. Developers who spend millions trying to build the world's tallest skyscraper suffer from *megalomania*.

mé-lange \\mā-'läⁿzh\\ (*n*) medley; miscellany. This anthology provides a *mélange* of the author's output in the fields of satire, criticism, and political analysis.

me-lee \\'mā-ˌlā\\ (*n*) fight. The captain tried to ascertain the cause of the *melee* that had broken out among the crew members.

\\ə\\ **abut** \\ᵊ\\ **kitten,** F **table** \\ər\\ **further** \\a\\ **ash** \\ā\\ **ace** \\ä\\ **cot, cart**
\\au̇\\ **out** \\ch\\ **chin** \\e\\ **bet** \\ē\\ **easy** \\g\\ **go** \\i\\ **hit** \\ī\\ **ice** \\j\\ **job**

mel-lif-lu-ous \me-'lif-lə-wəs\ (*adj*) flowing smoothly; smooth. Italian is a *mellifluous* language.

me-men-to \mi-'ment-(,)ō\ (*n*) token; reminder. Take this book as a *memento* of your visit.

me-mo-ri-al-ize \mə-'mōr-ē-ə-,līz\ (*v*) commemorate. Let us *memorialize* his great contribution by dedicating this library in his honor.

men-da-cious \men-'dā-shəs\ (*adj*) lying; false. He was a pathological liar, and his friends learned to discount his *mendacious* stories.

men-di-cant \'men-di-kənt\ (*n*) beggar. From the moment we left the ship, we were surrounded by *mendicants* and peddlers; also (*adj*).

me-ni-al \'mē-nē-əl\ (*adj*) suitable for servants; low. I cannot understand why a person of your ability and talent should engage in such *menial* activities; also (*n*).

men-tor \'men-,tȯ(ə)r\ (*n*) teacher, guide. During this very trying period, he could not have had a better *mentor,* for the teacher was sympathetic and understanding.

mer-can-tile \'mər-kən-,tēl\ (*adj*) concerning trade. I am more interested in the opportunities available in the *mercantile* field than I am in those in the legal profession.

mer-ce-nar-y \'mərs-ᵊn-,er-ē\ (*adj*) interested in money or gain. I am certain that your action was prompted by *mercenary* motives; also (*n*).

mer-cu-ri-al \(,)mər-'kyur-ē-əl\ (*adj*) fickle; changing. He was of a *mercurial* temperament and therefore unpredictable.

mer-e-tri-cious \,mer-ə-'trish-əs\ (*adj*) flashy; tawdry. Her jewels were inexpensive but not *meretricious.*

me-sa \'mā-sə\ (*n*) high, flat-topped hill. The *mesa,* rising above the surrounding desert, was the most conspicuous feature of the area.

mes-mer-ize \'mez-mə-,rīz\ (*v*) hypnotize. The incessant drone seemed to *mesmerize* him and place him in a hypnotic trance.

---

met-al-lur-gi-cal \,met-ᵊl-'ər-ji-kəl\ (*adj*) pertaining to the art of removing metals from ores. During the course of his *metallurgical* research, the scientist developed a steel alloy of tremendous strength.

met-a-mor-pho-sis \,met-ə-'mȯr-fə-səs\ (*n*) change of form. The *metamorphosis* of caterpillar to butterfly is typical of many such changes in animal life.

met-a-phor \'met-ə-,fȯ(ə)r\ (*n*) implied comparison. "He soared like an eagle" is an example of a simile; "He is an eagle in flight," a *metaphor*.

met-a-phys-i-cal \,met-ə-'fiz-i-kəl\ (*adj*) pertaining to speculative philosophy. The modern poets have gone back to the fanciful poems of the *metaphysical* poets of the seventeenth century for many of their images. **met-a-phys-ics** \,met-ə-'fiz-iks\ (*n*)

mete \'mēt\ (*v*) measure; distribute. He tried to be impartial in his efforts to *mete* out justice.

me-thod-i-cal \mə-'thäd-i-kəl\ (*adj*) systematic. An accountant must be *methodical* and maintain order among his financial records.

me-tic-u-lous \mə-'tik-yə-ləs\ (*adj*) excessively careful. He was *meticulous* in checking his accounts.

me-trop-o-lis \mə-'träp-(ə-)ləs\ (*n*) large city. Every evening this terminal is filled with the thousands of commuters who are going from this *metropolis* to their homes in the suburbs.

met-tle \'met-ᵊl\ (*n*) courage; spirit. When challenged by the other horses in the race, the thoroughbred proved its *mettle* by its determination to hold the lead.

mi-as-ma \mī-'az-mə\ (*n*) swamp gas; odor of decaying matter. I suspect that this area is infested with malaria as I can readily smell the *miasma*.

mi-cro-cosm \'mī-krə-,käz-əm\ (*n*) small world. In the *microcosm* of our small village, we find illustrations of all the evils that beset the universe.

---

mien \'mēn\ (*n*) demeanor; bearing. She had the gracious *mien* of a queen.

mi-grant \'mī-grənt\ (*adj*) changing its habitat; wandering. These *migrant* birds return every spring; also (*n*).

mi-gra-to-ry \'mī-grə-ˌtōr-ē\ (*adj*) wandering. The return of the *migratory* birds to the northern sections of this country is a harbinger of spring.

mi-lieu \mēl-'yə(r)\ (*n*) environment, means of expression. His *milieu* is watercolor although he has produced excellent oil paintings and lithographs.

mil-i-tant \'mil-ə-tənt\ (*adj*) combative; bellicose. Although at this time he was advocating a policy of neutrality, one could usually find him adopting a more *militant* attitude; also (*n*).

mil-i-tate \'mil-ə-ˌtāt\ (*v*) work against. Your record of lateness and absence will *militate* against your chances of promotion.

mil-len-ni-um \mə-'len-ē-əm\ (*n*) thousand-year period; period of happiness and prosperity. The next *millennium* will be here soon.

mim-ic-ry \'mim-i-krē\ (*n*) imitation. Her gift for *mimicry* was so great that her friends said that she should be in the theater.

min-a-ret \ˌmin-ə-'ret\ (*n*) slender tower attached to a mosque. From the balcony of the *minaret* we obtained an excellent view of the town and the neighboring countryside.

mi-na-to-ry \'min-ə-ˌtōr-ē\ (*adj*) threatening. All abusive and *minatory* letters received by the mayor and other public officials were examined by the police.

minc-ing \'min(t)-siŋ\ (*adj*) affectedly dainty. Yum-Yum walked across the stage with *mincing* steps.

min-ion \'min-yən\ (*n*) a servile dependent. He was always accompanied by several of his *minions* because he enjoyed their subservience and flattery.

\ŋ\ **sing** \ō\ **go** \ȯ\ **law** \ȯi\ **boy** \th\ **thin** \th̲\ **the** \ü\ **loot** \u̇\ **foot** \y\ **yet** \zh\ **vision** \à, k̲, ⁿ, œ, œ̄, ue, ūe, ʸ\ *see* Pronunciation Symbols

mi·nu·ti·ae \mə-'n(y)ü-shē-,ē\ (*n*) petty details. She would have liked to ignore the *minutiae* of daily living.

mi·rage \mə-'räzh\ (*n*) unreal reflection; optical illusion. The lost prospector was fooled by a *mirage* in the desert.

mire \'mī(ə)r\ (*v*) entangle; stick in swampy ground. Their rear wheels became *mired* in mud; also (*n*).

mirth \'mərth\ (*n*) merriment; laughter. Sober Malvolio found Sir Toby's *mirth* improper.

mis·ad·ven·ture \,mis-əd-'ven-chər\ (*n*) mischance; ill luck. The young explorer met death by *misadventure*.

mis·an·thrope \'mis-ᵊn-,thrōp\ (*n*) one who hates mankind. We thought the hermit was a *misanthrope* because he shunned our society.

mis·ap·pre·hen·sion \ₒmis-,ap-ri-'hen-chən\ (*n*) error; misunderstanding. To avoid *misapprehension*, I am going to ask all of you to repeat the instructions I have given.

mis·ce·ge·na·tion \ₒmis-,ej-ə-'nā-shən\ (*n*) intermarriage between races. Some states passed laws against *miscegenation*.

mis·cel·la·ny \'mis-ə-,lā-nē\ (*n*) mixture of writings on various subjects. This is an interesting *miscellany* of nineteenth-century prose.

mis·chance \⁽ᵒ⁾mis(h)-'chan(t)s\ (*n*) ill luck. By *mischance*, he lost his week's salary.

mis·con·cep·tion \,mis-kən-'sep-shən\ (*n*) misinterpretation; misunderstanding. I wrote a detailed explanation of the reasons for my decision so that there would be no *misconceptions* regarding my intent.

mis·con·strue \,mis-kən-'strü\ (*v*) interpret incorrectly; misjudge. She took the passage seriously rather than humorously because she *misconstrued* the author's ironic tone.

mis·cre·ant \'mis-krē-ənt\ (*n*) wretch; villain. His kindness to the *miscreant* amazed all of us who had expected to hear severe punishment pronounced; also (*adj*).

\ə\ **abut** \ᵊ\ **kitten,** F **table** \ər\ **further** \a\ **ash** \ā\ **ace** \ä\ **cot, cart**
\aú\ **out** \ch\ **chin** \e\ **bet** \ē\ **easy** \g\ **go** \i\ **hit** \ī\ **ice** \j\ **job**

mis-de-mean-or \\,mis-di-'mē-nər\\ (*n*) minor crime. The culprit pleaded guilty to a *misdemeanor* rather than face trial for a felony.

mis-giv-ing \\⁽ʰ⁾mis-'giv-iŋ\\ (*n*) doubt about a future event. Hamlet described his *misgivings* to Horatio but decided to fence with Laertes despite his foreboding of evil.

mis-hap \\'mis-,hap\\ (*n*) accident. With a little care you could have avoided this *mishap.*

mis-no-mer \\⁽ʰ⁾mis-'nō-mər\\ (*n*) wrong name; incorrect designation. His tyrannical conduct proved to all that his nickname, King Eric the Just, was a *misnomer.*

mi-sog-a-my \\mə-'sä-ga-mē\\ (*n*) hatred of marriage. He remained a bachelor not because of *misogamy* but because of ill fate; his fiancee died before the wedding.

mi-sog-y-nist \\mə-'säj-ə-nəst\\ (*n*) hater of women. She accused him of being a *misogynist* because he had been a bachelor all his life.

mis-sile \\'mis-əl\\ (*n*) object to be thrown or projected. Scientists are experimenting with guided *missiles;* also (*adj*).

mis-sive \\'mis-iv\\ (*n*) letter. The ambassador received a *missive* from the secretary of state.

mite \\'mīt\\ (*n*) very small object or creature; small coin. The criminal was so heartless that he even stole the widow's *mite.*

mit-i-gate \\'mit-ə-,gāt\\ (*v*) appease. Nothing he did could *mitigate* her wrath; she was unforgiving.

mne-mon-ic \\ni-'män-ik\\ (*adj*) pertaining to memory. He used *mnemonic* tricks to master new words; also (*n*).

mo-bile \\'mō-bəl\\ (*adj*) movable; not fixed. The *mobile* blood bank operated by the Red Cross visited our neighborhood today. **mo-bil-i-ty** \\mō-'bil-ət-ē\\ (*n*)

mode \\'mōd\\ (*n*) prevailing style. She was not used to their lavish *mode* of living.

\\ŋ\\ si**ng** \\ō\\ **go** \\ȯ\\ **law** \\ȯi\\ **boy** \\th\\ **thin** \\t̲h̲\\ **the** \\ü\\ **loot** \\u̇\\ **foot**
\\y\\ **yet** \\zh\\ **vision** \\à, k̲, ⁿ, œ, œ̄, ᵫ, ᵫ̄, ʸ\\ *see* Pronunciation Symbols

mod-i-cum \\'mäd-i-kəm\\ (*n*) limited quantity. Although his story is based on a *modicum* of truth, most of the events he describes are fictitious.

mod-ish \\'mōd-ish\\ (*adj*) fashionable. She always discarded all garments that were no longer *modish*.

mod-u-la-tion \\,mäj-ə-'lā-shən\\ (*n*) toning down; changing from one key to another. When she spoke, it was with quiet *modulation* of voice.

mo-gul \\'mō-₍ᵢ₎gəl\\ (*n*) powerful person. The oil *moguls* made great profits when the price of gasoline rose.

moi-e-ty \\'mȯi-ət-ē\\ (*n*) half; part. There is a *moiety* of the savage in her personality that is not easily perceived by those who do not know her well.

mol-e-cule \\'mäl-i-ˌkyü(ə)l\\ (*n*) the smallest part of a homogeneous substance. In chemistry, we study how atoms and *molecules* react to form new substances.

mol-li-fy \\'mäl-ə-'fī\\ (*v*) soothe. We tried to *mollify* the hysterical child by promising her many gifts.

molt \\'mōlt\\ (*v*) shed or cast off hair or feathers. The male robin *molted* in the spring; also (*n*).

mol-ten \\'mōlt-ᵊn\\ (*adj*) melted. The city of Pompeii was destroyed by volcanic ash rather than by *molten* lava flowing from Mount Vesuvius.

mo-men-tous \\mō-'ment-əs\\ (*adj*) very important. On this *momentous* occasion, we must be very solemn.

mo-men-tum \\mō-'ment-əm\\ (*n*) quantity of motion of a moving body; impetus. The car lost *momentum* as it tried to ascend the steep hill.

mon-ar-chy \\'män-ər-kē\\ (*n*) government under a single ruler. England today remains a *monarchy*.

mo-nas-tic \\mə-'nas-tik\\ (*adj*) related to monks. Wanting to live a religious life, he took his *monastic* vows.

mon-e-tar-y \\'män-ə-ˌter-ē\\ (*adj*) pertaining to money. She was in complete charge of all *monetary* matters affecting the household.

\\ə\\ **abut** \\ᵊ\\ **kitten, F table** \\ər\\ **further** \\a\\ **ash** \\ā\\ **ace** \\ä\\ **cot, cart**
\\au̇\\ **out** \\ch\\ **chin** \\e\\ **bet** \\ē\\ **easy** \\g\\ **go** \\i\\ **hit** \\ī\\ **ice** \\j\\ **job**

mon-o-lith-ic \ˌmän-ᵊl-'ith-ik\ (*adj*) solidly uniform; unyielding. The patriots sought to present a *monolithic* front.

mon-o-the-ism \'män-ə-ₒthē-ˌiz-əm\ (*n*) belief in one God. Abraham was the first to proclaim his belief in *monotheism.*

mo-not-o-ny \mə-'nät-ᵊn-ē\ (*n*) sameness leading to boredom. He took a clerical job, but soon grew to hate the *monotony* of his daily routine.

mon-u-men-tal \ˌmän-yə-'ment-ᵊl\ (*adj*) massive. Writing a dictionary is a *monumental* task.

mood-i-ness \'müd-ē-nəs\ (*n*) fits of depression or gloom. We could not discover the cause of his recurrent *moodiness.*

moor \'mu̇(ə)r\ (*n*) marshy wasteland. These *moors* can only be used for hunting; they are too barren for agriculture; also (*v*).

moot \'müt\ (*adj*) debatable. Our tariff policy is a *moot* subject.

mor-a-to-ri-um \ˌmȯr-ə-'tōr-ē-əm\ (*n*) legal delay of payment. If we declare a *moratorium* and delay collection of debts for six months, I am sure the farmers will be able to meet their bills.

mor-bid \'mȯr-bəd\ (*adj*) given to unwholesome thought; gloomy. These *morbid* speculations are dangerous; we must lighten our thinking by emphasis on more pleasant matters.

mor-dant \'mȯrd-ᵊnt\ (*adj*) biting; sarcastic; stinging. Actors feared the critic's *mordant* pen.

mo-res \'mȯ(ə)r-ˌāz\ (*n*) customs. The *mores* of Mexico are those of Spain with some modifications.

mor-i-bund \'mȯr-ə-ₒbənd\ (*adj*) at the point of death. The doctors called the family to the bedside of the *moribund* patient.

\ŋ\ sing \ō\ go \ȯ\ law \ȯi\ boy \th\ thin \t̲h̲\ the \ü\ loot \u̇\ foot
\y\ yet \zh\ vision \à, k̲, ⁿ, œ, œ̄, ᴜe, ɪ̄e, ʸ\ *see* Pronunciation Symbols

mo-rose \mə-'rōs\ (*adj*) ill-humored; sullen. When we first meet Hamlet, we find him *morose* and depressed.

mor-ti-cian \mȯr-'tish-ən\ (*n*) undertaker. The *mortician* prepared the corpse for burial.

mor-ti-fy \'mȯrt-ə-ˌfī\ (*v*) humiliate; punish the flesh. She was so *mortified* by her blunder that she ran to her room in tears.

mote \'mōt\ (*n*) small speck. The tiniest *mote* in the eye is very painful.

mo-tif \mō-'tēf\ (*n*) theme. This simple *motif* runs throughout the entire score.

mot-ley \'mät-lē\ (*adj*) parti-colored; mixed. The captain had gathered a *motley* crew to sail the vessel.

mot-tled \'mät-ᵊld\ (*adj*) spotted. When he blushed, his face took on a *mottled* hue.

moun-te-bank \'maůnt-i-ˌbaŋk\ (*n*) charlatan; boastful pretender. The patent medicine man was a *mountebank*.

mud-dle \'məd-ᵊl\ (*v*) confuse; mix up. His thoughts were *muddled* and chaotic; also (*n*).

mug-gy \'məg-ē\ (*adj*) warm and damp. August in New York City is often *muggy*.

mulct \'məlkt\ (*v*) defraud a person of something. The lawyer was accused of trying to *mulct* the boy of his legacy; also (*n*).

mul-ti-far-i-ous \ˌməl-tə-'far-ē-əs\ (*adj*) varied; greatly diversified. A career woman and mother, she was constantly busy with the *multifarious* activities of her daily life.

mul-ti-form \'məl-ti-ˌfȯrm\ (*adj*) having many forms. Snowflakes are *multiform* but always hexagonal.

mul-ti-lin-gual \ˌməl-ti-'liŋ-g(yə-)wəl\ (*adj*) having many languages. Because they are bordered by so many countries, the Swiss people are *multilingual*.

mul-ti-plic-i-ty \ˌməl-tə-'plis-ət-ē\ (*n*) state of being numerous. He was appalled by the *multiplicity* of details he had to complete before setting out on his mission.

\ə\ **abut** \ᵊ\ **kitten**, F **table** \ər\ **further** \a\ **ash** \ā\ **ace** \ä\ **cot, cart**
\aů\ **out** \ch\ **chin** \e\ **bet** \ē\ **easy** \g\ **go** \i\ **hit** \ī\ **ice** \j\ **job**

mun-dane \ˌmən-'dān\ (*adj*) worldly as opposed to spiritual. He was concerned only with *mundane* matters, especially the daily stock market quotations.

mu-nif-i-cent \myu̇-'nif-ə-sənt\ (*adj*) very generous. The *munificent* gift was presented to the bride.

murk-i-ness \'mər-kē-nəs\ (*n*) darkness; gloom. The *murkiness* and fog of the waterfront that evening depressed me.

muse \'myüz\ (*v*) ponder. For a moment he *mused* about the beauty of the scene, but his thoughts soon changed as he recalled his own personal problems; also (*n*).

musk-y \'məs-kē\ (*adj*) having the odor of musk. She left a trace of *musky* perfume behind her.

must-y \'məs-tē\ (*adj*) stale; spoiled by age. The attic was dark and *musty*.

mu-ta-ble \'myüt-ə-bəl\ (*adj*) changing in form; fickle. His opinions were *mutable* and easily influenced by anyone who had any powers of persuasion.

mu-ti-late \'myüt-ᵊl-ˌāt\ (*v*) maim. The torturer threatened to *mutilate* his victim.

mu-ti-nous \'myüt-ᵊn-əs\ (*adj*) unruly; rebellious. The captain had to use force to quiet his *mutinous* crew.

my-o-pic \mī-'ō-pik\ (*adj*) nearsighted. In thinking only of your present needs and ignoring the future, you are being rather *myopic*. **my-o-pi-a** \mī-'ō-pē-ə\ (*n*)

myr-i-ad \'mir-ē-əd\ (*n*) very large number. *Myriads* of mosquitoes from the swamps invaded our village every twilight; also (*adj*).

N

na-dir \'nā-,di(ə)r\ (*n*) lowest point. Although few people realized it, the Dow-Jones average had reached its *nadir* and would soon begin an upward surge.

na-iv-e-té \ ₍ᵢ₎nä-,ēv(-ə)-'tā\ (*n*) quality of being unsophisticated. I cannot believe that such *naiveté* is unassumed in a person of her age and experience.

nar-cis-sist \'när-sə-səst\ (*n*) conceited, self-centered person. A *narcissist* is his own best friend. **nar-cis-sism** \'när-sə-siz-əm\ (*n*); **nar-cis-sis-tic** \'när-sə-'sis-tik\ (*adj*)

na-scent \'nas-ᵊnt\ (*adj*) incipient; coming into being. If we could identify these revolutionary movements in their *nascent* state, we would be able to eliminate serious trouble in later years.

na-tal \'nāt-ᵊl\ (*adj*) pertaining to birth. He refused to celebrate his *natal* day because it reminded him of the few years he could look forward to.

nau-se-ate \'nȯ-z(h)ē-,āt\ (*v*) cause to become sick; fill with disgust. The foul smells began to *nauseate* him.

nau-ti-cal \'nȯt-i-kəl\ (*adj*) pertaining to ships or navigation. The Maritime Museum contains many models of clipper ships, logbooks, anchors, and many other items of a *nautical* nature.

nave \'nāv\ (*n*) main body of a church. The *nave* of the cathedral was empty at this hour.

neb-u-lous \'neb-yə-ləs\ (*adj*) cloudy; hazy. Your theories are too *nebulous;* please clarify them.

ne-crol-o-gy \nə-'kräl-ə-jē\ (*n*) obituary notice; list of the dead. The *necrology* of those buried in this cemetery is available in the office.

nec-ro-man-cy \'nek-rə-,man(t)-sē\ (*n*) black magic; dealings with the dead. Because he was able to perform feats of *necromancy,* the natives thought he was in league with the devil.

\ə\ **abut** \ᵊ\ **kitten, F table** \ər\ **further** \a\ **ash** \ā\ **ace** \ä\ **cot, cart**
\au̇\ **out** \ch\ **chin** \e\ **bet** \ē\ **easy** \g\ **go** \i\ **hit** \ī\ **ice** \j\ **job**

ne-far-i-ous \ni-'far-ē-əs\ (*adj*) very wicked. He was universally feared because of his many *nefarious* deeds.

ne-ga-tion \ni-'gā-shən\ (*n*) denial. I must accept his argument since you have been unable to present any *negation* of his evidence.

neg-li-gence \'neg-li-jən(t)s\ (*n*) carelessness. *Negligence* can prove costly near complicated machinery.

nem-e-sis \'nem-ə-səs\ (*n*) revenging agent. Captain Bligh vowed to be Christian's *nemesis*.

ne-o-phyte \'nē-ə-ˌfīt\ (*n*) recent convert; beginner. This mountain slope contains slides that will challenge experts as well as *neophytes*.

nep-o-tism \'nep-ə-ˌtiz-əm\ (*n*) favoritism (to a relative). John left his position with the company because he felt that advancement was based on *nepotism* rather than ability.

net-tle \'net-ᵊl\ (*v*) annoy; vex. Do not let him *nettle* you with his sarcastic remarks.

nex-us \'nek-səs\ (*n*) connection. I fail to see the *nexus* that binds these two widely separated events.

nib \'nib\ (*n*) beak; pen point. The *nibs* of fountain pens often became clotted and corroded.

ni-ce-ty \'nī-sət-ē\ (*n*) precision; minute distinction. I cannot distinguish between such *niceties* of reasoning.

nig-gard-ly \'nig-ərd-lē\ (*adj*) meanly stingy; parsimonious. The *niggardly* pittance the widow receives from the government cannot keep her from poverty.

nig-gle \'nig-əl\ (*v*) spend too much time on minor points; carp. Let's not *niggle* over details. **nig-gling** \'nig-(ə-)liŋ\ (*adj*)

ni-hil-ism \'nī-(h)ə-ˌliz-əm\ (*n*) denial of traditional values; total skepticism. *Nihilism* holds that existence has no meaning.

nir-va-na \ni(ə)r-'vän-ə\ (*n*) in Buddhist teachings, the ideal state in which the individual becomes lost in the

---

\ŋ\ sing \ō\ go \ȯ\ law \ȯi\ boy \th\ thin \<u>th</u>\ the \ü\ loot \u̇\ foot
\y\ yet \zh\ vision \à, <u>k</u>, ⁿ, œ, œ̄, ᴜe, ᴜ̄e, ʸ\ *see* Pronunciation Symbols

attainment of an impersonal beatitude. He tried to explain the concept of *nirvana* to his skeptical students.

noc·tur·nal \näk-'tərn-əl\ (*adj*) done at night. Mr. Jones obtained a watchdog to prevent the *nocturnal* raids on his chicken coops.

noi·some \'nöi-səm\ (*adj*) foul smelling; unwholesome. I never could stand the *noisome* atmosphere surrounding the slaughterhouses.

no·mad·ic \nō-'mad-ik\ (*adj*) wandering. Several *nomadic* tribes of Indians would hunt in this area each year.

no·men·cla·ture \'nō-mən-ˌklā-chər\ (*n*) terminology; system of names. She struggled to master scientific *nomenclature*.

non·age \'nän-ij\ (*n*) immaturity. She was embarrassed by the *nonage* of her contemporaries who never seemed to grow up.

non·cha·lance \ˌnän-shə-'län(t)s\ (*n*) indifference; lack of interest. Few people could understand how he could listen to the news of the tragedy with such *nonchalance;* the majority regarded him as callous and unsympathetic.

non·com·mit·tal \ˌnän-kə-'mit-əl\ (*adj*) neutral; unpledged; undecided. We were annoyed by his *noncommittal* reply for we had been led to expect definite assurances of his approval.

non·en·ti·ty \nä-'nen(t)-ət-ē\ (*n*) nonexistence; person of no importance. Of course you are a *nonentity;* you will continue to be one until you prove your value to the community.

non·plus \'nän-'pləs\ (*v*) bring to a halt by confusion. In my efforts to correct this situation I was *nonplussed* by the stupidity of my assistants; also (*n*).

non se·qui·tur \(ᐟ)nän-'sek-wət-ər\ (*n*) a conclusion that does not follow from the facts stated. Your term paper is full of *non sequiturs;* I cannot see how you reached the conclusions you state.

\ə\ **abut** \ᵊ\ kitten, F table \ər\ **further** \a\ **ash** \ā\ **ace** \ä\ **cot, cart**
\au̇\ **out** \ch\ **chin** \e\ **bet** \ē\ **easy** \g\ **go** \i\ **hit** \ī\ **ice** \j\ **job**

nose-gay \'nōz-,gā\ (*n*) fragrant bouquet. These spring flowers will make an attractive *nosegay*.

nos-tal-gia \nä-'stal-jə\ (*n*) homesickness; longing for the past. The first settlers found so much work to do that they had little time for *nostalgia*.

no-to-ri-ous \nō-'tōr-ē-əs\ (*adj*) outstandingly bad; unfavorably known. Captain Kidd was a *notorious* pirate.

nov-el-ty \'näv-əl-tē\ (*n*) something new; newness. The computer is no longer a *novelty* around the office. **nov-el** \'näv-əl\ (*adj*)

nov-ice \'näv-əs\ (*n*) beginner. Even *novices* can do good work if they follow these simple directions.

nox-ious \'näk-shəs\ (*adj*) harmful. We must trace the source of these *noxious* gases before they asphyxiate us.

nu-ance \'n(y)ü-,än(t)s\ (*n*) shade of difference in meaning or color. The unskilled eye of the layman has difficulty in discerning the *nuances* of color in the paintings.

nu-bile \'n(y)ü-bəl\ (*adj*) marriageable. Mrs. Bennet, in *Pride and Prejudice* by Jane Austen, was worried about finding suitable husbands for her five *nubile* daughters.

nu-ga-to-ry \'n(y)ü-gə-,tōr-ē\ (*adj*) futile; worthless. This agreement is *nugatory* for no court will enforce it.

nu-mis-ma-tist \n(y)ü-'miz-mət-əst\ (*n*) person who collects coins. The *numismatist* had a splendid collection of antique coins.

nup-tial \'nəp-shəl\ (*adj*) related to marriage. Their *nuptial* ceremony was performed in Golden Gate Park.

nur-ture \'nər-chər\ (*v*) bring up; feed; educate. We must *nurture* the young so that they will develop into good citizens; also (*n*).

nu-tri-ent \'n(y)ü-trē-ənt\ (*adj*) providing nourishment. During the convalescent period, the patient must be provided with *nutrient* foods; also (*n*).

O

oaf \'ōf\ (*n*) stupid, awkward person. He called the unfortunate waiter a clumsy *oaf*.

ob-du-rate \'äb-d(y)ə-rət\ (*adj*) stubborn. He was *obdurate* in his refusal to listen to our complaints.

o-bei-sance \ō-'bās-ᵊn(t)s\ (*n*) bow. She made an *obeisance* as the king and queen entered the room.

ob-e-lisk \'äb-ə-ˌlisk\ (*n*) tall column tapering and ending in a pyramid. Cleopatra's Needle is an *obelisk* in Central Park, New York City.

o-bese \ō-'bēs\ (*adj*) fat. It is advisable that *obese* people try to lose weight.

ob-fus-cate \'äb-fə-ˌskāt\ (*v*) confuse; muddle. Do not *obfuscate* the issues by dragging in irrelevant arguments.

o-bit-u-ar-y \ə-'bich-ə-ˌwer-ē\ (*n*) death notice. I first learned of his death when I read the *obituary* in the newspaper.

ob-jec-tive \əb-'jek-tiv\ (*adj*) not influenced by emotions; fair. Even though he was her son, she tried to be *objective* about his behavior.

ob-jec-tive \əb-'jek-tiv\ (*n*) goal; aim. A degree in medicine was her ultimate *objective*.

ob-jur-gate \'äb-jər-ˌgāt\ (*v*) scold; rebuke severely. I am afraid he will *objurgate* us publicly for this offense.

ob-jur-ga-tion \ˌäb-jər-'gā-shən\ (*n*) severe rebuke; scolding. *Objurgations* and even threats of punishment did not deter the young hoodlums.

o-blig-a-to-ry \ə-'blig-ə-ˌtōr-ē\ (*adj*) binding; required. It is *obligatory* that books borrowed from the library be returned within two weeks.

o-blique \ō-'blēk\ (*adj*) slanting; deviating from the perpendicular or from a straight line. The sergeant ordered the men to march "*Oblique* Right"; also (*n*).

o-bliq-ui-ty \ō-'blik-wət-ē\ (*n*) departure from right principles; perversity. His moral decadence was marked by his *obliquity* from the ways of integrity and honesty.

\ə\ **abut** \ᵊ\ **kitten, F table** \ər\ **further** \a\ **ash** \ā\ **ace** \ä\ **cot, cart**
\au̇\ **out** \ch\ **chin** \e\ **bet** \ē\ **easy** \g\ **go** \i\ **hit** \ī\ **ice** \j\ **job**

o-blit-er-ate \ə-'blit-ə-ˌrāt\ (v) destroy completely. The tidal wave *obliterated* several island villages.

o-bliv-i-on \ə-'bliv-ē-ən\ (n) forgetfulness. His works had fallen into a state of *oblivion;* no one bothered to read them.

ob-liv-i-ous \ə-'bliv-ē-əs\ (adj) unaware; forgetful. The distracted teacher was *oblivious* to the activities of the students in the back of the classroom.

ob-lo-quy \'äb-lə-kwē\ (n) slander; disgrace; infamy. I resent the *obloquy* that you are casting upon my reputation.

ob-nox-ious \äb-'näk-shəs\ (adj) offensive. I find your behavior *obnoxious;* please amend your ways.

ob-scure \äb-'skyu̇(ə)r, əb\ (adj) dark; vague; unclear. Even after I read the poem for the fourth time, its meaning was still *obscure.*

ob-scure \äb-'skyü(ə)r, əb\ (v) darken; make unclear. At times he seemed purposely to *obscure* his meaning, preferring mystery to clarity.

ob-se-qui-ous \əb-'sē-kwē-əs\ (adj) slavishly attentive; servile; sycophantic. Nothing is more annoying to me than the *obsequious* demeanor of some people who wait on me.

ob-ses-sion \äb-'sesh-ən\ (n) fixed idea; continued brooding. This *obsession* with the supernatural has made him unpopular with his neighbors.

ob-so-lete \ˌäb-sə-'lēt\ (adj) outmoded. That word is *obsolete;* do not use it.

ob-ste-tri-cian \ˌäb-stə-'trish-ən\ (n) physician specializing in delivery of babies. In modern times, the delivery of children has passed from the midwife to the more scientifically trained *obstetrician.*

ob-strep-er-ous \əb-'strep-(ə-)rəs\ (adj) boisterous; noisy. The crowd became *obstreperous* and shouted their disapproval of the proposals made by the speaker.

\ŋ\ sing \ō\ go \ȯ\ law \ȯi\ boy \th\ thin \t̲h̲\ the \ü\ loot \u̇\ foot
\y\ yet \zh\ vision \à, k̲, ⁿ, œ, œ̄, ᴜe, ᴜ̅e, ʸ\ *see* Pronunciation Symbols

ob-trude \əb-'trüd\ (*v*) push into prominence. The other members of the group object to the manner in which you *obtrude* your opinions into matters of no concern to you.

ob-tru-sive \əb-'trü-siv\ (*adj*) pushing forward. I found him a very *obtrusive* person, constantly seeking the center of the stage.

ob-tuse \äb-'t(y)üs\ (*adj*) blunt; stupid. Because he was so *obtuse,* he could not follow the teacher's reasoning and asked foolish questions.

ob-vi-ate \'äb-vē-ˌāt\ (*v*) make unnecessary; get rid of. I hope this contribution will *obviate* any need for further collections of funds.

oc-cult \ə-'kəlt\ (*adj*) mysterious; secret; supernatural. The *occult* rites of the organization were revealed only to members; also (*n*).

oc-u-list \'äk-yə-ləst\ (*n*) physician who specializes in treatment of the eyes. In many states, an *oculist* is the only one who may apply medicinal drops to the eyes for the purpose of examining them.

o-di-ous \'ōd-ē-əs\ (*adj*) hateful. I find the task of punishing you most *odious.*

o-di-um \'ōd-ē-əm\ (*n*) repugnance; dislike. I cannot express the *odium* I feel at your heinous actions.

o-dor-if-er-ous \ˌōd-ə-'rif-(ə-)rəs\ (*adj*) giving off an odor. The *odoriferous* spices stimulated his jaded appetite.

o-dor-ous \'ōd-ə-rəs\ (*adj*) having an odor. This variety of hybrid tea rose is more *odorous* than the one you have in your garden.

of-fal \'ȯ-fəl\ (*n*) waste; garbage. In America, we discard as *offal* that which could feed families in less fortunate parts of the world.

of-fi-cious \ə-'fish-əs\ (*adj*) meddlesome; excessively trying to please. Browning informs us that the Duke

---

\ə\ abut \ə\ kitten, F table \ər\ further \a\ ash \ā\ ace \ä\ cot, cart
\aȯ\ out \ch\ chin \e\ bet \ē\ easy \g\ go \i\ hit \ī\ ice \j\ job

resented the bough of cherries some *officious* fool brought to the Duchess.

o-gle \'ōg-əl\ (*v*) glance coquettishly at; make eyes at. Sitting for hours at the sidewalk cafe, the old gentleman would *ogle* the young girls and recall his youthful romances; also (*n*).

ol-fac-to-ry \äl-'fak-t(ə-)rē\ (*adj*) concerning the sense of smell. The *olfactory* organ is the nose.

ol-i-gar-chy \'äl-ə-ˌgär-kē\ (*n*) government by a few. The feudal *oligarchy* was supplanted by an autocracy.

om-i-nous \'äm-ə-nəs\ (*adj*) threatening. These clouds are *ominous;* they portend a severe storm.

om-nip-o-tent \äm-'nip-ət-ənt\ (*adj*) all-powerful. The monarch regarded himself as *omnipotent* and responsible to no one for his acts; also (*n*).

om-ni-pres-ent \ˌäm-ni-'prez-ᵊnt\ (*adj*) universally present; ubiquitous. On Christmas Eve, Santa Claus is *omnipresent.*

om-ni-scient \äm-'nish-ənt\ (*adj*) all-knowing. I do not pretend to be *omniscient,* but I am positive about this item.

om-niv-o-rous \äm-'niv-(ə-)rəs\ (*adj*) eating both plant and animal food, devouring everything. Some animals, including man, are *omnivorous* and eat both meat and vegetables; others are either carnivorous or herbivorous.

on-er-ous \'än-ə-rəs\ (*adj*) burdensome. He asked for an assistant because his work load was too *onerous.* **o-nus** \'ō-nəs\ (*n*)

on-o-mat-o-poe-ia \ˌän-ə-ˌmat-ə-'pē-(y)ə\ (*n*) words formed in imitation of natural sounds. Words like "rustle" and "gargle" are illustrations of *onomatopoeia.*

on-slaught \'än-ˌslȯt\ (*n*) vicious assault. We suffered many casualties during the unexpected *onslaught* of the enemy troops.

o-nus \'ō-nəs\ (*n*) burden; responsibility. The emperor was spared the *onus* of signing the surrender papers; instead, he relegated the assignment to his generals.

\ŋ\ sing \ō\ go \ȯ\ law \ȯi\ boy \th\ thin \th̲\ the \ü\ loot \u̇\ foot
\y\ yet \zh\ vision \ə, k̲, ⁿ, œ, œ̄, ᵫ, ᵫ̄, ʸ\ *see* Pronunciation Symbols

o-pal-es-cent \ˌō-pə-'les-ᵊnt\ (*adj*) iridescent. The Ancient Mariner admired the *opalescent* sheen on the water.

o-paque \ō-'pāk\ (*adj*) dark; not transparent. I want something *opaque* placed in this window so that no one will be able to watch me; also (*n*).

o-pi-ate \'ō-pē-ət\ (*n*) sleep producer; deadener of pain. By such *opiates,* he made the people forget their difficulties and accept their unpleasant circumstances; also (*adj*).

op-por-tune \ˌäp-ər-'t(y)ün\ (*adj*) timely; well chosen. You have come at an *opportune* moment for I need a new secretary.

op-por-tun-ist \ˌäp-ər-'t(y)ü-nəst\ (*n*) individual who sacrifices principles for expediency by taking advantage of circumstances. I do not know how he will vote on this question as he is an *opportunist.*

op-pro-bri-ous \ə-'prō-brē-əs\ (*adj*) disgraceful. I find your conduct so *opprobrious* that I must exclude you from classes.

op-pro-bri-um \ə-'prō-brē-əm\ (*n*) infamy; vilification. He refused to defend himself against the slander and *opprobrium* hurled against him by the newspapers; he preferred to rely on his record.

op-ti-cian \äp-'tish-ən\ (*n*) maker and seller of eyeglasses. The patient took the prescription given him by his oculist to the *optician.*

op-ti-mal \'äp-tə-məl\ (*adj*) most favorable. If you wait for the *optimal* moment to act, you may never begin your project. op-ti-mum \äp-tə-məm\ (*n*)

op-ti-mist \'äp-tə-məst\ (*n*) person who looks on the bright side. The pessimist says the glass is half-empty; the *optimist* says it is half-full.

op-tom-e-trist \äp-'täm-ə-trəst\ (*n*) one who fits glasses to remedy visual defects. Although an *optometrist* is qualified to treat many eye disorders, he may not use medicines or surgery in his examinations.

\ə\ abut \ᵊ\ kitten, F table \ər\ further \a\ ash \ā\ ace \ä\ cot, cart
\aů\ out \ch\ chin \e\ bet \ē\ easy \g\ go \i\ hit \ī\ ice \j\ job

op-u-lence \\'äp-yə-lən(t)s\\ (*n*) wealth. Visitors from Europe are amazed at the *opulence* of this country.

o-pus \\'ō-pəs\\ (*n*) work. Although many critics hailed his Fifth Symphony as his major work, he did not regard it as his major *opus.*

or-a-to-ri-o \\,or-ə-'tōr-ē-,ō\\ (*n*) dramatic poem set to music. The Glee Club decided to present an *oratorio* during their recital.

or-di-nance \\'ord-nən(t)s\\ (*n*) decree. Passing a red light is a violation of a city *ordinance.*

o-ri-en-ta-tion \\,ōr-ē-ən-'tā-shən\\ (*n*) act of finding oneself in society. Freshman *orientation* provides the incoming students with an opportunity to learn about their new environment and their place in it.

or-i-fice \\'or-ə-fəs\\ (*n*) mouthlike opening; small opening. The Howe Caverns were discovered when someone observed that a cold wind was issuing from an *orifice* in the hillside.

or-nate \\or-'nāt\\ (*adj*) excessively decorated; highly decorated. Furniture of the Baroque period can be recognized by its *ornate* carvings.

or-ni-thol-o-gist \\,or-nə-'thäl-ə-jəst\\ (*n*) scientific student of birds. Audubon's drawings of American bird life have been of interest not only to the *ornithologists* but also to the general public.

or-ni-thol-o-gy \\,or-nə-'thäl-ə-jē\\ (*n*) study of birds. Audubon's studies of American birds greatly influenced the course of *ornithology* in this country.

or-o-tund \\'or-ə-,tənd\\ (*adj*) having a round, resonant quality; inflated speech. The politician found that his *orotund* voice was an asset when he spoke to his constituents.

or-thog-ra-phy \\or-'thäg-rə-fē\\ (*n*) correct spelling. Many of us find English *orthography* difficult to master because so many of our words are not written phonetically.

\\ŋ\\ si**ng**   \\ō\\ **go**   \\o\\ **law**   \\oi\\ **boy**   \\th\\ **thin**   \\<u>th</u>\\ **the**   \\ü\\ **loot**   \\u\\ **foot**
\\y\\ **yet**   \\zh\\ **vision**   \\à, <u>k</u>, ⁿ, œ, œ̄, ɶ, ɶ̄, ʸ\\ *see* Pronunciation Symbols

os-cil-late \\'äs-ə-ˌlāt\\ (*v*) vibrate pendulumlike; waver. It is interesting to note how public opinion *oscillates* between the extremes of optimism and pessimism.

os-si-fy \\'äs-ə-ˌfī\\ (*v*) change or harden into bone. When he called his opponent a "bonehead," he implied that his adversary's brain had *ossified* and that he was not capable of clear thinking.

os-ten-si-ble \\ä-'sten(t)-sə-bəl\\ (*adj*) apparent; professed; pretended. Although the *ostensible* purpose of this expedition is to discover new lands, we are really interested in finding new markets for our products.

os-ten-ta-tious \\ˌäs-tən-'tā-shəs\\ (*adj*) showy; pretentious. The real hero is never *ostentatious*.

os-tra-cize \\'äs-trə-ˌsīz\\ (*v*) exclude from public favor; ban. As soon as the newspapers carried the story of his connection with the criminals, his friends began to *ostracize* him. **os-tra-cism** \\'äs-trə-ˌsiz-əm\\ (*n*)

oust \\'aust\\ (*v*) expel; drive out. The world wondered if the United States could *oust* Noriega from power.

o-vert \\ō-'vərt\\ (*adj*) open to view. According to the United States Constitution, a person must commit an *overt* act before he may be tried for treason.

o-ver-ween-ing \\ˌō-vər-'wē-niŋ\\ (*adj*) presumptuous; arrogant. His *overweening* pride in his accomplishments was not justified.

o-vine \\'ō-ˌvīn\\ (*adj*) like a sheep. How *ovine* these true-believers were, following their shepherds thoughtlessly.

o-void \\'ō-ˌvoid\\ (*adj*) egg-shaped. At Easter she had to cut out hundreds of brightly colored *ovoid* shapes.

\\ə\\ **abut** \\ə\\ **kitten**, F **table** \\ər\\ **further** \\a\\ **ash** \\ā\\ **ace** \\ä\\ **cot, cart**
\\au̇\\ **out** \\ch\\ **chin** \\e\\ **bet** \\ē\\ **easy** \\g\\ **go** \\i\\ **hit** \\ī\\ **ice** \\j\\ **job**

P

pach-y-derm \\'pak-i-ˌdərm\ (*n*) thick-skinned animal. The elephant is probably the best-known *pachyderm.*

pac-i-fist \\'pas-ə-fəst\ (*n*) one opposed to force; anti-militarist. The *pacifists* urged that we reduce our military budget and recall our troops stationed overseas.

pad-dock \\'pad-ək\ (*n*) saddling enclosure at race track; lot for exercising horses. The *paddock* is located directly in front of the grandstand so that all may see the horses being saddled and the jockeys mounted.

pae-an \\'pē-ən\ (*n*) song of praise or joy. They sang *paeans* for their safe arrival.

pains-tak-ing \\'pān-ˌstā-kiŋ\ (*adj*) showing hard work; taking great care. The new high-frequency word list is the result of *painstaking* efforts on the part of our research staff.

pal-at-able \\'pal-ət-ə-bəl\ (*adj*) agreeable; pleasing to the taste. Paying taxes can never be made *palatable.*

pa-la-tial \pə-'lā-shəl\ (*adj*) magnificent. He proudly showed us through his *palatial* home.

pa-la-ver \pə-'lav-ər\ (*n*) discussion; misleading speech; chatter. In spite of all the *palaver* before the meeting, the delegates were able to conduct serious negotiations when they sat down at the conference table; also (*v*).

pal-ette \\'pal-ət\ (*n*) board on which painter mixes pigments. At the present time, art supply stores are selling a paper *palette* that may be discarded after use.

pal-let \\'pal-ət\ (*n*) small, poor bed. The weary traveler went to sleep on his straw *pallet.*

pal-li-ate \\'pal-ē-ˌāt\ (*v*) ease pain; make less guilty or offensive. Doctors must *palliate* that which they cannot cure.

pal-li-a-tion \ˌpal-ē-'ā- shən\ (*n*) act of making less severe or violent. If we cannot find a cure for this disease at

---

\ŋ\ **sing** \ō\ **go** \ȯ\ **law** \ȯi\ **boy** \th\ **thin** \th\ **the** \ü\ **loot** \u̇\ **foot**
\y\ **yet** \zh\ **vision** \à, k̲, ⁿ, œ, œ̄, ᵫ, ᵫ̄, ʸ\ *see* Pronunciation Symbols

the present time, we can, at least, endeavor to seek its *palliation.*

pal·lid \'pal-əd\ (*adj*) pale; wan. Because his occupation required that he work at night and sleep during the day, he had an exceptionally *pallid* complexion.

pal·pa·ble \'pal-pə-bəl\ (*adj*) tangible; easily perceptible. I cannot understand how you could overlook such a *palpable* blunder. **pal·pa·bly** \'pal-pə-blē\ (*adv*)

pal·pi·tate \'pal-pə-ˌtāt\ (*v*) throb; flutter. As he became excited, his heart began to *palpitate* more and more erratically.

pal·try \'pȯl-trē\ (*adj*) insignificant; petty. This is a *paltry* sum to pay for such a masterpiece.

pan·a·ce·a \ˌpan-ə-'sē-ə\ (*n*) cure-all; remedy for all diseases. There is no easy *panacea* that will solve our complicated international situation.

pan·de·mo·ni·um \ˌpan-də-'mō-nē-əm\ (*n*) wild tumult. When the ships collided in the harbor, *pandemonium* broke out among the passengers.

pan·der \'pan-dər\ (*v*) cater to the low desires of others. Books that *pander* to man's lowest instincts should be banned.

pan·e·gy·ric \ˌpan-ə-'jir-ik\ (*n*) formal praise. The modest hero blushed as he listened to the *panegyrics* uttered by the speakers about his valorous act.

pan·o·ply \'pan-ə-plē\ (*n*) full set of armor. The medieval knight in full *panoply* found his movements limited by the weight of his armor.

pan·o·ra·ma \ˌpan-ə-'ram-ə\ (*n*) comprehensive view; unobstructed view in all directions. Tourists never forget the impact of their first *panorama* of the Grand Canyon.

pan·to·mime \'pant-ə-ˌmīm\ (*n*) acting without dialogue. Because he worked in *pantomime,* the clown could be understood wherever he appeared; also (*v*).

\ə\ abut \ᵊ\ kitten, F table \ər\ further \a\ ash \ā\ ace \ä\ cot, cart
\au̇\ out \ch\ chin \e\ bet \ē\ easy \g\ go \i\ hit \ī\ ice \j\ job

pa-py-rus \pə-'pī-rəs\ (*n*) ancient paper made from stem of papyrus plant. The ancient Egyptians were among the first to write on *papyrus*.

par-a-ble \'par-ə-bəl\ (*n*) short, simple story teaching a moral. Let us apply to our own conduct the lesson that this *parable* teaches.

par-a-digm \'par-ə-ˌdīm\ (*n*) model; example; pattern. Pavlov's experiment in which he trains a dog to salivate on hearing a bell is a *paradigm* of the conditioned-response experiment in behavioral psychology.

par-a-dox \'par-ə-ˌdäks\ (*n*) statement that looks false but is actually correct; a contradictory statement. Wordsworth's "The child is father to the man" is an example of *paradox*. **par-a-dox-i-cal** \ par-ə-'däk-si-kəl\ (*adj*); **par-a-dox-i-cal-ly** \ˌpar-ə-'däk-si-k(ə-)lē\ (*adv*)

par-a-gon \'par-ə-ˌgän\ (*n*) model of perfection. The class disliked him because the teacher was always pointing to him as a *paragon* of virtue.

par-al-lel-ism \'par-ə-ˌlel-ˌiz-əm\ (*n*) state of being parallel; similarity. There is a striking *parallelism* between the two ages.

pa-ram-et-er \pə-'ram-ət-ər\ (*n*) limit; independent variable. We need to define the *parameters* of the problem.

par-a-mour \'par-ə-ˌmù(ə)r\ (*n*) illicit lover. She sought a divorce on the grounds that her husband had a *paramour* in another town.

par-a-noi-a \ˌpar-ə-'nòi-ə\ (*n*) chronic form of insanity marked by delusions of grandeur or persecution. The psychiatrists analyzed his ailment as *paranoia*. **par-a-noid** \'par-ə-ˌnòid\ (*adj or n*)

par-a-pet \'par-ə-pət\ (*n*) low wall at edge of roof or balcony. The best way to attack the soldiers fighting behind the *parapets* on the roof is by bombardment from the air.

par-a-pher-na-lia \ˌpar-ə-fə(r)-'nāl-yə\ (*n*) equipment; odds and ends. His desk was cluttered with paper, pen,

---

ink, a dictionary, and other *paraphernalia* of the writing craft.

par-a-phrase \'par-ə-ˌfrāz\ (*v*) restate a passage in one's own words while retaining thought of author. In 250 words or less, *paraphrase* this article; also (*n*).

par-a-site \'par-ə-ˌsīt\ (*n*) animal or plant living on another; toady; sycophant. The tapeworm is an example of the kind of *parasite* that may infest the human body. par-a-sit-ic \ˌpar-ə-'sit-ik\ (*adj*); par-a-sit-ism \par-ə-sə-ˌtiz-əm\ (*n*); par-a-sit-ize \'par-ə-sə-ˌtīz\ (*v*)

pa-ri-ah \pə-'rī-ə\ (*n*) social outcast. I am not a *pariah* to be shunned and ostracized.

par-i-ty \'par-ət-ē\ (*n*) equality; close resemblance. I find your analogy inaccurate because I do not see the *parity* between the two illustrations.

par-lance \'pär-lən(t)s\ (*n*) language; idiom. All this legal *parlance* confuses me; I need an interpreter.

par-ley \'pär-lē\ (*n*) conference. The peace *parley* has not produced the anticipated truce; also (*v*).

par-o-dy \'par-əd-ē\ (*n*) humorous imitation; travesty. We enjoyed the clever *parodies* of popular songs that the chorus sang; also (*v*).

par-ox-ysm \'par-ək-ˌsiz-əm\ (*n*) fit or attack of pain, laughter, rage. When he heard of his sons' misdeeds, he was seized by a *paroxysm* of rage. par-ox-ys-mal \ˌpar-ək-'siz-məl\ (*adj*)

par-ri-cide \'par-ə-ˌsīd\ (*n*) person who murders his own close relative; murder of a close relative. The jury was shocked by the details of this vicious *parricide* and found the man who had killed his mother guilty of murder in the first degree.

par-ry \'par-ē\ (*v*) ward off a blow. He was content to wage a defensive battle and tried to *parry* his opponent's thrusts.

par-si-mo-ni-ous \ˌpär-sə-'mō-nē-əs\ (*adj*) stingy; excessively frugal. His *parsimonious* nature did not permit

---

\ə\ **abut** \ʼə\ **kitten**, F **table** \ər\ **further** \a\ **ash** \ā\ **ace** \ä\ **cot, cart**
\au̇\ **out** \ch\ **chin** \e\ **bet** \ē\ **easy** \g\ **go** \i\ **hit** \ī\ **ice** \j\ **job**

him to enjoy any luxuries. par-si-mo-ny \'pär-sə-ˌmō-nē\ (*n*); par-si-mo-ni-ous-ly \ˌpär-sə-'mō-nē-əs-lē\ (*adv*)

par-ti-al-i-ty \ˌpär-shē-'al-ət-ē\ (*n*) inclination; bias. As a judge, not only must I be unbiased, but I must also avoid any evidence of *partiality* when I award the prize. par-tial \'pär-shəl\ (*adj*); par-tial-ly \'pärsh-(ə-)lē\ (*adv*)

par-ti-san \'pärt-ə-zən\ (*adj*) one-sided; prejudiced; committed to a party. On certain issues of conscience, she refused to take a *partisan* stand; also (*n*).

par-tu-ri-tion \ˌpärt-ə-'rish-ən\ (*n*) delivery; childbirth. The difficulties anticipated by the obstetricians at *parturition* did not materialize; it was a normal delivery.

par-ve-nu \'pär-və-ˌn(y)ü\ (*n*) upstart; newly rich person. Although extremely wealthy, he was regarded as a *parvenu* by the aristocratic members of society.

pas-sé \pa-'sā\ (*adj*) old-fashioned; past the prime. His style is *passé* and reminiscent of the Victorian era.

pas-sive \'pas-iv\ (*adj*) not active; acted upon. Mahatma Gandhi urged his followers to pursue a program of *passive* resistance as he felt that it was more effective than violence and acts of terrorism; also (*n*). pas-sive-ly \'pas-iv-lē\ (*adv*); pas-siv-i-ty \pa-'siv-ət-ē\ (*n*)

pas-tiche \pas-'tēsh\ (*n*) imitation of another's style in musical composition or in writing. We cannot even say that his music is a *pastiche* of this composer or that; it is, rather, reminiscent of many musicians.

pas-to-ral \'pas-t(ə-)rəl\ (*adj*) rural. In these stories of *pastoral* life, we find an understanding of the daily tasks of country folk.

pa-tent \'pat-ᵊnt\ (*adj*) open for the public to read; obvious. It was *patent* to everyone that the witness spoke the truth; also (*n*).

pa-thet-ic \pa-'thet-ik\ (*adj*) causing sadness, compassion, pity; touching. Everyone in the auditorium was weeping

---

\ŋ\ sing \ō\ go \o\ law \oi\ boy \th\ thin \th\ the \ü\ loot \u\ foot
\y\ yet \zh\ vision \à, k, ⁿ, œ, œ̄, ue, ūe, ʸ\ *see* Pronunciation Symbols

by the time he finished his *pathetic* tale about the orphaned boy. pa-thet-i-cal-ly \pə-'thet-i-k(ə-)lē\ (*adv*)

path-o-log-i-cal \ˌpath-ə-'läj-i-kəl\ (*adj*) pertaining to disease. As we study the *pathological* aspects of this disease, we must not overlook the psychological elements. pa-thol-o-gy \pə-'thäl-ə-jē\ (*n*); pa-thol-o-gist \pə-'thäl-ə-jəst\ (*n*)

pa-thos \'pā-ˌthäs\ (*n*) tender sorrow; pity; quality in art or literature that produces these feelings. The quiet tone of *pathos* that ran through the novel never degenerated into the maudlin or the overly sentimental.

pa-ti-na \pə-'tē-nə\ (*n*) green crust on old bronze works; tone slowly taken by varnished painting. Judging by the *patina* on this bronze statue, we can conclude that this is the work of a medieval artist.

pa-tois \'pa-ˌtwä\ (*n*) local or provincial dialect. His years of study of the language at the university did not enable him to understand the *patois* of the natives.

pa-tri-arch \'pā-trē-ˌärk\ (*n*) father and ruler of a family or tribe. In many primitive tribes, the leader and lawmaker was the *patriarch*. pa-tri-ar-chal \ˌpā-trē-'är-kəl\ (*adj*); pa-tri-arch-ate \'pā-trē-ˌär-kət\ (*n*); pa-tri-ar-chy \'pā-trē-ˌär-kē\ (*n*)

pa-tri-cide \ˌpā-trə-'sīd\ (*n*) person who murders his father; murder of a father. A *patricide* is a type of parricide.

pa-tri-mo-ny \'pa-trə-ˌmō-nē\ (*n*) inheritance from father. As predicted by his critics, he spent his *patrimony* within two years of his father's death. pat-ri-mo-ni-al \ˌpa-trə-'mo-ne-əl\ (*adj*)

pa-tron-ize \'pā-trə-ˌnīz\ (*v*) support; act superior toward. Experts in a field sometimes appear to *patronize* people who are less knowledgeable of the subject.

pau-ci-ty \'pȯ-sət-ē\ (*n*) scarcity. The poor test papers indicate that the members of this class have a *paucity* of intelligence.

\ə\ abut \ᵊ\ kitten, F table \ər\ further \a\ ash \ā\ ace \ä\ cot, cart
\aᵫ\ out \ch\ chin \e\ bet \ē\ easy \g\ go \i\ hit \ī\ ice \j\ job

pec-ca-dil-lo \,pek-ə-'dil-(,)ō\ (*n*) slight offense. If we examine these escapades carefully, we will realize that they are mere *peccadilloes* rather than major crimes.

pe-cu-ni-ar-y \pi-'kyü-nē-,er-ē\ (*adj*) pertaining to money. I never expected a *pecuniary* reward for my work in this activity.

ped-a-gogue \'ped-ə-,gäg\ (*n*) teacher; dull and formal teacher. He could never be a stuffy *pedagogue;* his classes were always lively and filled with humor.

ped-ant \'ped-ᵊnt\ (*n*) scholar who overemphasizes book learning or technicalities. His insistence that the book be memorized marked the teacher as a *pedant* rather than a scholar. **ped-ant-ry** \'ped-ᵊn-trē\ (*n*)

pe-dan-tic \pi-'dant-ik\ (*adj*) showing off learning; bookish. What you say is *pedantic* and reveals an unfamiliarity with the realities of life. **ped-ant** \'ped-ᵊnt\ (*n*)

pe-des-tri-an \pə-'des-trē-ən\ (*adj*) ordinary; unimaginative. Unintentionally boring, he wrote page after page of *pedestrian* prose.

pe-di-a-tri-cian \,pēd-ē-ə-'trish-ən\ (*n*) expert in children's diseases. The family doctor advised the parents to consult a *pediatrician* about their child's ailment. **pe-di-at-rics** \,pēd-ē-'a-triks\ (*n*); **pe-di-at-ric** \,pēd-ē-'a-trik\ (*n*)

pe-jo-ra-tive \pi-'jȯr-ət-iv\ (*adj*) having a deteriorating or depreciating effect on the meaning of a word. His use of *pejorative* language indicated his contempt for his audience.

pell-mell \'pel-'mel\ (*adv*) in confusion; disorderly. The excited students dashed *pell-mell* into the stadium to celebrate the victory.

pel-lu-cid \pe-'lü-səd\ (*adj*) transparent; limpid; easy to understand. After reading these stodgy philosophers, I find his *pellucid* style very enjoyable.

pen-ance \'pen-ən(t)s\ (*n*) self-imposed punishment for sin. The Ancient Mariner said, "I have *penance* done

---

\ŋ\ **sing** \ō\ **go** \ȯ\ **law** \ȯi\ **boy** \th\ **thin** \t͟h\ **the** \ü\ **loot** \u̇\ **foot**
\y\ **yet** \zh\ **vision** \à, k̲, ⁿ, œ, œ̄, ᵫ, ū̃e, ʸ\ *see* Pronunciation Symbols

and *penance* more will do," to atone for the sin of killing the albatross.

pen·chant \'pen-chənt\ (*n*) strong inclination; liking. He had a *penchant* for sculpture.

pen·dant \'pen-dənt\ (*adj*) hanging down from something. Her *pendant* earrings glistened in the light.

pen·dent \'pen-dənt\ (*adj*) suspended; jutting; pending. The *pendent* rock hid the entrance to the cave.

pen·du·lous \'pen-jə-ləs\ (*adj*) hanging; suspended. The *pendulous* chandeliers swayed in the breeze and gave the impression that they were about to fall from the ceiling.

pen·i·tent \'pen-ə-tənt\ (*adj*) repentant. When he realized the enormity of his crime, he became remorseful and *penitent;* also (*n*). pen·i·tence \'pen-ə-ten(t)s\ (*n*); pen·i·ten·tial \,pen-ə-'ten-chəl\ (*adj*)

pen·sive \'pen(t)-siv\ (*adj*) dreamily thoughtful; thoughtful with a hint of sadness. The *pensive* youth gazed at the painting for a long time and then sighed. pen·sive·ly \'pen(t)-siv-lē\ (*adv*)

pen·um·bra \pə-'nəm-brə\ (*n*) partial shadow (in an eclipse). During an eclipse, we can see an area of total darkness and a lighter area that is the *penumbra.*

pe·nu·ri·ous \pə-'n(y)ur-ē-əs\ (*adj*) stingy; parsimonious. He was a *penurious* man, averse to spending money even for the necessities of life.

pen·u·ry \'pen-yə-rē\ (*n*) extreme poverty. We find much *penury* and suffering in this slum area.

pe·on \'pē-,än\ (*n*) unskilled laborer; drudge. He was doomed to be a *peon,* to live a lowly life of drudgery and toil.

per·cus·sion \pər-'kəsh-ən\ (*adj*) striking one object against another sharply. The drum is a *percussion* instrument.

per·di·tion \pər-'dish-ən\ (*n*) damnation; complete ruin. He was damned to eternal *perdition.*

\ə\ **abut** \ə\ **kitten**, F **table** \ər\ **further** \a\ **ash** \ā\ **ace** \ä\ **cot, cart**
\au̇\ **out** \ch\ **chin** \e\ **bet** \ē\ **easy** \g\ **go** \i\ **hit** \ī\ **ice** \j\ **job**

per-e-gri-na-tion \ˌper-ə-grə-'nā-shən\ (*n*) journey. His *peregrinations* in foreign lands did not bring understanding; he mingled only with fellow tourists and did not attempt to communicate with the native population.

pe-remp-to-ry \pə-'rem(p)-t(ə-)rē\ (*adj*) demanding and leaving no choice. I resent your *peremptory* attitude. **pe-remp-to-ri-ly** \pə-'rem(p)-t(ə-)rə-ly\ (*adv*)

pe-ren-ni-al \pə-'ren-ē-əl\ (*n*) something long-lasting. These plants are hardy *perennials* and will bloom for many years; also (*adj*). **pe-ren-ni-al-ly** \pə-'ren-ē-ə-lē\ (*adv*)

per-fid-i-ous \ₐpər-'fid-ē-əs\ (*adj*) basely false. Your *perfidious* gossip is malicious and dangerous. **per-fid-i-ous-ly** \pər-'fid-ē-əs-lē\ (*adv*)

per-fi-dy \'pər-fəd-ē\ (*n*) violation of a trust. When we learned of his *perfidy,* we were shocked and dismayed.

per-force \pər-'fō(ə)rs\ (*adv*) of necessity. I must *perforce* leave, as my train is about to start.

per-func-to-ry \pər-'fəŋ(k)-t(ə-)rē\ (*adj*) superficial; listless; not thorough. He overlooked many weaknesses when he inspected the factory in his *perfunctory* manner. **per-func-to-ri-ly** \pər-'fəŋ(k)-t(ə-)rə-lē\ (*adv*)

pe-rim-e-ter \pə-'rim-ət-ər\ (*n*) outer boundary. To find the *perimeter* of any quadrilateral, we add the four sides.

per-i-pa-tet-ic \ˌper-ə-pə-'tet-ik\ (*adj*) walking about; moving. The *peripatetic* school of philosophy derives its name from the fact that Aristotle walked with his pupils while discussing philosophy with them.

pe-riph-e-ry \pə-'rif-(ə-)rē\ (*n*) edge, especially of a round surface. He sensed that there was something just beyond the *periphery* of his vision. **pe-riph-er-al** \pə-'rif-(ə-)rəl\ (*adj*)

per-ju-ry \pərj-(ə-)rē\ (*n*) false testimony while under oath. When several witnesses appeared to challenge his

---

\ŋ\ **sing**   \ō\ **go**   \o\ **law**   \oi\ **boy**   \th\ **thin**   \t̲h̲\ **the**   \ü\ **loot**   \u̇\ **foot**
\y\ **yet**   \zh\ **vision**   \à, k̲, ⁿ, œ, œ̄, ue, ūe, ʸ\ *see* Pronunciation Symbols

story, he was indicted for *perjury.* per-jure \'pər-jər\ (*v*); per-jur-er \'pər-jər-ər\ (*n*)

per-me-a-ble \'pər-mē-ə-bəl\ (*adj*) porous; allowing passage through. Glass is *permeable* to light. per-me-a-bil-i-ty \,pər-mē-ə-'bil-ət-ē\ (*n*)

per-me-ate \'pər-mē-,āt\ (*v*) pass through, spread. The odor of frying onions *permeated* the air. per-me-a-tion \,pər-mē-'ā-shən\ (*n*)

per-ni-cious \pər-'nish-əs\ (*adj*) very destructive. He argued that these books had a *pernicious* effect on young and susceptible minds. per-ni-cious-ly \pər-'nish-əs-lē\ (*adv*)

per-or-a-tion \'per-ər-,ā-shən\ (*n*) conclusion of an oration. The *peroration* was largely hortatory and brought the audience to its feet clamoring for action at its close.

per-pe-trate \'pər-pə-,trāt\ (*v*) commit an offense. Only an insane person could *perpetrate* such a horrible crime. per-pe-tra-tion \,pər-pə-'trā-shən\ (*n*); per-pe-tra-tor \'pər-pə-,trāt-ər\ (*n*)

per-pet-u-al \pər-'pech-(ə-)wəl\ (*adj*) everlasting. Ponce de Leon hoped to find *perpetual* youth. per-pet-u-al-ly \pər-'pech-(ə-)wəl-lē\ (*adv*)

per-qui-site \'pər-kwə-zət\ (*n*) any gain above stipulated salary. The *perquisites* attached to this job make it even more attractive than the salary indicates.

per-se-vere \,pər-sə-'vi(ə)r\ (*v*) to persist in an attempt to accomplish a goal, despite difficulty. He was able to surpass his humble origins because he *persevered* in every project he attempted.

per-si-flage \'pər-si-,fläzh\ (*n*) flippant conversation; banter. This *persiflage* is not appropriate when we have such serious problems to discuss.

per-sist \pər-'sist\ (*v*) to continue; endure. You will receive poor grades if you *persist* in your poor study habits.

\ə\ abut \ə\ kitten, F table \ər\ further \a\ ash \ā\ ace \ä\ cot, cart
\aů\ out \ch\ chin \e\ bet \ē\ easy \g\ go \i\ hit \ī\ ice \j\ job

per-son-a-ble \'pərs-nə-bəl\ (*adj*) attractive. The man I am seeking to fill this position must be *personable* since he will be representing us before the public.

per-spi-ca-cious \,pər-spə-'kā-shəs\ (*adj*) having insight; penetrating; astute. We admired his *perspicacious* wisdom and sagacity. per-spi-cac-i-ty \,pər-spə-'kas-ət-ē\ (*n*)

per-spi-cu-i-ty \,pər-spə-'kyü-ət-ē\ (*n*) clearness of expression; freedom from ambiguity. One of the outstanding features of this book is the *perspicuity* of its author; his meaning is always clear.

per-spic-u-ous \pər-'spik-yə-wəs\ (*adj*) plainly expressed. His *perspicuous* comments eliminated all possibility of misinterpretation.

pert \'pərt\ (*adj*) impertinent; forward. I think your *pert* and impudent remarks call for an apology.

per-ti-na-cious \,pərt-ᵊn-'ā-shəs\ (*adj*) stubborn; persistent. He is bound to succeed because his *pertinacious* nature will not permit him to quit. per-ti-nac-i-ty \,pərt-ᵊn-'as-ət-ē\ (*n*)

per-ti-nent \'pərt-ᵊn-ənt\ (*adj*) suitable; to the point. The lawyer wanted to know all the *pertinent* details. per-ti-nence \'pərt-ᵊn-ən(t)s\ (*n*)

per-turb \pər-'tərb\ (*v*) disturb greatly. I am afraid this news will *perturb* him. per-tur-ba-tion \,pərt-ər-'bā-shən\ (*n*)

pe-rus-al \pə-'rü-zəl\ (*n*) reading. I am certain that you have missed important details in your rapid *perusal* of this document. pe-ruse \pə-'rüz\ (*v*)

per-va-sive \pər-'vā-siv\ (*adj*) spread throughout; permeating. The *pervasive* odor of mothballs clung to the clothes and did not fade away until they had been thoroughly aired. per-vade \pər-'vād\ (*adj*)

per-verse \(ᵢ)pər-'vərs\ (*adj*) stubborn; intractable. Because of your *perverse* attitude, I must rate you as

---

\ŋ\ **sing** \ō\ **go** \ò\ **law** \òi\ **boy** \th\ **thin** \t̲h̲\ **the** \ü\ **loot** \ù\ **foot**
\y\ **yet** \zh\ **vision** \à, k̲, ⁿ, œ, œ̄, ᵫ, ᵫ̄, ʸ\ *see* Pronunciation Symbols

deficient in cooperation. per-verse-ly \pər-'vərs-lē\
(*adv*); per-verse-ness \pər-'vərs-nəs\ (*n*)

per-ver-sion \pər-'vər-zhən\ (*n*) corruption; turning from
right to wrong. Inasmuch as he had no motive for his
crimes, we could not understand his *perversion.*

per-ver-si-ty \pər-'vər-sət-ē\ (*n*) stubborn maintenance of
a wrong cause. I cannot forgive your *perversity* in
repeating such an impossible story.

pes-si-mism \'pəs-ə-,miz-əm\ (*n*) belief that life is basically bad or evil; gloominess. The good news we have
been receiving lately indicates that there is little reason
for your *pessimism.* pes-si-mist \'pəs-ə-məst\ (*n*);
pes-si-mis-tic \,pes-ə-'mis-tik\ (*adj*)

pes-ti-len-tial \,pes-tə-'len-chəl\ (*adj*) causing plague;
baneful. People were afraid to explore the *pestilential*
swamp. pes-ti-lence \'pes-tə-lən(t)s\ (*n*); pes-ti-len-tial-ly
\,pes-tə-'lench-(ə-)lē\ (*adv*)

pet-ri-fy \'pe-trə-,fī\ (*v*) turn to stone. His sudden and unexpected appearance seemed to *petrify* her. pet-ri-fac-
tion \,pe-trə-'fak-shən\ (*n*)

pet-u-lant \'pech-ə-lənt\ (*adj*) touchy; peevish. The feverish patient was *petulant* and restless. pet-u-lance \'pech-
ə-lən(t)s\ (*n*); pet-u-lant-ly \'pech-ə-lənt-lē\ (*adv*)

phi-al \'fī(-ə)l\ (*n*) small bottle. Even though it is small,
this *phial* of perfume is expensive.

phi-lan-der \fə-'lan-dər\ (*v*) make love lightly, flirt. Do
not *philander* or trifle with my affections because love
is too serious. phi-lan-der-er \fə-'lan-dər-ər\ (*n*)

phi-lan-thro-pist \fə-'lan(t)-thrə-pəst\ (*n*) lover of
mankind; doer of good. As he grew older, he became
famous as a *philanthropist* and benefactor of the needy.
phi-lan-thro-py \fə-'lan(t)-thrə-pē\ (*n*); phil-an-throp-ic
\,fil-ən-'thräp-ik\ (*adj*)

phi-lis-tine \'fil-ə-,stēn\ (*n*) narrow-minded person, uncul-
tured and exclusively interested in material gain. We

\ə\ **abut** \ᵊ\ **kitten,** F **table** \ər\ **further** \a\ **ash** \ā\ **ace** \ä\ **cot, cart**
\aú\ **out** \ch\ **chin** \e\ **bet** \ē\ **easy** \g\ **go** \i\ **hit** \ī\ **ice** \j\ **job**

need more men of culture and enlightenment; we have too many *philistines* among us; also (*adj*).

phi-lol-o-gy \fə-'läl-ə-jē\ (*n*) study of language. The professor of *philology* advocated the use of Esperanto as an international language. **phil-o-log-i-cal** \,fil-ə-'läj-i-kəl\ (*adj*); **phi-lol-o-gist** \fə-'läl-ə-jəst\ (*n*)

phleg-mat-ic \fleg-'mat-ik\ (*adj*) calm; not easily disturbed. The nurse was a cheerful but *phlegmatic* person.

pho-bi-a \'fō-bē-ə\ (*n*) morbid fear. His fear of flying was more than mere nervousness; it was a real *phobia*.

phys-i-og-no-my \,fiz-ē-'ä(g)-nə-mē\ (*n*) face. He prided himself on his ability to analyze a person's character by studying his *physiognomy*.

phys-i-o-log-i-cal \,fiz-ē-ə-'läj-i-kəl\ (*adj*) pertaining to the science of the function of living organisms. To understand this disease fully, we must examine not only its *physiological* aspects but also its psychological elements. **phys-i-ol-o-gist** \,fiz-ē-'äl-ə-jəst\ (*n*); **phys-i-ol-o-gy** \,fiz-ē-'äl-ə-jē\ (*n*)

pi-ca-resque \,pik-ə-'resk\ (*adj*) pertaining to rogues in literature. *Tom Jones* has been hailed as one of the best *picaresque* novels in the English language.

pie-bald \'pī-,bȯld\ (*adj*) mottled; spotted. You should be able to identify this horse easily as it is the only *piebald* horse in the race; also (*n*).

pied \'pīd\ (*adj*) variegated; multicolored. The *Pied* Piper of Hamelin got his name from the multicolored clothing he wore.

pil-lage \'pil-ij\ (*v*) plunder. The enemy *pillaged* the quiet village and left it in ruins; also (*n*).

pil-lo-ry \'pil-(ə-)rē\ (*v*) punish by placing in a wooden frame and subjecting to ridicule. Even though he was mocked and *pilloried,* he maintained that he was correct in his beliefs; also (*n*).

---

pin·ion \\'pin-yən\\ (*v*) restrain. They *pinioned* his arms against his body but left his legs free so that he could move about; also (*n*).

pin·na·cle \\'pin-i-kəl\\ (*n*) peak. We could see the morning sunlight illuminate the *pinnacle* while the rest of the mountain lay in shadow.

pi·ous \\'pī-əs\\ (*adj*) devout. The *pious* parents gave their children a religious upbringing. pi·ous·ly \\'pī-əs-lē\\ (*adv*)

pi·quant \\'pē-kənt\\ (*adj*) pleasantly tart-tasting; stimulating. The *piquant* sauce added to our enjoyment of the meal. pi·quan·cy \\'pē-kən-sē\\ (*n*)

pique \\'pēk\\ (*n*) irritation; resentment. She showed her *pique* by her refusal to appear with the other contestants at the end of the contest; also (*v*).

pith·y \\'pith-ē\\ (*adj*) concise; meaty. I enjoy reading his essays because they are always compact and *pithy.*

pit·tance \\'pit-ᵊn(t)s\\ (*n*) a small allowance or wage. He could not live on the *pittance* he received as a pension and had to look for an additional source of revenue.

pla·cate \\'plāk-ˌāt\\ (*v*) pacify; conciliate. The teacher tried to *placate* the angry mother. pla·ca·ble \\'plak-ə-bəl\\ (*adj*)

plac·id \\'plas-əd\\ (*adj*) peaceful; calm. After his vacation in this *placid* section, he felt soothed and rested. pla·cid·i·ty \\ pla-'sid-ət-ē\\ (*n*); plac·id·ly \\'plas-əd-lē\\ (*adv*)

pla·gia·rism \\'plā-jə-ˌriz-əm\\ (*n*) theft of another's ideas or writings passed on as original. The editor recognized the *plagiarism* and rebuked the culprit who had presented the manuscript as original. pla·gia·rize \\'plā-jə-ˌrīz\\ (*v*); pla·gia·rist \\'plā-jə-ˌrəst\\ (*n*)

plain·tive \\'plānt-iv\\ (*adj*) mournful. The dove has a *plaintive* and melancholy call. plain·tive·ly \\'plānt-iv-lē\\ (*adv*)

\\ə\\ **abut** \\ᵊ\\ **kitten,** F **table** \\ər\\ **further** \\a\\ **ash** \\ā\\ **ace** \\ä\\ **cot, cart**
\\au̇\\ **out** \\ch\\ **chin** \\e\\ **bet** \\ē\\ **easy** \\g\\ **go** \\i\\ **hit** \\ī\\ **ice** \\j\\ **job**

plat-i-tude \\'plat-ə-,t(y)üd\\ (*n*) trite remark; commonplace statement. The *platitudes* in his speech were applauded by the vast majority in his audience; only a few people perceived how trite his remarks were. **plat-i-tu-di-nous** \\,plat-ə-'t(y)üd-nəs\\ (*adj*)

pla-ton-ic \\plə-'tän-ik\\ (*adj*) purely spiritual; theoretical; without sensual desire. Although a member of the political group, he took only a *platonic* interest in its ideals and goals.

plau-di-to-ry \\'plȯ-də-,tȯr-ē\\ (*adj*) approving; applauding. The theatrical company reprinted the *plauditory* comments of the critics in its advertisement.

plau-si-ble \\'plȯ-zə-bəl\\ (*adj*) having a show of truth but open to doubt; specious. Even though your argument is *plausible,* I still would like to have more proof. **plau-si-bil-i-ty** \\,plȯ-zə-'bil-ət-ē\\ (*n*); **plau-si-bly** \\'plȯ-zə-blē\\ (*adv*)

ple-be-ian \\pli-'bē-(y)ən\\ (*adj*) common; pertaining to the common people. His speeches were aimed at the *plebeian* minds and emotions; they disgusted the more refined.

pleb-i-scite \\'pleb-ə-,sīt\\ (*n*) expression of the will of a people by direct election. I think this matter is so important that it should be decided not by a handful of legislators but by a *plebiscite* of the entire nation.

ple-na-ry \\'plē-nə-rē\\ (*adj*) complete; full. The union leader was given *plenary* power to negotiate a new contract with the employers.

plen-i-po-ten-tia-ry \\,plen-ə-pə-'tench-(ə-)rē\\ (*adj*) fully empowered. Since he was not given *plenipotentiary* powers by his government, he could not commit his country without consulting his superiors; also (*n*).

plen-i-tude \\'plen-ə-,t(y)üd\\ (*n*) abundance; completeness. Looking in the pantry, we admired the *plenitude* of fruits and pickles we had preserved during the summer.

pleth-o-ra \\'pleth-ə-rə\\ (*n*) excess; overabundance. She offered a *plethora* of reasons for her shortcomings.

plumb \\'pləm\\ (*adj*) checking perpendicularity; vertical. Before hanging wallpaper it is advisable to drop a *plumb* line from the ceiling as a guide; also (*n*, *v*).

po-di-a-trist \\pə-'dī-ə-trəst\\ (*n*) doctor who treats ailments of the feet. He consulted a *podiatrist* about his fallen arches. po-di-a-try \\pə-'dī-ə-trē\\ (*n*)

po-di-um \\'pōd-ē-əm\\ (*n*) pedestal; raised platform. The audience applauded as the conductor made his way to the *podium.*

poi-gnant \\'poi-nyənt\\ (*adj*) keen; piercing; severe. Her *poignant* grief left her pale and weak. poi-gnan-cy \\'poi-nyən-sē\\ (*n*)

po-lem-ic \\pə-'lem-ik\\ (*n*) controversy; argument in support of a point of view. His essays were, for the main part, *polemics* in support of the party's policy; also (*adj*). po-lem-i-cist \\pə-'lem-ə-səst\\ (*n*)

pol-i-tic \\'päl-ə-ˌtik\\ (*adj*) expedient; prudent; well devised. Even though he was disappointed, he did not think it *politic* to refuse this offer.

pol-i-ty \\'päl-ət-ē\\ (*n*) form of government of nation or state. Our *polity* should be devoted to the concept that the government should strive for the good of all citizens.

po-lyg-a-mist \\pə-'lig-ə-məst\\ (*n*) one who has more than one spouse at a time. He was arrested as a *polygamist* when his two wives filed complaints about him. po-lyg-a-my \\pə-'lig-ə-mē\\ (*n*); po-lyg-a-mous \\pə-'lig-ə-məs\\ (*adj*)

pol-y-glot \\'päl-i-ˌglät\\ (*adj*) speaking several languages. New York City is a *polyglot* community because of the thousands of immigrants who settle there; also (*n*).

pon-der-ous \\'pän-d(ə-)rəs\\ (*adj*) weighty; unwieldy. His humor lacked the light touch; his jokes were always *ponderous.*

\\ə\\ abut \\ᵊ\\ kitten, F table \\ər\\ further \\a\\ ash \\ā\\ ace \\ä\\ cot, cart
\\aü\\ out \\ch\\ chin \\e\\ bet \\ē\\ easy \\g\\ go \\i\\ hit \\ī\\ ice \\j\\ job

por-tend \pȯr-'tend\ (*v*) foretell; presage. The king did not know what these omens might *portend* and asked his soothsayers to interpret them.

por-tent \'pȯ(ə)r-ˌtent\ (*n*) sign; omen; forewarning. He regarded the black cloud as a *portent* of evil.

por-ten-tous \pȯr-'tent-əs\ (*adj*) ominous; serious. I regard our present difficulties and dissatisfactions as *portentous* omens of future disaster.

port-ly \'pȯrt-lē\ (*adj*) stately; stout. The overweight gentleman was shown a size 44 *portly* suit.

pos-ter-i-ty \pä-'ster-ət-ē\ (*n*) descendants; future generations. We hope to leave a better world to *posterity.*

post-hu-mous \'päs-chə-məs\ (*adj*) after death (as of child born after father's death or book published after author's death). The critics ignored his works during his lifetime; it was only after the *posthumous* publication of his last novel that they recognized his great talent.

pos-tu-late \'päs-chə-lət\ (*n*) self-evident truth. We must accept these statements as *postulates* before pursuing our discussions any further; also (*v*).

po-ta-ble \'pȯt-ə-bəl\ (*adj*) suitable for drinking. The recent drought in the Middle Atlantic states has emphasized the need for extensive research in ways of making seawater *potable;* also (*n*).

po-tent \'pōt-ᵊnt\ (adj) powerful; persuasive; greatly influential. The jury was swayed by the highly *potent* testimony of the crime's sole eyewitness. po-ten-cy \'pōt-ᵊn-sē\ (*n*)

po-ten-tate \'pōt-ᵊn-ˌtāt\ (*n*) monarch; sovereign. The *potentate* spent more time at Monte Carlo than he did at home with his people.

po-ten-tial \pə-'ten-chəl\ (*adj*) expressing possibility; latent. This juvenile delinquent is a *potential* murderer; also (*n*). po-ten-ti-al-i-ty \pə-ˌten-chē-'al-ət-ē\ (*n*); po-ten-tial-ly \pə-'tench-(ə-)lē\ (*adv*)

\ŋ\ sing \ō\ go \ȯ\ law \ȯi\ boy \th\ thin \th\ the \ü\ loot \u̇\ foot
\y\ yet \zh\ vision \à, k̲, ⁿ, œ, œ̄, ue, ūe, ʸ\ *see* Pronunciation Symbols

po·tion \\'pō-shən\ (*n*) dose (of liquid). Tristan and Isolde drink a love *potion* in the first act of the opera.

pot·pour·ri \\,pō-pu̇-'rē\ (*n*) heterogeneous mixture; medley. He offered a *potpourri* of folk songs from many lands.

poul·tice \\'pōl-təs\ (*n*) soothing application applied to sore and inflamed portions of the body. He was advised to apply a flaxseed *poultice* to the inflammation; also (*v*).

prac·ti·ca·ble \\'prak-ti-kə-bəl\ (*adj*) feasible. The board of directors decided that the plan was *practicable* and agreed to undertake the project. **prac·ti·ca·bil·i·ty** \\,prak-ti-kə-'bil-ət-ē\ (*n*)

prac·ti·cal \\'prak-ti-kəl\ (*adj*) based on experience; useful. He was a *practical* man, opposed to theory. **prac·ti·cal·i·ty** \\,prak-ti-'kal-ət-ē\ (*n*); **prac·ti·cal·ly** \\'prak-ti-k(ə-)lē\ (*adv*)

prag·mat·ic \\prag-'mat-ik\ (*adj*) practical; concerned with practical values. This test should provide us with a *pragmatic* analysis of the value of this course.

prag·ma·tist \\'prag-mət-əst\ (*n*) practical person. No *pragmatist* enjoys becoming involved in a game he can never win.

prate \\'prāt\ (*v*) speak foolishly; boast idly. Let us not *prate* about our qualities; rather, let our virtues speak for themselves.

prat·tle \\'prat-ᵊl\ (*v*) babble. The little girl *prattled* endlessly about her dolls; also (*n*).

pre·am·ble \\'prē-,am-bəl\ (*n*) introductory statement. In the *Preamble* to the Constitution, the purpose of the document is set forth.

pre·car·i·ous \\pri-'kar-ē-əs\ (*adj*) uncertain; risky. I think this stock is a *precarious* investment and advise against its purchase. **pre·car·i·ous·ly** \\pri-'kar-ē-əs-lē\ (*adv*); **pre·car·i·ous·ness** \\pri-'kar-ē-əs-nəs\ (*n*)

prec·e·dent \\'pres-əd-ənt\ (*n*) something preceding in time that may be used as an authority or guide for future

---

\ə\ abut \ᵊ\ kitten, F table \ər\ further \a\ ash \ā\ ace \ä\ cot, cart
\au̇\ out \ch\ chin \e\ bet \ē\ easy \g\ go \i\ hit \ī\ ice \j\ job

action. This decision sets a *precedent* for future cases of a similar nature.

pre-ce-dent \pri-'sēd-ᵊnt\ (*adj*) preceding in time, rank, etc. Our discussions, *precedent* to this event, certainly did not give you any reason to believe that we would adopt your proposal.

pre-cept \'prē-₁sept\ (*n*) practical rule guiding conduct. "Love thy neighbor as thyself" is a worthwhile *precept*.

prec-i-pice \'pres-(ə-)pəs\ (*n*) cliff; dangerous position. Suddenly Indiana Jones found himself dangling from the edge of a *precipice*.

pre-cip-i-tate \pri-'sip-ət-ət\ (*adj*) headlong; rash. Do not be *precipitate* in this matter; investigate further. **pre-cip-i-tate-ly** \pri-'sip-ət-ət-lē\ (*adv*); **pre-cip-i-tate-ness** \pri-'sip-ət-ət-nəss\ (*n*)

pre-cip-i-tate \pri-'sip-ə-₁tāt\ (*v*) throw headlong; hasten. We must be patient as we cannot *precipitate* these results.

pre-cip-i-tous \pri-'sip-ət-əs\ (*adj*) steep. This hill is difficult to climb because it is so *precipitous*. **pre-cip-i-tous-ly** \pri-'sip-ət-əs-lē\ (*adv*)

pre-clude \pri-'klüd\ (*v*) make impossible; eliminate. This contract does not *preclude* my being employed by others at the same time that I am working for you.

pre-co-cious \pri-'kō-shəs\ (*adj*) developed ahead of time. By his rather adult manner of discussing serious topics, the child demonstrated that he was *precocious*. **pre-co-cious-ly** \pri-'kō-shəs-lē\ (*adv*); **pre-coc-i-ty** \pri-'käs-ət-ē\ (*n*)

pre-cur-sor \pri-'kər-sər\ (*n*) forerunner. Gray and Burns were *precursors* of the Romantic Movement in English literature.

pred-a-to-ry \'pred-ə-₁tōr-ē\ (*adj*) plundering. The hawk is a *predatory* bird. **pred-a-tor** \'pred-ət-ər\ (*n*)

\ŋ\ si**ng** \ō\ g**o** \o'\ l**aw** \oi\ b**oy** \th\ **th**in \t̲h̲\ **the** \ü\ l**oo**t \u'\ f**oo**t
\y\ **y**et \zh\ vi**sion** \à, k̲, ⁿ, œ, œ̄, ue, ūe, ʸ\ *see* Pronunciation Symbols

pre-di-lec-tion \ˌpred-ᵊl-'ek-shən\ (*n*) partiality; preference. Although the artist used various media from time to time, he had a *predilection* for watercolor.

pre-em-i-nent \prē-'em-ə-nənt\ (*adj*) outstanding; superior. The king traveled to Boston because he wanted the *preeminent* surgeon in the field to perform the operation. **pre-em-i-nence** \prē-'em-ə-nən(t)s\ (*n*); **pre-em-i-nent-ly** \prē-'em-ə-nənt-lē\ (*adv*)

pre-empt \prē-'em(p)t\ (*v*) appropriate beforehand. Your attempt to *preempt* this land before it is offered to the public must be resisted. **pre-emp-tion** \pre-'em(p)-shən\ (*n*)

pref-a-to-ry \'pref-e-ˌtōr-ē\ (*adj*) introductory. The chairman made a few *prefatory* remarks before he called on the first speaker.

pre-hen-sile \prē-'hen(t)-səl\ (*adj*) capable of grasping or holding. Monkeys use not only their arms and legs but also their *prehensile* tails in traveling through the trees.

pre-lude \'prel-ˌ(y)üd\ (*n*) introduction; forerunner. I am afraid that this border raid is the *prelude* to more serious attacks.

pre-med-i-tate \pri-'med-ə-tāt\ (*v*) plan in advance. She had *premeditated* the murder for months, reading about common poisons and buying weed killer that contained arsenic.

pre-mo-ni-tion \ˌprē-mə-'nish-ən\ (*n*) forewarning. We ignored these *premonitions* of disaster because they appeared to be based on childish fears.

pre-mon-i-to-ry \pri-'män-ə-ˌtōr-ē\ (*adj*) serving to warn. You should have visited a doctor as soon as you felt these *premonitory* chest pains.

pre-pon-der-ance \pri-'pän-d(ə-)rən(t)s\ (*n*) superiority of power, quantity, etc. The rebels sought to overcome the *preponderance* of strength of the government forces by engaging in guerrilla tactics. **pre-pon-der-ant** \pri-'pän-

---

\ə\ **abut** \ᵊ\ **kitten**, F **table** \ər\ **further** \a\ **ash** \ā\ **ace** \ä\ **cot, cart** \aù\ **out** \ch\ **chin** \e\ **bet** \ē\ **easy** \g\ **go** \i\ **hit** \ī\ **ice** \j\ **job**

d(ə-)rənt\ (*adj*); pre-pon-der-ant-ly \pri-'pän-d(ə-)rənt-lē\ (*adv*)

pre-pon-der-ate \pri-'pän-də-ˌrāt\ (*v*) be superior in power; outweigh. I feel confident that the forces of justice will *preponderate* eventually in this dispute.

pre-pos-ter-ous \pri-'päs-t(ə-)rəs\ (*adj*) absurd; ridiculous. The excuse he gave for his lateness was so *preposterous* that everyone laughed.

pre-rog-a-tive \pri-'räg-ət-iv\ (*n*) privilege; unquestionable right. The president cannot levy taxes; that is the *prerogative* of the legislative branch of government.

pres-age \'pres-ij\ (*v*) foretell. The vultures flying overhead *presaged* the discovery of the corpse in the desert.

pre-sen-ti-ment \pri-'zent-ə-mənt\ (*n*) premonition; foreboding. Hamlet felt a *presentiment* about his meeting with Laertes.

pres-tige \pre-'stēzh\ (*n*) impression produced by achievements or reputation. The wealthy man sought to obtain social *prestige* by contributing to popular charities. **pres-ti-gious** \pre-'stij-əs\ (*adj*)

pre-sump-tion \pri-'zəm(p)-shən\ (*n*) arrogance; effrontery. She had the *presumption* to disregard our advice. **pre-sump-tive** \pri-'zəm(p)-tiv\ (*adj*)

pre-ten-tious \pri-'ten-chəs\ (*adj*) ostentatious; ambitious. I do not feel that your limited resources will permit you to carry out such a *pretentious* program. **pre-ten-tious-ly** \pri-'ten-chəs-lē\ (*adv*); **pre-ten-tious-ness** \pri-'ten-chəs-nəs\ (*n*)

pre-ter-nat-u-ral \ˌprēt-ər-'nach(-ə)-rəl\ (*adj*) beyond that which is normal in nature. John's mother's total ability to tell when he was lying struck him as almost *preternatural*.

pre-text \'prē-ˌtekst\ (*n*) excuse. He looked for a good *pretext* to get out of paying a visit to his aunt.

pre-vail \pri-'vā(e)l\ (*v*) induce; triumph over. He tried to *prevail* on her to type his essay for him.

prev-a-lent \'prev(-ə)-lənt\ (*adj*) widespread; generally accepted. A radical committed to social change, Reed had no patience with the conservative views *prevalent* in the America of his day.

pre-var-i-cate \pri-'var-ə-ˌkāt\ (*v*) lie. Some people believe that to *prevaricate* in a good cause is justifiable and regard the statement as a "white lie." pre-var-i-ca-tion \pri-ˌvar-ə-'kā-shən\ (*n*); pre-var-i-ca-tor \pri-'var-ə-ˌkāt-ər\ (*n*)

prim \'prim\ (*adj*) very precise and formal; exceedingly proper. Many people commented on the contrast between the *prim* attire of the young lady and the inappropriate clothing worn by her escort. prim-ly \'prim-lē\ (*adv*); prim-ness \'prim-nəs\ (*n*)

pri-mo-gen-i-ture \ˌprī-mō-'jen-ə-ˌchù(ə)r\ (*n*) seniority by birth. By virtue of *primogeniture,* the first-born child has many privileges denied his brothers and sisters.

pri-mor-di-al \prī-'mȯrd-ē-əl\ (*adj*) existing at the beginning (of time); rudimentary. The Neanderthal Man is one of our *primordial* ancestors.

primp \'primp\ (*v*) dress or groom oneself with care. She *primps* for hours before a dance.

pris-tine \'pris-ˌtēn\ (*adj*) characteristic of earlier times; primitive; unspoiled. This area has been preserved in all its *pristine* wildness.

pri-va-tion \prī-'vā-shən\ (*n*) hardship; want. In his youth, he knew hunger and *privation.*

privy \'priv-ē\ (*adj*) secret; hidden; not public. We do not care for *privy* chamber government. priv-i-ly \'priv-ə-lē\ (*adv*)

probe \'prōb\ (*v*) explore with tools. The surgeon *probed* the wound for foreign matter before suturing it; also (*n*).

pro-bi-ty \'prō-bət-ē\ (*n*) uprightness; incorruptibility. Everyone took his *probity* for granted; his defalcations, therefore, shocked us all.

\ə\ abut \ᵊ\ kitten, F table \ər\ **further** \a\ **ash** \ā\ **ace** \ä\ **cot, cart**
\aú\ **out** \ch\ **chin** \e\ bet \ē\ **easy** \g\ go \i\ **hit** \ī\ **ice** \j\ **job**

prob-lem-at-ic \,präb-lə-'mat-ik\ (*adj*) perplexing; unsettled; questionable. Given the many areas of conflict still awaiting resolution, the outcome of the peace talks remains *problematic.*

pro-bos-cis \prə-'bäs-əs\ (*n*) long snout; nose. The elephant uses its *proboscis* to handle things and carry them from place to place.

pro-cliv-i-ty \prō-'kliv-ət-ē\ (*n*) inclination; natural tendency. He has a *proclivity* to grumble.

pro-cras-ti-nate \p(r)ə-'kras-tə-ˌnāt\ (*v*) postpone; delay. It is wise not to *procrastinate;* otherwise, we find ourselves bogged down in a mass of work that should have been finished long ago. **pro-cras-ti-na-tion** \p(r)ə-ˌkras-tə-'nā-shən\ (*n*); **pro-cras-ti-na-tor** \p(r)ə-'kras-tə-ˌnāt-ər\ (*n*)

prod \'präd\ (*v*) poke; stir up; urge. If you *prod* him hard enough, he'll eventually clean his room.

prod-i-gal \'präd-i-gəl\ (*adj*) wasteful; reckless with money. The *prodigal* son squandered his inheritance; also (*n*). **prod-i-gal-i-ty** \ˌpräd-ə-'gal-ət-ē\ (*n*)

pro-di-gious \prə-'dij-əs\ (*adj*) marvelous; enormous. He marveled at her *prodigious* appetite. **pro-di-gious-ly** \prə-'dij-əs-lē\ (*adv*)

prod-i-gy \'präd-ə-jē\ (*n*) marvel; highly gifted child. Menuhin was a *prodigy,* performing wonders on his violin when he was barely eight years old.

pro-fane \prō-'fān\ (*v*) violate; desecrate. Tourists are urged not to *profane* the sanctity of holy places by wearing improper garb; also (*adj*). **prof-a-na-tion** \ˌpräf-ə-'nā-shən\ (*n*)

prof-li-gate \'präf-li-gət\ (*adj*) dissipated; wasteful; licentious. In this *profligate* company, he lost all sense of decency; also (*n*). **prof-li-ga-cy** \'präf-li-gə-sē\ (*n*); **prof-li-gate-ly** \'präf-li-gət-lē\ (*adv*)

pro-fu-sion \prə-'fyü-zhən\ (*n*) lavish expenditure; overabundant condition. Seldom have I seen food and drink served in such *profusion*. pro-fuse \prə-'fyüs\ (*adj*); pro-fuse-ly \prə-'fyüs-lē\ (*adv*)

pro-gen-i-tor \prō-'jen-ət-ər\ (*n*) ancestor. We must not forget the teachings of our *progenitors* in our desire to appear modern.

prog-e-ny \'präj-(ə-)nē\ (*n*) children; offspring. He was proud of his *progeny* but regarded George as the most promising of all his children.

prog-no-sis \präg-'nō-səs\ (*n*) forecasted course of a disease; prediction. If the doctor's *prognosis* is correct, the patient will be in a coma for at least twenty-four hours.

prog-nos-ti-cate \präg-'näs-tə-ˌkāt\ (*v*) predict. I *prognosticate* disaster unless we change our wasteful ways. prog-nos-ti-ca-tion \ˌ(ˌ)präg-ˌnäs-tə-'kā-shən\ (*n*); prog-nos-ti-ca-tor \präg-'näs-tə-ˌkāt-ər\ (*n*)

pro-jec-tile \prə-'jek-tᵊl\ (*n*) missile. Man has always hurled *projectiles* at his enemy, whether in the form of stones or of highly explosive shells.

pro-le-tar-i-an \ˌprō-lə-'ter-ē-ən\ (*n*) member of the working class. The aristocrats feared mob rule and gave the right to vote only to the wealthy, thus depriving the *proletarians* of a voice in government; also (*adj*).

pro-lif-ic \prə-'lif-ik\ (*adj*) abundantly fruitful. He was a *prolific* writer and wrote as many as three books a year. pro-lif-i-cal-ly \prə-'lif-i-k(ə-)lē\ (*adv*)

pro-lix \prō-'liks\ (*adj*) verbose; drawn out. His *prolix* arguments irritated the jury. pro-lix-i-ty \prō-'lik-sət-ē\ (*n*)

pro-mis-cu-ous \prə-'mis-kyə-wəs\ (*adj*) mixed indiscriminately; haphazard; irregular. In the opera *La Bohème,* we get a picture of the *promiscuous* life led by the young artists of Paris. pro-mis-cu-it-y \ˌpräm-əs-'kyü-ət-ē\ (*n*); pro-mis-cu-ous-ly \prə-'mis-kyə-wəs-lē\ (*adv*); pro-mis-cu-ous-ness \prä-'mis-kyə-wəs-nəs\ (*n*)

prom-on-to-ry \'präm-ən-ˌtōr-ē\ (*n*) headland. They erected a lighthouse on the *promontory* to warn approaching ships of their nearness to the shore.

\ə\ abut \ᵊ\ kitten, F table \ər\ **further** \a\ **ash** \ā\ **ace** \ä\ **cot, cart** \au̇\ **out** \ch\ **chin** \e\ **bet** \ē\ **easy** \g\ **go** \i\ **hit** \ī\ **ice** \j\ **job**

pro-mote \prə-'mōt\ (*v*) further; encourage. The company launched a major new advertising campaign in order to *promote* its sales.

pro-mul-gate \'präm-əl-ˌgāt\ (*v*) make known by official proclamation or publication. As soon as the Civil Service Commission *promulgates* the names of the successful candidates, we shall begin to hire members of our staff. **pro-mul-ga-tion** \ˌpräm-əl-'gā-shən\ (*n*)

prone \'prōn\ (*adj*) inclined to; prostrate. She was *prone* to sudden fits of anger.

prop-a-gate \'präp-ə-ˌgāt\ (*v*) multiply; spread. I am sure disease must *propagate* in such unsanitary and crowded areas. **prop-a-ga-tion** \ˌpräp-ə-'gā-shən\ (*n*)

pro-pel-lants \prə-'pel-ənts\ (*n*) substances that propel or drive forward. The development of our missile program has forced our scientists to seek more powerful *propellants*.

pro-pen-si-ty \prə-'pen(t)-sət-ē\ (*n*) natural inclination. I dislike your *propensity* to belittle every contribution he makes to our organization.

pro-phy-lac-tic \ˌprō-fə-'lak-tik\ (*adj*) used to prevent disease. Despite all *prophylactic* measures introduced by the authorities, the epidemic raged until cool weather set in; also (*n*).

pro-pin-qui-ty \pra-'piŋ-kwət-ē\ (*n*) nearness; kinship. Their relationship could not be explained as being based on mere *propinquity;* they were more than relatives; they were true friends.

pro-pi-ti-ate \prō-'pish-ē-ˌāt\ (*v*) appease. The natives offered sacrifices to *propitiate* the gods. **pro-pi-ti-a-tion** \prō-ˌpis(h)-ē-'ā-shən\ (*n*); **pro-pi-ti-a-to-ry** \prō-'pish-(ē-)ə-ˌtōr-ē\ (*adj*)

pro-pi-tious \prə-'pish-əs\ (*adj*) favorable; kindly. I think it is advisable that we wait for a more *propitious* occasion to announce our plans.

---

pro-pound \prə-'paúnd\ (*v*) put forth for analysis. In your discussion, you have *propounded* several questions; let us consider each one separately.

pro-pri-ety \p(r)ə-'pri-ət-ē\ (*n*) fitness; correct conduct. I want you to behave at this dinner with *propriety;* don't embarrass me.

pro-pul-sive \prə-'pel-siv\ (*adj*) driving forward. The jet plane has a greater *propulsive* power than the engine-driven plane. pro-pul-sion \prə-'pel-shən\ (*n*)

pro-sa-ic \prō-'zā-ik\ (*adj*) commonplace; dull. I do not like this author because he is so unimaginative and *prosaic.*

pro-scribe \prō-'skrīb\ (*v*) ostracize; banish; outlaw. Antony, Octavius, and Lepidus *proscribed* all those who had conspired against Julius Caesar. pro-scrip-tion \prō-'skrip-shən\ (*n*)

pros-e-ly-tize \'präs-(ə-)lə-ˌtīz\ (*v*) convert to a religion or belief. In these interfaith meetings, there must be no attempt to *proselytize;* we must respect all points of view.

pros-o-dy \'präs-əd-ē\ (*n*) the art of versification. This book on *prosody* contains a rhyming dictionary as well as samples of the various verse forms.

pros-trate \'präs-ˌtrāt\ (*v*) stretch out full on ground. He *prostrated* himself before the idol; also (*adj*). pros-tra-tion \prä-'strā-shən\ (*n*)

pro-té-gé \'prōt-ə-ˌzhā\ (*n*) person under the protection and support of a patron. Cyrano de Bergerac refused to be a *protégé* of Cardinal Richelieu. pro-té-gée \'prōt-ə-ˌzhā\ (*n*)

pro-to-col \'prōt-ə-ˌkol\ (*n*) diplomatic etiquette. We must run this state dinner according to *protocol* if we are to avoid offending any of our guests.

pro-to-type \'prōt-ə-ˌtīp\ (*n*) original work used as a model by others. The crude typewriter on display in this museum is the *prototype* of the elaborate machines in use today.

\ə\ **abut** \ˀə\ **kitten, F table** \ər\ f**urther** \a\ **ash** \ā\ **ace** \ä\ **cot, cart**
\aú\ **out** \ch\ **chin** \e\ **bet** \ē\ **easy** \g\ **go** \i\ **hit** \ī\ **ice** \j\ **job**

pro-tract \prō-'trakt\ (*v*) prolong. Do not *protract* this phone conversation as I expect an important business call within the next few minutes.

pro-trude \prō-'trüd\ (*v*) stick out. His fingers *protruded* from the holes in his gloves. pro-tru-sion \prō-'trü-zhən\ (*n*); pro-tru-sive \prō-'trü-siv\ (*adj*)

prov-e-nance \'präv(-ə)-nən(t)s\ (*n*) origin or source of something. I am not interested in its *provenance;* I am more concerned with its usefulness than with its source.

prov-en-der \'präv-ən-dər\ (*n*) dry food; fodder. I am not afraid of a severe winter because I have stored a large quantity of *provender* for the cattle.

prov-i-dent \'präv-əd-ənt\ (*adj*) displaying foresight; thrifty; preparing for emergencies. In his usual *provident* manner, he had insured himself against this type of loss. prov-i-dent-ly \'präv-əd-ənt-lē\ (*adv*)

pro-vin-cial \pra-'vin-chəl\ (*adj*) pertaining to a province; limited. We have to overcome their *provincial* attitude and get them to become more cognizant of world problems. pro-vin-cial-ism \prə-'vin-chəl-ˌiz-əm\ (*n*)

pro-vi-so \prə-'vī-ˌ(ı)zo\ (*n*) stipulation. I am ready to accept your proposal with the *proviso* that you meet your obligations within the next two weeks.

prov-o-ca-tion \ˌpräv-ə-'kā-shən\ (*n*) cause for anger or retaliation. In order to prevent a sudden outbreak of hostilities, we must give our foe no *provocation*. pro-voc-a-tive \prə-'väk-ət-iv\ (*n*)

prox-im-i-ty \präk-'sim-ət-ē\ (*n*) nearness. The deer sensed the hunter's *proximity* and bounded away.

prox-y \'präk-sē\ (*n*) authorized agent. Please act as my *proxy* and vote for this slate of candidates; also (*adj*).

pru-dent \'prüd-ənt\ (*adj*) cautious; careful. A miser hoards money not because he is *prudent* but because he is greedy. pru-dence \'prüd-ən(t)s\ (*n*)

prune \\'prün\\ (*v*) cut away; trim. With the help of her editor, she was able to *prune* her manuscript into publishable form.

pru-ri-ent \\'prùr-ē-ənt\\ (*adj*) based on lascivious thoughts. The police attempted to close the theater where the *prurient* film was being presented. **pru-ri-ence** \\'prùr-ē-ən(t)s\\ (*n*)

pseud-o-nym \\'süd-ᵊn-,im\\ (*n*) pen name. Samuel Clemens's *pseudonym* was Mark Twain. **pseud-on-y-mous** \\sü-'dän-ə-məs\\ (*adj*)

psy-che \\'sī-kē\\ (*n*) soul; mind. It is difficult to delve into the *psyche* of a human being.

psy-chi-a-trist \\sə-'kī-ə-trəst\\ (*n*) a doctor who treats mental diseases. A *psychiatrist* often needs long conferences with his patient before a diagnosis can be made. **psy-chi-a-try** \\sə-'kī-ə-trē\\ (*n*); **psy-chi-at-ric** \\,sī-kē-'a-trik\\ (*adj*)

psy-cho-path-ic \\,sī-kə-'path-ik\\ (*adj*) pertaining to mental derangement. The *psychopathic* patient suffers more frequently from a disorder of the nervous system than from a diseased brain. **psy-cho-path** \\'sī-kə-,path\\ (*n*)

psy-cho-sis \\sī-'kō-səs\\ (*n*) mental disorder. We must endeavor to find an outlet for the patient's repressed desires if we hope to combat this *psychosis*.

pu-er-ile \\'pyù(-ə)r-al\\ (*adj*) childish. His *puerile* pranks sometimes offended his serious-minded friends. **pu-er-il-i-ty** \\,pyù(-ə)r-'il-ət-ē\\ (*n*)

pu-gi-list \\'pyü-jə-ləst\\ (*n*) boxer. The famous *pugilist* Cassius Clay changed his name to Muhammed Ali.

pug-na-cious \\,pəg-'nā-shəs\\ (*adj*) combative; disposed to fight. As a child he was *pugnacious* and fought with everyone. **pug-nac-i-ty** \\,pəg-'nas-ət-ē\\ (*n*)

puis-sant \\'pwis-ᵊnt\\ (*adj*) powerful; strong; potent. We must keep his friendship for he will make a *puissant* ally. **puis-sance** \\'pwis-ᵊn(t)s\\ (*n*)

\\ə\\ **abut** \\ᵊ\\ **kitten**, F **table** \\ər\\ **further** \\a\\ **ash** \\ā\\ **ace** \\ä\\ **cot, cart**
\\aù\\ **out** \\ch\\ **chin** \\e\\ **bet** \\ē\\ **easy** \\g\\ **go** \\i\\ **hit** \\ī\\ **ice** \\j\\ **job**

pul-chri-tude \\'pəl-krə-ˌt(y)üd\ (*n*) beauty; comeliness. I do not envy the judges who have to select this year's Miss America from this collection of female *pulchritude.* pul-chri-tu-di-nous \ˌpəl-krə-'t(y)üd-nəs\ (*adj*)

pul-mo-nar-y \\'pùl-mə-ˌner-ē\ (*adj*) pertaining to the lungs. In his research on *pulmonary* diseases, he discovered many facts about the lungs of animals and human beings.

pul-sate \\'pəl-ˌsāt\ (*v*) throb. We could see the blood vessels in his temple *pulsate* as he became more angry. pul-sa-tion \ˌpəl-'sā-shən\ (*n*)

pum-mel \\'pəm-əl\ (*v*) beat. The severity with which he was *pummeled* was indicated by the bruises he displayed on his head and face.

punc-til-i-ous \ˌpəŋ(k)-'til-ē-əs\ (*adj*) laying stress on niceties of conduct, form; precise. We must be *punctilious* in our planning of this affair, for any error may be regarded as a personal affront.

pun-dit \\'pən-dət\ (*n*) learned Hindu; any learned man; authority on a subject. Even though he discourses on the matter like a *pundit,* he is actually rather ignorant about this topic.

pun-gent \\'pən-jənt\ (*adj*) stinging; caustic. The *pungent* aroma of the smoke made me cough. pun-gen-cy \\'pən-jən-sē\ (*n*); pun-gent-ly \pən-jənt-lē\ (*adv*)

pu-ni-tive \\'pyü-nət-iv\ (*adj*) punishing. He asked for *punitive* measures against the offender.

pu-ny \\'pyü-nē\ (*adj*) insignificant; tiny; weak. Our *puny* efforts to stop the flood were futile.

pur-ga-to-ry \\'pər-gə-ˌtōr-ē\ (*n*) place of spiritual expiation. In this *purgatory,* he could expect no help from his comrades. pur-ga-tor-i-al \ˌpər-gə-'tōr-ē-əl\ (*adj*)

purge \\'pərj\ (*v*) clean by removing impurities; to clear of charges. If you are to be *purged* of the charge of contempt of Congress, you must be willing to answer the questions previously asked; also (*n*).

\ŋ\ sing \ō\ go \ò\ law \òi\ boy \th\ thin \t͟h\ the \ü\ loot \ù\ foot
\y\ yet \zh\ vision \à, k̲, ⁿ, œ, œ̄, ue, ūe, ʸ\ *see* Pronunciation Symbols

pur-loin \\(ₗ)pər-'lȯin\ (*v*) steal. In the story, "The *Purloined* Letter," Poe points out that the best hiding place is often the most obvious place.

pur-port \'pər-ˌpō(ə)rt\ (*n*) intention; meaning. If the *purport* of your speech was to arouse the rabble, you succeeded admirably; also (*v*).

pur-vey-or \\(ₗ)pər-'vā-ər\ (*n*) furnisher of foodstuffs; caterer. As *purveyor* of rare wines and viands, he traveled through France and Italy every year in search of new products to sell. pur-vey \\(ₗ)pər-'vā\ (*v*); pur-vey-ance \\(ₗ)pər-'vā-ən(t)s\ (*n*)

pur-view \'pər-ˌvyü\ (*n*) scope. The sociological implications of these inventions are beyond the *purview* of this book.

pu-sil-lan-i-mous \ˌpyü-sə-'lan-ə-məs\ (*adj*) cowardly; fainthearted. You should be ashamed of your *pusillanimous* conduct during this dispute. pu-sil-la-nim-i-ty \ˌpyü-sə-lə-'nim-ət-ē\ (*n*)

pu-ta-tive \'pyüt-ət-iv\ (*adj*) supposed; reputed. Although there are some doubts, the *putative* author of this work is Massinger.

pu-trid \'pyü-trəd\ (*adj*) foul; rotten; decayed. The gangrenous condition of the wound was indicated by the *putrid* smell when the bandages were removed. pu-trid-i-ty \pyü-'trid-ət-ē\ (*n*)

py-ro-ma-ni-ac \ˌpī-rō-'mā-nē-ˌak\ (*n*) person with an irresistible desire to set things on fire. The detectives searched the area for the *pyromaniac* who had set these costly fires. py-ro-ma-ni-a \ˌpī-rō-'mā-nē-ə\ (*n*)

\ə\ **abut** \ᵊ\ **kitten, F table** \ər\ **further** \a\ **ash** \ā\ **ace** \ä\ **cot, cart**
\au̇\ **out** \ch\ **chin** \e\ **bet** \ē\ **easy** \g\ **go** \i\ **hit** \ī\ **ice** \j\ **job**

Q

quack \\'kwak\\ (*n*) charlatan; imposter. Do not be misled by the exorbitant claims of this *quack;* also (*adj*).

quad-ru-ped \\'kwäd-ˌrə-ped\\ (*n*) four-footed animal. Most mammals are *quadrupeds.*

quaff \\'kwäf\\ (*v*) drink with relish. As we *quaffed* our ale, we listened to the gay songs of the students in the tavern; also (*n*).

quag-mire \\'kwag-ˌmī(ə)r\\ (*n*) bog; marsh. Our soldiers who served in Vietnam will never forget the drudgery of marching through the *quagmires* of the delta country.

quail \\'kwā(ə)l\\ (*v*) cower; lose heart. He was afraid that he would *quail* in the face of danger.

qual-i-fied \\'kwäl-ə-ˌfīd\\ (*adj*) limited; restricted. Unable to give the candidate full support, the mayor gave him only a *qualified* endorsement. (secondary meaning) qual-i-fy \\'kwäl-ə-ˌfī\\ (*v*)

qualm \\'kwäm\\ (*n*) misgiving. His *qualms* of conscience had become so great that he decided to abandon his plans.

quan-da-ry \\'kwän-d(ə-)rē\\ (*n*) dilemma. When the two colleges to which he had applied accepted him, he was in a *quandary* as to which one he should attend.

quar-an-tine \\'kwȯr-ən-ˌtēn\\ (*n*) isolation of person or ship to prevent spread of infection. We will have to place this house under *quarantine* until we determine the exact nature of the disease; also (*v*).

quar-ry \\'kwȯr-ē\\ (*n*) victim; object of a hunt. The police closed in on their *quarry.*

quar-ry \\'kwȯr-ē\\ (*v*) dig into. They *quarried* blocks of marble out of the hillside; also (*n*).

quay \\kē\\ (*n*) dock; landing place. Because of the captain's carelessness, the ship crashed into the *quay.*

quea-sy \\'kwē-zē\\ (*adj*) easily nauseated; squeamish. As the ship left the harbor, he became *queasy* and thought that he was going to suffer from seasickness.

---

quell \'kwel\ (*v*) put down; quiet. The police used fire hoses and tear gas to *quell* the rioters.

quer-u-lous \'kwer-(y)ə-ləs\ (*adj*) fretful; whining. His classmates were repelled by his *querulous* and complaining statements.

queue \'kyü\ (*n*) line. They stood patiently in the *queue* outside the movie theater.

quib-ble \'kwib-əl\ (*v*) equivocate; play on words. Do not *quibble; I* want a straightforward and definite answer; also (*n*).

qui-es-cent \kwī-'es-ənt\ (*adj*) at rest; dormant. After this geyser erupts, it will remain *quiescent* for twenty-four hours.

qui-e-tude \'kwī-ə-ˌt(y)üd\ (*n*) tranquillity. He was impressed by the air of *quietude* and peace that pervaded the valley.

quin-tes-sence \kwin-'tes-ən(t)s\ (*n*) purest and highest embodiment. These books display the *quintessence* of wit.

quip \'kwip\ (*n*) taunting remark. You are unpopular because you are too free with your *quips* and sarcastic comments; also (*v*).

quirk \'kwərk\ (*n*) startling twist; caprice. By a *quirk* of fate, he found himself working for the man whom he had discharged years before.

quix-ot-ic \kwik-'sät-ik\ (*adj*) idealistic but impractical. He is constantly presenting these *quixotic* schemes.

quiz-zi-cal \'kwiz-i-kəl\ (*adj*) bantering; comical; humorously serious. Will Rogers's *quizzical* remarks endeared him to his audiences.

quo-rum \'kwōr-əm\ (*n*) number of members necessary to conduct a meeting. The senator asked for a roll call to determine whether a *quorum* was present.

\ə\ **abut** \ᵊ\ **kitten, F table** \ər\ **further** \a\ **ash** \ā\ **ace** \ä\ **cot, cart**
\aù\ **out** \ch\ **chin** \e\ **bet** \ē\ **easy** \g\ **go** \i\ **hit** \ī\ **ice** \j\ **job**

R

ra-bid \\'rab-əd\\ (*adj*) like a fanatic; furious. He was a *rabid* follower of the Dodgers and watched them play whenever he could go to the ball park.

ra-con-teur \\,rak-,än-'tər\\ (*n*) storyteller. My father was a gifted *raconteur* with an unlimited supply of anecdotes.

rail \\'rā(ə)l\\ (*v*) scold; rant. You may *rail* at him all you want; you will never change him.

rai-ment \\'rā-mənt\\ (*n*) clothing. "How can I go to the ball?" asked Cinderella. "I have no *raiment* to wear."

rak-ish \\'rā-kish\\ (*adj*) stylish; sporty. He wore his hat at a *rakish* and jaunty angle.

ram-i-fi-ca-tion \\,ram-ə-fə-'kā-shən\\ (*n*) branching out; subdivision. We must examine all the *ramifications* of this problem.

ram-i-fy \\'ram-ə-,fī\\ (*v*) divide into branches or subdivisions. When the plant begins to *ramify,* it is advisable to nip off most of the new branches.

ramp \\'ramp\\ (*n*) slope; inclined plane. The house was built with *ramps* instead of stairs in order to enable the man in the wheelchair to move easily from room to room and floor to floor.

ram-pant \\'ram-pənt\\ (*adj*) rearing up on hind legs; unrestrained. The *rampant* weeds in the garden killed all the flowers that had been planted in the spring.

ram-part \\'ram-,pärt\\ (*n*) defensive mound of earth. From the *ramparts* we watched the fighting continue.

ran-cid \\'ran(t)-səd\\ (*adj*) having the odor of stale fat. A *rancid* odor filled the ship's galley.

ran-cor \\'raŋ-kər\\ (*n*) bitterness; hatred. Let us forget our *rancor* and cooperate in this new endeavor.

ran-kle \\'raŋ-kəl\\ (*v*) irritate; fester. The memory of having been jilted *rankled* him for years.

rant \\'rant\\ (*v*) rave; speak bombastically. As we heard him *rant* on the platform, we could not understand his strange popularity with many people; also (*n*).

\\ŋ\\ sing \\ō\\ go \\ȯ\\ law \\ȯi\\ boy \\th\\ thin \\<u>th</u>\\ the \\ü\\ loot \\u̇\\ foot
\\y\\ yet \\zh\\ vision \\à, <u>k</u>, ⁿ, œ, œ̄, ᵫ, ᵫ̄, ʸ\\ *see* Pronunciation Symbols

ra-pa-cious \rə-'pā-shəs\ (*adj*) excessively grasping; plundering. Hawks and *rapacious* birds play an important role in the "balance of nature"; therefore, they are protected throughout North America.

rap-proche-ment \rap-ˌrōsh-'mäⁿ\ (*n*) reconciliation. Both sides were eager to effect a *rapprochement* but did not know how to undertake a program designed to bring about harmony.

rar-e-fied \'rar-ə-ˌfid\ (*adj*) made less dense [of a gas]. The mountain climbers had difficulty breathing in the *rarefied* atmosphere.

raspy \'ras-pē\ (*adj*) grating; harsh. The sergeant's *raspy* voice grated on the recruits' ears.

ra-ti-o-ci-na-tion \ˌrat-ē-ˌōs-ᵊn-'ā-shən\ (*n*) reasoning; act of drawing conclusions from premises. Poe's "The Gold Bug" is a splendid example of the author's use of *ratiocination*.

ra-tio-nal-i-za-tion \ˌrash-nə-lə-'zā-shən\ (*n*) bringing into conformity with reason. All attempts at *rationalization* at this time are doomed to failure; tempers and emotions run too high for intelligent thought to prevail.

ra-tio-na-lize \'rash-nə-ˌlīz\ (*v*) reason; justify an improper act. Do not try to *rationalize* your behavior by blaming your companions.

rau-cous \'ro-kəs\ (*adj*) harsh and shrill. His *raucous* laughter irritated me.

rav-age \'rav-ij\ (*v*) plunder; despoil. The marauding army *ravaged* the countryside; also (*n*).

rav-en-ous \'rav-(ə-)nəs\ (*adj*) extremely hungry. The *ravenous* dog upset several garbage pails in its search for food.

raze \'rāz \ (*v*) destroy completely. The owners intend to *raze* the hotel and erect an office building on the site.

re-ac-tion-ar-y \rē-'ak-shə-ˌner-ē\ (*adj*) recoiling from progress; retrograde. His program was *reactionary*

\ə\ **abut** \ᵊ\ **kitten**, F **table** \ər\ **further** \a\ **ash** \ā\ **ace** \ä\ **cot, cart**
\aú\ **out** \ch\ **chin** \e\ **bet** \ē\ **easy** \g\ **go** \i\ **hit** \ī\ **ice** \j\ **job**

since it sought to abolish many of the social reforms instituted by the previous administration; also (*n*).

realm \relm\ (*n*) kingdom; sphere. The *realm* of possibilities for the new invention was endless.

re-bate \'re-ˌbāt\ (*n*) discount. We offer a *rebate* of ten percent to those who pay cash; also (*v*).

re-buff \ri-'bəf\ (*v*) reject sharply; snub. She *rebuffed* his invitation so smoothly that he did not realize he had been snubbed.

re-cal-ci-trant \ri-'kal-sə-trənt\ (*adj*) obstinately stubborn. Donkeys are reputed to be the most *recalcitrant* of animals.

re-cant \ri-'kant\ (*v*) repudiate; withdraw previous statement. Unless you *recant* your confession, you will be punished severely.

re-ca-pit-u-late \ˌrē-kə-'pich-ə-ˌlāt\ (*v*) summarize. Let us *recapitulate* what has been said thus far before going ahead.

re-ces-sion \ri-'sesh-ən\ (*n*) withdrawal; retreat. The *recession* of the troops from the combat area was completed in an orderly manner.

re-cid-i-vism \ri-'sid-ə-ˌviz-əm\ (*n*) habitual return to crime. Prison reformers in the United States are disturbed by the high rate of *recidivism;* the number of men serving second and third terms in prison indicates the failure of the prisons to rehabilitate the inmates.

re-cip-i-ent \ri-'sip-ē-ənt\ (*n*) receiver. Although he had been the *recipient* of many favors, he was not grateful to his benefactor.

re-cip-ro-cal \ri-'sip-rə-kəl\ (*adj*) mutual; exchangeable; interacting. The two nations signed a *reciprocal* trade agreement; also (*n*).

re-cip-ro-cate \ri-'sip-rə-ˌkāt\ (*v*) repay in kind. If they attack us, we shall be compelled to *reciprocate* and bomb their territory.

\ŋ\ sing \ō\ go \ȯ\ law \ȯi\ boy \th\ thin \th\ the \ü\ loot \u̇\ foot
\y\ yet \zh\ vision \à, k̲, ⁿ, œ, œ̄, ue, ūe, ʸ\ *see* Pronunciation Symbols

re-cluse \'rek-ˌlüs\ (*n*) hermit. The *recluse* lived in a hut in the forest; also (*adj*).

rec-on-cile \'rek-ən-ˌsīl\ (*v*) make friendly after quarrel; correct inconsistencies. Each month we *reconcile* our checkbook with the bank statement.

re-con-dite \'rek-ən-ˌdīt\ (*adj*) abstruse; profound; hidden from view. He read many *recondite* books in order to obtain the material for his scholarly thesis.

re-con-nais-sance \ri-'kän-ə-zən(t)s\ (*n*) survey of enemy by soldiers; reconnoitering. If you encounter any enemy soldiers during your *reconnaissance,* capture them for questioning.

re-count \(ˌ)re-'kaúnt\ (*v*) tell; narrate. We always looked forward to our visits to my grandfather's home because he would *recount* fascinating stories from his youth; also (*n*).

re-course \'rē-ˌkō(ə)rs\ (*n*) resorting to help when in trouble. The boy's only *recourse* was to appeal to his father for aid.

rec-re-ant \'rek-rē-ənt\ (*n*) coward; betrayer of faith. The religious people ostracized the *recreant* who had abandoned their faith; also (*adj*).

re-crim-i-na-tion \ri-ˌkrim-ə-'nā-shən\ (*n*) countercharges. Loud and angry *recriminations* were her answer to his accusations.

rec-ti-fy \'rek-tə-ˌfī\ (*v*) correct. I want to *rectify* my error before it is too late.

rec-ti-tude \'rek-tə-ˌt(y)üd\ (*n*) uprightness. He was renowned for his *rectitude* and integrity.

re-cum-bent \ri-'kəm-bənt\ (*adj*) reclining; lying down completely or in part. The command "AT EASE" does not permit you to take a *recumbent* position.

re-cu-per-ate \ri-'k(y)ü-pə-ˌrāt\ (*v*) recover. The doctors were worried because the patient did not *recuperate* as rapidly as they had expected.

\ə\ abut \ə\ kitten, F table \ər\ further \a\ ash \ā\ ace \ä\ cot, cart
\aú\ out \ch\ chin \e\ bet \ē\ easy \g\ go \i\ hit \ī\ ice \j\ job

re-cur-rent \ri-'kər-ənt\ (*adj*) occurring again and again. These *recurrent* attacks disturbed us and we consulted a physician.

re-cu-sant \'rek-yə-zənt\ (*n*) person who refuses to comply; applied specifically to those who refused to attend Anglican services. In that religious community, the *recusant* was shunned as a pariah; also (*adj*). **re-cu-san-cy** \'rek-yə-zən-sē\ (*n*)

red-o-lent \'red-ᵊl-ənt\ (*adj*) fragrant; odorous; suggestive of an odor. Even though it is February, the air is *redolent* of spring.

re-doubt-a-ble \ri-'daut-ə-bəl\ (*adj*) formidable; causing fear. The neighboring countries tried not to offend the Russians because they could be *redoubtable* foes.

re-dress \ri-'dres\ (*n*) remedy; compensation. Do you mean to tell me that I can get no *redress* for my injuries?; also (*v*).

re-dun-dant \ri-'dən-dənt\ (*adj*) superfluous; excessively wordy; repetitious. Your composition is *redundant;* you can easily reduce its length.

reek \'rēk\ (*v*) emit (odor). The room *reeked* with stale tobacco smoke; also (*n*).

re-fec-tion \ri-'fek-shən\ (*n*) slight refreshment. In our anxiety to reach our destination as rapidly as possible, we stopped on the road for only a quick *refection.*

re-fec-to-ry \ri-'fek-t(ə-)rē\ (*n*) dining hall. In this huge *refectory,* we can feed the entire monastic order at one sitting.

re-frac-tion \ri-'frak-shən\ (*n*) bending of a ray of light. When you look at a stick inserted in water, it looks bent because of the *refraction* of the light by the water.

re-frac-to-ry \ri-'frak-t(ə-)rē\ (*adj*) stubborn; unmanageable. The *refractory* horse was eliminated from the race.

\ŋ\ sing \ō\ go \ȯ\ law \ȯi\ boy \th\ thin \<u>th</u>\ the \ü\ loot \u̇\ foot
\y\ yet \zh\ vision \à, <u>k</u>, ⁿ, œ, œ̄, ᵫe, ᵫē, ʸ\ *see* Pronunciation Symbols

re-fur-bish \ri-'fər-bish\ (*v*) renovate; make bright by polishing. The flood left a deposit of mud on everything; it was necessary to *refurbish* our belongings.

ref-u-ta-tion \,ref-yù-'tā-shən\ (*n*) disproof of opponents' arguments. I will wait until I hear the *refutation* before deciding whom to favor.

re-fute \ri-'fyüt\ (*v*) disprove. The defense called several respectable witnesses who were able to *refute* the false testimony of the prosecution's only witness.

re-gal \'rē-gəl\ (*adj*) royal. The young prince has a *regal* manner.

re-gale \ri-'gā(ə)l\ (*v*) entertain. John *regaled* us with tales of his adventures in Africa.

re-gat-ta \ri-'gät-ə\ (*n*) boat or yacht race. Many boating enthusiasts followed the *regatta* in their own yachts.

re-gen-er-a-tion \ri-jen-ə-'rā-shən\ (*n*) spiritual rebirth. Modern penologists strive for the *regeneration* of the prisoners.

reg-i-cide \'rej-ə-sīd\ (*n*) murder of a king or queen. The death of Mary Queen of Scots was an act of *regicide*.

re-gime \'rā-'zhēm\ (*n*) method or system of government. When a Frenchman mentions the Old *Regime,* he refers to the government existing before the revolution.

reg-i-men \'rej-ə-mən\ (*n*) systematic plan, especially for improving health. I hope the results warrant our living under this strict and inflexible *regimen* of exercise.

re-ha-bil-i-tate \,rē-(h)ə-'bil-ə-,tāt\ (*v*) restore to proper condition. We must *rehabilitate* those whom we send to prison.

re-im-burse \,rē-əm-'bərs\ (*v*) repay. Let me know what you have spent and I will *reimburse* you.

re-it-er-ate \rē-'it-ə-rāt\ (*v*) repeat. I shall *reiterate* this message until all have understood it.

\ə\ **abut** \ə\ **kitten, F table** \ər\ **further** \a\ **ash** \ā\ **ace** \ä\ **cot, cart** \aù\ **out** \ch\ **chin** \e\ **bet** \ē\ **easy** \g\ **go** \i\ **hit** \ī\ **ice** \j\ **job**

re-ju-ve-nate \ri-'jü-və-ˌnāt\ (*v*) make young again. The charlatan claimed that his elixir would *rejuvenate* the aged and weary.

rel-e-gate \'rel-ə-ˌgāt\ (*v*) banish; consign to inferior position. If we *relegate* these experienced people to positions of unimportance because of their political persuasions, we shall lose the services of valuably trained personnel.

rel-e-van-cy \'rel-ə-vən-sē\ (*n*) pertinence; reference to the case in hand. I was impressed by the *relevancy* of your remarks. **rel-e-vant** \'rel-ə-vənt\ (*adj*)

re-lin-quish \ri-'liŋ-kwish\ (*v*) abandon. I will *relinquish* my claims to this property if you promise to retain my employees.

rel-ish \'rel-ish\ (*v*) savor; enjoy. I *relish* a good joke as much as anyone else; also (*n*).

re-luc-tant \ri-'lək-tənt\ (*adj*) unwilling; hesitant. I was *reluctant* to run for office a second time after my first unsuccessful attempt.

re-me-di-a-ble \ri-'mēd-ē-ə-bəl\ (*adj*) reparable. Let us be grateful that the damage is *remediable*.

re-me-di-al \ri-'mēd-ē-əl\ (*adj*) curative; corrective. Because he was a slow reader, he decided to take a course in *remedial* reading.

rem-i-nis-cence \ˌrem-ə-'nis-ᵊn(t)s\ (*n*) recollection. Her *reminiscences* of her experiences are so fascinating that she ought to write a book.

re-miss \ri-'mis\ (*adj*) negligent. He was accused of being *remiss* in his duty.

rem-nant \'rem-nənt\ (*n*) remainder. I suggest that you wait until the store places the *remnants* of these goods on sale.

re-mon-strate \ri-'män-ˌstrāt \ (*v*) protest. I must *remonstrate* about the lack of police protection in this area.

re-morse \ri-'mȯ(ə)rs\ (*n*) guilt; self-reproach. The murderer felt no *remorse* for his crime.

\ŋ\ sing \ō\ go \ȯ\ law \ȯi\ boy \th\ thin \th\ the \ü\ loot \u̇\ foot
\y\ yet \zh\ vision \à, ḵ, ⁿ, œ, œ̄, ᴜe, ᴜ̄e, ʸ\ *see* Pronunciation Symbols

re-mu-ner-a-tive \ri-'myü-nə-rət-iv\ (*adj*) compensating; rewarding. I find my new work so *remunerative* that I may not return to my previous employment. **re-mu-ner-a-tion** \ri-ˌmyü-nə-rā-shən\ (*n*)

rend \'rend\ (*v*) split; tear apart. In his grief, he tried to *rend* his garments.

ren-der \'ren-dər\ (*v*) deliver; provide; represent. He *rendered* aid to the needy and indigent.

ren-dez-vous \'rän-di-ˌvü\ (*n*) meeting place. The two fleets met at the *rendezvous* at the appointed time; also (*v*).

ren-di-tion \ren-'dish-ən\ (*n*) translation; artistic interpretation of a song, etc. The audience cheered enthusiastically as she completed her *rendition* of the aria.

ren-e-gade \'ren-i-ˌgād\ (*n*) deserter; apostate. Because he refused to support his fellow members in their drive, he was shunned as a *renegade*.

re-nounce \ri-'naun(t)s\ (*v*) abandon; discontinue; disown; repudiate. Joan of Arc refused to *renounce* her statements even though she knew she would be burned at the stake as a witch.

ren-o-vate \'ren-ə-ˌvāt\ (*v*) restore to good condition; renew. They claim that they can *renovate* worn shoes so that they look like new ones.

re-nun-ci-a-tion \ri-ˌnən(t)-sē-ˌā-shən\ (*n*) giving up; renouncing. Do not sign this *renunciation* of your right to sue until you have consulted a lawyer.

rep-a-ra-ble \'rep-(ə-)rə-bəl\ (*adj*) capable of being repaired. Fortunately, the damages we suffered in the accident were *reparable*.

rep-a-ra-tion \ˌrep-ə-'rā-shən\ (*n*) amends; compensation. At the peace conference, the defeated country promised to pay *reparations* to the victors.

rep-ar-tee \ˌrep-ər-'tē\ (*n*) clever reply. He was famous for his witty *repartee* and his sarcasm.

\ə\ **abut** \ᵊ\ **kitten, F table** \ər\ **further** \a\ **ash** \ā\ **ace** \ä\ **cot, cart**
\au̇\ **out** \ch\ **chin** \e\ **bet** \ē\ **easy** \g\ **go** \i\ **hit** \ī\ **ice** \j\ **job**

re-pel-lent \ri-'pel-ənt\ (*adj*) driving away; unattractive. Mosquitoes find the odor so *repellent* that they leave any spot where this liquid has been sprayed; also (*n*).

re-per-cus-sion \rē-pər-'kəsh-ən\ (*n*) rebound; reverberation; reaction. I am afraid that this event will have serious *repercussions.*

rep-er-toire \'rep-ə(r)-ˌtwär\ (*n*) list of works of music, drama, etc., a performer is prepared to present. The opera company decided to include *Madame Butterfly* in its *repertoire* for the following season.

re-plen-ish \ri-'plen-ish\ (*v*) fill up again. The end of rationing enabled us to *replenish* our supply of canned food.

re-plete \ri-'plēt\ (*adj*) filled to capacity; abundantly supplied. This book is *replete* with humorous situations.

rep-li-ca \'rep-li-kə\ (*n*) copy. Are you going to hang this *replica* of the Declaration of Independence in the classroom or in the auditorium?

re-pos-i-to-ry \ri-'päz-ə-ˌtōr-ē\ (*n*) storehouse. Libraries are *repositories* of the world's best thoughts.

rep-re-hen-si-ble \ˌrep-ri-'hen(t)-sə-bəl\ (*adj*) deserving blame. Your vicious conduct in this situation is *reprehensible.*

re-prieve \ri-'prēv\ (*n*) temporary stay. During the twenty-four-hour *reprieve,* the lawyers sought to make the stay of execution permanent; also (*v*).

rep-ri-mand \'rep-rə-ˌmand\ (*v*) reprove severely. I am afraid that my parents will *reprimand* me when I show them my report card; also (*n*).

re-pri-sal \ri-'prī-zəl\ (*n*) retaliation. I am confident that we are ready for any *reprisals* the enemy may undertake.

rep-ro-bate \'rep-rə-ˌbāt\ (*n*) person hardened in sin, devoid of a sense of decency. I cannot understand why he has so many admirers if he is the *reprobate* you say he is; also (*adj*).

\ŋ\ sing \ō\ go \ò\ law \òi\ boy \th\ thin \th̲\ the \ü\ loot \u̇\ foot
\y\ yet \zh\ vision \à, k̲, ⁿ, œ, œ̄, ue, ūe, ʸ\ *see* Pronunciation Symbols

rep-ro-ba-tion \rep-rə-'bā-shən\ (*n*) severe disapproval. The students showed their *reprobation* of his act by refusing to talk with him.

re-prove \ri-'prüv\ (*v*) censure; rebuke. The principal *reproved* the students when they became unruly in the auditorium.

re-pu-di-ate \ri-'pyüd-ē-ˌāt\ (*v*) disown; disavow. He announced that he would *repudiate* all debts incurred by his wife.

re-pug-nance \ri-'pəg-nən(t)s\ (*n*) loathing. She looked at the snake with *repugnance.*

re-qui-em \'rek-wē-əm\ (*n*) mass for the dead; dirge. They played Mozart's *Requiem* at the funeral.

req-ui-site \'rek-wə-zət\ (*n*) necessary requirement. Many colleges state that a student must offer three years of a language as a *requisite* for admission; also (*adj*).

re-quite \ri-'kwīt\ (*v*) repay; revenge. The wretch *requited* his benefactors by betraying them.

re-scind \ri-'sind \ (*v*) cancel. Because of public resentment, the king had to *rescind* his order.

re-scis-sion \ri-'sizh-ən\ (*n*) abrogation; annulment. The *rescission* of the unpopular law was urged by all political parties.

re-serve \ri-'zərv\ (*n*) self-control; care in expressing oneself. She was outspoken and uninhibited; he was cautious and inclined to *reserve.* (secondary meaning) re-served \ri-'zərvd\ (*adj*)

res-i-due \'rez-ə-ˌd(y)ü\ (*n*) remainder; balance. In his will, he requested that after payment of debts, taxes, and funeral expenses, the *residue* be given to his wife.

re-signed \ri-'zīnd\ (*adj*) unresisting; patiently submissive. Bob Cratchit was too *resigned* to his downtrodden existence to protest Scrooge's bullying. res-ig-na-tion \rez-ig-'nā-shən\ (*n*)

\ə\ **abut** \ᵊ\ **kitten, F table** \ər\ **further** \a\ **ash** \ā\ **ace** \ä\ **cot, cart** \aů\ **out** \ch\ **chin** \e\ **bet** \ē\ **easy** \g\ **go** \i\ **hit** \ī\ **ice** \j\ **job**

re-sil-ient \ri-'zil-yənt\ (*adj*) elastic; having the power of springing back. Steel is highly *resilient* and therefore is used in the manufacture of springs.

re-solve \ri-'zälv\ (*v*) settle; determine. The couple went to a counselor in order to *resolve* their differences.

re-solve \ri-'zälv\ (*n*) determination. Nothing could shake his *resolve* that his children would get the best education that money could buy; also (*v*).

res-o-nant \'rez-ᵊn-ənt\ (*adj*) echoing; resounding; possessing resonance. His *resonant* voice was particularly pleasing.

re-spite \'res-pət\ (*n*) delay in punishment; interval of relief; rest. The judge granted the condemned man a *respite* to enable his attorneys to file an appeal.

re-splen-dent \ri-'splen-dənt\ (*adj*) brilliant; lustrous. The toreador wore a *resplendent* costume.

re-spon-sive-ness \ri-'spän(t)-siv-nəs\ (*n*) state of reacting readily to appeals, orders, etc. The audience cheered and applauded, delighting the performers by its *responsiveness*.

res-ti-tu-tion \res-tə-'t(y)ü-shən\ (*n*) reparation; indemnification. He offered to make *restitution* for the window broken by his son.

res-tive \'res-tiv\ (*adj*) unmanageable; fretting under control. We must quiet the *restive* animals.

re-strained \ri-'strānd\ (*adj*) held in check; under control; limited. The artist's *restrained* use of color was considered subtle by some, and dull by others.

re-sur-gent \ri-'sər-jənt\ (*adj*) rising again after defeat, etc. The *resurgent* nation surprised everyone by its quick recovery after total defeat.

re-sus-ci-tate \ri-'səs-ə-ˌtāt\ (*v*) revive. The lifeguard tried to *resuscitate* the drowned child by applying artificial respiration.

\ŋ\ sing   \ō\ go   \ò\ law   \òi\ boy   \th\ thin   \t̲h̲\ the   \ü\ loot   \u̇\ foot
\y\ yet   \zh\ vision   \à, k̲, ⁿ, œ, œ̄, ᵾe, ᵾē, ʸ\ *see* Pronunciation Symbols

re-tal-i-ate \ri-'tal-ē-,āt\ (*v*) repay in kind (usually for bad treatment). Fear that we will *retaliate* immediately deters our foe from attacking us.

re-ten-tive \ri-'tent-iv\ (*adj*) holding; having a good memory. The pupil did not need to spend much time in study as he had a *retentive* mind.

ret-i-cence \'ret-ə-sən(t)s\ (*n*) reserve; uncommunicativeness; inclination to be silent. Because of the *reticence* of the key witness, the case against the defendant collapsed.

ret-i-nue \'ret-ᵊn-,(y)ü\ (*n*) following; attendants. The queen's *retinue* followed her down the aisle.

re-tir-ing \ri-'tī(ə)r-iŋ\ (*adj*) modest; shy. Given Susan's *retiring* personality, no one expected her to take up public speaking.

re-tort \ri-'tȯ(ə)rt\ (*n*) quick, sharp reply. Even when it was advisable for her to keep her mouth shut, she was always ready with a quick *retort;* also (*v*).

re-trac-tion \ri-'trak-shən\ (*n*) withdrawal. He dropped his libel suit after the newspaper published a *retraction* of its statement.

re-trench \ri-'trench\ (*v*) cut down; economize. If they were to be able to send their children to college, they would have to *retrench.*

ret-ri-bu-tion \,re-trə-'byü-shən\ (*n*) vengeance; compensation; punishment for offenses. The evangelist maintained that an angry deity would exact *retribution* from the sinners.

re-trieve \ri-'trēv\ (*v*) recover; find and bring in. The dog was intelligent and quickly learned to *retrieve* the game killed by the hunter; also (*n*).

ret-ro-ac-tive \,re-trō-'ak-tiv\ (*adj*) of a law that dates back to a period before its enactment. Because the law was *retroactive* to the first of the year, we found he was eligible for the pension.

\ə\ **abut** \ᵊ\ **kitten, F table** \ər\ **further** \a\ **ash** \ā\ **ace** \ä\ **cot, cart**
\aů\ **out** \ch\ **chin** \e\ **bet** \ē\ **easy** \g\ **go** \i\ **hit** \ī\ **ice** \j\ **job**

ret-ro-grade \re-trə-ˌgrād\ (*v*) go backwards; degenerate. Instead of advancing, our civilization seems to have *retrograded* in ethics and culture; also (*adv, adj*).

ret-ro-spec-tive \re-trə-'spek-tiv\ (*adj*) looking back on the past. It is only when we become *retrospective* that we can appreciate the tremendous advances made during this century; also (*n*).

rev-el-ry \'rev-əl-rē\ (*n*) boisterous merrymaking. New Year's Eve is a night of *revelry.*

re-ver-ber-ate \ri-'vər-bə-ˌrāt\ (*v*) echo; resound. The entire valley *reverberated* with the sound of the church bells.

re-vere \ri-'vi(ə)r\ (*v*) respect; honor. In Asian societies, people *revere* their elders.

rev-er-ie \'rev-(ə-)rē\ (*n*) daydream; musing. He was awakened from his *reverie* by the teacher's question.

re-vile \ri-'vī(ə)l\ (*v*) slander; use verbal abuse. He was avoided by all who feared that he would *revile* and abuse them if they displeased him.

re-vul-sion \ri-'vəl-shən\ (*n*) sudden violent change of feeling; reaction. Many people in this country who admired dictatorships underwent a *revulsion* when they realized what Hitler and Mussolini were trying to do.

rhap-so-dize \'rap-sə-ˌdīz\ (*v*) to speak or write in an exaggeratedly enthusiastic manner. She greatly enjoyed her Hawaiian vacation and *rhapsodized* about it for weeks.

rhet-o-ric \'ret-ə-rik\ (*n*) art of effective communication; insincere language. All writers, by necessity, must be skilled in *rhetoric.* rhe-tor-i-cal \ri-'tȯr-i-kəl\ (*adj*)

rheum-y \'rü-mē\ (*adj*) pertaining to a discharge from nose and eyes. His *rheumy* eyes warned us that he was coming down with a cold.

rib-ald \'rib-əld\ (*adj*) wanton; profane. He sang a *ribald* song that offended many of us.

---

rife \rīf\ (*adj*) abundant; current. In the face of the many rumors of scandal, which are *rife* at the moment, it is best to remain silent.

rift \rift\ (*n*) opening; break. The plane was lost in the stormy sky until the pilot saw the city through a *rift* in the clouds.

rig-or \rig-ər\ (*n*) severity. Many settlers could not stand the *rigors* of the New England winters.

ris-i-ble \riz-ə-bəl\ (*adj*) inclined to laugh; ludicrous. His remarks were so *risible* that the audience howled with laughter. **ris-i-bil-i-ty** \riz-ə-'bil-ət-ē\ (*n*)

ris-qué \ri-'skā\ (*adj*) verging upon the improper; off-color. Please do not tell your *risqué* anecdotes at this party.

roan \rōn\ (*adj*) brown mixed with gray or white. You can distinguish this horse in a race because it is *roan* while all the others are bay or chestnut; also (*n*).

ro-bust \rō-'bəst\ (*adj*) vigorous; strong. The candidate for the football team had a *robust* physique.

ro-co-co \rə-'kō-ˌkō\ (*adj*) ornate; highly decorated. The *rococo* style in furniture and architecture, marked by scrollwork and excessive decoration, flourished during the middle of the eighteenth century; also (*n*).

ro-se-ate \rō-zē-ət\ (*adj*) rosy; optimistic. I am afraid you will have to alter your *roseate* views in the light of the distressing news that has just arrived.

ros-ter \räs-tər\ (*n*) list. They print the *roster* of players in the season's program.

ros-trum \räs-trəm\ (*n*) platform for speech-making; pulpit. The crowd murmured angrily and indicated that they did not care to listen to the speaker who was approaching the *rostrum*.

rote \rōt\ (*n*) repetition. He recited the passage by *rote* and gave no indication he understood what he was saying.

\ə\ **abut** \ᵊ\ **kitten, F table** \ər\ **further** \a\ **ash** \ā\ **ace** \ä\ **cot, cart**
\au̇\ **out** \ch\ **chin** \e\ **bet** \ē\ **easy** \g\ **go** \i\ **hit** \ī\ **ice** \j\ **job**

ro-tun-da \rō-'tən-də\ (*n*) circular building or hall covered with a dome. His body lay in state in the *rotunda* of the Capitol.

ro-tun-di-ty \rō-'tən-dət-ē\ (*n*) roundness; sonorousness of speech. Washington Irving emphasized the *rotundity* of the governor by describing his height and circumference. ro-tund \rō-'tənd\ (*adj*)

rout \raüt\ (*v*) stampede; drive out; defeat decisively. The reinforcements were able to *rout* the enemy; also (*n*).

rub-ble \'rəb-əl\ (*n*) fragments. Ten years after World War II, some of the *rubble* left by enemy bombings could still be seen.

ru-bi-cund \'rü-bi-ₐkənd\ (*adj*) having a healthy reddish color; ruddy; florid. His *rubicund* complexion was the result of an active outdoor life.

rud-dy \'rəd-ē\ (*adj*) reddish; healthy-looking. His *ruddy* features indicated that he had spent much time in the open.

ru-di-men-ta-ry \ₐrüd-ə-'ment ə-rē\ (*adj*) not developed; elementary. His dancing was limited to a few *rudimentary* steps.

rue-ful \'rü-fəl\ (*adj*) regretful; sorrowful; dejected. The artist has captured the sadness of childhood in his portrait of the boy with the *rueful* countenance.

ruf-fi-an \'rəf-ē-ən\ (*n*) bully; scoundrel. The *ruffians* threw stones at the police.

ru-mi-nate \'rü-mə-ₐnāt\ (*v*) chew the cud; ponder. We cannot afford to wait while you *ruminate* upon these plans.

rum-mage \'rəm-ij\ (*v*) ransack; thoroughly search. When we *rummaged* through the trunks in the attic, we found many souvenirs of our childhood days; also (*n*).

ruse \'rüs\ (*n*) trick; stratagem. You will not be able to fool your friends with such an obvious *ruse*.

\ŋ\ sing \ō\ go \ȯ\ law \ȯi\ boy \th\ thin \t̲h̲\ the \ü\ loot \u̇\ foot
\y\ yet \zh\ vision \à, k̲, ⁿ, œ, œ̄, ue, ūe, ʸ\ *see* Pronunciation Symbols

rus-tic \'rəs-tik\ (*adj*) pertaining to country people; uncouth. The backwoodsman looked out of place in his *rustic* attire; also (*n*).

rus-ti-cate \'rəs-ti-ˌkāt\ (*v*) banish to the country, dwell in the country. I like city life so much that I can never understand how people can *rusticate* in the suburbs.

ruth-less \'rüth-ləs\ (*adj*) pitiless. The escaped convict was a dangerous and *ruthless* murderer.

S

sac·cha·rine \\'sak-(ə-)rən\\ (*adj*) cloyingly sweet. She tried to ingratiate herself, speaking sweetly and smiling a *saccharine* smile.

sac·er·do·tal \\sas-ər-'dōt-ᵊl\\ (*adj*) priestly. The priest decided to abandon his *sacerdotal* duties and enter the field of politics.

sac·ri·le·gious \\sak-rə-'lij-əs\\ (*adj*) desecrating; profane. His stealing of the altar cloth was a very *sacrilegious* act.

sac·ro·sanct \\'sak-rō-,saŋ(k)t\\ (*adj*) most sacred; inviolable. The brash insurance salesman invaded the *sacrosanct* privacy of the office of the president of the company.

sa·dis·tic \\sə-'dis-tik\\ (*adj*) inclined to cruelty. If we are to improve conditions in this prison, we must first get rid of the *sadistic* warden. **sa·dism** \\'sa-,diz-əm\\ (*n*)

saf·fron \\'saf-rən\\ (*adj*) orange-colored; colored like the autumn crocus. The Halloween cake was decorated with *saffron*-colored icing.

sa·ga \\'säg-ə\\ (*n*) Scandinavian myth; any legend. This is a *saga* of the sea and the men who risk their lives on it.

sa·ga·cious \\sə-'gā-shəs\\ (*adj*) keen; shrewd; having insight. He is much too *sagacious* to be fooled by a trick like that.

sa·lient \\'sā-lyənt\\ (*adj*) prominent. One of the *salient* features of that newspaper is its excellent editorial page; also (*n*).

sa·line \\'sā-,lēn\\ (*adj*) salty. The slighty *saline* taste of this mineral water is pleasant; also (*n*).

sal·low \\'sal-(ₒ)ō\\ (*adj*) yellowish; sickly in color. We were disturbed by his *sallow* complexion.

sa·lu·bri·ous \\sə-'lü-brē-əs\\ (*adj*) healthful. Many people with hay fever move to more *salubrious* sections of the country during the months of August and September.

\\ŋ\\ sing \\ō\\ go \\ȯ\\ law \\ȯi\\ boy \\th\\ thin \\t̲h̲\\ the \\ü\\ loot \\u̇\\ foot
\\y\\ yet \\zh\\ vision \\à, k̲, ⁿ, œ, œ̄, ᴜe, ᴜ̄e, ʸ\\ *see* Pronunciation Symbols

sal-u-ta-ry \\'sal-yə-ˌter-ē\ (*adj*) tending to improve; beneficial; wholesome. The punishment had a *salutary* effect on the boy, as he became a model student; also (*n*).

sal-vage \\'sal-vij\ (*v*) rescue from loss. All attempts to *salvage* the wrecked ship failed; also (*n*).

sanc-ti-mo-ni-ous \ˌsaŋ(k)-tə-'mō-nē-əs\ (*adj*) displaying ostentatious or hypocritical devoutness. You do not have to be so *sanctimonious* to prove that you are devout.

sanc-tion \\'saŋ(k)-shən\ (*v*) approve; ratify. Nothing will convince me to *sanction* the engagement of my daughter to such a worthless young man.

san-gui-nar-y \\'saŋ-gwə-ˌner-ē\ (*adj*) bloody. The battle of Iwo Jima was unexpectedly *sanguinary*.

san-guine \\'saŋ-gwən\ (*adj*) cheerful; hopeful. Let us not be too *sanguine* about the outcome.

sa-pi-ent \\'sā-pē-ənt\ (*adj*) wise; shrewd. The students enjoyed the professor's *sapient* digressions more than his formal lectures.

sar-casm \\'sär-ˌkaz-əm\ (*n*) scornful remarks; stinging rebuke. His feelings were hurt by the *sarcasm* of his supposed friends. **sar-cas-tic** \ sär-'kas-tik\ (*adj*)

sar-coph-a-gus \sär-'käf-ə-gəs\ (*n*) stone coffin, often highly decorated. The display of the *sarcophagus* in the art museum impresses me as a morbid exhibition.

sar-don-ic \sär-'dän-ik\ (*adj*) disdainful; sarcastic; cynical. The *sardonic* humor of nightclub comedians who satirize or ridicule patrons in the audience strikes some people as amusing and others as rude.

sar-to-ri-al \sär-'tōr-ē-əl\ (*adj*) pertaining to tailors or tailored clothes. He was as famous for the *sartorial* splendor of his attire as he was for his acting.

sate \\'sāt\ (*v*) satisfy to the full; cloy. Its hunger *sated,* the lion dozed.

---

sat-el-lite \'sat-ᵊl-ˌīt\ (*n*) small body revolving around a larger one. During the first few years of the Space Age, hundreds of *satellites* were launched by Russia and the United States.

sa-ti-ate \'sā-shē-ˌāt\ (*v*) surfeit; satisfy fully. The guests, having eaten until they were *satiated,* now listened inattentively to the speakers. **sa-ti-ate** \'sā-sh(ē-)ət\ (*adj*)

sa-ti-e-ty \sə-'tī-ət-ē\ (*n*) condition of being crammed full; glutted state; repletion. The *satiety* of the guests at the sumptuous feast became apparent when they refused the delicious dessert.

sat-ire \'sa-ˌtī(ə)r\ (*n*) form of literature in which irony, sarcasm, and ridicule are employed to attack vice and folly. *Gulliver's Travels,* which is regarded by many as a tale for children, is actually a bitter *satire* attacking man's folly.

sat-u-rate \'sach-ə-ˌrāt\ (*v*) soak. Their clothes were *saturated* by the rain. **sat-u-rate** \'sach-(ə-)rət\ (*adj*)

sat-ur-nine \'sat-ər-ˌnīn\ (*adj*) gloomy. Do not be misled by his *saturnine* countenance; he is not as gloomy as he looks.

sa-tyr \'sāt-ər\ (*n*) half-human, half-bestial being in the court of Dionysos, portrayed as wanton and cunning. He was like a *satyr* in his lustful conduct.

saun-ter \'sȯnt-ər\ (*v*) stroll slowly. As we *sauntered* through the park, we stopped frequently to admire the spring flowers.

sa-vant \sa-'vänt\ (*n*) scholar. Our faculty includes many world-famous *savants.*

sa-voir faire \ˌsav-ˌwär-'fa(ə)r\ (*n*) tact; poise; sophistication. I envy his *savoir faire;* he always knows exactly what to do and say.

sa-vor \'sā-vər\ (*v*) have a distinctive flavor, smell, or quality. I think your choice of a successor *savors* of favoritism; also (*n*).

\ŋ\ sing \ō\ go \ȯ\ law \ȯi\ boy \th\ thin \th̲\ the \ü\ loot \u̇\ foot
\y\ yet \zh\ vision \à, k̲, ⁿ, œ, œ̄, ue, ūe, ʸ\ *see* Pronunciation Symbols

scant-y \\'skant-ē\ (*adj*) meager; insufficient. Thinking his helping of food was *scanty,* Oliver Twist asked for more.

scape-goat \\'skāp-,gōt\ (*n*) someone who bears the blame for others. After the *Challenger* disaster, NASA searched for *scapegoats* on whom it could cast the blame.

scav-en-ger \\'skav-ən-jər\ (*n*) collector and disposer of refuse; animal that devours refuse and carrion. The Oakland *Scavenger* Company is responsible for the collection and disposal of the community's garbage.

schism \\'siz-əm\ (*n*) division; split. Let us not widen the *schism* by further bickering.

scin-til-la \sin-'til-ə\ (*n*) shred; least bit. You have not produced a *scintilla* of evidence to support your argument.

scin-til-late \\'sint-ᵊl-,āt\ (*v*) sparkle; flash. I enjoy her dinner parties because the food is excellent and the conversation *scintillates.*

sci-on \\'sī-ən\ (*n*) offspring. The farm boy felt out of place in the school attended by the *scions* of the wealthy and noble families.

scourge \\'skərj\ (*n*) lash; whip; severe punishment. They feared the plague and regarded it as a deadly *scourge;* also (*v*).

scru-pu-lous \\'skrü-pyə-ləs\ (*adj*) conscientious; extremely thorough. I can recommend him for a position of responsibility for I have found him a very *scrupulous* young man.

scru-ti-nize \\'skrüt-ᵊn-,īz\ (*v*) examine closely and critically. Searching for flaws, the sergeant *scrutinized* every detail of the private's uniform.

scul-lion \\'skəl-yən\ (*n*) menial kitchen worker. Lynette was angry because she thought she had been given a *scullion* to act as her defender.

scur-ri-lous \\'skər-ə-ləs\ (*adj*) obscene; indecent. Your *scurrilous* remarks are especially offensive because they are untrue.

\ə\ **abut** \ᵊ\ **kitten,** F **table** \ər\ **further** \a\ **ash** \ā\ **ace** \ä\ **cot, cart**
\aů\ **out** \ch\ **chin** \e\ **bet** \ē\ **easy** \g\ **go** \i\ **hit** \ī\ **ice** \j\ **job**

scut-tle \\'skət-ᵊl\\ (*v*) sink by cutting holes in. The sailors decided to *scuttle* their vessel rather than surrender it to the enemy; also (*n*).

se-ba-ceous \\si-'bā-shəs\\ (*adj*) oily; fatty. The *sebaceous* glands secrete oil to the hair follicles.

se-ces-sion \\si-'sesh-ən\\ (*n*) withdrawal. The *secession* of the Southern states provided Lincoln with his first major problem after his inauguration.

sec-u-lar \\'sek-yə-lər\\ (*adj*) worldly; not pertaining to church matters; temporal. The church leaders decided not to interfere in *secular* matters; also (*n*).

se-date \\si-'dāt\\ (*adj*) composed; grave. The parents were worried because they felt their son was too quiet and *sedate;* also (*v*).

sed-en-tar-y \\'sed-ᵊn-ˌter-ē\\ (*adj*) requiring sitting. Because he had a *sedentary* occupation, he decided to visit a gymnasium weekly.

se-di-tion \\si-'dish-ən\\ (*n*) resistance to authority; insubordination. His words, though not treasonous in themselves, were calculated to arouse thoughts of *sedition.*

sed-u-lous \\'sej-ə-ləs\\ (*adj*) diligent. Stevenson said that he played the "*sedulous* ape" and diligently imitated the great writers of the past.

seethe \\'sēth\\ (*v*) be disturbed; boil. The nation was *seething* with discontent as the noblemen continued their arrogant ways.

sem-blance \\'sem-blən(t)s\\ (*n*) outward appearance; guise. Although this book has a *semblance* of wisdom and scholarship, a careful examination will reveal many errors and omissions.

se-nil-i-ty \\si-'nil-ət-ē\\ (*n*) old age; feeblemindedness of old age. Most of the decisions are being made by the junior members of the company because of the *senility* of the president.

\\ŋ\\ **sing** \\ō\\ **go** \\ȯ\\ **law** \\ȯi\\ **boy** \\th\\ **thin** \\th\\ **the** \\ü\\ **loot** \\u̇\\ **foot**
\\y\\ **yet** \\zh\\ **vision** \\à, k̲, ⁿ, œ, œ̄, ɷe, ɷ̄e, ʸ\\ *see* Pronunciation Symbols

sen-su-al \'sench-(ə-)wəl\ (*adj*) devoted to the pleasures of the senses; carnal; voluptuous. I cannot understand what caused him to drop his *sensual* way of life and become so ascetic.

sen-su-ous \'sench-(ə-)wəs\ (*adj*) pertaining to the physical senses; operating through the senses. He was stimulated by the sights, sounds, and smells about him; he was enjoying his *sensuous* experience.

sen-ten-tious \sen-'ten-chəs\ (*adj*) terse; concise; aphoristic. After reading so many redundant speeches, I find his *sententious* style particularly pleasing.

sep-tic \'sep-tik\ (*adj*) putrid; producing putrefaction. The hospital was in such a filthy state that we were afraid that many of the patients would suffer from *septic* poisoning.

sep-ul-cher \'sep-əl-kər\ (*n*) tomb. Annabel Lee was buried in the *sepulcher* by the sea.

se-qua-cious \si-'kwā-shəs\ (*adj*) eager to follow; ductile. The *sequacious* members of Parliament were only too willing to do the bidding of their leader.

se-ques-ter \si-'kwes-tər\ (*v*) retire from public life; segregate; seclude. Although he had hoped for a long time to *sequester* himself in a small community, he never was able to drop his busy round of activities in the city.

ser-en-dip-i-ty \ser-ən-'dip-ət-ē\ (*n*) gift for finding valuable things not searched for. Many scientific discoveries are a matter of *serendipity*.

se-ren-i-ty \sə-'ren-ət-ē\ (*n*) calmness; placidity. The *serenity* of the sleepy town was shattered by a tremendous explosion.

ser-pen-tine \'sər-pən-ˌtēn\ (*adj*) winding; twisting. The car swerved at every curve in the *serpentine* road.

ser-rate \'se(ə)r-ˌāt\ (*adj*) having a sawtoothed edge. The beech tree is one of many plants that has *serrate* leaves. ser-rate \se-'rāt\ (*v*)

ser-vile \'sər-vəl\ (*adj*) slavish; cringing. Uriah Heep was a very *servile* individual.

sev-er-ance \'sev-(ə-)rən(t)s\ (*n*) the act of dividing or separating. A factory accident resulted in the *severance* of two of the worker's fingers. **sev-er** \'sev-ər\ (*v*)

se-ver-i-ty \sə-'ver-ət-ē\ (*n*) harshness; plainness. The newspapers disapproved of the *severity* of the sentence.

shack-le \'shak-əl\ (*v*) chain; fetter. The criminal's ankles were *shackled* to prevent his escape; also (*n*).

sham \'sham\ (*v*) pretend. He *shammed* sickness to get out of going to school; also (*n*).

sham-bles \'sham-bəlz\ (*n*) slaughterhouse; scene of carnage. By the time the police arrived, the room was a *shambles.*

sheaf \'shēf\ (*n*) bundle of stalks of grain; any bundle of things tied together. The lawyer picked up a *sheaf* of papers as he rose to question the witness.

sheathe \'shēth\ (*v*) place into a case. As soon as he recognized the approaching men, he *sheathed* his dagger and hailed them as friends.

sher-bet \'shər-bət\ (*n*) flavored dessert ice. I prefer raspberry *sherbet* to ice cream since it is less fattening.

shib-bo-leth \'shib-ə-ləth\ (*n*) watchword; slogan. We are often misled by *shibboleths.*

shim-mer \'shim-ər\ (*v*) glimmer intermittently. The moonlight *shimmered* on the water as the moon broke through the clouds for a moment; also (*n*).

shoal \'shōl\ (*n*) shallow place. The ship was stranded on a *shoal* and had to be pulled off by tugs; also (*v*).

shod-dy \'shäd-ē\ (*adj*) sham; not genuine; inferior. You will never get the public to buy such *shoddy* material.

shrew \'shrü\ (*n*) scolding woman. No one wanted to marry Shakespeare's Kate because she was a *shrew.*

\ŋ\ **sing** \ō\ **go** \o\ **law** \oi\ **boy** \th\ **thin** \th\ **the** \ü\ **loot** \u\ **foot**
\y\ **yet** \zh\ **vision** \à, k̲, ⁿ, œ, œ̄, ᵫe, ᵫē, ʸ\ *see* Pronunciation Symbols

sib-ling \\'sib-ling\\ (*n*) brother or sister. We may not enjoy being *siblings,* but we cannot forget that we still belong to the same family.

sib-yl-line \\'sib-ə-ˌlin\\ (*adj*) prophetic; oracular. Until their destruction by fire in 83 B.C., the *sibylline* books were often consulted by the Romans.

si-de-re-al \\sī-'dir-ē-əl\\ (*adj*) relating to the stars. The study of *sidereal* bodies has been greatly advanced by the new telescope.

silt \\'silt\\ (*n*) sediment deposited by running water. The harbor channel must be dredged annually to remove the *silt;* also (*v*).

sim-i-an \\'sim-ē-ən\\ (*adj*) monkeylike. Lemurs are nocturnal mammals and have many *simian* characteristics, although they are less intelligent than monkeys; also (*n*).

sim-i-le \\'sim-ə-ˌlē\\ (*n*) comparison of one thing with another, using the word *like* or *as*. We are constantly using *similes* and metaphors to convey our thoughts to others.

si-mil-i-tude \\sə-'mil-ə-ˌt(y)üd\\ (*n*) similarity; using comparisons such as similes, etc. Although the critics deplored his use of mixed metaphors, he continued to write in *similitudes.*

sim-per-ing \\'sim-p(ə-)riŋ\\ (*adj*) smirking. I can overlook his *simpering* manner, but I cannot ignore his stupidity.

sim-u-late \\'sim-yə-ˌlāt\\ (*v*) feign. He *simulated* insanity in order to avoid punishment for his crime.

si-ne-cure \\'sī-ni-ˌkyu̇(ə)r\\ (*n*) well-paid position with little responsibility. My job is no *sinecure;* I work long hours and have much responsibility.

sin-ew-y \\'sin-yə-wē\\ (*adj*) tough; strong and firm. The steak was too *sinewy* to chew.

sin-is-ter \\'sin-əs-tər\\ (*adj*) evil. We must defeat the *sinister* forces that seek our downfall.

\\ə\\ **abut** \\ᵊ\\ **kitten, F table** \\ər\\ **further** \\a\\ **ash** \\ā\\ **ace** \\ä\\ **cot, cart**
\\au̇\\ **out** \\ch\\ **chin** \\e\\ **bet** \\ē\\ **easy** \\g\\ **go** \\i\\ **hit** \\ī\\ **ice** \\j\\ **job**

sin-u-ous \\'sin-yə-wəs\\ (*adj*) winding; bending in and out; not morally honest. The snake moved in a *sinuous* manner.

skep-tic \\'skep-tik\\ (*n*) doubter; person who suspends judgment until he has examined the evidence supporting a point of view. In this matter, I am a *skeptic;* I want proof.

skimp \\'skimp\\ (*v*) provide scantily; live very economically. They were forced to *skimp* on necessities in order to make their limited supplies last the winter.

skit-tish \\'skit-ish\\ (*adj*) lively; frisky. He is as *skittish* as a kitten playing with a piece of string.

skul-dug-ge-ry \\skəl-'dəg-(ə-)rē\\ (*n*) dishonest behavior. The investigation into municipal corruption turned up new instances of *skulduggery* daily.

skulk \\'skəlk\\ (*v*) move furtively and secretly. He *skulked* through the less fashionable sections of the city in order to avoid meeting any of his former friends; also (*n*).

slack-en \\'slak-ən\\ (*v*) slow up; loosen. As they passed the finish line, the runners *slackened* their pace.

slake \\'slāk\\ (*v*) quench; sate. When we reached the oasis, we were able to *slake* our thirst.

slan-der \\'slan-dər\\ (*n*) defamation; utterance of false and malicious statements. Unless you can prove your allegations, your remarks constitute *slander;* also (*v*).

slat-tern \\'slat-ərn\\ (*n*) untidy or slovenly person. If you persist in wearing such sloppy clothes, people will call you a *slattern;* also (*adj*).

slea-zy \\'slē-zē\\ (*adj*) flimsy; unsubstantial. This is a *sleazy* material; it will not wear well.

sleep-er \\'slē-pər\\ (*n*) something originally of little value or importance that in time becomes very valuable. Unnoticed by the critics at its publication, the eventual Pulitzer Prize winner was a classic *sleeper.*

sleight \\'slīt\\ (*n*) dexterity. The magician amazed the audience with his *sleight* of hand.

\\ŋ\\ **sing**   \\ō\\ **go**   \\ȯ\\ **law**   \\ȯi\\ **boy**   \\th\\ **thin**   \\t͟h\\ **the**   \\ü\\ **loot**   \\u̇\\ **foot**
\\y\\ **yet**   \\zh\\ **vision**   \\à, k̲, ⁿ, œ, œ̄, ue, ūe, ʸ\\ *see* Pronunciation Symbols

slith-er \'slith-ər\ (*v*) slip or slide. After the mud slide, many people *slithered* down this hill as they left their homes.

sloth \'slȯth\ (*n*) laziness. Such *sloth* in a young person is deplorable.

slough \'sləf\ (*v*) cast off. Each spring, the snake *sloughs* off its skin; also (*n*).

slov-en-ly \'sləv-ən-lē\ (*adj*) untidy; careless in work habits. Such *slovenly* work habits will never produce good products.

slug-gard \'sləg-ərd\ (*n*) lazy person. "You are a *sluggard,* a drone, a parasite," the angry father shouted at his lazy son.

slug-gish \'sləg-ish\ (*adj*) slow; lazy; lethargic. After two nights without sleep, she felt *sluggish* and incapable of exertion.

sluice \'slüs\ (*n*) artificial channel for directing or controlling the flow of water. This *sluice* gate is opened only in times of drought to provide water for irrigation; also (*v*).

smat-ter-ing \'smat-ə-riŋ\ (*v*) slight knowledge. I don't know whether it is better to be ignorant of a subject or to have a mere *smattering* of information about it.

smirk \'smərk\ (*n*) conceited smile. Wipe that *smirk* off your face!; also (*v*).

smol-der \'smōl-dər\ (*v*) burn without flame; be liable to break out at any moment. The rags *smoldered* for hours before they burst into flame.

snick-er \'snik-ər\ (*n*) half-stifled laugh. The boy could not suppress a *snicker* when the teacher sat on the tack; also (*v*).

sniv-el \'sniv-əl\ (*v*) run at the nose; snuffle; whine. Don't you come *sniveling* to me complaining about your big brother.

so-bri-e-ty \sə-'brī-ət-ē\ (*n*) soberness. The solemnity of the occasion filled us with *sobriety.*

\ə\ **abut** \ə\ **kitten, F table** \ər\ **further** \a\ **ash** \ā\ **ace** \ä\ **cot, cart**
\au̇\ **out** \ch\ **chin** \e\ **bet** \ē\ **easy** \g\ **go** \i\ **hit** \ī\ **ice** \j\ **job**

so-bri-quet \\'sō-bri-ˌkā\\ (*n*) nickname. Despite all his protests, his classmates continued to call him by that unflattering *sobriquet.*

sod-den \\'säd-ᵊn\\ (*adj*) soaked; dull, as if from drink. He set his *sodden* overcoat near the radiator to dry.

so-journ \\'sō-jərn\\ (*n*) temporary stay. After his *sojourn* in Florida, he began to long for the colder climate of his native New England home; also (*v*).

so-lace \\'säl-əs\\ (*n*) comfort in trouble. I hope you will find *solace* in the thought that all of us share your loss.

so-le-cism \\'säl-ə-ˌsiz-əm\\ (*n*) construction that is flagrantly incorrect grammatically. I must give this paper a failing mark because it contains many *solecisms.*

so-lem-ni-ty \\sə-'lem-nət-ē\\ (*n*) seriousness; gravity. The minister was concerned that nothing should disturb the *solemnity* of the marriage service. sol-emn \\'säl-əm\\ (*adj*)

so-lic-i-tous \\sə-'lis-ət-əs\\ (*adj*) worried; concerned. The employer was very *solicitous* about the health of his employees as replacements were difficult to get.

so-lil-o-quy \\sə-'lil-ə-kwē\\ (*n*) the act of talking to oneself. The *soliloquy* is a device used by the dramatist to reveal a character's innermost thoughts and emotions.

sol-stice \\'säl-stəs\\ (*n*) point at which the sun is farthest from the equator. The winter *solstice* usually occurs on December 21.

sol-vent \\'säl-vənt\\ (*adj*) able to pay all debts. By dint of very frugal living, he was finally able to become *solvent* and avoid bankruptcy proceedings; also (*n*).

so-mat-ic \\sō-'mat-ik\\ (*adj*) pertaining to the body; physical. Why do you ignore the spiritual aspects and emphasize only the corporeal and the *somatic?*

som-nam-bu-list \\säm-'nam-byə-ləst\\ (*n*) sleepwalker. The most famous *somnambulist* in literature is Lady Macbeth; her monologue in the sleepwalking scene is one of the highlights of Shakespeare's play.

---

som-no-lent \'säm-nə-lənt\ (*adj*) half asleep. The heavy meal and the overheated room made us all *somnolent* and indifferent to the speaker.

so-no-rous \sə-'nōr-əs\ (*adj*) resonant. His *sonorous* voice resounded through the hall.

soph-ist \'säf-əst\ (*n*) quibbler; employer of fallacious reasoning. You are using all the devices of a *sophist* in trying to prove your case; your argument is specious.

so-phis-ti-ca-tion \sə-ˌfis-tə-'kā-shən\ (*n*) artificiality; unnaturalness; act of employing sophistry in reasoning. *Sophistication* is an acquired characteristic, found more frequently among city dwellers than among residents of rural areas.

soph-ist-ry \'säf-ə-strē\ (*n*) seemingly plausible but fallacious reasoning. Instead of advancing valid arguments, he tried to overwhelm his audience with a flood of *sophistries*. **soph-ist** \'säf-əst\ (*n*)

soph-o-mor-ic \ˌsäf-ə-'mōr-ik\ (*adj*) immature; shallow. Your *sophomoric* remarks indicate that you have not given much thought to the problem.

so-po-ri-fic \ˌsäp-ə-'rif-ik\ (*n*) sleep producer. I do not need a *soporific* when I listen to one of his speeches; also (*adj*).

sor-did \'sòrd-əd\ (*adj*) filthy; base; vile. The social worker was angered by the *sordid* housing provided for the homeless.

soup-çon \süp-'sōⁿ\ (*n*) suggestion; hint; taste. A *soupçon* of garlic will improve this dish.

span-gle \'spaŋ-gəl\ (*n*) small metallic piece sewn to clothing for ornamentation. The thousands of *spangles* on her dress sparkled in the glare of the stage lights; also (*v*).

sparse \'spärs\ (*adj*) not thick; thinly scattered; scanty. He had moved from the densely populated city to the remote countryside where the population was *sparse*.

\ə\ **abut** \ᵊ\ **kitten**, F **table** \ər\ **further** \a\ **ash** \ā\ **ace** \ä\ **cot, cart**
\au̇\ **out** \ch\ **chin** \e\ **bet** \ē\ **easy** \g\ **go** \i\ **hit** \ī\ **ice** \j\ **job**

spas-mod-ic \spaz-'mäd-ik\ (*adj*) fitful; periodic. The *spasmodic* coughing in the auditorium annoyed the performers.

spate \'spāt\ (*n*) large amount. She commented on the *spate* of exercise books now on the market.

spa-tial \'spā-shəl\ (*adj*) relating to space. It is difficult to visualize the *spatial* extent of our universe.

spat-u-la \'spach-(ə-)lə\ (*n*) broad-bladed instrument used for spreading or mixing. The manufacturers of this frying pan recommend the use of a rubber *spatula* to avoid scratching the specially treated surface.

spawn \spȯn\ (*v*) lay eggs. Fish ladders had to be built in the dams to assist the salmon returning to *spawn* in their native streams; also (*n*).

spe-cious \'spē-shəs\ (*adj*) seemingly reasonable but incorrect. Let us not be misled by such *specious* arguments.

spec-tral \'spek-trəl\ (*adj*) ghostly. We were frightened by the *spectral* glow that filled the room.

spec-trum \'spek-trəm\ (*n*) colored band produced when beam of light passes through a prism. The visible portion of the *spectrum* includes red at one end and violet at the other.

spec-u-la-tion \spek-yə-'lā-shən\ (*n*) conjecture; contemplation. The discovery of Hester's pregnancy caused much *speculation* as to the identity of the father of her child.

sple-net-ic \spli-'net-ik\ (*adj*) spiteful; irritable; peevish. People shunned him because of his *splenetic* temper. **spleen** \'splēn\ (*n*)

spo-li-a-tion \spō-lē-'ā-shən\ (*n*) pillaging; depredation. We regard this unwarranted attack on a neutral nation as an act of *spoliation* and we demand that it cease at once and that proper restitution be made.

spo-rad-ic \spə-'rad-ik\ (*adj*) occurring irregularly. Although there are *sporadic* outbursts of shooting, we may report that the major rebellion has been defeated.

\ŋ\ sing \ō\ go \ȯ\ law \ȯi\ boy \th\ thin \th\ the \ü\ loot \u̇\ foot
\y\ yet \zh\ vision \à, k̲, ⁿ, œ, œ̄, ᵫ, ᵫ̄, ʸ\ *see* Pronunciation Symbols

sport-ive \'spōrt-iv\ (*adj*) playful. Such a *sportive* attitude is surprising in a person as serious as you usually are.

spume \'spyüm\ (*n*) froth; foam. The *spume* at the base of the waterfall extended for a quarter of a mile downriver; also (*v*).

spu-ri-ous \'spyùr-ē-əs\ (*adj*) false; counterfeit. He tried to pay the check with a *spurious* ten-dollar bill.

spurn \'spərn\ (*v*) reject; scorn. The heroine *spurned* the villain's advances.

squal-id \'skwäl-əd\ (*adj*) dirty; neglected; poor. It is easy to see how crime can breed in such a *squalid* neighborhood.

squan-der \'skwän-dər\ (*v*) waste. The prodigal son *squandered* the family estate; also (*n*).

stac-ca-to \sta-'kät-(ˌ)ō\ (*adj*) played in an abrupt manner; marked by abrupt sharp sound. His *staccato* speech reminded one of the sound of a machine gun.

stag-nant \'stag-nənt\ (*adj*) motionless; stale; dull. The *stagnant* water was a breeding ground for disease. **stag-nate** \'stag-ˌnāt\ (*v*)

staid \'stād\ (*adj*) sober; sedate. His conduct during the funeral ceremony was *staid* and solemn.

stale-mate \'stā(ə)l-ˌmāt\ (*n*) deadlock. Negotiations between the union and the employers have reached a *stalemate;* neither side is willing to budge from previously stated positions; also (*v*).

stal-wart \'stȯl-wərt\ (*adj*) strong, brawny; steadfast. His consistent support of the party has proved that he is a *stalwart* and loyal member; also (*n*).

stam-i-na \'stam-ə-nə\ (*n*) strength; staying power. I doubt that he has the *stamina* to run the full distance of the marathon race.

stanch \'stȯnch\ (*v*) check flow of. It is imperative that we *stanch* the gushing wound before we attend to the other injuries.

\ə\ **abut** \ᵊ\ **kitten,** F **table** \ər\ **further** \a\ **ash** \ā\ **ace** \ä\ **cot, cart**
\aù\ **out** \ch\ **chin** \e\ **bet** \ē\ **easy** \g\ **go** \i\ **hit** \ī\ **ice** \j\ **job**

stat-ic \\'stat-ik\\ (*adj*) unchanging; lacking development. Nothing had changed at home; things were *static*. **sta-sis** \\'stā-səs\\ (*n*)

stat-ute \\'stach-ₒüt\\ (*n*) law. We have many *statutes* in our law books that should be repealed.

stat-u-to-ry \\'stach-ə-ˌtōr-ē\\ (*adj*) created by statute or legislative action. This is a *statutory* crime.

stead-fast \\'sted-ˌfast\\ (*adj*) loyal. I am sure you will remain *steadfast* in your support of the cause.

stein \\'stīn\\ (*n*) beer mug. He thought of college as a place where one drank beer from *steins* and sang songs of lost lambs.

stel-lar \\'stel-ər\\ (*adj*) pertaining to the stars; outstanding. He was the *stellar* attraction of the entire performance.

sten-to-ri-an \\sten-'tōr-ē-ən\\ (*adj*) extremely loud. The town crier had a *stentorian* voice.

ste-re-o-typed \\'ster-ē-ə-ˌtīpt\\ (*adj*) fixed and unvarying representation. My chief objection to the book is that the characters are *stereotyped.*

stig-ma \\'stig-mə\\ (*n*) token of disgrace; brand. I do not attach any *stigma* to the fact that you were accused of this crime; the fact that you were acquitted clears you completely.

stig-ma-tize \\'stig-mə-ˌtīz\\ (*v*) brand; mark as wicked. I do not want to *stigmatize* this young offender for life by sending him to prison.

stilt-ed \\'stil-təd\\ (*adj*) bombastic; inflated. His *stilted* rhetoric did not impress the college audience; they were immune to bombastic utterances.

stint \\'stint\\ (*n*) supply; allotted amount; assigned portion of work. After his *stint* in the Army he will join his father's company; also (*v*).

sti-pend \\'stī-ˌpend\\ (*n*) pay for services. There is a nominal *stipend* attached to this position.

\\ŋ\\ **sing** \\ō\\ **go** \\ȯ\\ **law** \\ȯi\\ **boy** \\th\\ **thin** \\t͟h\\ **the** \\ü\\ **loot** \\ u̇\\ **foot**
\\y\\ **yet** \\zh\\ **vision** \\à, k̲, ⁿ, œ, œ̄, ue, ūe, ʸ\\ *see* Pronunciation Symbols

sto·ic \\'stō-ik\\ (*n*) person who is indifferent to pleasure or pain. The doctor called her patient a *stoic* because he had borne the pain of the examination without whimpering; also (*adj*).

stoke \\'stōk\\ (*v*) provide with fuel; feed abundantly. They swiftly *stoked* themselves, knowing they would not have another meal until they reached camp.

stol·id \\'stäl-əd\\ (*adj*) dull; impassive. I am afraid that this imaginative poetry will not appeal to such a *stolid* person.

strat·a·gem \\'strat-ə-jəm\\ (*n*) deceptive scheme. We saw through his clever *stratagem*.

stra·tum \\'strāt-əm\\ (*n*) layer of earth's surface; layer of society. Unless we alleviate conditions in the lowest *stratum* of our society, we may expect grumbling and revolt.

stri·at·ed \\'strī-ˌāt-əd\\ (*adj*) marked with parallel bands. The glacier left many *striated* rocks.

stric·ture \\'strik-chər\\ (*n*) critical comments; severe and adverse criticism. His *strictures* on the author's style are prejudiced and unwarranted.

stri·dent \\'strīd-ᵊnt\\ (*adj*) loud and harsh. She scolded him in a *strident* voice.

strin·gent \\'strin-jənt\\ (*adj*) binding; rigid. I think these regulations are too *stringent*.

strut \\'strət\\ (*n*) pompous walk. His *strut* as he marched about the parade ground revealed him for what he was: a pompous buffoon; also (*v*).

strut \\'strət\\ (*n*) supporting bar. The engineer calculated that the *strut* supporting the rafter needed to be reinforced. (secondary meaning)

stul·ti·fy \\'stəl-tə-ˌfī\\ (*v*) cause to appear foolish or inconsistent. By changing your opinion at this time, you will *stultify* yourself.

stu·por \\'st(y)ü-pər\\ (*n*) state of apathy; daze; lack of awareness. In his *stupor,* the addict was unaware of the events taking place around him.

\\ə\\ **abut** \\ᵊ\\ **kitten, F table** \\ər\\ **further** \\a\\ **ash** \\ā\\ **ace** \\ä\\ **cot, cart**
\\au̇\\ **out** \\ch\\ **chin** \\e\\ **bet** \\ē\\ **easy** \\g\\ **go** \\i\\ **hit** \\ī\\ **ice** \\j\\ **job**

sty-gi-an \\'stij-(ē-)ən\\ (*adj*) gloomy; hellish; deathly. They descended into the *stygian,* half-lit subbasement.

sty-mie \\'stī-mē\\ (*v*) present an obstacle; stump. The detective was *stymied* by the contradictory evidence in the robbery investigation; also (*n*).

suave \\'swäv\\ (*adj*) smooth; bland. He is the kind of individual who is more easily impressed by a *suave* approach than by threats or bluster.

sua-vi-ty \\'swäv-ət-ē\\ (*n*) urbanity; polish. He is particularly good in roles that require *suavity* and sophistication.

sub-al-tern \\sə-'bȯl-tərn\\ (*n*) subordinate. The captain treated his *subalterns* as though they were children rather than commissioned officers; also (*adj*).

sub-jec-tive \\ₒsəb-'jek-tiv\\ (*adj*) occurring or taking place within the subject; unreal. Your analysis is highly *subjective;* you have permitted your emotions and your opinions to color your thinking.

sub-ju-gate \\'səb ji-ₒgāt\\ (*v*) conquer; bring under control. It is not our aim to *subjugate* our foe; we are interested only in establishing peaceful relations.

sub-li-mate \\'səb-lə-ₒmāt\\ (*v*) refine; purify. We must strive to *sublimate* these desires and emotions into worthwhile activities; also (*n*).

sub-lime \\sə-'blīm\\ (*adj*) exalted; noble; uplifting. We must learn to recognize *sublime* truths; also (*v*).

sub-lim-i-nal \\ₒsəb-'lim-ən-ᵊl\\ (*adj*) below the threshold. We may not be aware of the *subliminal* influences that affect our thinking.

sub-se-quent \\'səb-si-kwənt\\ (*adj*) following; later. In *subsequent* lessons, we shall take up more difficult problems.

sub-ser-vi-ent \\səb-'sər-vē-ənt\\ (*adj*) behaving like a slave; servile; obsequious. He was proud and dignified; he refused to be *subservient to* anyone.

\\ŋ\\ si**ng** \\ō\\ **go** \\ȯ\\ **law** \\ȯi\\ **boy** \\th\\ **thin** \\t̲h̲\\ **the** \\ü\\ **loot** \\u̇\\ **foot**
\\y\\ **yet** \\zh\\ **vision** \\à, k̲, ⁿ, œ, œ̄, ᵫ, ūe, ʸ\\ *see* Pronunciation Symbols

sub-sid-i-ar-y \səb-'sid-ē-,er-ē\ (*adj*) subordinate; secondary. This information may be used as *subsidiary* evidence but is not sufficient by itself to prove your argument; also (*n*).

sub-si-dy \'səb-səd-ē\ (*n*) direct financial aid by government, etc. Without this *subsidy,* American ship operators would not be able to compete in world markets.

sub-sis-tence \səb-'sis-tən(t)s\ (*n*) existence; means of support; livelihood. In these days of inflated prices, my salary provides a mere *subsistence.*

sub-stan-ti-ate \səb-'stan-chē-,āt\ (*v*) verify; support. I intend to *substantiate* my statement by producing witnesses.

sub-stan-tive \'səb-stən-tiv\ (*adj*) essential; pertaining to the substance. Although the delegates were aware of the importance of the problem, they could not agree on the *substantive* issues.

sub-ter-fuge \'səb-tər-,fyüj\ (*n*) pretense; evasion. As soon as we realized that you had won our support by *subterfuge,* we withdrew our endorsement of your candidacy.

sub-tle-ty \'sət-ᵊl-tē\ (*n*) nicety; cunning; guile; delicacy. The *subtlety* of his remarks was unnoticed by most of his audience.

sub-ver-sive \səb-'vər-siv\ (*adj*) tending to overthrow or ruin. We must destroy such *subversive* publications; also (*n*).

suc-cinct \(ₗ)sək-'siŋ(k)t\ (*adj*) brief; terse; compact. His remarks are always *succinct* and pointed.

suc-cor \'sək-ər\ (*n*) aid; assistance; relief. We shall be ever grateful for the *succor* your country gave us when we were in need; also (*v*).

suc-cu-lent \'sək-yə-lənt\ (*adj*) juicy; full of richness. The citrus foods from Florida are more *succulent* to some people than those from California; also (*n*).

\ə\ abut \ᵊ\ kitten, F table \ər\ further \a\ ash \ā\ ace \ä\ cot, cart
\aů\ out \ch\ chin \e\ bet \ē\ easy \g\ go \i\ hit \ī\ ice \j\ job

suc-cumb \sə-'kəm\ (*v*) yield; give in; die. I *succumb* to temptation whenever it comes my way.

suf-fuse \sə-'fyüz\ (*v*) spread over. A blush *suffused* her cheeks when we teased her about her love affair.

sul-ly \'səl-ē\ (*v*) tarnish; soil. He felt that it was beneath his dignity to *sully* his hands in such menial labor.

sul-try \'səl-trē\ (*adj*) sweltering. He could not adjust himself to the *sultry* climate of the tropics.

sum-ma-tion \(ͺ)sə-'mā-shən\ (*n*) act of finding the total; summary. In his *summation,* the lawyer emphasized the testimony given by the two witnesses.

sump-tu-ous \'səm(p)-ch(ə-w)əs\ (*adj*) lavish; rich. I cannot recall when I have had such a *sumptuous* feast.

sun-der \'sən-dər\ (*v*) separate; part. Northern and southern Ireland are politically and religiously *sundered.*

sun-dry \'sən-drē\ (*adj*) various; several. My suspicions were aroused when I read *sundry* items in the newspapers about your behavior.

su-per-an-nu-at-ed \ͺsü-pə-'ran-yə-ͺwāt-əd\ (*adj*) retired on pension because of age. The *superannuated* man was indignant because he felt that he could still perform a good day's work.

su-per-cil-i-ous \ͺsü-pər-'sil-ē-əs\ (*adj*) contemptuous; haughty. I resent your *supercilious* and arrogant attitude.

su-per-fi-cial \ͺsü-pər-'fish-əl\ (*adj*) trivial; shallow. Since your report gave only a *superficial* analysis of the problem, I cannot give you more than a passing grade.

su-per-flu-it-y \ͺsü-per-'flü-ət-ē\ (*n*) excess; overabundance. We have a definite lack of sincere workers and a *superfluity* of leaders.

su-per-im-pose \ͺsü-pə-rim-'pōz\ (*v*) place over something else. Your attempt to *superimpose* another agency in this field will merely increase the bureaucratic nature of our government.

\ŋ\ sing \ō\ go \ȯ\ law \ȯi\ boy \th\ thin \<u>th</u>\ the \ü\ loot \u̇\ foot
\y\ yet \zh\ vision \à, <u>k</u>, ⁿ, œ, œ̄, ue, ūe, ʸ\ *see* Pronunciation Symbols

su-per-nal \su̇-'pərn-ᵊl\ (*adj*) heavenly; celestial. His tale of *supernal* beings was skeptically received.

su-per-nu-mer-ar-y \sü-pər-'n(y)ü-mə-ˌrer-ē\ (*n*) person or thing in excess of what is necessary; extra. His first appearance on the stage was as a *supernumerary* in a Shakespearean tragedy.

su-per-sede \ˌsü-pər-'sēd\ (*v*) cause to be set aside; replace. This regulation will *supersede* all previous rules.

su-pine \su̇-'pīn\ (*adj*) lying on back. The defeated pugilist lay *supine* on the canvas.

sup-plant \sə-'plant\ (*v*) replace; usurp. Richard II was *supplanted* by Bolingbroke who later became King Henry IV.

sup-ple \'səp-əl\ (*adj*) flexible; pliant. The angler found a *supple* limb and used it as a fishing rod; also (*v*).

sup-pli-ant \'səp-lē-ənt\ (*adj*) entreating; beseeching. He could not resist the dog's *suppliant* whimpering and he gave it some food; also (*n*).

sup-pli-cate \'səp-lə-ˌkāt\ (*v*) petition humbly; pray to grant a favor. We *supplicate* your majesty to grant him amnesty.

sup-pos-i-ti-tious \sə-ˌpäz ə-'tish-əs\ (*adj*) assumed; counterfeit; hypothetical. I find no similarity between your *supposititious* illustration and the problem we are facing.

sup-press \sə-'pres\ (*v*) crush; subdue; inhibit. After the armed troops had suppressed the rebellion, the city was placed under martial law.

sur-cease \'sər-ˌsēs\ (*n*) cessation. He begged the doctors to grant him *surcease* from his suffering. **sur-cease** \ˌ₍ˌ₎sər-'sēs\ (*v*)

sur-feit \'sər-fət\ (*v*) cloy; overfeed. I am *surfeited* with the sentimentality of the average motion picture film; also (*n*).

\ə\ **abut** \ᵊ\ **kitten, F table** \ər\ **further** \a\ **ash** \ā\ **ace** \ä\ **cot, cart**
\au̇\ **out** \ch\ **chin** \e\ **bet** \ē\ **easy** \g\ **go** \i\ **hit** \ī\ **ice** \j\ **job**

sur-ly \\'sər-lē\ (*adj*) rude; cross. Because of his *surly* attitude, many people avoided his company.

sur-mise \sər-'mīz\ (*v*) guess. I *surmise* that he will be late for this meeting; also (*n*).

sur-mount \sər-'maúnt\ (*v*) overcome. He had to *surmount* many obstacles in order to succeed.

sur-rep-ti-tious \ˌsər-əp-'tish-əs\ (*adj*) secret. News of their *surreptitious* meeting gradually leaked out.

sur-ro-gate \\'sər-ə-ˌgät\ (*n*) substitute. For a fatherless child, a male teacher may become a father *surrogate*.

sur-veil-lance \sər-'vā-lən(t)s\ (*n*) watching; guarding. The FBI kept the house under constant *surveillance* in the hope of capturing all the criminals at one time.

sus-te-nance \\'səs-tə-nən(t)s\ (*n*) means of support, food, nourishment. In the tropics, the natives find *sustenance* easy to obtain.

su-ture \\'sü-chər\ (*n*) stitches sewn to hold the cut edges of a wound or incision; material used in sewing. We will remove the *sutures* as soon as the wound heals; also (*v*).

swar-thy \\'swȯr-thē\ (*adj*) dark; dusky. Despite the stereotypes, not all Italians are *swarthy;* many are fair-skinned and blond-haired.

swathe \\'swäth\ (*v*) wrap around; bandage. When I visited him in the hospital, I found him *swathed* in bandages.

swel-ter \\'swel-tər\ (*v*) be oppressed by heat. I am going to buy an air conditioning unit for my apartment as I do not intend to *swelter* through another hot and humid summer; also (*n*).

swin-dler \\'swin-(d)lər\ (*n*) cheat. She was gullible and trusting, an easy victim for the first *swindler* who came along.

syb-a-rite \\'sib-ə-ˌrīt\ (*n*) lover of luxury. Rich people are not always *sybarites;* some of them have little taste for a life of luxury.

\ŋ\ si**ng**   \ō\ **go**   \ȯ\ **law**   \ȯi\ **boy**   \th\ **thin**   \t͟h\ **the**   \ü\ **loot**   \u̇\ **foot**
\y\ **yet**   \zh\ **vision**   \à, k̲, ⁿ, œ, œ̄, ᵫ, ᵫ̄, ʸ\ *see* Pronunciation Symbols

sy·co·phan·tic \sik-ə-'fant-ik\ (*adj*) servilely flattering. The king enjoyed the *sycophantic* attentions of his followers.

syl·lo·gism \'sil-ə-jiz-əm\ (*n*) logical formula utilizing a major premise, a minor premise, and a conclusion. There must be a fallacy in this *syllogism;* I cannot accept the conclusion.

syl·van \'sil-vən\ (*adj*) pertaining to the woods; rustic. His paintings of nymphs in *sylvan* backgrounds were criticized as overly sentimental; also (*n*).

sym·me·try \'sim-ə-trē\ (*n*) arrangement of parts so that balance is obtained; congruity. The addition of a second tower will give this edifice the *symmetry* it now lacks.

syn·chro·nous \'siŋ-krə-nəs\ (*adj*) similarly timed; simultaneous with. We have many examples of scientists in different parts of the world who have made *synchronous* discoveries.

syn·the·sis \'sin(t)-thə-səs\ (*n*) combining parts into a whole. Now that we have succeeded in isolating this drug, our next problem is to plan its *synthesis* in the laboratory.

syn·thet·ic \sin-'thet-ik\ (*adj*) artificial; resulting from synthesis. During the twentieth century, many *synthetic* products have replaced the natural products; also (*n*).

\ə\ **abut** \ə\ **kitten**, F **table** \ər\ **further** \a\ **ash** \ā\ **ace** \ä\ **cot, cart**
\au̇\ **out** \ch\ **chin** \e\ **bet** \ē\ **easy** \g\ **go** \i\ **hit** \ī\ **ice** \j\ **job**

T

tac·it \'tas-ət\ (*adj*) understood; not put into words. We have a *tacit* agreement.

tac·i·turn \'tas-ə-ˌtərn\ (*adj*) habitually silent; talking little. New Englanders are reputedly *taciturn* people.

tact \'takt\ (*n*) diplomacy; good taste. Once must use *tact* when providing criticism in order to avoid hurting the feelings of the person one is trying to help.

tac·tile \'tak-tᵊl\ (*adj*) pertaining to the organs or sense of touch. His calloused hands had lost their *tactile* sensitivity.

taint \'tānt\ (*v*) contaminate; corrupt. Health authorities are always trying to prevent the sale and use of food *tainted* by bacteria.

tal·is·man \'tal-ə-smən\ (*n*) charm. She wore the *talisman* to ward off evil.

tal·on \'tal-ən\ (*n*) claw of a bird. The falconer wore a leather gauntlet to avoid being clawed by the hawk's *talons*.

tan·ta·lize \'tant-ᵊl-ˌīz\ (*v*) tease; torture with disappointment. Tom loved to *tantalize* his younger brother.

tan·ta·mount \'tant-ə-ˌmau̇nt\ (*adj*) equal in value. Your ignoring their pathetic condition is *tantamount* to murder.

tan·trum \'tan-trəm\ (*n*) fit of petulance; caprice. The child learned that he could have almost anything if he went into a *tantrum*.

ta·ran·tu·la \tə-'ranch-(ə-)lə\ (*n*) venomous spider. We need an antitoxin to counteract the bite of the *tarantula*.

tat·ter·de·ma·lion \tat-ərd-i-'māl-yən\ (*n*) ragged fellow. Do you expect an army of *tatterdemalions* and beggars to put up a real fight?

taut \'tȯt\ (*adj*) tight; ready. The captain maintained that he ran a *taut* ship.

tau·to·log·i·cal \tȯt-ᵊl-'äj-i-kəl\ (*adj*) needlessly repetitious. In the sentence "It was visible to the eye," the phrase "to the eye" is *tautological*.

\ŋ\ sing \ō\ go \ȯ\ law \ȯi\ boy \th\ thin \th̲\ the \ü\ loot \u̇\ foot
\y\ yet \zh\ vision \à, k̲, ⁿ, œ, œ̄, ᵫ, ᵫ̄, ʸ\ *see* Pronunciation Symbols

tau-tol-o-gy \to-'täl-ə-jē\ (*n*) unnecessary repetition; pleonasm. "Joyful happiness" is an illustration of *tautology*.

taw-dry \'tod-rē\ (*adj*) cheap and gaudy. He won a few *tawdry* trinkets in Coney Island; also (*n*).

te-di-um \'tēd-ē-əm\ (*n*) boredom; weariness. We hope this radio will help overcome the *tedium* of your stay in the hospital.

te-mer-i-ty \tə-'mer-ət-ē\ (*n*) boldness; rashness. Do you have the *temerity* to argue with me?

tem-per \'tem-pər\ (*v*) restrain; blend; toughen. His hard times in the army served only to *temper* his strength.

tem-po \'tem-₍ᵢ₎pō\ (*n*) speed of music. I find the conductor's *tempo* too slow for such a brilliant piece of music.

tem-po-ral \'tem-p(ə-)rəl\ (*adj*) not lasting forever; limited by time; secular. At one time in our history, *temporal* rulers assumed that they had been given their thrones by divine right.

tem-po-rize \'tem-pə-,rīz\ (*v*) avoid committing oneself; gain time. I cannot permit you to *temporize* any longer; I must have a definite answer today.

te-na-cious \tə-'nā-shəs\ (*adj*) holding fast. I had to struggle to break his *tenacious* hold on my arm.

te-nac-i-ty \tə-'nas-ət-ē\ (*n*) firmness; persistency; adhesiveness. It is extremely difficult to overcome the *tenacity* of a habit such as smoking.

ten-den-tious \ten-'den-chəs\ (*adj*) having an aim; biased. The editorials in this periodical are *tendentious* rather than truth-seeking.

te-net \'ten-ət\ (*n*) doctrine; dogma. I cannot accept the *tenets* of your faith.

ten-sile \'ten(t)-səl\ (*adj*) capable of being stretched. Mountain climbers must know the *tensile* strength of their ropes.

ten-ta-tive \'tent-ət-iv\ (*adj*) provisional; experimental. Your *tentative* plans sound plausible.

\ə\ abut \ᵊ\ kitten, F table \ər\ **further** \a\ ash \ā\ ace \ä\ cot, **cart**
\au̇\ **out** \ch\ **chin** \e\ bet \ē\ **easy** \g\ go \i\ hit \ī\ ice \j\ **job**

ten-u-ous \'ten-yə-wəs\ (*adj*) thin; rare; slim. The allegiance of our allies is held by rather *tenuous* ties.

ten-ure \'ten-yər\ (*n*) holding of an office; time during which such an office is held. He has permanent *tenure* in this position.

tep-id \'tep-əd\ (*adj*) lukewarm. During the summer, I like to take a *tepid* bath.

ter-ma-gant \'tər-mə-gənt\ (*n*) shrew; scolding, brawling woman. *The Taming of the Shrew* is one of many stories of the methods used in changing a *termagant* into a demure lady; also (*adj*).

ter-mi-nol-o-gy \ ˌtər-mə-'näl-ə-jē\ (*n*) terms used in a science or art. The special *terminology* developed by some authorities in the field has done more to confuse laypeople than to enlighten them.

ter-mi-nus \'tər-mə-nəs\ (*n*) last stop of railroad. After we reached the railroad *terminus,* we continued our journey into the wilderness on saddle horses.

ter-res-tri-al \tə-'res-t(r)ē-əl\ (*adj*) of the earth. We have been able to explore the *terrestrial* regions much more thoroughly than the aquatic or celestial regions.

terse \'tərs\ (*adj*) concise; abrupt; pithy. I admire his *terse* style of writing.

ter-ti-ar-y \'tər-shē-ˌer-ē\ (*adj*) third. He is so thorough that he analyzes *tertiary* causes where other writers are content with primary and secondary reasons.

tes-sel-lat-ed \'tes-ə-ˌlāt-əd\ (*adj*) inlaid; mosaic. I recall seeing a table with a *tessellated* top of bits of stone and glass in a very interesting pattern.

tes-ta-tor \'tes-ˌtāt-ər\ (*n*) maker of a will. The attorney called in his secretary and his partner to witness the signature of the *testator.*

tes-ty \'tes-tē\ (*adj*) irritable; short-tempered. My advice is to avoid discussing this problem with him today as he is rather *testy.*

\ŋ\ **sing** \ō\ **go** \ȯ\ **law** \ȯi\ **boy** \th\ **thin** \th̲\ **the** \ü\ **loot** \u̇\ **foot**
\y\ **yet** \zh\ **vision** \ȧ, k̲, ⁿ, œ, œ̄, ᵾe, ᵾē, ʸ\ *see* Pronunciation Symbols

teth-er \\'te<u>th</u>-ər\\ (*v*) tie with a rope. Before we went to sleep, we *tethered* the horses to prevent their wandering off during the night; also (*v*).

thau-ma-tur-gist \\'thȯ-mə-ˌtər-jəst\\ (*n*) miracle worker; magician. I would have to be a *thaumaturgist* and not a mere doctor to find a remedy for this disease.

the-oc-ra-cy \\thē-'äk-rə-sē\\ (*n*) government of a community by religious leaders. Some Pilgrims favored the establishment of a *theocracy* in New England.

the-os-o-phy \\thē-'äs-ə-fē\\ (*n*) wisdom in divine things. *Theosophy* seeks to embrace the essential truth in all religions.

ther-a-peu-tic \\ther-ə-'pyüt-ik\\ (*adj*) curative. These springs are famous for their *therapeutic* qualities.

ther-mal \\'thər-məl\\ (*adj*) pertaining to heat. The natives discovered that the hot springs gave excellent *thermal* baths and began to develop their community as a health resort; also (*n*).

thrall \\'thrȯl\\ (*n*) slave; bondage. The captured soldier was held in *thrall* by the conquering army.

thren-o-dy \\'thren-əd-ē\\ (*n*) song of lamentation; dirge. When he died, many poets wrote *threnodies* about his passing.

thrifty \\'thrif-tē\\ (*adj*) careful about money; economical. A *thrifty* shopper compares prices before making major purchases.

throe \\'thrō\\ (*n*) violent anguish. The *throes* of despair can be as devastating as the spasms accompanying physical pain.

throng \\'thrȯŋ\\ (*n*) crowd. *Throngs* of shoppers jammed the aisles; also (*v*).

throt-tle \\'thröt-ᵊl\\ (*v*) strangle. The criminal tried to *throttle* the old man; also (*n*).

thwart \\'thwȯ(ə)rt\\ (*v*) baffle; frustrate. He felt that everyone was trying to *thwart* his plans.

\\ə\\ **abut** \\ᵊ\\ **kitten, F table** \\ər\\ **further** \\a\\ **ash** \\ā\\ **ace** \\ä\\ **cot, cart**
\\aů\\ **out** \\ch\\ **chin** \\e\\ **bet** \\ē\\ **easy** \\g\\ **go** \\i\\ **hit** \\ī\\ **ice** \\j\\ **job**

tim-bre \'tam-bər\ (*n*) quality of a musical tone produced by a musical instrument. We identify the instrument producing a musical sound by its *timbre.*

ti-mid-i-ty \tə-'mid-ət-ē\ (*n*) lack of self-confidence or courage. If you are to succeed as a salesman, you must first lose your *timidity.*

tim-o-rous \'tim-(ə-)rəs\ (*adj*) fearful; demonstrating fear. His *timorous* manner betrayed the fear he felt at the moment.

ti-rade \tī-'rād\ (*n*) extended scolding; denunciation. Long before he had finished his *tirade,* we were sufficiently aware of the seriousness of our misconduct.

ti-tan-ic \tī-'tan-ik\ (*adj*) gigantic. *Titanic* waves beat against the shore during the hurricane.

tithe \'fīth\ (*n*) tax of one-tenth. Because he was an agnostic, he refused to pay his *tithe* to the clergy; also (*v*).

tit-il-late \'tit-ᵊl-ˌāt\ (*v*) tickle. I am here not to *titillate* my audience but to enlighten it.

tit-u-lar \'tich-(ə-)lər\ (*adj*) nominal holding of title without obligations. Although he was the *titular* head of the company, the real decisions were made by his general manager.

toad-y \'tōd-ē\ (*v*) flatter for favors. I hope you see through those who are *toadying* you for special favors; also (*n*).

to-ga \'tō-gə\ (*n*) Roman outer robe. Marc Antony pointed to the slashes in Caesar's *toga.*

tol-er-ant \'täl(-ə)-rənt\ (*adj*) immune; forbearing. Because of restrictions on water use, we purchased drought-*tolerant* plants for our yard.

tome \'tōm\ (*n*) large volume. He spent much time in the libraries poring over ancient *tomes.*

to-pog-ra-phy \tə-'päg-rə-fē\ (*n*) physical features of a region. Before the generals gave the order to attack, they ordered a complete study of the *topography* of the region.

\ŋ\ sing \ō\ go \o\ law \oi\ boy \th\ thin \t͟h\ the \ü\ loot \u̇\ foot
\y\ yet \zh\ vision \à, k̲, ⁿ, œ, œ̄, ue, ūe, ʸ\ *see* Pronunciation Symbols

tor-pid \\tȯr-pəd\ (*adj*) dormant; dull; lethargic. The *torpid* bear had just come out of his cave after his long hibernation.

tor-por \\tȯr-pər\ (*n*) lethargy; sluggishness; dormancy. Nothing seemed to arouse him from his *torpor:* he had wholly surrendered himself to lethargy. tor-pid \\tȯr-pəd\ (*adj*)

tor-so \\tȯr-₍ₒ₎sō\ (*n*) trunk of statue with head and limbs missing; human trunk. This torso, found in the ruins of Pompeii, is now on exhibition in the museum in Naples.

tor-tu-ous \\tȯrch-(ə-)wəs\ (*adj*) winding; full of curves. Because this road is so *tortuous,* it is unwise to go faster than twenty miles an hour on it.

touch-stone \\təch-ˌstōn\ (*n*) stone used to test the fineness of gold alloys; criterion. What *touchstone* can be used to measure the character of a person?

touchy \\təch-ē\ (*adj*) sensitive; irascible. Do not discuss this phase of the problem as he is very *touchy* about it.

tox-ic \\täk-sik\ (*adj*) poisonous. We must seek an antidote for whatever *toxic* substance he has eaten.

tract \\trakt\ (*n*) pamphlet; a region of indefinite size. The king granted William Penn a *tract* of land in the New World.

trac-ta-ble \\trak-tə-bəl\ (*adj*) docile. You will find the children in this school very *tractable* and willing to learn.

tra-duce \\trə-'d(y)üs\ (*v*) expose to slander. His opponents tried to *traduce* the candidate's reputation by spreading rumors about his past.

tra-jec-to-ry \\trə-'jek-t(ə-)rē\ (*n*) path taken by a projectile. The police tried to locate the spot from which the assassin had fired the fatal shot by tracing the *trajectory* of the bullet.

tran-quil-li-ty \\tran-'kwil-ət-ē\ (*n*) calmness; peace. After the commotion and excitement of the city, I appreciate the *tranquillity* of these fields and forests.

\ə\ **abut** \ᵊ\ **kitten,** F **table** \ər\ **further** \a\ **ash** \ā\ **ace** \ä\ **cot, cart**
\aù\ **out** \ch\ **chin** \e\ **bet** \ē\ **easy** \g\ **go** \i\ **hit** \ī\ **ice** \j\ **job**

tran-scend \tran(t)s-'end\ (*v*) exceed; surpass. This accomplishment *transcends* all our previous efforts. tran-scen-den-tal \tran(t)s-‚en-'dent-ᵊl\ (*adj*)

tran-scribe \tran(t)s-'krīb\ (*v*) make a copy of. When you *transcribe* your notes, please send a copy to Mr. Smith and keep the original for our files. tran-scrip-tion \tran(t)s-'krip-shən\ (*n*)

trans-gres-sion \tran(t)s-'gresh-ən\ (*n*) violation of a law; sin. Forgive us our *transgressions.*

tran-sient \'tranch-ənt\ (*adj*) fleeting; quickly passing away; staying for a short time. This hotel caters to a *transient* trade; also (*n*).

tran-si-tion \tran(t)s-'ish-ən\ (*n*) going from one state of action to another. During the period of *transition* from oil heat to gas heat, the furnace will have to be shut off.

trans-lu-cent \tran(t)s-'lüs-ᵊnt\ (*adj*) partly transparent. We could not recognize the people in the next room because of the *translucent* curtains that separated us.

trans-mute \tran(t)s-'myüt\ (*v*) change; convert to something different. He was unable to *transmute* his dreams into actualities.

trans-par-ent \tran(t)s-'par-ənt\ (*adj*) permitting light to pass through freely; easily detected. Your scheme is so *transparent* that it will fool no one.

tran-spire \tran(t)s-'pī(ə)r\ (*v*) exhale; become known; happen. In spite of all our efforts to keep the meeting a secret, news of our conclusions *transpired.*

trau-mat-ic \trȯ-'mat-ik\ (*adj*) pertaining to an injury caused by violence. In his nightmares, he kept recalling the *traumatic* experience of being wounded in battle.

tra-vail \trə-'vā(ə)l\ (*n*) painful labor. How long do you think a man can endure such *travail* and degradation without rebelling?; also (*v*).

---

tra-verse \trə-'vərs\ (*v*) go through or across. When you *traverse* this field, be careful of the bull. tra-verse \'tra-vərs\ (*n*)

trav-es-ty \'trav-ə-stē\ (*n*) comical parody; treatment aimed at making something appear ridiculous. The decision the jury has arrived at is a *travesty* of justice; also (*v*).

trea-cle \'trē-kəl\ (*n*) syrup obtained in refining sugar. *Treacle* is more highly refined than molasses.

trea-tise \'trēt-əs\ (*n*) article treating a subject systematically and thoroughly. He is preparing a *treatise* on the Elizabethan playwrights for his graduate degree.

trek \'trek\ (*v*) travel with difficulty. The tribe *trekked* further north that summer in search of available game; also (*n*).

trem-or \'trem-ər\ (*n*) trembling; slight quiver. She had a nervous *tremor* in her right hand.

trem-u-lous \'trem-yə-ləs\ (*adj*) trembling; wavering. She was *tremulous* more from excitement than from fear.

tren-chant \'tren-chənt\ (*adj*) cutting; keen. I am afraid of his *trenchant* wit for it is so often sarcastic.

tren-cher-man \'tren-chər-mən\ (*n*) good eater. He is not finicky about his food; he is a *trencherman*.

trep-i-da-tion \trep-ə-'dā-shən\ (*n*) fear; trembling agitation. We must face the enemy without *trepidation* if we are to win this battle.

trib-u-la-tion \trib-yə-'lā-shən\ (*n*) distress; suffering. After all the trials and *tribulations* we have gone through, we need this rest.

tri-bu-nal \trī-,byün-ᵊl\ (*n*) court of justice. The decision of the *tribunal* was final.

trib-ute \'trib-₍₎yüt\ (*n*) tax levied by a ruler; mark of respect. The colonists refused to pay *tribute* to a foreign despot.

\ə\ **abut** \ᵊ\ **kitten, F table** \ər\ **further** \a\ **ash** \ā\ **ace** \ä\ **cot, cart**
\aù\ **out** \ch\ **chin** \e\ **bet** \ē\ **easy** \g\ **go** \i\ **hit** \ī\ **ice** \j\ **job**

tri-dent \'trīd-ᵊnt\ (*n*) three-pronged spear. Neptune is usually depicted as rising from the sea, carrying his *trident* on his shoulder; also (*adj*).

tril-o-gy \'tril-ə-jē\ (*n*) group of three works. Romain Rolland's novel *Jean Christophe* was first published as a *trilogy.*

trite \'trīt\ (*adj*) hackneyed; commonplace. The *trite* and predictable situations in many television programs alienate many viewers.

tri-vi-a \'triv-ē-ə\ (*n*) trifles; unimportant matters. Too many magazines ignore newsworthy subjects and feature *trivia.*

troth \'träth\ (*n*) pledge of good faith especially in betrothal. He gave her his *troth* and vowed he would cherish her always.

truck-le \'trək-əl\ (*v*) curry favor; act in an obsequious way. If you *truckle* to the lord, you will be regarded as a sycophant; if you do not, you will be considered arrogant.

tru-cu-lent \'trək-yə-lənt\ (*adj*) aggressive; savage. They are a *truculent* race, ready to fight at any moment.

tru-ism \'trü-ˌiz-əm\ (*n*) self-evident truth. Many a *truism* is well expressed in a proverb.

trum-pe-ry \'trəm-p(ə-)rē\ (*n*) objects that are showy, valueless, deceptive. All this finery is mere *trumpery.*

trun-cate \'trəŋ-ˌkāt\ (*v*) cut the top off. The top of a cone that has been *truncated* in a plane parallel to its base is a circle.

tryst \'trist\ (*n*) appointed meeting. The lovers kept their *tryst* even though they realized their danger.

tu-mult \'t(y)ü-ˌməlt\ (*n*) commotion; riot; noise. She could not make herself heard over the *tumult* of the mob.

tun-dra \'tən-drə\ (*n*) rolling, treeless plain in Siberia and arctic North America. Despite the cold, many geologists are trying to discover valuable mineral deposits in the *tundra.*

\ŋ\ sing \ō\ go \ò\ law \òi\ boy \th\ thin \th̲\ the \ü\ loot \ů\ foot
\y\ yet \zh\ vision \à, k̲, ⁿ, œ, œ̄, ue, ūe, ʸ\ *see* Pronunciation Symbols

tur-bid \'tər-bəd\ (*adj*) muddy; having the sediment disturbed. The water was *turbid* after the children had waded through it.

tur-bu-lence \'tər-byə-lən(t)s\ (*n*) state of violent agitation. We were frightened by the *turbulence* of the ocean during the storm.

tu-reen \tə-'rēn\ (*n*) deep table dish for holding soup. The waiters brought the soup to the tables in silver *tureens.*

tur-gid \'tər-jəd\ (*adj*) swollen; distended. The *turgid* limb was sore and painful.

turn-key \'tərn-ˌkē\ (*n*) jailer. By bribing the *turnkey,* the prisoner arranged to have better food brought to him in his cell.

tur-pi-tude \'tər-pə-ˌt(y)üd\ (*n*) depravity. A visitor may be denied admittance to this country if he has been guilty of moral *turpitude.*

tu-te-lage \'t(y)üt-ᵊl-ij\ (*n*) guardianship; training. Under the *tutelage* of such masters of the instrument, he made rapid progress as a virtuoso.

tu-te-lar-y \'t(y)üt-ᵊl-ˌer-ē\ (*adj*) protective; pertaining to a guardianship. I am acting in my *tutelary* capacity when I refuse to grant you permission to leave the campus; also (*n*).

ty-ro \'tī-ˌ(ₒ)rō\ (*n*) beginner; novice. For a mere *tyro,* you have produced some marvelous results.

U

u·biq·ui·tous \yü-'bik-wət-əs\ (*adj*) being everywhere; omnipresent. You are *ubiquitous;* I meet you wherever I go.

ul·te·ri·or \əl-'tir-ē-ər\ (*adj*) situated beyond; unstated. You must have an *ulterior* motive for your behavior.

ul·ti·mate \'əl-tə-mət\ (*adj*) final; not susceptible to further analysis. Scientists are searching for the *ultimate* truths; also (*n*).

ul·ti·ma·tum \əl-tə-'māt-əm\ (*n*) last demand; warning. Since they have ignored our *ultimatum,* our only recourse is to declare war.

um·brage \'əm-brij\ (*n*) resentment; anger; sense of injury or insult. She took *umbrage* at his remarks.

u·na·nim·i·ty \yü-nə-'nim-ət-ē\ (*n*) complete agreement. We were surprised by the *unanimity* with which our proposals were accepted by the different groups. **u·nan·i·mous** \yù-nan-ə-məs\ (*adj*)

un·as·suag·able \ˌən-ə-'swā-jə-bəl\ (*adj*) unable to be soothed. He was *unassuagable;* the apology did no good.

un·as·sum·ing \ˌən-ə-'sü-miŋ\ (*adj*) modest. He is so *unassuming* that some people fail to realize how great a man he really is.

un·bri·dled \ˌən-'brīd-ᵊld\ (*adj*) unrestrained. He had a sudden fit of *unbridled* rage.

un·can·ny \ən-'kan-ē\ (*adj*) strange; mysterious. You have the *uncanny* knack of reading my innermost thoughts.

un·con·scio·na·ble \ən-'känch-(ə-)nə-bəl\ (*adj*) unscrupulous; excessive. He found the loan shark's demands *unconscionable* and impossible to meet.

un·couth \ən-'küth\ (*adj*) outlandish; clumsy; boorish. Most biographers portray Lincoln as an *uncouth* and ungainly young man.

---

unc-tion \\'əŋ(k)-shən\ (*n*) the act of anointing with oil. The anointing with oil of a person near death is called extreme *unction.*

unc-tu-ous \\'əŋ(k)-chə(-wə)s\ (*adj*) oily; bland; insincerely suave. Uriah Heep disguised his nefarious actions by *unctuous* protestations of his "'umility."

un-du-late \\'ən jə-ˌlāt\ (*v*) move with a wavelike motion. The waters *undulated* in the breeze. un-du-late \\'ən-jə-lət\ (*adj*)

un-earth \ən-'ərth\ (*v*) dig up. When they *unearthed* the city, the archaeologists found many relics of an ancient civilization.

un-earth-ly \ən-'ərth-lē\ (*adj*) not earthly; weird. There is an *unearthly* atmosphere about his work that amazes the casual observer.

un-e-quiv-o-cal \ˌən-i-'kwiv-ə-kəl\ (*adj*) plain; obvious. My answer to your proposal is an *unequivocal* and absolute "No."

un-err-ing-ly \ˌən-'e(ə)r-iŋ-lē\ (*adv*) infallibly. My teacher *unerringly* pounced on the one typographical error in my essay.

un-fal-ter-ing \ən-'fȯl-t(ə-)riŋ\ (*adj*) steadfast. She approached the guillotine with *unfaltering* steps.

un-feigned \ən-'fānd\ (*adj*) genuine; real. I am sure her surprise was *unfeigned.*

un-fledged \ən-'flejd\ (*adj*) immature. It is hard for an *unfledged* writer to find a sympathetic publisher.

un-gain-ly \ən 'gān-lē\ (*adj*) awkward. He is an *ungainly* young man.

un-guent \\'ən-gwənt\ (*n*) ointment. Apply this *unguent* to the sore muscles before retiring.

u-ni-for-mi-ty \ˌyü-nə-'fȯr-mət-ē\ (*n*) sameness; consistency; monotony. After a while, the *uniformity* of TV situation comedies becomes boring. u-ni-form \\'yü-nə-ˌfȯrm\ (*adj*)

\ə\ **abut** \ᵊ\ **kitten, F table** \ər\ **further** \a\ **ash** \ā\ **ace** \ä\ **cot, cart**
\aú\ **out** \ch\ **chin** \e\ **bet** \ē\ **easy** \g\ **go** \i\ **hit** \ī\ **ice** \j\ **job**

u·ni·lat·er·al \yü-ni-'lat-ə-rəl\ (*adj*) one-sided. This legislation is *unilateral* since it binds only one party in the controversy.

un·im·peach·a·ble \ˌən-im-'pē-chə-bəl\ (*adj*) blameless and exemplary. His conduct in office was *unimpeachable.*

un·in·hib·it·ed \ˌən-in-'hib-ət-əd\ (*adj*) unrepressed. The congregation was shocked by her *uninhibited* laughter during the sermon.

u·nique \yü-'nēk\ (*adj*) without an equal; single in kind. You have the *unique* distinction of being the first student whom I have had to fail in this course.

u·ni·son \'yü-nə-sən\ (*n*) unity of pitch; complete accord. The choir sang in *unison.*

un·kempt \ən-'kem(p)t\ (*adj*) disheveled; with uncaredfor appearance. The beggar was dirty and *unkempt.*

un·mit·i·gat·ed \ˌən-'mit-ə-ˌgāt-əd\ (*adj*) harsh; severe; not lightened. I sympathize with you in your *unmitigated* sorrow.

un·ob·tru·sive \ˌən-əb-'trü-siv\ (*adj*) inconspicuous; not blatant. The secret service agents in charge of protecting the president tried to be as *unobtrusive* as possible.

un·prec·e·dent·ed \ˌən-'pres-ə-ˌdent-əd\ (*adj*) novel; unparalleled. Margaret Mitchell's book *Gone with the Wind* was an *unprecedented* success.

un·ru·ly \ən-'rü-lē\ (*adj*) disobedient; lawless. The only way to curb this *unruly* mob is to use tear gas.

un·sa·vo·ry \ˌən-'sāv-(ə-)rē\ (*adj*) distasteful; morally offensive. People with *unsavory* reputations should not be allowed to work with young children.

un·seem·ly \ən-'sēm-lē\ (*adj*) unbecoming; inappropriate. Your levity is *unseemly* at this time.

un·sul·lied \ən-'səl-ēd\ (*adj*) untarnished. I am happy that my reputation is *unsullied.*

---

un-ten-a-ble \ən-'ten-ə-bəl\ (*adj*) unsupportable. I find your theory *untenable* and must reject it.

un-to-ward \ˌən-'tō(-ə)rd\ (*adj*) unfortunate; annoying. *Untoward* circumstances prevent me from being with you on this festive occasion.

un-wit-ting \ən-'wit-iŋ\ (*adj*) unintentional; not knowing. He was the *unwitting* tool of the swindlers.

un-wont-ed \ən-'wȯnt-əd\ (*adj*) unaccustomed by experience. He hesitated to assume the *unwonted* role of master of ceremonies at the dinner.

up-braid \ˌəp-'brād\ (*v*) scold; reproach. I must *upbraid* him for his misbehavior.

up-shot \'əp-ˌshät\ (*n*) outcome. The *upshot* of the rematch was that the former champion proved that he still possessed all the skills of his youth.

ur-bane \ˌər-'bān\ (*adj*) suave; refined; elegant. The courtier was *urbane* and sophisticated. ur-ban-i-ty \ˌər-'ban-ət-ē\ (*n*)

ur-chin \'ər-chən\ (*n*) mischievous child (usually a boy). Get out! This store is no place for grubby *urchins!*

ur-sine \'ər-ˌsīn\ (*adj*) bearlike; pertaining to a bear. Because of its *ursine* appearance, the great panda has been identified with the bears; actually, it is closely related to the raccoon.

u-sur-pa-tion \ˌyü-sər-'pā-shən\ (*n*) act of seizing power and rank of another. The revolution ended with the *usurpation* of the throne by the victorious rebel leader.

u-su-ry \'yüzh-(ə-)rē\ (*n*) lending money at illegal rates of interest. The loan shark was found guilty of *usury*.

u-to-pi-a \yu-'tō-pē-ə\ (*n*) imaginary land with perfect social and political system. Shangri-la was the name of James Hilton's Tibetan *utopia*.

V

vac·il·la·tion \'vas-ə-'lā-shən\ (*n*) fluctuation; wavering. His *vacillation* when confronted with a problem annoyed all of us who had to wait until he made his decision.

vac·u·ous \'vak-yə-wəs\ (*adj*) empty; inane. The *vacuous* remarks of the politician annoyed the audience, who had hoped to hear more than empty platitudes.

vag·a·bond \'vag-ə-ˌbänd\ (*n*) wanderer; tramp. In summer, college students wander the roads of Europe like carefree *vagabonds; also* (*adj*).

va·ga·ry \'vā-gə-rē\ (*n*) caprice; whim. She followed every *vagary* of fashion.

va·grant \'vā-grənt\ (*adj*) stray; random. He tried to study, but could not collect his *vagrant* thoughts. **va·gran·cy** \'va-grən(t)-sē\ (*n*)

vague \'vāg\ (*adj*) unclear. The politician gave *vague* answers to the reporters' questions in order to avoid offending any voters.

vain·glo·ri·ous \(ᵗ)van-'glōr-ē-əs\ (*adj*) boastful; excessively conceited. He was a *vainglorious* and arrogant individual.

val·e·dic·to·ry \'val-ə-'dik-t(ə-)rē\ (*adj*) pertaining to farewell. I found the *valedictory* address too long; leave-taking should be brief; *also* (*n*).

val·i·date \'val-ə-ˌdāt\ (*v*) confirm; ratify. I will not publish my findings until I *validate* my results.

val·or \'val-ər\ (*n*) bravery. He received the Medal of Honor for his *valor* in battle. **val·iant** \'val-yənt\ (*adj*)

vam·pire \'vam-ˌpī(ə)r\ (*n*) ghostly being that sucks the blood of the living. Children were afraid to go to sleep at night because of the many legends of *vampires*.

van·guard \'van-ˌgärd\ (*n*) forerunners; advance forces. We are the *vanguard* of a tremendous army that is following us.

\ŋ\ sing \ō\ go \ȯ\ law \ȯi\ boy \th\ thin \<u>th</u>\ the \ü\ loot \u̇\ foot
\y\ yet \zh\ vision \à, <u>k</u>, ⁿ, œ, œ̄, ɯe, ɯē, ʸ\ *see* Pronunciation Symbols

van-tage \'vant-ij\ (*n*) position giving an advantage. They fired upon the enemy from behind trees, walls, and any other point of *vantage* they could find.

va-pid \'vap-əd\ (*adj*) insipid; inane. He delivered an uninspired and *vapid* address.

var-i-e-gat-ed \'ver-ē-ə-ˌgāt-əd\ (*adj*) many-colored. He will not like this blue necktie as he is addicted to *variegated* clothing.

vas-sal \'vas-əl\ (*n*) in feudalism, one who held land of a superior lord. The lord demanded that his *vassals* contribute more to his military campaign.

vaunt \'vȯnt\ (*v*) boast; brag; highly publicize. To *vaunt* this project now that its failure is known is pointless; also (*n*).

veer \'vi(ə)r\ (*v*) change in direction. After what seemed an eternity, the wind *veered* to the east and the storm abated; also (*n*).

veg-e-tate \'vej-ə-ˌtāt\ (*v*) live in a monotonous way. I do not understand how you can *vegetate* in this quiet village after the adventurous life you have led.

ve-he-ment \'vē-ə-mənt\ (*adj*) impetuous; with marked vigor. He spoke with *vehement* eloquence in defense of his client.

vel-lum \'vel-əm\ (*n*) parchment. Bound in *vellum* and embossed in gold, this book is a beautiful example of the binder's craft; also (*adj*).

ve-loc-i-ty \və-'läs-ət-ē\ (*n*) speed. The train went by at a considerable *velocity*.

ve-nal \'vēn-əl\ (*adj*) capable of being bribed. The *venal* policeman accepted the bribe offered him by the speeding motorist whom he had stopped.

ven-det-ta \ven-'det-ə\ (*n*) feud; private warfare. The *vendetta* continued for several generations despite all attempts by authorities to end the killings.

ven-dor \'ven-dər\ (*n*) seller. The fruit *vendor* sold her wares from a stall on the sidewalk.

\ə\ **abut** \ə\ **kitten, F table** \ər\ **further** \a\ **ash** \ā\ **ace** \ä\ **cot, cart**
\au̇\ **out** \ch\ **chin** \e\ **bet** \ē\ **easy** \g\ **go** \i\ **hit** \ī\ **ice** \j\ **job**

ve-neer \və-'ni(ə)r\ (*n*) thin layer; cover. Casual acquaintances were deceived by his *veneer* of sophistication and failed to recognize his fundamental shallowness; also (*v*).

ven-er-a-ble \'ven-ər(-ə)-bəl\ (*adj*) deserving high respect. We do not mean to be disrespectful when we refuse to follow the advice of our *venerable* leader.

ven-er-ate \'ven-ə-ˌrāt\ (*v*) revere. In China, the people *venerate* their ancestors.

ve-ni-al \'vē-nē-əl\ (*adj*) forgivable; trivial. We may regard a hungry man's stealing as a *venial* crime.

vent \'vent\ (*n*) a small opening outlet. The wine did not flow because the air *vent* in the barrel was clogged; also (*v*).

ven-tril-o-quist \ven-'tril-ə-kwəst\ (*n*) someone who can make his or her voice seem to come from another person or thing. This *ventriloquist* does an act in which she has a conversation with a wooden dummy.

ven-ture-some \'ven-chər-səm\ (*adj*) bold. A group of *venturesome* women were the first to scale Mt. Annapurna.

ven-tur-ous \'vench-(ə-)rəs\ (*adj*) daring. The five *venturous* young men decided to look for a new approach to the mountain top.

ven-ue \'ven-ˌyü\ (*n*) location. The attorney asked for a change of *venue;* he thought his client would do better if the trial were held in a less conservative county.

ve-ra-cious \və-'rā-shəs\ (*adj*) truthful. I can recommend him for this position because I have always found him *veracious* and reliable. **ve-rac-i-ty** \və-'ras-ət-ē\ (*n*)

ver-bal-ize \'vər-bə-ˌlīz\ (*v*) to put into words. I know you don't like to talk about these things, but please try to *verbalize* your feelings.

ver-ba-tim \ˌ(ˌ)vər-'bāt-əm\ (*adv*) word for word. He repeated the message *verbatim;* also (*adj*).

ver-bi-age \'vər-bē-ij\ (*n*) pompous array of words. After we had waded through all the *verbiage,* we discovered that the writer had said very little.

\ŋ\ sing \ō\ go \ȯ\ law \ȯi\ boy \th\ **thin** \th̲\ **the** \ü\ loot \u̇\ foot
\y\ yet \zh\ vision \à, k̲, ⁿ, œ, œ̄, ue, ūe, ʸ\ *see* Pronunciation Symbols

ver-bose \\(ᵢ)vər-'bōs\ (*adj*) wordy. This article is too *verbose;* we must edit it.

ver-dant \'vərd-ᵊnt\ (*adj*) green; fresh. The *verdant* meadows in the spring are always an inspiring sight.

verge \'vərj\ (*n*) border; edge. Madame Curie knew she was on the *verge* of discovering the secrets of radioactive elements; also (*v*).

ver-i-si-mil-i-tude \ver-ə-sə-'mil-ə-ˌt(y)üd\ (*n*) appearance of truth; likelihood. Critics praised her for the *verisimilitude* of her performance as Lady Macbeth. She was completely believable.

ver-i-ty \'ver-ət-ē\ (*n*) truth; reality. The four *verities* were revealed to Buddha during his long meditation.

ver-nac-u-lar \və(r)-'nak-yə-lər\ (*n*) living language; natural style. Cut out those old-fashioned thee's and thou's and write in the *vernacular;* also (*adj*).

ver-nal \'vərn-ᵊl\ (*adj*) pertaining to spring. We may expect *vernal* showers all during the month of April.

ver-sa-tile \'vər-sət-ᵊl\ (*adj*) having many talents; capable of working in many fields. He was a *versatile* athlete; at college he had earned varsity letters in baseball, football, and track.

ver-tex \'vər-ˌteks\ (*n*) summit. Let us drop a perpendicular line from the *vertex* of the triangle to the base.

ver-tig-i-nous \\(ᵢ)vər-'tij-ə-nəs\ (*adj*) giddy; causing dizziness. I do not like the rides in the amusement park because they have a *vertiginous* effect on me.

ver-ti-go \'vərt-i-gō\ (*n*) dizziness. We test potential plane pilots for susceptibility to spells of *vertigo*.

verve \'vərv\ (*n*) enthusiasm; liveliness. She approached her studies with such *verve* that it was impossible for her to do poorly.

ves-tige \'ves-tij\ (*n*) trace; remains. We discovered *vestiges* of early Indian life in the cave.

vex \'veks\ (*v*) annoy; distress. Please try not to *vex* your mother; she is doing the best she can.

\ə\ **abut** \ᵊ\ kitten, F table \ər\ **further** \a\ **ash** \ā\ **ace** \ä\ **cot, cart**
\aú\ **out** \ch\ **chin** \e\ **bet** \ē\ **easy** \g\ **go** \i\ **hit** \ī\ **ice** \j\ **job**

vi-a-ble \'vī-ə-bəl\ (*adj*) capable of maintaining life. The infant, though prematurely born, is *viable* and has a good chance to survive.

vi-ands \'vī-əndz\ (*n*) food; provisions. There was a cache of *viands* at the campsite.

vi-car-i-ous \vī-'ker-ē-əs\ (*adj*) acting as a substitute; done by a deputy. Many people get a *vicarious* thrill at the movies by imagining they are the characters on the screen.

vi-cis-si-tude \və-'sis-ə-ˌt(y)üd\ (*n*) change of fortune. I am accustomed to life's *vicissitudes,* having experienced poverty and wealth, sickness and health, and failure and success.

vict-uals \'vit-ᵊlz\ (*n*) food. I am very happy to be able to provide you with these *victuals.*

vie \'vī\ (*v*) contend; compete. When we *vie* with each other for his approval, we are merely weakening ourselves and strengthening him.

vig-i-lance \'vij-ə-lən(t)s\ (*n*) watchfulness. Eternal *vigilance* is the price of liberty.

vi-gnette \vin-'yet\ (*n*) picture; short literary sketch. *The New Yorker* published her latest *vignette.*

vig-or \'vig-ər\ (*n*) active strength. Although he was over seventy years old, Jack had the *vigor* of a man in his prime. **vig-or-ous** \'vig-(ə-)rəs\ (*adj*)

vil-i-fy \'vil-ə-ˌfī\ (*v*) slander. Why is he always trying to *vilify* my reputation?

vin-di-cate \'vin-də-ˌkāt\ (*v*) clear of charges. I hope to *vindicate* my client and return him to society as a free man.

vin-dic-tive \vin-'dik-tiv\ (*adj*) revengeful. He was very *vindictive* and never forgave an injury.

vi-per \'vī-pər\ (*n*) poisonous snake. The habitat of the horned *viper,* a particularly venomous snake, is in sandy regions like the Sahara or the Sinai peninsula.

vi-ra-go \və-'räg-ˌ(ˌ)ō\ (*n*) shrew. Rip Van Winkle's wife was a veritable *virago.*

\ŋ\ sing   \ō\ go   \ȯ\ law   \ȯi\ boy   \th\ thin   \<u>th</u>\ the   \ü\ loot   \u̇\ foot
\y\ yet   \zh\ vision   \à, <u>k</u>, ⁿ, œ, œ̄, ᵫ, ᵫ̄, ʸ\ *see* Pronunciation Symbols

vir-ile \'vir-əl\ (*adj*) manly. I do not accept the premise that a man is *virile* only when he is belligerent.

vir-tu-o-so \ˌvər-chə-'wō-ₔ)sō\ (*n*) highly skilled artist. Heifetz is a violin *virtuoso*.

vir-u-lent \'vir-(y)ə-lənt\ (*adj*) extremely poisonous. The virus is highly *virulent* and has made many of us ill for days.

vi-rus \'vī-rəs\ (*n*) disease communicator. The doctors are looking for a specific medicine to control this *virus*.

vis-age \'viz-ij\ (*n*) face; appearance. The stern *visage* of the judge indicated that he had decided to impose a severe penalty.

vis-cer-al \'vis-ə-rəl\ (*adj*) felt in one's inner organs. She disliked the *visceral* sensations she had whenever she rode the roller coaster.

vis-cous \'vis-kəs\ (*adj*) sticky; gluey. Melted tar is a *viscous* substance. **vis-cos-i-ty** \vis-'käs-ət-ē\ (*n*)

vi-sion-ar-y \'vizh-ə-ˌner-ē\ (*adj*) produced by imagination; fanciful; mystical. He was given to *visionary* schemes that never materialized; also (*n*).

vi-ti-ate \'vish-ē-ˌāt\ (*v*) spoil the effect of; make inoperative. Fraud will *vitiate* the contract.

vit-re-ous \'vi-trē-əs\ (*adj*) pertaining to or resembling glass. Although this plastic has many *vitreous* qualities such as transparency, it is unbreakable.

vit-ri-ol-ic \vi-trē-'äl-ik\ (*adj*) corrosive; sarcastic. Such *vitriolic* criticism is uncalled for.

vi-tu-per-a-tive \vī-'t(y)ü-p(ə-)rət-iv\ (*adj*) abusive; scolding. He became more *vituperative* as he realized that we were not going to grant him his wish.

vi-va-cious \və-'vā-shəs\ (*adj*) animated; gay. She had always been *vivacious* and sparkling.

vi-vi-sec-tion \viv-ə-'sek-shən\ (*n*) act of dissecting living animals. The Society for the Prevention of Cruelty to Animals opposed *vivisection* and deplored the practice of using animals in scientific experiments.

vix-en \'vik-sən\ (*n*) female fox; ill-tempered woman. Aware that she was right once again, he lost his temper and called her a shrew and a *vixen*.

vo-cif-er-ous \vō-'sif-(ə-)rəs\ (*adj*) clamorous; noisy. The crowd grew *vociferous* in its anger and threatened to take the law into its own hands.

vogue \'vōg\ (*n*) popular fashion. Slacks became the *vogue* on many college campuses.

vol-a-tile \'väl-ət-ᵊl\ (*adj*) evaporating rapidly; lighthearted; mercurial. Ethyl chloride is a very *volatile* liquid.

vo-li-tion \vō-'lish-ən\ (*n*) act of making a conscious choice. She selected this dress of her own *volition*.

vol-u-ble \'väl-yə-bəl\ (*adj*) fluent; glib. He was a *voluble* speaker, always ready to talk.

vo-lu-mi-nous \və-'lü-mə-nəs\ (*adj*) bulky; large. Despite her family burdens, she kept up a *voluminous* correspondence with her friends.

vo-lup-tu-ous \və-'ləp-chə-(-wə)s\ (*adj*) gratifying the senses. The nobility during the Renaissance led *voluptuous* lives.

vo-ra-cious \vȯ-'rā-shəs\ (*adj*) ravenous. The wolf is a *voracious* animal.

vo-ta-ry \'vōt-ə-rē\ (*n*) follower of a cult. He was a *votary* of every new movement in literature and art.

vouch-safe \vaȯch-'sāf\ (*v*) grant condescendingly; guarantee. I can safely *vouchsafe* you a fair return on your investment.

vul-ner-a-ble \'vəln-(ə-)rə-bəl\ (*adj*) susceptible to wounds. Achilles was *vulnerable* only in his heel.

vy-ing \'vī-iŋ\ (*v*) contending. Why are we *vying* with each other for his favors? **vie** \'vī\ (*v*)

W

waft \'wäft\ (*v*) move gently, as if impelled by wind or waves. Daydreaming, he gazed at the leaves that *wafted* past his window; also (*n*).

wag-gish \'wag-ish\ (*adj*) mischievous; humorous; tricky. He was a prankster who, unfortunately, often overlooked the damage he could cause with his *waggish* tricks.

waif \'wāf\ (*n*) homeless child or animal. Although he already had eight cats, he could not resist adopting yet another feline *waif*.

waive \'wāv\ (*v*) give up temporarily; yield. I will *waive* my rights in this matter in order to expedite our reaching a proper decision.

wal-low \'wäl-(ˌ)ō\ (*v*) roll in; indulge in; become helpless. The hippopotamus loves to *wallow* in the mud.

wan \'wän\ (*adj*) having a pale or sickly color; pallid. Suckling asked, "Why so pale and *wan*, fond lover?"; also (*v*).

wane \'wān\ (*v*) grow gradually smaller. From now until December 21, the winter equinox, the hours of daylight will *wane*; also (*n*).

wan-gle \'waŋ-gəl\ (*v*) bring about by manipulation or trickery. She tried to *wangle* an invitation to the party.

wan-ton \'wȯnt-ᵊn\ (*adj*) unruly; unchaste, excessive. His *wanton* pride cost him many friends; also (*n*).

war-ble \'wȯr-bəl\ (*v*) sing melodiously; trill. Every morning the birds *warbled* outside her window; also (*n*).

war-rant \'wȯr-ənt\ (*v*) justify; authorize. Before the judge issues the injunction, you must convince her this action is *warranted*.

war-ran-ty \'wȯr-ənt-ē\ (*n*) guarantee; assurance by seller. The purchaser of this automobile is protected by the manufacturer's *warranty* that he will replace any defective part for five years or 50,000 miles.

\ə\ **abut** \ʼə\ **kitten**, F **table** \ər\ **further** \a\ **ash** \ā\ **ace** \ä\ **cot, cart**
\au̇\ **out** \ch\ **chin** \e\ **bet** \ē\ **easy** \g\ **go** \i\ **hit** \ī\ **ice** \j\ **job**

war-y \'wa(ə)r-ē\ *(adj)* very cautious. The spies grew *wary* as they approached the sentry.

wast-rel \'wā-strəl\ *(n)* profligate. He was denounced as a *wastrel* who had dissipated his inheritance.

wax \'waks\ *(v)* increase; grow. With proper handling, his fortunes *waxed* and he became rich.

way-lay \'wā-ˌlā\ *(v)* ambush; lie in wait. They agreed to *waylay* their victim as he passed through the dark alley going home.

wean \'wēn\ *(v)* accustom a baby not to nurse; give up a cherished activity. He decided he would *wean* himself away from eating junk food and stick to fruits and vegetables.

weath-er \'weth̲-ər\ *(v)* endure the effects of weather or other forces. He *weathered* the changes in his personal life with difficulty, as he had no one in whom to confide.

welt \'welt\ *(n)* mark from a beating or whipping. The evidence of child abuse was very clear; Jennifer's small body was covered with *welts* and bruises.

wel-ter \'wel-tər\ *(v)* wallow. At the height of the battle, the casualties were so numerous that the victims *weltered* in their blood while waiting for medical attention; also *(n)*.

whee-dle \'hwēd-ᵊl\ *(v)* cajole; coax; deceive by flattery. She knows she can *wheedle* almost anything she wants from her father.

whelp \'hwelp\ *(n)* young wolf, dog, tiger, etc. This collie *whelp* won't do for breeding, but he'd make a fine pet.

whet \'hwet\ *(v)* sharpen; stimulate. The odors from the kitchen are *whetting* my appetite; I will be ravenous by the time the meal is served.

whim-si-cal \'hwim-zi-kəl\ *(adj)* capricious; fanciful; quaint. *Peter Pan* is a *whimsical* play.

whin-ny \'hwin-ē\ *(v)* neigh like a horse. When he laughed through his nose, it sounded as if he *whinnied;* also *(n)*.

\ŋ\ si**ng** \ō\ g**o** \o\ l**aw** \oi\ b**oy** \th\ **th**in \th̲\ **the** \ü\ l**oo**t \u\ f**oo**t
\y\ **y**et \zh\ vi**s**ion \à, k̲, ⁿ, œ, œ̄, ue, ūe, ʸ\ *see* Pronunciation Symbols

whit \'hwit\ (*n*) smallest speck. There is not a *whit* of intelligence or understanding in your observations.

whorl \'hwȯr(ə)l\ (*n*) ring of leaves around stem; ring. Identification by fingerprints is based on the difference in shape and number of the *whorls* on the fingers.

wi-ly \'wī-lē\ (*adj*) cunning; artful. He is as *wily* as a fox in avoiding trouble.

wince \'win(t)s\ (*v*) shrink back; flinch. The screech of the chalk on the blackboard made her *wince*.

wind-fall \'win(d)-ˌfȯl\ (*n*) unexpected lucky event. This huge tax refund is quite a *windfall*.

win-now \'win-ₒō\ (*v*) sift; separate good parts from bad. This test will *winnow* out the students who study from those who don't bother.

win-some \'win(t)-səm\ (*adj*) agreeable; gracious; engaging. By her *winsome* manner, she made herself liked by everyone who met her.

with-er \'with-ər\ (*v*) shrivel; decay. Cut flowers are beautiful for a day, but all too soon they *wither.*

wit-less \'wit-ləs\ (*adj*) foolish; idiotic. Such *witless* and fatuous statements will create the impression that you are an ignorant individual.

wit-ti-cism \'wit-ə-ˌsiz-əm\ (*n*) witty saying; facetious remark. What you regard as *witticisms* are often offensive to sensitive people.

wiz-ard-ry \'wiz-ə(r)-drē\ (*n*) sorcery; magic. Merlin amazed the knights with his *wizardry.*

wiz-en \'wiz-ᵊn\ (*v*) wither; shrivel. The hot sun *wizened* all the trees and plants.

wont \'wȯnt\ (*n*) custom; habitual procedure. As was his *wont,* he jogged two miles every morning before going to work.

world-ly \'wər(-ə)l-dlē\ (*adj*) engrossed in matters of this earth; not spiritual. You must leave your *worldly* goods behind you when you go to meet your Maker.

\ə\ **abut** \ᵊ\ kitten, F table \ər\ **further** \a\ ash \ā\ **ace** \ä\ cot, cart
\au̇\ **out** \ch\ chin \e\ bet \ē\ **easy** \g\ go \i\ hit \ī\ ice \j\ job

wraith \ˈrāth \ (*n*) ghost; phantom of a living person. It must be a horrible experience to see a ghost; it is even more horrible to see the *wraith* of a person we know to be alive.

wran·gle \ˈraŋ-gəl\ (*v*) quarrel; obtain through arguing; herd cattle. They *wrangled* over their inheritance.

wrath \ˈrath\ (*n*) anger; fury. She turned to him, full of *wrath,* and said, "What makes you think I'll accept lower pay for this job than you get?"

wreak \ˈrēk\ (*v*) inflict. I am afraid he will *wreak* his wrath on the innocent as well as the guilty.

wrench \ˈrench\ (*v*) pull; strain; twist. She *wrenched* free of her attacker and landed a powerful kick to his kneecap.

wrest \ˈrest\ (*v*) pull away; take by violence. With only ten seconds left to play, our team *wrested* victory from their grasp.

writhe \ˈrīth\ (*v*) squirm, twist. He was *writhing* in pain, desperate for the drug his body required.

wry \ˈrī\ (*adj*) twisted; with a humorous twist. We enjoy Dorothy Parker's verse for its *wry* wit.

XYZ

xe-no-phile \'zen-ə-ˌfil\ (*n*) one attracted to foreign people, manners, and styles. She was a *xenophile* who spent all her time exploring foreign cultures.

xe-no-pho-bi-a \ˌzen-ə-'fō-bē-ə\ (*n*) fear and hatred of anything foreign. His *xenophobia* prevented him from learning anything about the customs of people in other countries.

yearn \'yərn\ (*v*) desire; long. After the long run I *yearned* to sit down and soak my throbbing feet.

yen \'yen\ (*n*) longing; urge. She had a *yen* to get away and live on her own for a while.

yeo-man \'yō-mən\ (*n*) man owning small estate; middle-class farmer. It was not the aristocrat but the *yeoman* who determined the nation's policies.

yoke \'yōk\ (*v*) join together, unite. I don't wish to be *yoked* to him in marriage, as if we were cattle pulling a plow; also (*n*).

yo-kel \'yō-kəl\ (*n*) country bumpkin. At school, his classmates regarded him as a *yokel* and laughed at his rustic mannerisms.

za-ny \'zā-nē\ (*adj*) crazy; comic. I can watch the Marx brothers' *zany* antics for hours.

zeal-ot \'zel-ət\ (*n*) fanatic; person who shows excessive zeal. It is good to have a few *zealots* in our group for their enthusiasm is contagious.

ze-nith \'zē-nəth\ (*n*) point directly overhead in the sky; summit. When the sun was at its *zenith,* the glare was not as strong as at sunrise and sunset.

zeph-yr \'zef-ər\ (*n*) gentle breeze; west wind. When these *zephyrs* blow, it is good to be in an open boat under a full sail.

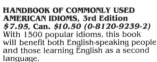

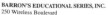

Macbeth

At last! Shakespeare in Language everyone can understand...
SHAKESPEARE MADE EASY Series

Scene 7	Scene 7
*Macbeth's castle. Enter a **sewer** directing divers servants. Then enter **Macbeth**.*	*A room in **Macbeth's** castle. A **Butler** and several **Waiters** cross, carrying dishes of food. Then **Macbeth** enters. He is thinking about the proposed murder of **King Duncan**.*
Macbeth If it were done, when 'tis done, then 'twere well It were done quickly: if th' assassination Could trammel up the consequence, and catch, With his surcease, success; that but this blow 5 Might be the be-all and the end-all here, But here, upon this bank and shoal of time, We'd jump the life to come. But in these cases We still have judgement here: that we but teach Bloody instructions, which being taught return 10 To plague th'inventor: this even-handed justice Commends th'ingredience of our poisoned chalice To our own lips. He's here in double trust: First, as I am his kinsman and his subject, Strong both against the deed: then, as his host, 15 Who should against his murderer shut the door, Not bear the knife myself. Besides, this Duncan Hath borne his faculties so meek, hath been So clear in his great office, that his virtues Will plead like angels, trumpet-tounged, against 20 The deep damnation of his taking-off; And pity, like a naked new-born babe, Striding the blast, or Heaven's cherubin, horsed Upon the sightless couriers of the air, Shall blow the horrid deed in every eye, 25 That tears shall drown the wind. I have no spur To prick the sides of my intent, but only Vaulting ambition, which o'erleaps itself, And falls on th'other –	**Macbeth** If we could get away with the deed after it's done, then the quicker it were done, the better. If the murder had no consequences, and his death ensured success...If, when I strike the blow, that would be the end of it – here, right here, on this side of eternity – we'd willingly chance the life to come. But usually, we get what's coming to us here on earth. We teach the art of bloodshed, then become the victims of our own lessons. This evenhanded justice makes us swallow our own poison. *[Pause]* Duncan is here on double trust: first, because I'm his kinsman and his subject (both good arguments against the deed); then, because I'm his host, who should protect him from his murderer–not bear the knife. Besides, this Duncan has used his power so gently, he's been so incorruptible his great office, that his virtues will plead like angels, their tongues trumpeting the damnable horror of his murder. And pity, like a naked newborn babe or Heaven's avenging angels riding the winds, will cry the deed to everyone so that tears will blind the eye. I've nothing to spur me on but high-leaping ambition, which can often bring about one's downfall.

A simplified modern translation appears side-by-side with the original Elizabethan text...plus there's helpful background material, study questions, and other aids to better grades. Yes, up-to-date language now makes it easier to score well on tests *and* enjoy the ageless beauty of the master's works.

Shakespeare is Made Easy for these titles:

Hamlet, $6.95

Henry IV, Part One, $4.95

Julius Caesar, $6.95

King Lear, $6.95

Macbeth, $6.95

The Merchant of Venice, $6.95

A Midsummer's Night's Dream, $6.95

Romeo & Juliet, $6.95

The Tempest, $6.95

Twelfth Night, $6.95

Books may be purchased at your bookstore, or by mail from Barron's. Enclose check or money order for the total amount plus sales tax where applicable and 15% for postage and handling charge (minimum charge $4.95). Prices subject to change without notice.

Barron's Educational Series, Inc.
250 Wireless Boulevard
Hauppauge, New York 11788

(#16) R 4/97

Notes